Teach Yourself Great Web Design in a Week

Anne-Rae Vasquez-Peterson

Paul Chow

Sams.net Publishing
201 W. 103rd Street
Indianapolis, IN 46290

Teach Yourself Great Web Design in a Week

Copyright ©1997 by Sams.net Publishing

FIRST EDITION

International Standard Book Number: 1-57521-253-6

Library of Congress Catalog Card Number: 96-71501

2000   99   98   97   4   3   2   1

Interpretation of the printing code: the rightmost double-digit number is the year of the book's printing; the rightmost single-digit, the number of the book's printing. For example, a printing code of 97-1 shows that the first printing of the book occurred in 1997.

Composed in *American Typewriter*, *Bembo*, *Officina*, and *MCPdigital* by Macmillan Computer Publishing

Printed in the United States of America

Publisher and President:	Richard K. Swadley
Publishing Manager:	Mark Taber
Acquisitions Manager	Beverly M. Eppink
Director of Editorial Services:	Cindy Morrow
Assistant Marketing Managers:	Kristina Perry
	Rachel Wolfe

Acquisitions Editor
Kelly Murdock

Development Editor
Kelly Murdock

Software Development Specialist
Bob Correll

Production Editor
Fran Blauw

Indexer
Bruce Clingaman

Technical Reviewer
Brett Bonnerberger

Editorial Coordinator
Katie Wise

Technical Edit Coordinator
Lorraine Schaffer

Resource Coordinator
Deborah Frisby

Editorial Assistants
*Carol Ackerman, Andi Richter,
Rhonda Tinch-Mize*

Cover Designer
Tim Amrhein

Book Designer
Gary Adair

Copy Writer
Peter Fuller

Production Team Supervisors
Brad Chinn, Charlotte Clapp

Production
*Mona Brown, Jennifer Dierdorff, Michael Dietsch,
Polly Lavrick, Erich J. Richter*

Overview

Contents

Teach Yourself Great Web Design in a Week

Teach Yourself Great Web Design in a Week

8 Creating Graphics to Spice Up Your Page   187

Dedication

We dedicate this book to God for answering our prayers and giving us the strength to stick with it, and to our families for their continued love and support.

Acknowledgments

We have just finished spitting out more than 400 pages of our blood, sweat, and tears, pouring out our heartfelt stories, painstaking graphics, and every ounce of information we had left in our heads. And through it all, we laughed, we cried, we whined.

And now it's time to give our thanks... So go ahead, Paul...

—I'd like to thank Anne-Rae's mom for all the home-cooked meals and the entertaining commentaries she made while watching her daily talk shows, and for taking me in as one of her own. And to Anne-Rae's dad for fixing my mirror and other things, for giving me the cool Grizzlies sweatshirt, and also for unknowingly giving up his parking spot in the driveway for me. Over to you, Anne-Rae.

—And let's not forget Brad. Thank you for providing us with enough ice cream to calm our frayed nerves, especially before deadlines. I'd also like to thank Paul's parents, Mr. and Mrs. Chow. Thank you for the salmon and for letting Paul hang out with us so much. He wrote, he slept, he ate, he even played video games. He became one of us.

—Okay, enough already. We'd like to give a HUGE thanks to Andrew for helping us out with the appendixes, the creative stories, the songs, and all the cool graphics he designed. We will never forget his renditions of Beatles' songs, his blunt criticisms, and his sarcastic wit that inspired us throughout the book. Andrew, thanks, and may the shwartz be with you. Oh—and thanks to little Brandon for bringing us Kit Kats from our stash, and also for drawing those cute little pictures for our book.

—I'd like to thank my pal and mentor Brian Waring for getting me into this bizness in the first place. And from the both of us, a super-huge thanks to Kelly Murdock for his encouragement, guidance, and trust in us. Thank you to everyone at Sams.net. A super big thank you to our wonderful production editor, Fran Blauw, for all her hard work and entertaining e-mails. We still owe you dinner, Fran. And, finally, for all our friends who thought we fell off the face of the earth but were with us in spirit and prayers: JDC, LF, JDR, PS, CM, AL, TL, SL, LL, and everyone else who believed in us.

As a stale fortune cookie saying once read,

You will go far, but be sure to come back.

'Til the next book, Peace.

—*Anne-Rae and Paul*

About the Authors

Anne-Rae Vasquez-Peterson is President of AR&B Internet Site & Publishing Inc., a vibrant, innovative Web design company specializing in site designs, Internet consulting, and virtual-hosting services for individuals and corporations. Anne-Rae also plays the role of Web site administrator, chief Web designer, and CGI and HTML consultant. Her expertise in HTML authoring, Web and multimedia design, project and database management, and Internet marketing is a major contribution to the success of the company. In addition, Anne-Rae is co-founder of a freelance artist directory that brings together the talents of various media artists, Web designers, and programmers from the University of British Columbia. Her background in the Internet Publishing Certificate Program at the university has given her the opportunity to work with many talented people in the industry.

Anne-Rae provides consulting services and training in Web and HTML design for university instructors and students. Her down-to-earth speaking and writing style appeals even to the most non-technical members of her audience.

On a personal note, Anne-Rae loves participating in the performing arts. She does freelance work as a writer, singer, songwriter, and artist. On her days off, you can find her directing or performing in independent theater and movie productions.

Paul Chow was enticed into computer programming at a very young age when he first got his hands on a brand new Commodore Pet computer. Soon after, he designed his first computer graphic by creating an image using ASCII text. Ever since then, Paul has never looked back.

Paul is Vice-President and Chief Graphic Designer for AR&B Internet Site and Publishing Inc. From the days when he was a freelance graphic artist, multimedia developer, and computer programmer, Paul brings to the company a strong background in digital video production, graphic design, computer animation, and user-interface development. In addition, he is co-founder of the computer consulting company Advantage Consulting, a division of Advantage Holdings Group Limited. Paul graduated from the department of Computer Information Systems at Langara College in Vancouver, British Columbia, Canada. For several years, he worked as a computer programmer/systems analyst for a large Canadian corporation.

On the side, Paul provides consulting services in Web page design at the University of British Columbia. He also enjoys every aspect of the performing arts—acting, singing, directing, and screenwriting. When he is not working, Paul can be found performing with his rock band at various events.

Teach Yourself Great Web Design in a Week

Tell Us What You Think!

As a reader, you are the most important critic and commentator of our books. We value your opinion and want to know what we're doing right, what we could do better, what areas you'd like to see us publish in, and any other words of wisdom you're willing to pass our way. You can help us make strong books that meet your needs and give you the computer guidance you require.

Do you have access to CompuServe or the World Wide Web? Then check out our CompuServe forum by typing GO SAMS at any prompt. If you prefer the World Wide Web, check out our site at http://www.mcp.com.

Note

If you have a technical question about this book, call the technical support line at 317-581-3833.

As the publishing manager of the group that created this book, I welcome your comments. You can fax, e-mail, or write me directly to let me know what you did or didn't like about this book—as well as what we can do to make our books stronger. Here's the information:

Fax: 317-581-4669

E-mail: newtech_mgr@sams.samspublishing.com

Mail: Mark Taber
Sams.net Publishing
201 W. 103rd Street
Indianapolis, IN 46290

Introduction

With the exploding popularity of the Internet, many people want to learn how to design their own Web pages. A majority of Web-authoring books today concentrate mainly on the technical aspect of HTML coding. Knowing HTML does not necessarily make someone a Web designer, though. Many sites we see on the Web are hard to read, difficult to navigate, or just plain ugly. Because of the lack of basic design elements, such as white space, appropriate background/foreground design, and text size/font choice, many Web sites send out optical and information overload. They might have a usable basic design but, unfortunately, lack the flair and style to set them apart from thousands of other Web pages. This book gives novice Web designers the basics for designing an organized, appealing, user-friendly Web site. As Web designers ourselves, we found very few resources on good Web design techniques.

We derived the techniques for the effective Web designs we use in this book from basic principles of typography, layout, design, and publication. We hope that this book will be the first in its category to help novice Web designers out there on the Net who want to learn the tricks of the trade.

What Will You Learn in Just One Week?

The truth is that anyone can learn HTML and publish his or her own Web pages on the Internet. The fact is, however, that *not* everyone knows how to design a good Web page. *Teach Yourself Great Web Design in a Week* shows you how to design your Web site from the initial planning stages to the online testing and publishing stage. You will learn the steps to create a good Web site and the common errors you should avoid. You'll find out more about making your Web site one that makes you proud to be called a Web designer. Just follow this book's seven-day strategy for designing a great Web site.

How Is This Book Structured?

This book is designed to be read over seven days. Each day of reading is clearly outlined into two chapters a day. Of course, if you are like us, you might want to read ahead, which is entirely up to you. We do encourage you to apply the techniques you learn in each chapter, even if you are just designing a sample Web site for starters. You'll find that it will be more enjoyable and easier to understand the information if you are actually designing a site yourself. With this book, you will get the knowledge that good Web designers have to design an exceptional Web site—all in one week!

- ✦ On Day 1, we introduce you to the elements and the basics of Web design. You learn about the structure of a Web page and the importance of design elements on a Web page.

- ✦ On Day 2, we focus on the planning stages of Web design, from time-management issues to designing the user interface and navigation.

- ✦ On Day 3, we show you great page-layout techniques using HTML tables and frames. We also spend some time applying text and typographical techniques to Web page design.

✦ On Day 4, we teach you about what color really means to your site and show you how to create the graphics that will spice up your Web pages.

✦ On Day 5, we show you how to manipulate your graphics to add special effects, and we also spend some time showing you how to design cool, animated GIFs.

✦ On Day 6, we go through the design of an actual Web site step by step, showing you the implementation of a user interface design. You also learn tips to improve your future Web designs.

✦ Finally, on Day 7, we talk about adding multimedia to make your Web pages come alive, and we discuss the future of Web design.

Unlike other design books, which are in plain black and white, this book is chockful of four-color graphics and examples. You will find instructions, summaries, exercises, and tips in every chapter to help you design your Web site.

Who Should Read This Book?

Whether you are a novice or experienced Web designer, or if you have an understanding of HTML but want to know more about the designing aspects of a Web site, *Teach Yourself Great Web Design in a Week* will help you learn the techniques to design an effective and aesthetically appealing Web site. Whatever category you are in, you definitely will enjoy learning how to avoid common design errors from our fun examples of what *not* to do with your Web design. In the next seven days, we will take you through every twist and turn, every nook and cranny of the Web design process. If you want a fun, non-technical, laid-back approach to learning more about Web design concepts, you most certainly have come to the right book.

We're on the Web!

You can find examples and information about Web design techniques discussed in this book at our Web site at

`http://www.arnb.com/webdesign/`

Now you'll begin your mission learning about Web design concepts. If you choose to accept this mission, you will further your knowledge and Web design skills. This book will self-instruct in 10 seconds. Good luck, and may the source be with you.

Web Page Basics and Anatomy

Chapter 1

Web Page Elements: What Design Elements Go into a Web Page?

What goes into the design of a Web page? No, we're not talking about mastering the art of HTML (or even Java, for that matter). In this chapter, we are going to focus on the aspect of design itself. We will introduce you to the basic elements of design and discuss the importance of design elements on a Web page. After that, we will talk a little bit about cross-platform design issues and what designing a flexible layout scheme means. So let's not waste another moment! Strap on your seat belts and get ready, because in just a couple of seconds, we will be taking you into The Intriguing World of Web Design.

So You Wanna Design a Web Site?

So does every other person who can get his hands on a good HTML tutorial. Sure, everybody and his grandmother can call themselves Web designers (actually, there are lots of grandmothers designing their own Web pages out there. Hi, Grandma!). We prefer to call them *HTML enabled*. It takes more than personal flair to design something—ask the person who designed the magnetic bank card holder.

Note

For those of you who consider yourselves HTML enabled, we have a special button just for you! (See Figure 1.1.) Join the HTML Enabled Society by cutting out the HTML Enabled button. Now you can wear it and show it off to all your friends. **(Warning: Don't cut out the button if this book belongs to the library!)**

Where does that leave those of you who really want to learn the process of Web designing? Well, my friend, in order to learn the process of design, you'll have to learn about the basics. Like any well-thought-out brochure, newsletter, newspaper, magazine, or book, the presentation of the overall printed publication is what makes one publication stand out from the others.

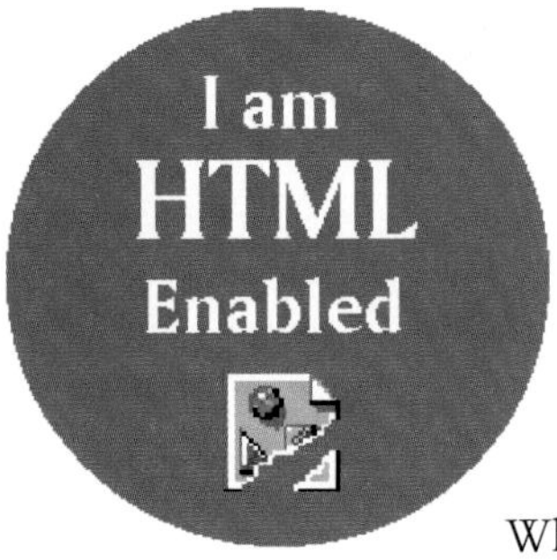

I am HTML Enabled

Figure 1.1.
Your HTML Enabled button. Repeat after me: I am not a Web designer, I am only HTML enabled.

Why should the information on the Web be any different? We are assuming that you want to publish your information on the Web because you have something to say about a topic, a hobby, or your business. You use design elements to organize your ideas and present them to your audience in the way you intended. These elements divide your ideas into smaller sections for better readability. Information is easier to digest if served in tasty amounts.

You don't need to be a design artist to be a good Web designer. You just need to understand the basics of design elements before you start.

Similar to elements on a printed page, a Web page's skeleton consists of three parts: the header, the body, and the footer. (See Figure 1.2.) Headers and footers provide the flow of continuity from one page to the next.

Within the skeleton, there are a number of other elements, such as a page title, a top-of-the-page graphics header, text, graphics, links to appropriate pages, and e-mail contact and copyright information.

The arrangement of text, use of different fonts, blending of color, addition of background and foreground images, and use of white space are simple design elements that you will apply to your Web site to bring style and flair to your Web pages.

But What About Sites That Don't Use Design Elements?

You might have noticed that some Web sites do not use Web design elements such as header graphics or e-mail contact information. You might land on a home page that simply contains an image map with several hot links. The lack of basic page elements can be used as a technique to create an effect or mood. You should be cautious when omitting Web design elements from your pages, though. Whenever you purposely remove basic elements from your design, you should consider whether the benefits of achieving a certain effect outweigh the benefits of the functionality of the elements.

Note

Figure 1.2 shows an example of a Web-page skeleton. Notice that the header contains a company logo graphic for The Magnetic Emporium. The body of the site contains the main content for the company, and the footer contains company copyright information.

Header, Body, and Footer

Now that we've introduced the basic elements, let's focus on each part of the Web-page skeleton and find out what it does. Understanding each part's role in a Web page will help you with your design.

Using Your Head Wisely

The *header* of your Web page is what a person sees when he first lands on your site.

Tip

Your Web page may include 1,000 useful household magnetic devices, but if your home page doesn't have a header that tells people that your site is about magnets, how many people do you think will wait for the page to load to find out? (See Figure 1.3.)

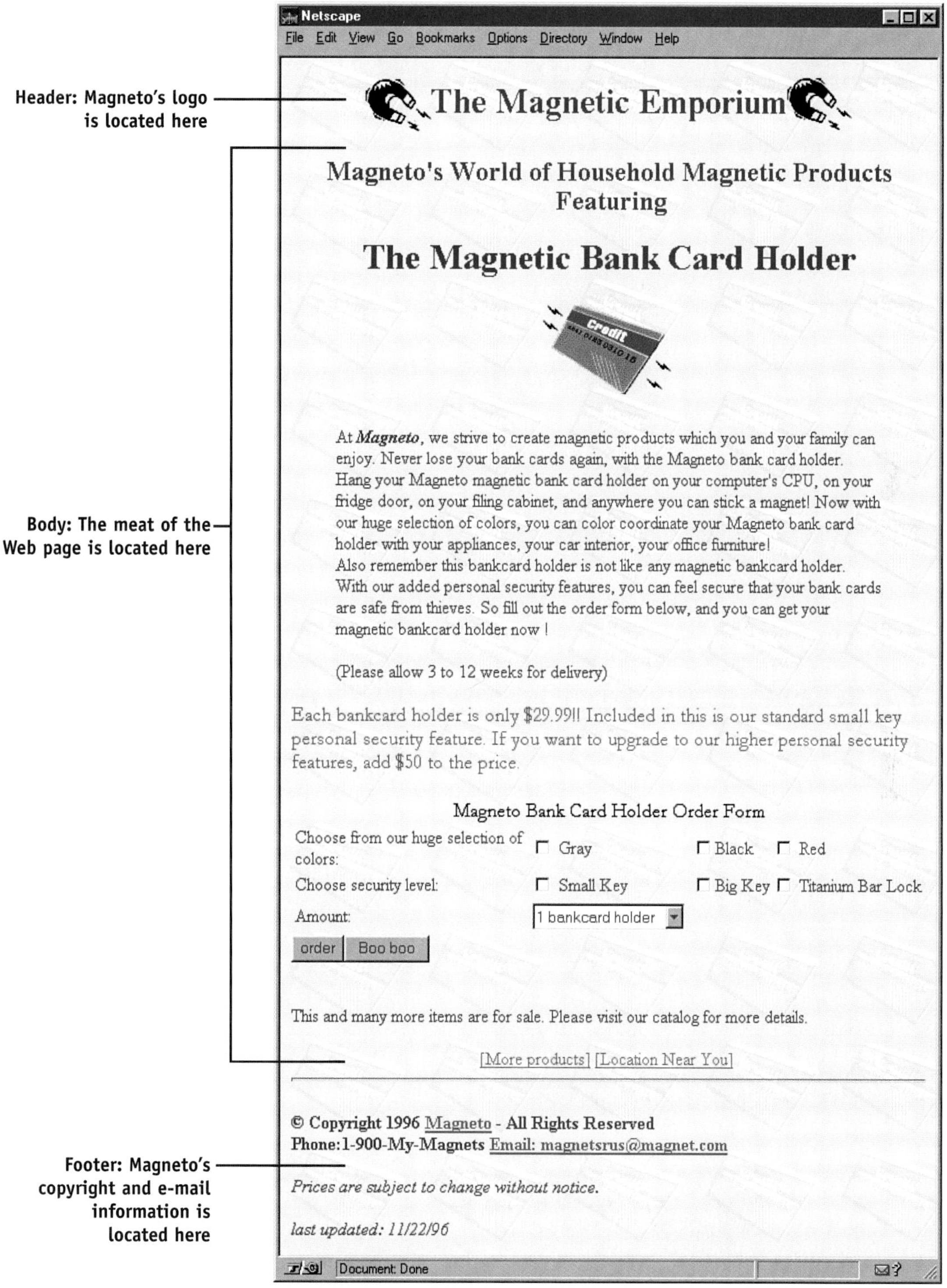
Header: Magneto's logo is located here
Body: The meat of the Web page is located here
Footer: Magneto's copyright and e-mail information is located here
Netscape
File Edit View Go Bookmarks Options Directory Window Help
The Magnetic Emporium
Magneto's World of Household Magnetic Products Featuring
The Magnetic Bank Card Holder
Credit
At Magneto, we strive to create magnetic products which you and your family can enjoy. Never lose your bank cards again, with the Magneto bank card holder. Hang your Magneto magnetic bank card holder on your computer's CPU, on your fridge door, on your filing cabinet, and anywhere you can stick a magnet! Now with our huge selection of colors, you can color coordinate your Magneto bank card holder with your appliances, your car interior, your office furniture!
Also remember this bankcard holder is not like any magnetic bankcard holder. With our added personal security features, you can feel secure that your bank cards are safe from thieves. So fill out the order form below, and you can get your magnetic bankcard holder now !
(Please allow 3 to 12 weeks for delivery)
Each bankcard holder is only $29.99!! Included in this is our standard small key personal security feature. If you want to upgrade to our higher personal security features, add $50 to the price.
Magneto Bank Card Holder Order Form
Choose from our huge selection of colors:
Gray
Black
Red
Choose security level:
Small Key
Big Key
Titanium Bar Lock
Amount:
1 bankcard holder
order
Boo boo
This and many more items are for sale. Please visit our catalog for more details.
[More products] [Location Near You]
© Copyright 1996 Magneto - All Rights Reserved
Phone:1-900-My-Magnets Email: magnetsrus@magnet.com
Prices are subject to change without notice.
last updated: 11/22/96
Document: Done

Figure 1.2.

Magneto's Magnetic Bank Card Holder Web site gives you an example of a basic Web-page skeleton.

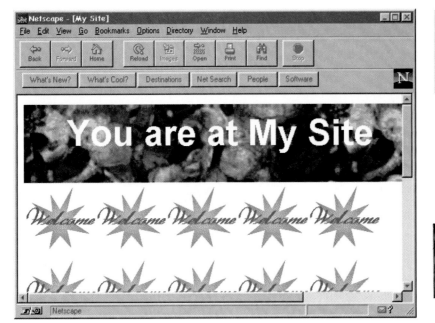

Figure 1.3.

Colorful, but what the...?! A header graphic that doesn't say much.

Bad Design

The header section usually contains a header graphic that displays the title of your Web site or your company logo. Because it is the first thing anyone sees, it is important to make this section interesting yet informative. Some people with slower modems don't have the patience to wait for the whole page to load. If they see a crummy graphic taking forever to load and nothing on the graphic that really helps explain what the site is about, they will, in most cases, click the Back button faster than you can say "Yahoo!" (See Figure 1.4.)

Bad Design

Figure 1.4.

A header's graphic loading on a computer with a slow modem connection.

Although they are not absolutely essential, you should include navigational elements such as a navigational bar or text links in the header of your page. For people who have visited your site before, having the navigational tools at the top of the page makes it easier to get to a specific page without having to wait for the current page to completely load.

Headers on all your pages should be consistent. People should be able to tell at a glance that they are still on the same site just by looking at the top of the page.

Do You Like My Body?

The *body* section of the Web page contains the main content of your page. The content can consist of text, graphics, animation, links, tables, navigation, and forms. Consider the body of your Web page as the living guts of all that your site has to say. Designing this section is the most important part of the design process, because this is where all the design elements—such as style, proportions, structure, dimension, and balance—come into play. We go into greater detail about the body section in upcoming chapters.

Who Reads Your Bottom?

You'd be surprised at how many people read the information at the bottom of a Web page. The *footer* section usually contains the last revision date, credits, contact, disclaimer, and copyright information. Often, counters, banner advertisements, and other elements find their way into footers. The footer should contain, at a minimum, contact information such as the Webmaster's Web URL and e-mail address. People need to know that they

can contact someone about a question or comment they might have about your site or organization. Footers also are useful for providing you, the Webmaster, with a sense of authorship. (See Figures 1.5 through 1.8.)

Some sites include footer information on the main home page only. You should place minimum contact information in the footer section on all the Web pages on a site, though, because not everyone lands on a site via the home page. People can arrive at a page on your site through a bookmarked link, an open text search engine, or even just by accident. Never assume that your home page will be seen by everyone who lands on your site. The easier it is for someone to contact you, the more likely it is that they will be able to give you feedback.

Additional Elements: Titles, Links, Lists, Callouts, and Indexes

Adding focus to a Web site can be as easy as using a few additional design elements to enhance the readability of your information.

Choosing Your Titles

The *title* of your document appears in the title bar at the top of your browser and in the head of your Web page. Search engines often use the words in a title to find keywords for the site. People using search engine lists to find sites will want to know in a few words what a site is about before they decide to visit it. Your title therefore should be descriptive and meaningful. (See Figures 1.9 and 1.10.)

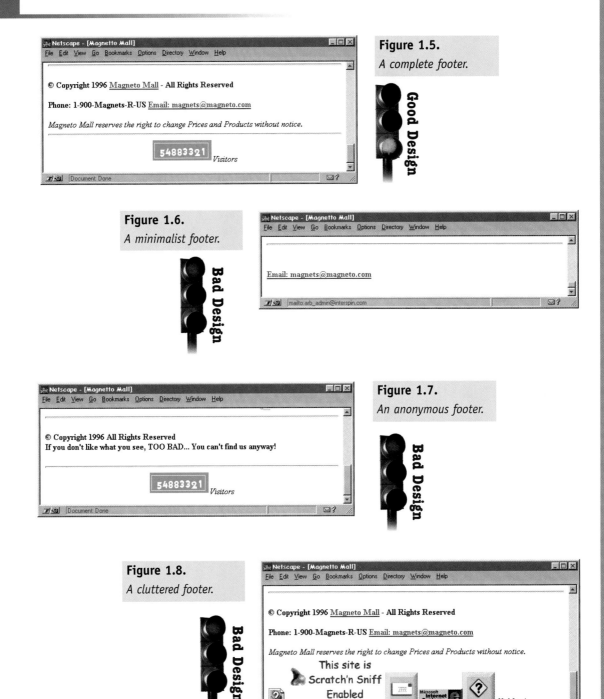

Figure 1.5.
A complete footer.

Good Design

Figure 1.6.
A minimalist footer.

Bad Design

Figure 1.7.
An anonymous footer.

Bad Design

Figure 1.8.
A cluttered footer.

Bad Design

Figure 1.9.

A descriptive title in the title bar and header.

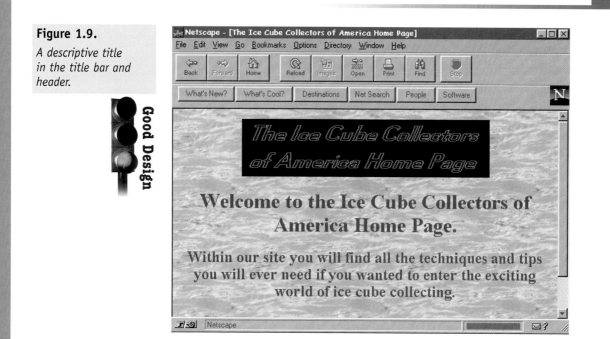

Good Design

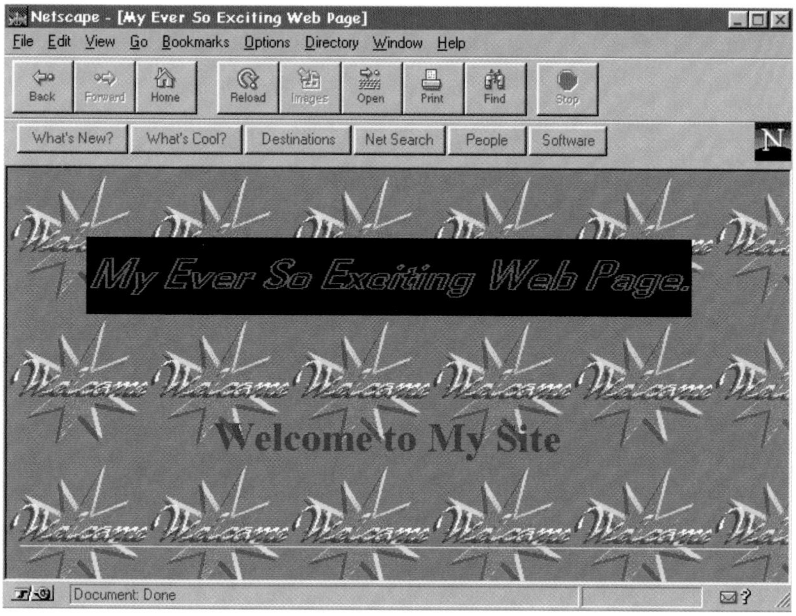

Figure 1.10.

A generic title in the title bar and header.

Bad Design

Don't use titles such as "My Favorite Links" or "Our Home Page." This "My" person and the "Our" guy have enough Web sites dedicated to them. I'm sure if you do a search on My Home Page, you'll probably get tens of thousands of Web sites. Instead, try to include a content keyword that describes what your favorite links are or what your home page is about—for example, "Favorite Links to Ice Carving Sites." (See Figure 1.11.)

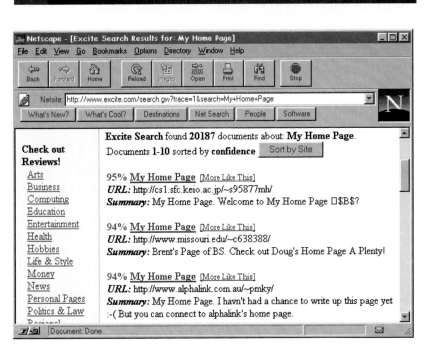

Figure 1.11.
The ever-popular "My" guy. (Note: We pulled up 20,187 sites with a My Home Page search.)

Linking Your Information Smoothly

One great thing about the Web is the capability to link information from one page to another, whether it be on the same site or a different site. When done properly, making a word or phrase come alive by hot linking it to a relevant site or document can be very effective in getting your message across. Unlike printed mediums, where information is static, readers can move instantly to a different page with just one click.

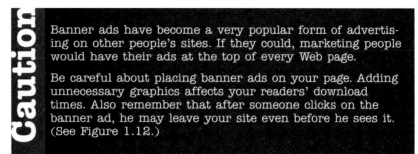

Banner ads have become a very popular form of advertising on other people's sites. If they could, marketing people would have their ads at the top of every Web page.

Be careful about placing banner ads on your page. Adding unnecessary graphics affects your readers' download times. Also remember that after someone clicks on the banner ad, he may leave your site even before he sees it. (See Figure 1.12.)

Figure 1.12.

A banner-ad emporium. (Where's the page?)

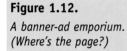

Bad Design

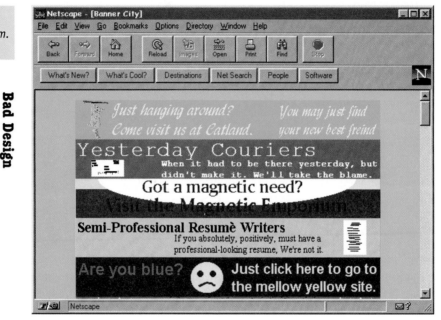

You, as a designer, must try to balance the benefits of including outside links on your Web page with the probable consequences of losing your audience halfway through the information being presented. Usually, an author's goal does not include any interruption in the flow of text. It is hard enough to keep a reader focused on your page without having an outside link entice him away from your topic. This is not to say that you should never use outside links; just plan your links carefully. What might seem like a logical link to you might not be so obvious to your readers. (See Figures 1.13 and 1.14.)

Outside links: Numerous outside links in Magneto Mall's first paragraph take the focus away from the Web page's overall message.

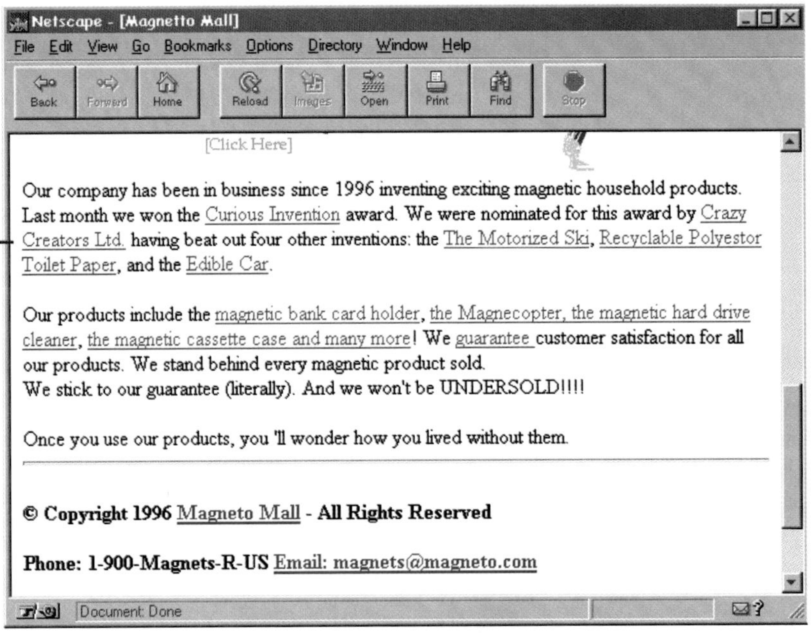

Netscape - [Magnetto Mall]

File Edit View Go Bookmarks Options Directory Window Help

Back | Forward | Home | Reload | Images | Open | Print | Find | Stop

[Click Here]

Our company has been in business since 1996 inventing exciting magnetic household products. Last month we won the Curious Invention award. We were nominated for this award by Crazy Creators Ltd. having beat out four other inventions: the The Motorized Ski, Recyclable Polyestor Toilet Paper, and the Edible Car.

Our products include the magnetic bank card holder, the Magnecopter, the magnetic hard drive cleaner, the magnetic cassette case and many more! We guarantee customer satisfaction for all our products. We stand behind every magnetic product sold.
We stick to our guarantee (literally). And we won't be UNDERSOLD!!!!

Once you use our products, you 'll wonder how you lived without them.

© Copyright 1996 Magneto Mall - **All Rights Reserved**

Phone: 1-900-Magnets-R-US Email: magnets@magneto.com

Document: Done

Figure 1.13.
Magneto Mall includes several interrupting links to outside Web sites in its first paragraph.

Bad Design

Note

Figure 1.14 shows how Magneto Mall removed distracting links from its main paragraph. Now, a sentence set off in a separate paragraph asks readers to visit the sponsor's outside link if they want to see more inventions. In addition to this, Magneto Mall placed the rest of its outside links on an Other Links page.

Our company has been in business since 1996 inventing exciting magnetic household products. Last month we won the Curious Invention award. We were nominated for this award by Crazy Creators Ltd. having beat out four other inventions: the The Motorized Ski, Recyclable Polyestor Toilet Paper, and the Edible Car.

Our products include the magnetic bank card holder, the Magnecopter, the magnetic hard drive cleaner, the magnetic cassette case and many more! We guarantee customer satisfaction for all our products. We stand behind every magnetic product sold. We stick to our guarantee (literally). And we won't be UNDERSOLD!!!!

Please visit our sponsors Crazy Creators Ltd. to find out more about other inventions.

Once you use our products, you 'll wonder how you lived without them.

[Other Links]

Outside link: Magneto Mall removed all its distracting links and replaced them with one outside link that is separated from the main paragraph. The focus of the main paragraph remains intact.

Other links: Magneto Mall moved the rest of its outside links to an Other Links page.

Figure 1.14.
Magneto Mall's first paragraph is more focused now that the outside links have been removed from the first paragraph.

Also try to consider that after the reader clicks on a link, it might be difficult for him to realize that he is going to a different site unless he is given a hint of warning beforehand. (See Figure 1.15.) If appropriate, keep all outside links on a separate links page. That way, readers know that after they click on these links, they will be leaving your site.

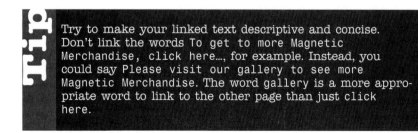

Try to make your linked text descriptive and concise. Don't link the words To get to more Magnetic Merchandise, click here..., for example. Instead, you could say Please visit our gallery to see more Magnetic Merchandise. The word gallery is a more appropriate word to link to the other page than just click here.

Lists, Callouts, and Indexes

You can arrange smaller groups of information into elements such as lists, callouts, or indexes.

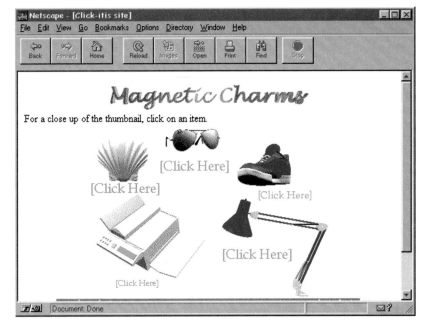

Figure 1.15.
The Click Here syndrome.

Bad Design

A *list* separates information into smaller references. Lists visually aid readers by presenting the information in an orderly fashion. Instead of choosing from a series of choices or examples in a sentence, the user can quickly reference information in a list. A sentence that simply lists a variety of beneficial magnetic devices in the sentence is less effective than an actual list that concentrates the information into separate lines, for example. (See Figures 1.16 and 1.17.)

> **Note**
> Using indexes as navigational tools is discussed in greater detail in Chapter 4, "Planning Navigation Techniques & Building the User Interface Framework."

Indexes give readers a quick overview or outline of the information presented. Information is divided into levels: the first is the main category or section, the second is a sublevel, and so on. Levels often are used as navigational tools; levels in an index can be hot linked to the section in the document where the information is located. Indexes are familiar elements to readers and should be considered when designing a navigational tool for the user interface.

A graphic sometimes needs text to help explain what is depicted. A *callout* is the extra textual information that corresponds with a graphic or text. (See Figure 1.18.) Often, a callout is used as a sidebar or commentary relating to the graphic or text beside it. You can design a callout by using tables in HTML and the <ALIGN> tag.

> **Note**
> Visit the World Wide Web Consortium's Web site at http://www.htmlhelp.com/reference/wilbur/overview.html for a more complete resource on HTML standards and tags.

Bad Design

Figure 1.16.

Using a sentence to list information.

Good Design

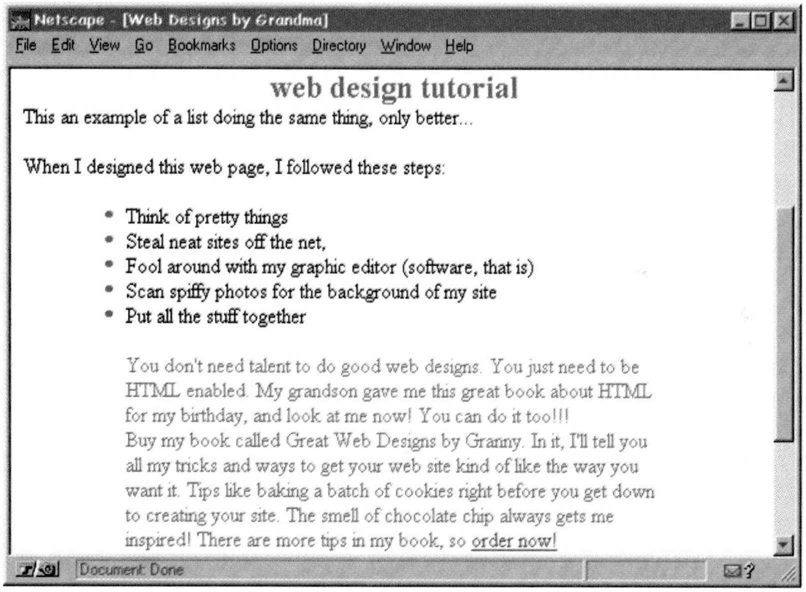

Figure 1.17.

A list that does the same thing as the sentence in Figure 1.16, only better.

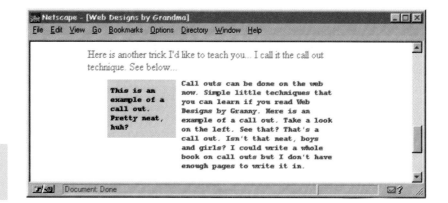

Figure 1.18.

The callout: Extra textual information.

> **Note**
>
> Achieving the callout effect is discussed in greater detail in Chapter 5, "Page-Layout Techniques Using Tables & Frames."

Text Arrangement: Using Margins and Spacing

Margins are used to make line lengths shorter. The shorter the distance a reader's eyes have to travel from left to right, the easier it is to read the text. When you read a newspaper, for example, you will notice that the text is arranged in columns. If you had to read a newspaper line from the left margin all the way to the right margin, you might find it hard to keep your place on the line.

Columns provide shorter lines to read and also aid in the flow of the text. (See Figures 1.19 and 1.20.)

Columns and margins are very useful in Web design, because they make the onscreen text legible. Readers may have their browser set at a smaller font or their screen resolution set very high, thus producing very small text. Reading small text with no margin space onscreen can cause eye fatigue. Adding margin space helps reduce eye stress and also adds style to your page. Space creates pleasant pauses and adds rhythm to your page. (See Figures 1.21 and 1.22.)

Currently, HTML is limited to only a few tags that can add space to a Web page. We will show you ways to work around this problem in Chapters 5 and 6, "Text & Typography: What Do They Really Mean to Web Page Design?"

Figure 1.19.

A newspaper page with no columns.

Bad Design

CONSPIRACY AT MAGNETTO MALL

An insider from Magnetto Mall has stepped forward and provided incriminating information which pertains to the Magnetto Mall. The source states that the Magnetto Mall is really an undercover militia group bent on attempting to demagnetize the world. They are accused of setting up a world-wide system in which they would steal large amounts of information from disks, hard drives, video tapes, bank cards and then throw the switch, demagnetizing everything in the process. With all this information stored only by Magneto Mall, they will be able to demand large amounts of financial compensation for delivery of information lost due to the demagnetization. This would cause a crisis the proportion of which we cannot comprehend. Magnetto Mall will have nations in the grip of their hands, totally at their mercy. A very frightening proposition, indeed! Sure they appear to be just another household invention company. But think about it. Doesn't almost all of the most important information in our lives live in objects that are susceptible to such a dastardly act. What will Magneto products do? They will demagnetize our information! Think about! If Magnet Mall took over the world, how could we do our banking, our shopping, our every day things, like watching videos, listening to tapes, and playing games on our computers? An insider from Magnetto Mall has stepped forward and provided incriminating information which pertains to the Magnetto Mall. The source states that the Magnetto Mall is really an undercover militia group bent on attempting to demagnetize the world. They are accused of setting up a world-wide system in which they would steal large amounts of information from disks, hard drives, video tapes, bank cards and then throw the switch, demagnetizing everything in the process. With all this information stored only by Magneto Mall, they will be able to demand large amounts of financial compensation for delivery of information lost due to the demagnetization. This would cause a crisis the proportion of which we cannot comprehend. Magnetto Mall will have nations in the grip of their hands, totally at their mercy. A very frightening proposition, indeed! Sure they appear to be just another household invention company. But think about it. Doesn't almost all of the most important information in our lives live in objects that are susceptible to such a dastardly act. What will Magneto products do? They will demagnetize our information! Think about! If Magnet Mall took over the world, how could we do our banking, our shopping, our every day things, like watching videos, listening to tapes, and playing games on our computers? An insider from Magnetto Mall has stepped forward and provided incriminating information which pertains to the Magnetto Mall. The source states that the Magnetto Mall is really an undercover militia group bent on attempting to demagnetize the world. They are accused of setting up a world-wide system in which they would steal large amounts of information from disks,

Figure 1.20.

A newspaper page with columns.

Good Design

CONSPIRACY AT MAGNETTO MALL

An insider from Magnetto Mall has stepped forward and provided incriminating information which pertains to the Magnetto Mall. The source states that the Magnetto Mall is really an undercover militia group bent on attempting to demagnetize the world. They are accused of setting up a world-wide system in which they would steal large amounts of information from disks, hard drives, video tapes, bank cards and then throw the switch, demagnetizing everything in the process. With all this information stored only by Magneto Mall, they will be able to demand large amounts of financial compensation for delivery of information lost due to the demagnetization. This would cause a crisis the proportion of which we cannot comprehend. Magnetto Mall will have nations in the grip of their hands, totally at their mercy. A very frightening proposition, indeed! Sure they appear to be just another household invention company. But think about it. Doesn't almost all of the most important information in our lives live in objects that are susceptible to such a dastardly act. What will Magneto products do? They will demagnetize our information! Think about! If Magnet Mall took over the world, how could we do our banking, our shopping, our every day things, like watching videos, listening to tapes, and playing games on our computers?

Figure 1.21.

Text on a Web page with no columns.

Bad Design

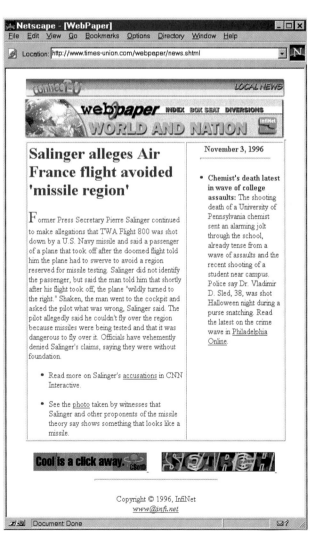

An insider from Magnetto Mall has informed us that Magnetto Mall is really an undercover militia group out to try and demagnetize the world. In the process, they are stealing large amounts of information from disks, hard drives, video tapes, bank cards and anything that can be demagnetized. With all this information, Magnetto Mall will be able to take over nations. Very frightening indeed! Sure they appear to be just another household invention company. But think about it... Isn't most information stored on some form of magnetic device, such as a computer, disk, or bank card? If Magnetto Mall took over the world, could we do our banking, our shopping, our everyday things, like watch videos, listen to tapes, play on our computers? An insider from Magnetto Mall has informed us that Magnetto Mall is really an undercover militia group out to demagnetize the world. In the process, they are stealing large amounts of information from disks, hard drives, video tapes, bank cards and anything that can be demagnetized. With all this information, Magnetto Mall will be able to take over nations. Very frightening indeed! Sure they appear to be just another household invention company. But think about it... Isn't most information stored on some form of magnetic device, such as a computer, disk, or bank card? If Magnetto Mall took over the world, could we do our banking, our shopping, our everyday things, like watch videos, listen to tapes, play on our computers? An insider from Magnetto Mall has informed us that Magnetto Mall is really an undercover militia group out to demagnetize the world. In the process, they are stealing large amounts of information from disks, hard drives, video tapes, bank cards and anything that can be

Figure 1.22.

Text on a Web page with columns at `http://www.times-union.com/webpaper/news.shtml.`

Good Design

Salinger alleges Air France flight avoided 'missile region'

Former Press Secretary Pierre Salinger continued to make allegations that TWA Flight 800 was shot down by a U.S. Navy missile and said a passenger of a plane that took off after the doomed flight told him the plane had to swerve to avoid a region reserved for missile testing. Salinger did not identify the passenger, but said the man told him that shortly after his flight took off, the plane "wildly turned to the right." Shaken, the man went to the cockpit and asked the pilot what was wrong, Salinger said. The pilot allegedly said he couldn't fly over the region because missiles were being tested and that it was dangerous to fly over it. Officials have vehemently denied Salinger's claims, saying they were without foundation.

- Read more on Salinger's accusations in CNN Interactive.

- See the photo taken by witnesses that Salinger and other proponents of the missile theory say shows something that looks like a missile.

November 3, 1996

- Chemist's death latest in wave of college assaults: The shooting death of a University of Pennsylvania chemist sent an alarming jolt through the school, already tense from a wave of assaults and the recent shooting of a student near campus. Police say Dr. Vladimir D. Sled, 38, was shot Halloween night during a purse snatching. Read the latest on the crime wave in Philadelphia Online.

Copyright © 1996, InfiNet
www@infi.net

Fonts, Fonts, Fonts: Size, Face, and Color

The capability to manipulate your fonts in HTML is a Web designer's wish come true. With the <FONT> tag, designers now have some control over how their documents appear on someone else's browser. But don't get overly excited yet. Browsers still can override font tag attributes if a reader chooses that option. Nonetheless, we won't need to use the HTML default heading tags anymore! You now can manipulate headlines and body text into stylish formats using different font attributes. (See Figure 1.23.)

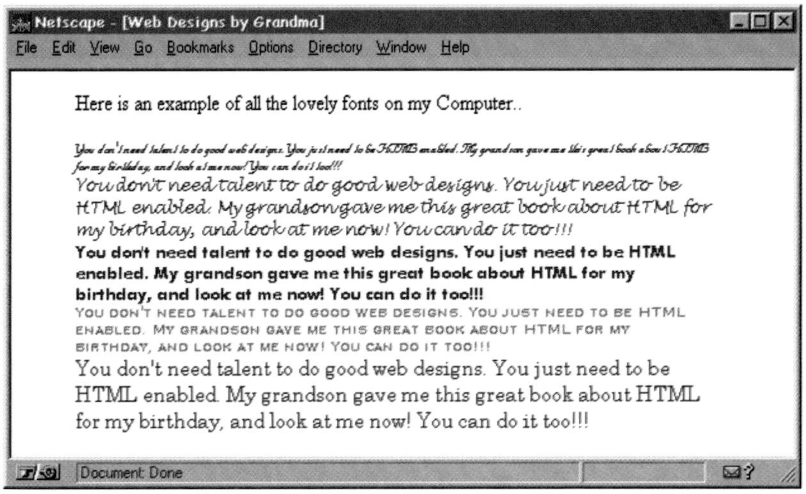

Figure 1.23.
Fonts galore!

Adding color to your fonts can bring focus to a word or line. Changing your body font also can make your document easier to read. Currently, the font types you should use for your Web designs are the fonts that come as defaults with your computer. If you use a font that is exclusive to your computer, you will be the only one who will be able to enjoy it. (See Figure 1.24.)

Figure 1.24.

Using an exclusive font.

An exclusive font seen on my computer —

The same exclusive font seen on Grandma Neddy's computer —

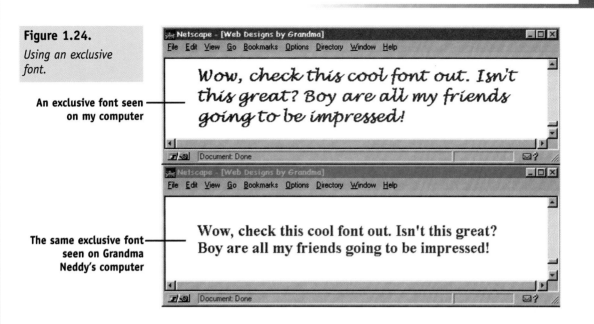

Using Space as a Design Tool

White space is a design element that seems to be the least-used element on the Web. Many sites have a "Let's jam everything into the header of our page" attitude. Because the header is the first thing a person sees when he arrives at a site, it seems logical to cram every inch of a person's screen with information. However, on a design level, too much information at once can cause information overload. The human brain can take in only so much information at one time. (See Figure 1.25.)

Bad Design

Figure 1.25.

How much information can you cram into one page?

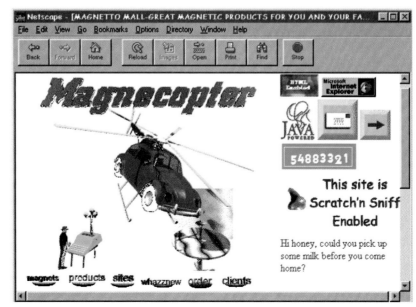

Imagine trying to read a ticker tape. After reading a few sentences, your eyes will want to call a time-out. When information is continuously fed to your eyes, your eyes need to rest to let your brain digest the information. Now apply this concept to the Web. Reading information on a monitor can be very tiring on the eyes, especially when the text goes on and on without any breaks. When text and graphics are broken up with gaps of white space, the information becomes easier to read and gives your eyes a break.

Caution

Don't get carried away with adding excessive amounts of white space. The flow of your information will become disjointed, and too many gaps between topics will drown your readers into boredom. (See Figure 1.26.)

Color in Design

In many design mediums, color is an important factor in bringing the design to life. People associate places, events, and objects with certain colors. When you think of a rose, the color red usually comes to mind. You can say a lot with color. If you are trying to achieve a mood, your choice of colors should reflect the message of the mood. If you are designing a site for children, for example, you might use the primary colors red, green, and blue.

If you are trying to portray a serious, dark mood, gray and black might be your choice of colors for your site. You should consider your color choice carefully. Don't get carried away with throwing in color wherever you feel like it. If you were redecorating your house, you wouldn't run down to the paint store, start buying paint, and just start

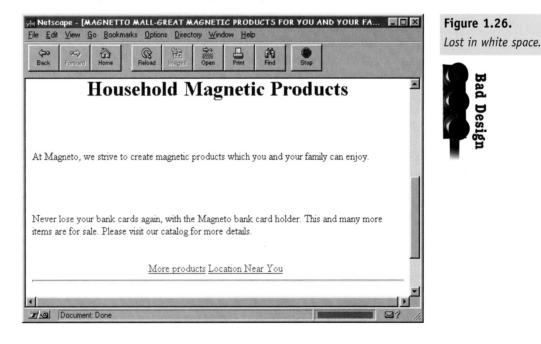

Figure 1.26.
Lost in white space.

Bad Design

painting each wall, based not on the uniform color but on the closest open paint can. You should carefully plan a color scheme to begin with. (If, in fact, that is how you do your redecorating, you'd better put this book down right now and check out your walls.) Choosing a color scheme for your Web site is a very delicate task of balancing shades, hues, and blends. When choosing colors, you also should consider that not everyone has the same resolution on their monitors as you do, so what looks like a light pink on your screen might look bright red on someone else's screen. (See Figure 1.27.)

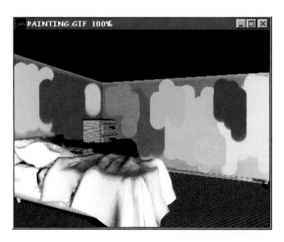

Figure 1.27.
Home design with an à la paint-sale flair.

> **Note**
>
> We will go deeper into designing with color in Chapter 7, "Splashing on the Color: Effective Color Schemes for Your Web Site."

Background: Colors, Textures, and Patterns

Behind all the things that go into a Web page, the background can be either the added touch to your site or the design disaster of the century. (See Figure 1.28.) The purpose of good design is to use the elements of design to help your audience focus on your content, not to distract them from it. One of the biggest design mistakes seen on the Web is the improper use of background images and colors. No matter how well your page is laid out or how wonderful your graphics are, when the background image upstages the contents on the page, all the elements of design get chucked out the window.

Just as in designing a stage set for a television situation comedy, the background should enhance the atmosphere of the scene and not take away from it. An actor's nightmare is when he is being upstaged by a background prop. You can't focus on the actor's dialogue when the stove behind him is in flames. (If you can, you probably belong to the TV's Tunnel Vision Society.) The best background images are those that blend quietly with the other design elements.

Texture is a nice effect to use as a background. But, even then, this design element can be abused. If the background texture serves no purpose for the overall aesthetic quality of a Web page, you should have no reason to use it. Why have blue-colored plaster in your bedroom if it doesn't coordinate with your bedding or curtains? Don't put texture into your Web pages unless it adds to the overall design.

Using the Color attribute in the background tag also can provide a background effect. And, here again, we face the same dilemma. Coordinating the background color with the rest of the elements on your page is a somewhat tricky thing. Color combinations that work well definitely will add to your design, though.

One of the main points you should keep in mind is that, when using any of these design elements, you always should plan ahead and not be afraid to experiment. Test out your site using different color and background combinations and see which one is the most effective. It never hurts to get an outside opinion—preferably, an opinion from someone who is not working on or associated with the project.

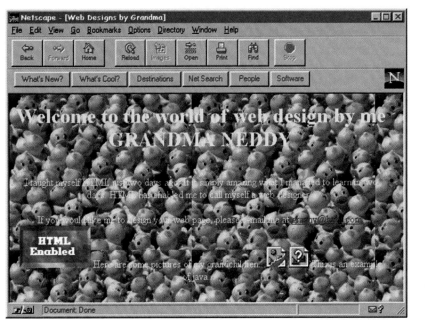

Figure 1.28.
Love my background? Welcome to Grandma Neddy's home page.

Bad Design

Finally, a word of wisdom: A dash of color can make the difference, but one too many dashes can make a disaster. Balance a few colors, shades, and backgrounds that complement each other and work with them throughout your site. The fewer the colors, the easier it is to maintain the continuity on all your pages. (See Figure 1.29.)

Note

You can find more information on color and color combinations in Chapter 7 and Appendix B, "Color Reference Guide."

23

Chapter 1: Web Page Elements: What Design Elements Go into a Web Page?

Figure 1.29.

A background that won't take away the limelight.

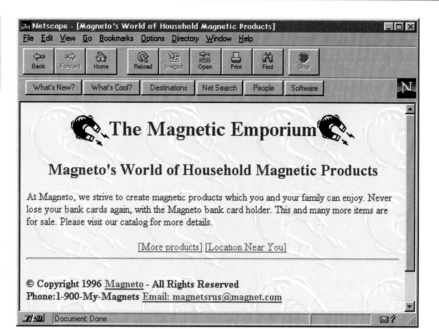

Good Design

Images, Graphics, and Icons

Humans are very visual creatures by nature. Even when our eyes are closed, our brains can create images in our minds. When we dream, we tend to see things visually and not in textual form.

In the world of design, an image is a powerful tool because it can convey a message without any words. An image can cross language barriers and communicate its message to people of many different nations. The English language can reach only so many people on the Internet, but a graphic can send its message to many more. (See Figures 1.30 and 1.31.)

Choosing an image or a graphic to communicate a message to your audience is not a task to be taken lightly. Images and graphics should not be treated simply as ornamental pieces for your pages. First of all, graphics take a long time to load, so any unnecessary graphics on your page will only frustrate your readers. Use images or graphics that add focus to your site rather than take away from it. If the graphic serves a purpose on your page, go for it. But if it is on your page because you think it looks cool, consider taking it out.

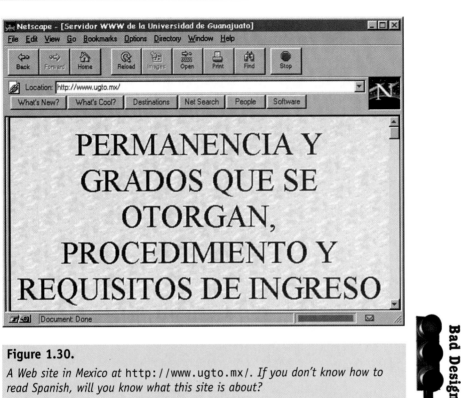

Figure 1.30.

A Web site in Mexico at http://www.ugto.mx/. *If you don't know how to read Spanish, will you know what this site is about?*

Bad Design

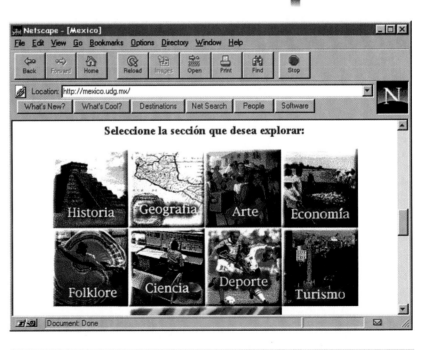

Good Design

Figure 1.31.

A graphic on a Web site in Mexico at http://mexico.udg.mx/. *If you don't know how to read Spanish, can you guess what this site is about?*

Note

Downloading a small, well-designed graphic might be worth the wait when you're using a slow modem. A huge, ugly graphic that hogs up bandwidth time won't be. Graphic size is not based on the actual dimension of the graphic but on the byte size of the file.

Since the days of cavemen, humans have used drawings or icons to communicate with each other. The interpretation of each icon is based on an association of the icon with a particular item or experience. When you use a piece of software, a set of buttons probably will be included to help you perform certain tasks. Drawings are usually on these buttons to help you to distinguish what each button does. The button with a picture of a printer on it, for example, usually is the button that sends the document to the printer. These drawings or icons help you find your way around.

As in software user interfaces, icons can be used in your site to help your readers navigate. Designing icons is discussed in Chapter 11, "Completing the Core Web Site: Implementing the User Interface."

Tip

When designing your icons, keep them simple. Icons do not need to look realistic. Don't try to squeeze a masterpiece onto one little icon. Icons are meant to be small, and adding too many things to one can be confusing to the reader. (See Figure 1.32.)

Typical icons you see on the Web

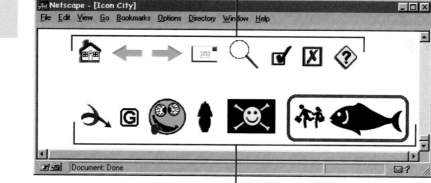

Figure 1.32.
Various icons.

Icon't understand it—confusing icons

Cross-Platform Design Issues: Do You See What I See?

Web design is unique because the reader is in control of the final outcome of the design. This makes it difficult for a Web site to appear in the exact way the designer intended.

A Melting Pot of Browsers, Computers, and Gadgets

The Web is a true platform-independent community. People can design and publish Web pages no matter what kind of computer they use. This means that stuff produced for the Web on a PC can be viewed by someone on his or her Mac or UNIX station. Although the technical intricacies of designing and viewing Web sites with various machines may differ, overall design issues still apply. In your design, you still must deal with proportion, structure, balance, alignment, graphics, flow, contrast, functionality, and other issues.

The differences don't stop there. Imagine the number of browsers out there that interpret each Web site in their own special ways. The problem with all these different machines and browsers viewing the same information is exactly that: they are different machines, viewing the same information, with different hardware and different browsers. What might look awesome on one machine or browser might look dull or even downright unappealing on another. (See Figures 1.33 and 1.34.) Many types of video cards and monitors are out there, and they may have their own little differences in settings. A page designed for a 640×480 pixel screen looks quite different on a 1,280×1,024 screen. With the difference in screen settings, the graphics on the original Web page could shrink to a dot or expand out and fill quite a lot of space. Without line breaks, the text that once wrapped around and filled five lines might be a single line on a larger screen (so much for spending all that time on layout).

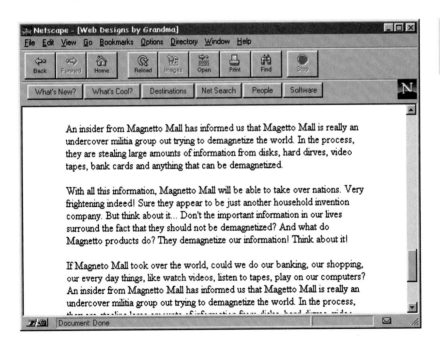

Figure 1.33.
Viewing a page in Netscape.

If you feel that you know your audience, you could design your site with the assumption that your readers will have all the necessary plug-ins and gizmos you'll need to get your site working exactly the way you want it. But, like my momma always told me, "Never assume anything. If you do, you make an ashtray out of U and me…" Who really knows what kind of browsers or plug-ins your audience will have?

(See Figure 1.35.) If you want to be Mr. or Ms. Nice, you can create different versions of your site so that all the browsers in the world can see your stuff. This is great if you have the time and the desire to duplicate your work 30 different ways. When you finish duplicating your work over and over and over again, be prepared for someone else to point out that you didn't make versions for the other elite browsers out there in Timbuktu.

Figure 1.34.

Viewing the same page shown in Figure 1.33 in a Lynx browser.

Figure 1.35.

How plugged in can you get?

Color Me Bad

Color is another cross-platform issue to address. You have just spent hours pouring over a cool photo, touching up the image pixel by pixel until it is a tribute to perfection. You place it on the Web and run to the phone to call your friend. You proudly announce to him that your *image de resistance* is up, and that he should now feast on the beauty of it. He calls back in five minutes (unless he has a separate line for his computer, in which case you get immediate feedback). He tries to sound enthused, but you can hear the disappointment in his voice. You wonder why this 24-bit masterpiece would only bring forced enthusiasm from your friend. "What did you say? What do you mean you only have a 4-bit color palette?!?" (See Figures 1.36 and 1.37.)

Note

In order for a reader to enjoy a Web site that incorporates multimedia files such as Shockwave, RealAudio, or QuickTime Video, his browser needs the required plug-in, which he can download from the Net.

Figure 1.36.

Your 24-bit masterpiece.

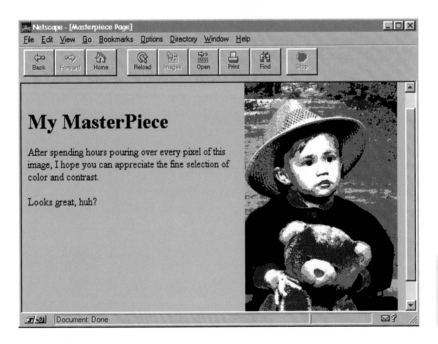

Figure 1.37.

Your 24-bit masterpiece with a 4-bit color palette.

H-e-e-e-e-e-l-l-l-l-l-l-p!!!!!

So how are struggling Web designers like us supposed to create great Web design when we have little control over how our work is going to appear on another person's computer or browser? We suggest that you approach this problem with these considerations in mind:

◆ When you are putting your site together, consider the different platforms out there.

◆ Figure out who your main audience is.

◆ Try to use tags that most popular browsers support. Stay away from tags that are supported by specific browsers only.

◆ Never assume anything about your audience. Let them know what to expect at your site. And remember: If it doesn't add to it, don't use it.

A designer must take into consideration every member of the audience. If possible, be sure to check the masterpiece on different platforms for cross-platform translation of your work. A designer must be imaginative and creative enough to design something that is at least suitable for a majority of the audience. It's impossible to please everyone (trust us, you won't), but if you let your readers know what to expect at your site and try to steer away from anything that is supported only by specific browsers, your readers will appreciate it.

Flexible Layout Schemes

Web sites designed specifically for one browser might look great on that particular browser but awful on another. Your site should be flexible enough to be viewed by many different browsers. You can accomplish this by designing your site with the lowest common denominator in mind. If you use tags that are non-browser specific, a majority of your audience will be able to view your site without having to download yet another browser. Interrupting readers with a

```
You can't see this site unless you
have the latest and greatest version
of Scratch & Sniff Version 3004
```

message is not only going to annoy them, but also might sidetrack them from your site forever. Remember: Don't distract your readers.

When achieving certain layout effects on your page, try to work around the HTML limitations. Don't leap in and start using the latest and greatest HTML tags (such as cascading style sheet tags). If you do, you might alienate a majority of readers who only have previous versions of a browser. Instead, try to achieve page-layout effects by using HTML tags such as the <TABLE>, <BR>, <P>, and <FONT> tags, which are supported by HTML 2.0 standards.

Set the standards for your designs. Determine which common denominator your site will be designed for. If you decide that your site will be viewed best in Netscape and Internet Explorer, make sure that this standard is consistent in all your designs. Also determine the type of bandwidth speed at which your audience will be accessing your graphics. If you decide that your graphics should be accessed quickly with a 14.4Kbps modem, make sure that your graphics meet those standards.

Remember: Your readers, not you, control the ultimate outcome of your Web design. The more browser-friendly your site, the more likely readers will stay and visit it.

Summary

Now that you have become familiar with basic design elements, let's review the major points in this chapter:

◆ Before designing your site, remember to plan and organize your ideas, keeping the design elements of the header, body, and footer in mind.

◆ Be concise and complete with all your design elements.

◆ Maintain continuity on your Web pages by being consistent with your design elements.

◆ Make sure that your titles and links are descriptive. The more descriptive they are, the easier it will be for your readers to determine what your site is about.

◆ Try to avoid unnecessary outside links in your main documents, because they might distract your audience from your topic.

◆ Be consistent with your fonts and break up your text with space to make your information more legible.

◆ Make sure that the fonts you use are not exclusive to your computer.

◆ Don't cram everything into a small area on your page.

◆ Planning your color scheme ensures that the color combinations add to your design rather than take away from it.

◆ Make sure that the background is not louder than the content of the Web page.

◆ Use graphics that effectively convey your message. Avoid adding unnecessary graphics to your page.

◆ Keep your icons and graphics simple.

◆ Test out your site on different platforms to ensure that your page is laid out in the way you intended.

◆ Designing with the lowest common denominator in mind will properly convey your message to a majority of your audience.

Q&A

Q **Why should I bother following a structured format for my designs? I thought that *designing* meant being creative. Won't a formal structure diminish my creativity?**

A Web design uses the traditional elements of design to convey creativity in a more effective way. Remember that the Web is new to many people. Why alienate them by making it harder to understand your site? Designing with your audience in mind brings focus to your creativity. What's the point of being creative if no one else understands it? If you understand the elements of design, it's up to you to decide whether you should use them.

Q **Why do I need text on my Web site? If I use graphics, I won't have to worry about my page layout changing on other platforms.**

A As we mentioned earlier, graphics take a long time to load compared to HTML text. The more graphics on your site, the longer it takes to load your page on someone's browser. Also remember that, to decrease download time, people sometimes turn off their graphics-viewing capabilities while surfing the Web. Landing on a site with only graphics-based text means that graphically disabled people will not be able to see the content on your page.

Q You mentioned in this chapter that people should avoid putting outside links in their main Web pages. What if I want to link to someone else's page and someone else wants to link to mine?

A If possible, limit all your outside links to an Other Links page. That way, when people click on a link on this page, they will be aware that they will be leaving your site.

Challenge Yourself

An important part of design is familiarizing yourself with various designs—good and bad. You need to surf the Net and view a variety of Web sites created by different designers. Go to a number of sites and answer the following questions for each site:

- ✦ Is the site aesthetically pleasing?
- ✦ If the site is not aesthetically pleasing, what elements make it unappealing?
- ✦ Which design items discussed in this chapter are used? Which design items are left out?
- ✦ Do you think the site achieved its objective? If not, why do you think it does not achieve its objective?

As you view more Web sites, you will begin to pick up on the items that make a successful Web site appealing, as well as realize what elements make an unsuccessful Web site unappealing. This experience will be a great asset in helping you judge how to design your Web sites for maximum effectiveness and results.

Chapter 2

The Basics of Web Page Design

Proportion, *balance*, *consistency*, *contrast*, and *rhythm* are words you will hear quite often in the design world. In this chapter, we will explain to you their importance and how to apply them to your Web designs. We also will spend some time talking about creating effective headings and pull-quotes, using lines and boxes to control focus, and more. So stick around and learn about the basics of Web design.

Proportions of Your Page

Peripheral vision makes our range of view fairly wide. That is, when we look ahead, we see not only what is directly in our line of vision, but also above our line of vision, below it, beside it, and even out of the corners of our eyes. One thing that our eyes can't do (and no, the answer does not have anything to do with X-ray vision) is focus completely on more than one thing at a time. (Again, if you are a member of the Tunnel Vision Society, never mind.)

Stimulate Me

Our eyes and minds need visual stimuli to attract our attention. We zoom in on objects that capture our focus. That is why a page layout containing rhythm and contrast stimulates our eyes and minds more than a page full of straight text. When laid out in a certain way, different sizes and shapes of elements on a Web page can make or break a reader's desire to stay on that page. Our eyes like to focus on pages that are pleasantly laid out. (See Figure 2.1.)

Big Doesn't Always Mean Better

When the contrast of elements on your page, such as graphics, headers, and text, relate with each other intuitively and proportionally, it provides a pleasant stimulus to a reader's eyes. On the other hand, if you load up your page with same-sized elements beside each other, your Web page will lack the visual contrasts needed to keep a reader interested.

Figure 2.1.

HomeArts Network's home page (http://homearts.com/) is an example of how the elements of a page can be arranged to create an appealing design. Notice how the colors and shapes create rhythm with each other.

Good Design

The sizes of the elements on your Web page should relate to each other based on what their functions are on the page. The size of your header usually will be larger than the body text of your Web page. A graphic that you want your readers to focus on should be sized a bit larger so that it stands out from the body of text beside it. Every element of the Web page should relate to or connect with the other elements around it, based on the amount of emphasis you want to give each element.

Laying It Out on Paper

When you lay out your elements, take into consideration how the sizes of your graphics relate to the text and other graphics around them. If placed beside smaller elements, large elements can attract a reader's attention. Smaller elements can do the same thing, if they are surrounded by white space and pulled slightly away from the other elements. The main thing is to experiment first by arranging your elements. Take a piece of paper and draw squares and rectangular boxes to represent the elements of your page. Arrange them on your paper in the way you imagine your page to be. Try increasing or decreasing the sizes and shapes of certain elements. See which arrangements and sizes complement each other. Then test them out by showing them to other people.

> **Tip**
> Analyze which arrangements are more appealing or less appealing to your readers. The more you understand why someone likes or dislikes a particular arrangement, the more likely you will be to develop an effective design.

Structure: Organizing Your Design Elements

To achieve an effective layout for your Web page, we will start by doing it the old-fashioned way: by drawing it out on paper. So get your crayons out, boys and girls, coz now it's time to draw!

So How Do the Professionals Do It?

You see a really cool Web site and you wonder, "How did they align their graphics and text like that?" Well, for starters, the designer didn't just start typing HTML code and shoving in graphics wherever he felt like putting them. He took the time to draw his design out on paper first (we hope).

One difficult aspect of Web design is the fact that when you are creating HTML code on a text editor, you can't really see what your Web page looks like until you view it on your browser. You end up typing your HTML code, checking it out on your browser, finding something that is not correct, and then revising and editing your code again in your text editor. This bouncing back and forth from editor to browser becomes pretty dizzying after a while. If you are trying to type HTML code and design the layout of your Web page *on-the-fly* (without having a plan on paper), you'll never get anywhere. (It's like continuously laying down railroad tracks a second before the train travels over them.) It is better to have an outline of how the elements of your Web page are going be laid out before you start any HTML work. That way, you can look at the layout on the paper while you are typing the HTML code without stopping to check out what you're doing on the browser all the time.

Keeping all those things in mind, it's now time to put your thoughts onto paper.

To help you align your elements, draw a huge table or grid on your paper. We'll start with three columns first, and later we can move to four or five. The lines on the page in front of you will serve as an outline for your design. Now try drawing your design elements with the size and shape combinations you chose earlier, using the column widths as guides for alignment. (See Figure 2.2.) After you complete the drawing, take another page and try changing your elements around. Keep experimenting until you find an arrangement that works. After checking out your design in a variety of formats, start all over again using a four-column table. ("Huh? Start all over," you say?! "When does the fun stuff start?") This is the time to experiment by arranging and rearranging your design elements. Although this might seem like a time-consuming process, the results will make it easier for your Web design process in the long run. The alignment combination you choose also will be the first real step toward your Web site creation.

Note

What-You-See-Is-What-You-Get (WYSIWYG) HTML editors enable you to see what your site looks like while you are typing text and adding graphics. Currently, though, WYSIWYG editors are limited when it comes to controlling alignment. You get the most control over your page layout when you use a regular HTML text editor. Most WYSIWYG editors don't support all HTML tags and aren't sophisticated or flexible enough to do everything we want them to do (not yet, that is). In addition, these editors add unnecessary HTML coding to your pages, which makes the site cumbersome to maintain in the future.

Note

We will discuss a number of typographical issues in this chapter, including typographical terms that might not be familiar to you.

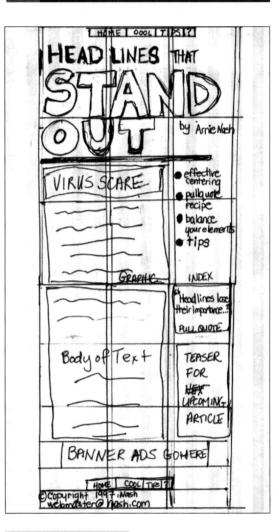

Figure 2.2.

A first sketch of elements on paper.

Alignment (Center, Left, Right, and Justified)

When you land on a professional-looking Web site, you usually don't say, "Hey, this guy did a great job aligning his text and graphics!" (Unless your boss designed it and is standing behind you while you test his site.) It is not something a person usually goes out looking for when he visits a site. When you land on a crummy site, though, your eyes quickly pick up boo-boos such as inconsistent alignment of headers, graphics, and text. You want your readers to focus on the content you are presenting, not on the presentation itself, especially if it sucks. Minimum distraction from the design means that maximum attention is given to your content. So the moral of the story is this: Good designing gets overlooked while bad designing gets looked over.

Center This, Justify That

> **Note**
>
> You should follow certain rules of thumb when aligning elements on your page. Sometimes, rules are made to be broken, and yes, we do it ourselves all the time. But before you take us literally, here is a word of advice: Understand the rule first before you break it.

Before the HTML `<CENTER>` tag came to be, Web designers were limited in their ability to control text alignment. They had to be content with left-aligning all their text and graphics on their Web pages. Now that the popular browsers support the `<ALIGN>` attribute and the `<CENTER>` tag, people on the Web are having a hay day trying to use them all over their pages—sometimes, with frightening results. (See Figure 2.3.)

Some Web-page designers like to show their readers how creative they are by using the center-my-whole-page technique. Centering the text might seem cool and artsy in the first sentence, but, after a while, it just becomes too darn hard to read. Centering sentences in a paragraph makes the starting and ending point of every line different from one line to the next. Instead of having your eyes logically look to the left margin for the beginning of a line, your eyes finish off one sentence and then search for the beginning of the next. Remember to use alignment techniques to aid your readers—not make them go cross-eyed.

Figure 2.3.

Centering our focus down the middle of the page, the Mid-State Midwives site shows us the over-centering effect.

Bad Design

To be effective, your alignment technique must bring focus to your element, whether it be a header or a callout box. Centering can be effective when used with headers, navigational bars, table contents, footers, and large graphics. You should not use centering for callout text, body text, lists, and singular small graphics. It is safe to say that the rest of the elements work best left aligned.

Justifying your text on paper or on the Web is a big no-no in our books. When sentences are justified, inconsistent gaps of white space show up between each word, which breaks up the flow of the text. This technique usually gives a box-like effect to the body of text, because the text aligns flush with the left and right margins. This means that the shorter the line, the bigger the white space between each word. Fortunately, the <JUSTIFY> tag is not an attribute supported by HTML 2.0 standards. Suffice it to say, we're pretty sure that the <JUSTIFY> tag will surface one day, and, when it does, you'd better justify the use of it before you use it!

Columns of Text

Columns are useful for organizing your elements and giving visual contrast to your page. A Web page of text that reads from the left margin of the page all the way to the right margin is not only difficult to read but pretty ugly to look at. A body of text with no breaks can drown out your message. Columns provide white space between different elements, giving contrast to your page. (See Figure 2.4.)

Figure 2.4.

The Sandman Hotels site (http://www.sandman.ca/starplus.html) displays text in two columns. Note how the text size is smaller in the left-hand column than it is in the right. Usually, for better readability, the narrower the column, the smaller the text size and type.

Column Widths and Lengths

The width of your column should determine the font size and type of your text. Narrow columns require smaller font sizes and types. Wider columns require larger font sizes and types. If you try to squeeze big text type into a narrow column, your sentences will look short and choppy. In contrast, if you put small text type in a wide column, your reader will have to use a magnifying glass to read it.

In this designing phase of your site, try using columns on Web pages that contain large amounts of text. Varying column widths adds variety and contrast to the page. Take a look at a few magazines to get some ideas of what kinds of variations on column widths work well with the elements in them. After leafing through a few magazines, you will get a sense of how the column widths control the flow of the text. Now try to find sites on the Web that contain columns of text and graphics. Note which ones you find visually appealing and try to see whether the column widths contribute to the appearance.

A narrow column on the left of your Web page can be used as a margin that can contain elements such as small graphics, callout information, text links, and so on. (See Figure 2.5.)

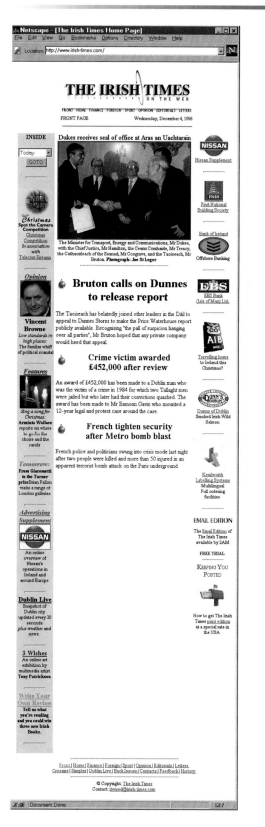

Figure 2.5.

The Irish Times (`http://www.irish-times.com`) *shows you the effectiveness of placing smaller elements into narrow columns to separate them from larger elements.*

Tip

Keep in mind that a number of people might be seeing your site on a 14-inch monitor. Keep the total of your column widths to no more than 600 pixels wide. When page widths are wider than the monitor, the reader has to scroll the page to the right in order to see the whole thing.

A page on the Web should be seen as a whole, so our word of advice is this: Don't make 'em scroll!

Placing Your Graphics in Columns

Unless you plan your site to be completely dominated by text, you most likely will be adding some visual images to your pages. Graphical elements are important in helping to convey the information you are presenting. If your text is laid out in columns for easy readability, your images should be placed strategically to enhance the meaning and flow of the text. (See Figure 2.6.)

Graphic images should relate to the surrounding text. You wouldn't want to place a picture of an ocean beside text that talks about the Sahara desert. In columns, the text should work its way around graphics and continue without disrupting the flow. You can set alignment between text and graphics by using alignment tags or by placing the text and graphics directly into a table.

Figure 2.6.

The graphics at Nando Times (`http://www.nando.net`) are placed in columns and aligned consistently to the left of the column to present a smooth flow of text and graphics.

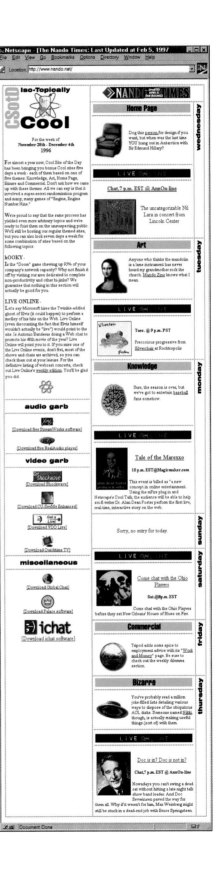

Balance: Don't Let One Element Overpower Another

Planning the layout of a Web page requires a designer to achieve many things. A Web page designer must make sure that his page has readable line lengths, visual contrast, proportion, and proper alignment. He also has to ensure that the page contains balance.

Balance is achieved when elements do not overpower one another (whether they are elements of a story, architecture, music, or fashion). Dressing in an expensive suit and wearing a trendy cologne might make a guy great date material (for some women). But if he can empty a theater full of people when he enters the room, it doesn't matter how great he thinks he looks. No one will notice his new $1,000 Armani suit if his new cologne overpowers him, his clothes, and everyone in the theater.

When applying this idea to Web design, a great Java applet won't improve your page if it overpowers the amazing graphics you spent hours creating. (See Figure 2.7.) With so much going on in your Web page, you, as a designer, must ensure that the elements work with, rather than against, each other. A unified page of elements brings focus to your content. (See Figure 2.8.)

Bad Design

Figure 2.7.

The Cause To Save All Causes site would have been a nice layout example except for the distracting Welcome to the Java polka dot creator applet picture that is shoved beside the Save the Cause graphic. This one element (no matter how cool it was to the designer) destroys the balance on the page.

Good Design

Figure 2.8.

There is a whole lotta balance happening at the Women's Edge (http://www.womensedge.com/children/index.html) site, with every element of design contributing to the overall flow of the Web page.

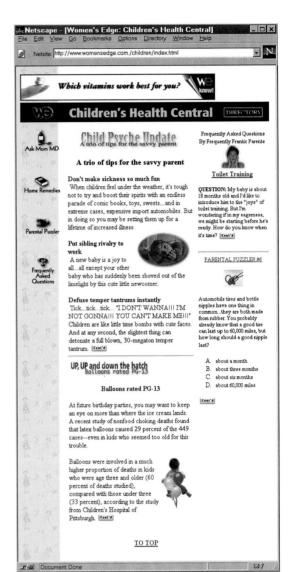

Consistency of Text and Graphics

The overall look and feel of a Web site should be consistent throughout. Consistency is critical in allowing your readers to become familiar with your site. Familiarity of the elements helps readers feel more comfortable and makes them receptive to the information presented. Consistency is achieved by proper selection and use of text and graphics, and by repeating elements such as headers, footers, and navigational tools on every page. (See Figure 2.9.)

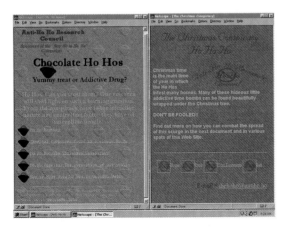

Figure 2.9.

The Chocolate Ho Hos site shows you how inconsistency can create confusion. Notice how the basic color, layout, and location of elements are significantly different on both pages. A reader will be thrown off by the change of style throughout the site.

Bad Design

Textual Consistency

You can make text consistent by using only one or a small number of similar font types and sizes. The sizes of the fonts for each type of element should be uniform. This means that all header text, footer text, body text, callouts, captions, and text links should be consistent in font size and type. If you are using 8-point Arial for your body text on your home page, for example, don't start changing to 10-point Garamond halfway through the page. Similarly, try to stick to the same font size and type for the body text on all your pages. The same goes for the other elements on your page, such as headers, callouts, and so on.

Header Consistency

The header is the first element the reader sees, so it is important to keep this element consistent throughout your site. A reader should be able to tell that he is on the same site by looking at the header of the page. If you constantly change the headers in your site, the reader might become disoriented, confused, and frustrated. If he has to adjust his eyes to a new look every time he lands on a page, he might ask himself, "Where the heck am I going?," or more likely, "What the heck are these guys doing here?" Your headers should reassure your reader that he is at the same site and not confuse him.

Graphics Consistency

Graphics come in a variety of shapes, sizes, and colors. Although the graphics may vary, you can achieve consistency by making sure that all the graphics have a similar theme, alignment, and color tone. Be creative—go wild and woolly with your graphics—but make sure that each graphic has a place and purpose on the page. Again, if the graphic is not necessary, get it out of there!

Navigational Consistency

Navigational elements always should be consistent throughout your site. Remember that a reader needs to be familiar with the navigational elements to be able to freely move around your site without getting confused or lost. You should help your reader by placing your navigational elements in the same area of each page.

You can use standard navigational icons that are recognizable to most surfers on the Net or create your own graphics. Just make sure that the graphics you decide to use are consistent on every page of your site.

Tip

If you place your navigational elements at the top of your home page, try to keep them in the same place on your other Web pages. Don't throw in your navigational elements wherever you feel like it. If you were driving in a foreign city, you wouldn't want to have the street signs located on the left side of the road for part of the street, on the right side of the road at another part, behind a tree at another part, and so on. Your readers shouldn't have to search all over your Web page to figure out where your navigational elements are. The design should give the reader free access to roam around your site—not hinder his travel.

Consistency, Consistency, Consistency (You Get What We Mean)

Web designers should strive to design their sites with consistency. Consistency brings a sense of style to your pages. A Web site that has a similar feel to all its pages is a site that will be remembered and bookmarked. Unless you want your readers to feel like they've reached the Twilight Zone, where anything can happen, you should keep radical changes to a minimum.

Flow of Text and Objects

The relationship between the elements on your page should enhance the *flow* of your text and objects. Don't put road blocks on your Web page. A huge graphic floating in the middle of your page for no rhyme or reason (and saying that it looks cool doesn't count) distracts your readers from the content of your page. We once saw a site where a guy was selling his boat, for example. He had this huge animation of a boat moving away from the dock and then backing up toward it, moving away and backing up, away and back, over and over again. No matter how cool that might seem to him, what the heck does that animation have to do with the fact that he is trying to sell his boat? If he wanted to display a photo of his boat, why did he have to animate it? Not only does the animation serve no purpose on the page, but it distracts the reader from the content of the page and increases the download time of the page tremendously.

The elements on your Web page should work harmoniously with each other. As a

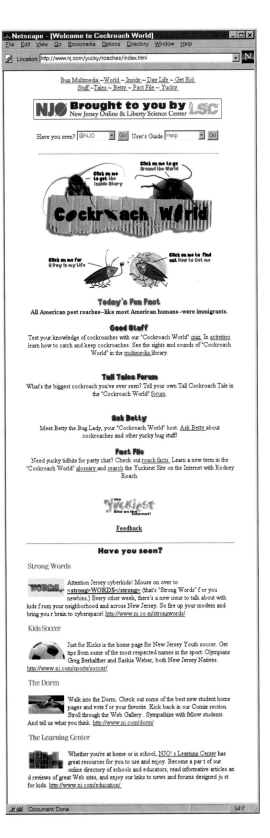

Figure 2.10.

A reader does not have to search around the Cockroach World site (http://www.nj.com/yucky/roaches/index.html) to find information. This is a well laid-out page where all the elements work together harmoniously.

designer, it is your job to ensure that a reader can go through your Web pages with ease. The easier it is for the reader, the more he will opt to stay at your site. (See Figure 2.10.)

Visual Contrast: Rhythm in Your Pages

Again, we bring up the importance of *visual contrast* on your Web pages. A page that contains no contrast can be quite a boring experience indeed.

Visual contrast enhances the rhythm of a Web page by creating a flow that helps guide the reader's eyes. Without rhythm, a page becomes stagnant and stale. Those who are guilty of stale design condemn their Web pages to become yet more deposits of unread information floating around cyberspace. Rhythm is a vital part in the forward flow and movement of the page. You can achieve rhythm through the orderly repetition of any element—line, shape, tone, and texture. Emphasis and repetition of certain elements help get your message across to your reader. (See Figure 2.11.)

Headlines That Stand Out

Headlines, or headings, do three main things on a Web page. They inform the reader what the text is about, focus his attention on a particular section of the page, and divide the content of the page into levels of importance.

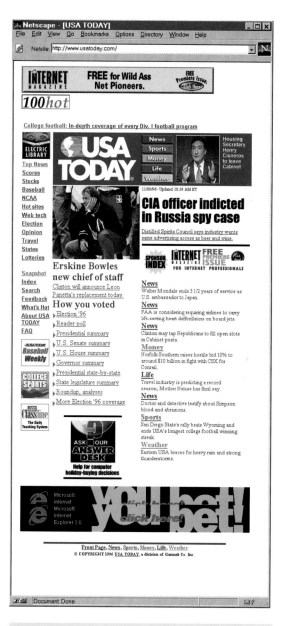

Figure 2.11.

A reader's visual senses are awakened by the contrast of color, shapes, and sizes on USA Today's (http://www.usatoday.com) home page.

A Few Words Go a Long Way

On the Web, we usually describe headlines as headings, because people usually associate headlines with newspaper media. Headings, just like headlines, can sell a story. So choose your words carefully. On the home page of a Web site, the heading `Hot Dog Vendors Save Exposed Buns from Cold` is eye catching but confusing to the reader. A heading that says `The Internet Connects Millions All Over the World` is only stating the obvious and has no impact at all. Wordy headings such as `Computer Virus Scare Shuts Down Whole City Block After Hacker Announces His Intentions` put your reader to sleep, not to mention that it takes up half his screen just to read it. (See Figure 2.12.) A heading should focus on one point. You don't have to convey the whole message in your heading. Just put enough into it so that your reader can sense what to expect next. (See Figure 2.13.)

Bad Design

Figure 2.12.
Cool News shows you examples of poorly written headlines.

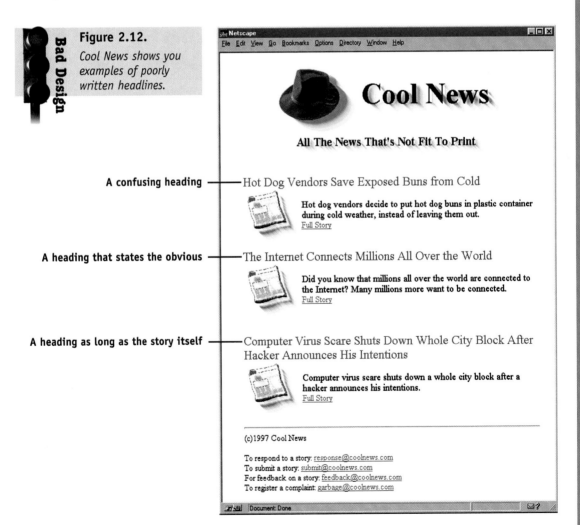

A confusing heading

A heading that states the obvious

A heading as long as the story itself

Cool News

All The News That's Not Fit To Print

Hot Dog Vendors Save Exposed Buns from Cold

Hot dog vendors decide to put hot dog buns in plastic container during cold weather, instead of leaving them out.
Full Story

The Internet Connects Millions All Over the World

Did you know that millions all over the world are connected to the Internet? Many millions more want to be connected.
Full Story

Computer Virus Scare Shuts Down Whole City Block After Hacker Announces His Intentions

Computer virus scare shuts down a whole city block after a hacker announces his intentions.
Full Story

(c)1997 Cool News

To respond to a story: response@coolnews.com
To submit a story: submit@coolnews.com
For feedback on a story: feedback@coolnews.com
To register a complaint: garbage@coolnews.com

Figure 2.13.

The Neely home page (`http://`
`users.vnet.net/bookbiz/`
`homepage.html`*) shows you examples
of concise and humorous headlines.*

Good Design

Levels of Importance

Headings also provide visual contrast on your
Web page. A large heading usually denotes
the importance of the content after it. A
smaller heading usually highlights points of
lesser importance. Font types and point sizes
should relate to the level of the heading. The
higher the level of the heading, the bigger
the font size and type. To maintain consistency on the page, try to refrain from using too
many font types and sizes. Choose one font
and type size for all your main headings, one
font and type size for all your subheadings,
and so on. The more consistent you are, the
more your reader will be able to judge the
level of importance for each section.

When Do We Use Pullquotes?

Pullquotes are short excerpts taken from portions of text that grab your reader's attention
and draw him to a particular body of text.
Because the text usually is bolder and larger
than the body text, the pullquote also helps
break up huge blocks of text and adds a nice
visual contrast to the whole Web page.

A Pullquote Recipe

When creating a pullquote, Web designers
should try to keep the message short and
sweet. A reader should be able to read the
pullquote at a glance. If it takes a reader
more than three seconds to read, you might
as well not call it a pullquote. A lengthy pullquote loses its purpose as an attention-
grabber if a reader decides that it would take
too long to read it and moves on to something else.

A good pullquote, on the other hand, takes an interesting phrase from a body of text that, taken out of context, piques the curiosity of a reader. If you read a tabloid paper, you will notice that many of its pull-quotes consist of controversial phrases. Few people will argue with the fact that most of us are very curious people or people hungry for information. When we create a pullquote, we want to trigger a reader's desire to find out more about something. Tabloid, magazine, and newspaper media hope to trigger their readers' need to know things, such as why the latest and greatest software has proven to be a dud in the software industry, or whether it is scientifically possible for gorillas to give birth to human babies, or something as irrelevant as how much Oprah really makes. It might not be information that a reader necessarily wanted to know before he picked up the magazine or paper, but the writer can use pullquotes to encourage the reader to decide that the topic might be worth the read.

This concept applies even more on the Web. If a reader is surfing for long periods of time, everything he reads can become monotonous. His eyes will yearn to find some way to focus on bits of information that interest him. A good pullquote can be a lifesaver for a reader who doesn't have the time to scroll all over the page to find what he is looking for. If a pullquote is right to the point and presented with a little wit, it usually is well appreciated. So the thing to remember when creating your pullquotes is to try to make them fun and savvy without taking away the meaning of the message. (See Figures 2.14 and 2.15.)

Pullquote Restraints

The location of your pullquotes is vital for the message of your Web page to come through. If you place the pullquote too early on a page, the story is given away. If you place the pullquote too late, the relevance of the quote is lost and ends up becoming just a space filler.

Also, when designing your layout, you must consider the number of pullquotes to use for your Web page. Too many pullquotes causes the page to become fragmented, disrupting the flow of your elements. Too many pullquotes also give away too much information to the reader. This is like watching an extremely long movie trailer that tries to show you all the good and funny scenes of the movie from beginning to end. Why would anyone bother watching the real movie when he or she could probably figure out the plot, the characters, and what happens at the end just by watching the trailer? The same idea goes with having too many pullquotes. If you put most of your witty lines and messages in your pullquotes, the reader won't bother reading the text. The proper extraction and placement of pullquotes should enhance the anticipation of reading the real text—not destroy it.

Figure 2.14.

The Sharlatan Romance site shows examples of several types of ineffective pullquotes.

Bad Design

Figure 2.15.

A review at Kewlbeans (http://pages.prodigy.com/kewlbeans/) shows an example of an effective pullquote that is well worded and enticing.

Good Design

Using Lines and Boxes to Control the Focus on Your Page

You can use lines and boxes to break up your elements into logical sections. These elements draw the reader's attention to special areas on your Web page.

Crossing the Line

You generally use *lines* to break up large amounts of text into smaller, manageable sections. Each of these sections usually has a self-contained idea or item the author wants the reader to address. You can break up your Web page with white space, but sometimes that might not be enough. A line can add the necessary focus to an area. Again, don't overdo it. Too many lines disrupt the flow of text on your page, which causes the reader to stop and go every time he hits a line.

Boxing Event

Boxes usually signal to the reader that the enclosed text or graphic has a special relationship to the adjacent element. By drawing the reader's eyes to it, a box emphasizes the contents in it. You can add color in a box to further focus a reader to a particular area. (See Figure 2.16.)

Caution

Don't go overboard adding boxes or lines to your Web page. A page with too many lines and boxes draws focus *away* from the page rather than *to* it.

You should use boxes only when you want a small amount of important information to stand out from the rest of the text. Remember that too much of one element can make your page cluttered and redundant. The same concept applies to adding too many boxes. Boxing too much information causes a reader to quickly dismiss the information in the boxes. Boxes lose their purpose when a reader sees one too many on a page. If he sees 10 boxes on the same page, he might become desensitized to the visual redundancy and dismiss their importance altogether.

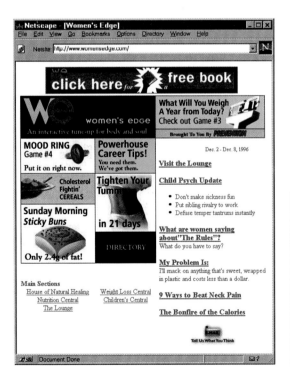

Figure 2.16.

The Women's Edge home page (`http://www.womensedge.com`) uses boxes around certain elements to emphasize their importance. Note how the colored boxes focus attention on what's inside them.

Adding Dimension with Shapes

If graphics came only in the form of squares, Web pages would become very blocky and boring. The advantage of computer graphics on the Web is that you can design the graphics in countless shapes, sizes, and colors. With proper color coordination and transparent background capabilities, you can design graphics to show up in any wild shape you can imagine. (See Figure 2.17.)

Figure 2.17.

Cute animal shapes enhance the checkboxes on the survey form at the Burrito Page (http://www.infobahn.com/pages/rito.html) site.

When you design different graphics with various shapes and sizes, you provide contrast to the page and add to the flow of the page. Designers also can use graphics to add meaning to a message by using shapes that are associated with certain activities or information (a red octagon usually is associated with a stop sign, for example).

Caution

Try to refrain from adding too many shapes to your Web page. As mentioned earlier, too much of one thing usually destroys the effect. Use shapes that are proportionate to the other elements and add to the visual flow of your page.

Adding Texture

Adding *texture* to a printed page adds visual and physical contrast to the presentation. When designing a résumé or an important report, you can set it apart from other documents by printing it on special, textured paper (cream colored with little flecks in the

paper or spotted with tiny polka dots). Although the texture of the paper does not add to the content of the page, it does provide an overall special look and feel to the document. The same thing applies to Web page backgrounds and images. A plain white background might be suitable for the page, but occasionally adding the appearance of texture to it might enhance the design. (See Figure 2.18.)

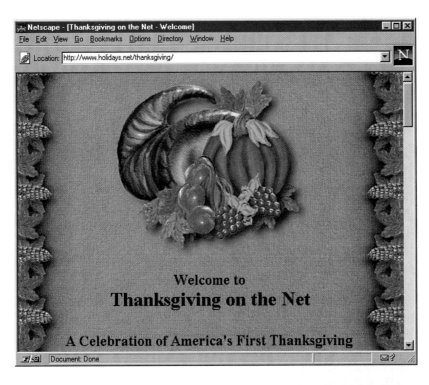

Figure 2.18.

A section of the Holiday Celebrations on the World Wide Web (`http://www.holidays.net/thanksgiving/`*) site has a pleasant texture in the background of the page that adds to the Thanksgiving feel of the design.*

Tip

Whenever you add texture to an element, make sure that the texture is appropriate and does not overshadow it. Don't use a wooden-grain texture for your navigational buttons, for example, if there is no reason for this. Texture can become an ugly distraction if used haphazardly.

Using Captions, Photo Credits, & Bylines

Captions, photo credits, and bylines are likely to be the most-read elements in written media. Unfortunately, we just don't see enough of them on the Web. Readers often look to captions, photo credits, or bylines for information on the element beside them. How many times have you found a photo image on a Web page and wanted to know exactly what the photo was about or the name of the photographer who took it?

A *caption* is the wording usually shown below or beside a graphic. Captions work as design elements to help bring graphics and photos together with the rest of the Web page. As an extension of the graphic itself, a caption gives the reader an explanation of what is being presented. Without this literal aid, a graphic's meaning can be misinterpreted and can confuse the reader. Helping your readers by providing capsules of information that help describe graphics makes them more easily understood. Some designers assume that their graphics speak for themselves and choose to refrain from using captions, or they use captions that are not helpful and are cryptic. We tend to see the caption as being as important as the graphic itself. What you put in your captions should be as well thought out as what you put in any other element on your Web page. (See Figure 2.19.)

A *photo credit* is a short phrase that gives credit to the photographer or artist of an image. Sometimes a photo credit states who the person is in the photo. A simple "Photo taken by Riko Suave" is all the information a photo credit needs.

A *byline* is a short phrase that gives credit to the author—usually for an article or story he has written. In most cases, the byline is located right after the heading at the top of the story or article. The byline can simply say "by Grandma Neddy" and should be a smaller font than the heading text but larger than the body text.

Tip

Try to add captions to graphics that show examples of something stated in your text. In your caption, try to explain what the graphic is about without stating the obvious. (Example: This is a car.) Be descriptive in as few words as possible.

Figure 2.19.

A caption and photo credit at The Irish Times (`http://www.irish-times.com`) *site.*

Caption

Photo credit

Summary

Now that you are familiar with the basics of Web page design, let's review the major points in this chapter:

- ✦ Add visual contrast by using different-size elements on your page. The sizes of your elements should relate to each other based on their functions on the page.

- ✦ Remember to organize your elements on paper before venturing near your HTML editor.

- ✦ Use alignment techniques that bring focus to your elements.

- ✦ Refrain from justifying your text to avoid creating ugly white gaps between words.

- ✦ Use columns to help break up large amounts of text for easier readability.

- ✦ Don't let one element overpower another. The elements on your Web page should work together to help deliver your message clearly—not to distract from it.

- ✦ The overall look and feel of a Web site should be consistent throughout. Consistency helps readers become familiar with the elements in the site and adds style to your pages.

- ✦ Add texture to your elements only if it contributes to the overall design. Texture can become an ugly distraction if used haphazardly.

- ✦ Don't put roadblocks on your Web page. The harder you make readers look for information, the faster people leave your site.

- ✦ Repeat lines, shapes, tones, and textures to enhance the flow of your content.

- ✦ Use headings that grab your reader's attention.

- ✦ Keep your headings, pullquotes, and captions short, informative, and creative. A good teaser attracts a reader to your information.

- ✦ Use lines and boxes only to focus attention on a few elements. Don't distract your readers with too many lines and boxes all over your page.

- ✦ Use shapes that are proportionate to the other elements and add to the visual flow of your page.

- ✦ Don't forget to give credit to the authors and designers of artwork, photos, and articles. Your artists will appreciate it, and so will your readers.

Q&A

If different browsers don't see all Web pages the same way, why do I need to worry about the layout of a page?

Again, depending on who your audience is, it is to your benefit that your page look its best to a majority of the people who visit your site. Your page might not look exactly the same on another browser, but you can keep the differences to a minimum if you keep your layout flexible.

How do I know whether my headlines or headings are effective? I usually read them, not write them.

If you are not a writer by profession, sometimes it is difficult to capture what you want to say on paper. We use a few techniques for writing headings. First, ask yourself, "How can I describe this section in as few words as possible?" List them out and then start playing around with different combinations of words. Then say them out loud and see which ones sound better to you. Finally, test them out on other people. It's always good to get feedback when you are creating anything. If all else fails, you might want to consider hiring a professional to help you with your writing. If you want your site to be as effective as possible, it might be worth the investment.

You mentioned in this chapter that I should understand a rule before breaking it. What does that mean?

I guess we're trying to say that many novice Web designers break design rules without knowing it. The outcome of this usually is an ineffective, unprofessional-looking Web site. On the other hand, an experienced designer might decide to stray from following conventional design techniques to achieve an effect by weighing the benefits of the effect he is trying to create against the benefits of his Web site's functionality. Rules are there to help you. Learn them, live them, love them, and break them only when you have a really good reason.

Challenge
Yourself

Now that you are acquainted with the elements of design, you are going to apply what you've learned to design a trial Web site. This section does not require any HTML coding; the concentration here is on the arrangement of the design elements that you can plan on paper.

Case Study

Grandma Neddy has designed her Web page: Chocolate Ho Hos— Grandma Neddy's Drug Design. She wants to divide her information into two separate pages.

Your Mission

To design two effective and aesthetically pleasing page layouts for Grandma Neddy's Web site.

You can complete this project in two ways. You can sketch and arrange the elements on paper. Or, you can print the elements from the CD-ROM. Then create the layouts by cutting and arranging the elements on paper. Try out different arrangements until you find something you like. You can paste the elements onto the page after you achieve the desired effect.

When you finish this assignment, you should understand how the elements contribute to your overall design. You can keep these page layouts handy for future challenges in upcoming chapters.

Required Tools

Pencil, paper, crayons, or colored felts

Optional Tools

Tape or glue stick

Supplied Elements

If you look at the CD-ROM at the back of this book, you will find the elements for this site in the "Chapter 2: Challenge Yourself" section.

The supplied elements follow:

- Two paragraphs of content
- Three cheesy headlines (you will determine whether they should be reworded or destroyed)
- Two pullquotes
- A selection of navigational bars (that you can choose from)
- Four photos of various sizes
- Four captions (you will determine which ones belong to which photos)
- One byline
- Three background images to use or destroy (as you see fit)
- Three headers and footers (that you can choose from)

Beginnings of a Great Web Page

Chapter 3

Where to Start: The Planning Stages of Web Design

Designing a great Web site means going into the design process with a good game plan. Careful planning ahead of time helps make the design process run smoother. In this chapter, we will show you how to target your audience and define your content, as well as give you some tips on time management.

Research: Who Is Your Audience?

You need to do a lot of pre-production work before you actually begin your design phase. The more you plan before starting to design the site, the easier it is when you actually do begin. One of the first things you need to determine is who the main audience of your site will be.

Is Anybody Out There?

When determining the audience for your site, you should ask yourself these questions:

- ✦ Who is the primary audience for this site?
- ✦ Should this site be exclusive to the primary audience, or do I want to aim for the widest possible range of people? Try to determine who is your main focus or target group.
- ✦ What types of images and graphics would appeal to my audience? Cool, funky, bandwidth-hogging graphics or simple, small, quick-loading graphics?
- ✦ What type of style would most appeal to my audience (formal, professional, trendy, casual, or just plain crazy)?
- ✦ Will the site provide free information or products to my readers, or is it a site where people are encouraged to send money? If it is a commercial site, will people be willing to purchase products online?

◆ What is the best format for the audience to access the information? Do they mind frames? Do they want basic text navigation or navigational image maps?

◆ What is the best way to convey my information to the target audience? (Children probably want more visuals, whereas adults might want less distraction and more information.)

Finally, ask yourself what the attention span of the audience will be. Don't laugh; this is a question a marketer asks himself every time he tries to sell something. Whether or not you like the idea, as a Web designer, you must learn how to think like a marketing professional. The ultimate goal in Web design is for the site to sell itself to the target audience (and beyond). If the designer can't keep his visitors entertained long enough for them to see what he has to say, his site will disappear into virtual Never-Never Land.

> **Tip**
>
> You should anticipate whether the attention span of your audience will be short or long. If it is short, make the message and the elements of your site concise and to the point. If you know that your site is one where people will expect a lot of high-tech gadgetry, you can concentrate on including a lot of flashy elements to keep their interests going. If your site is mainly an information source, you might get away with including larger amounts of textual information on your pages.

What Is the Unknown Factor?

When determining your audience, you always must do a balancing act of trying to target your audience while maintaining the user-friendliness of your site for all.

You never know exactly who is going to be looking at your site; therefore, it is a bit risky to assume too much of your audience. A site aimed at youths with short attention spans and an interest in high-tech items might also attract older, sophisticated baby boomers. (See Figure 3.1.) You always should plan your design with an awareness that people outside your target audience might visit your site.

Figure 3.1.
Hey, that's a great site, Dad!

High and Low Bandwidth Considerations

During rush hour, after a long day of work, you sit in a traffic nightmare as you inch your way to your destination at speeds a turtle could pass. Getting home around this time can seem so agonizingly slow. You look around at the other drivers and see the frustration on their faces. You sit and wait for the car in front of you to move. Any movement, even an inch, is cause for a mini-celebration. Sitting in your car for hours, bored out of your mind, you suddenly notice a large button on your dashboard. The button says that it has the special power to transport you out of this infernal traffic jam. Would *you* press that button?

You can apply the same idea to Web pages. If loading a Web page takes an intolerably long time, most people will press any button to get out of there. When designing a site, you must consider the speed at which your readers can load your pages. How quickly your readers can load your pages has a direct impact on the popularity of your site. If the reader has to wait too long, he probably will punch the STOP button and disappear from your site forever. This is where bandwidth considerations come into play while designing your pages. A super-huge page with a ton of graphics might look great and load quickly off your hard drive, but if the reader has a low bandwidth connection, downloading that same site off the Net isn't as enjoyable. A user's bandwidth is calculated by the speed of the server connection he has to the Internet divided by the number of people using that particular server connection. Remember that the Internet also experiences periods of rush-hour traffic. During those times, the bandwidth for each user becomes lower because of the number of people zapping around cyberspace causing cyber traffic jams. You should design your page to accommodate such occurrences.

A tradeoff exists between a huge page with many cool graphics and a smaller page that doesn't offer as many fancy items on it. The huge page with a lot of stuff happening on it might look cooler, but the smaller one probably loads faster. You must determine which type of audience you want your site to cater to. If a reader knows that your page contains useful and helpful information, he might tolerate the longer wait for your page to load. A reader who arrives at your page out of curiosity, however, might start clicking buttons left and right to leave as quickly as possible as soon as he realizes that the page is going to take forever to load. You can offer readers a way out of this dilemma by giving them the option to choose which type of Web pages they want to view. (See Figure 3.2.) You can alert your readers by telling them that they can choose a high-bandwidth or low-bandwidth view of your site. This option not only is helpful to your readers, but it also adds to your site's popularity.

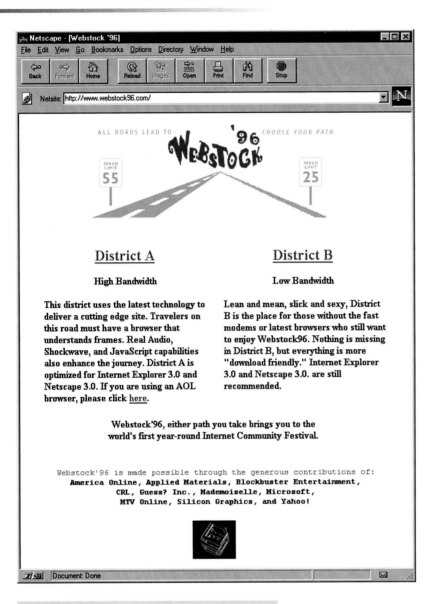

Figure 3.2.

Webstock (`http://www.webstock96.com/`) *gives readers the option to view the site at a high bandwidth or a low bandwidth.*

Where to Start: The Planning Stages of Web Design

Defining the purpose of your Web site is crucial to the success of your design. Knowing the message you are trying to convey on your Web page before you begin the design process helps you determine the organization of your elements. Remember that the reader ultimately came to your site to see the *content*. Without that content, your site is just an empty shell.

> **Tip**
>
> A site full of incredible Java applets, Shockwave, and CGI capabilities without any content is almost equivalent to a completely blank page on the Web. It really gets annoying when you land on a site that has absolutely nothing to say except *Hey everyone! Look at me! Isn't this great that I got my Web page on the Internet?* Few of us have the time to download a Web page that is void of any content. Of course, a few exceptions out there enjoy looking at useless Web sites all day long. All we can say to them is, "All the power to ya!"

To help you focus on your objectives in the planning stage of your design, you should ask yourself these questions:

- ✦ How do I want to present the information? Will it be fun, straightforward, splashy, teasing, or a combination of all?

- ✦ What amount of information should my site contain? Just because your company has a 50-page brochure doesn't mean that you have to put all that information on the Web. You might want to design a few, smaller, to-the-point pages for those who don't want to wade through a tidal wave of information.

- ✦ What type of images should I include to enhance the information presented on my pages? Make sure that your images enhance the page and do not distract or confuse your readers.

- ✦ Does my site require fancy-dancy elements to liven up my pages (animation, forms, Java, ActiveX, CGI scripts, and

so on)? If so, why? If you can't answer that question (and saying that you saw something like it on another site doesn't count), your site doesn't need those elements. Remember that if they don't add to your site, you should leave them out.

- ✦ What type of image or presentation do I want to convey? Select the information, writing style, graphics, background, and color scheme that will enhance the overall image or presentation of your site. (A professional look might require a simple yet classy presentation, for example. A casual, tongue-in-cheek look might require a more outrageous presentation.)

> **Caution**
>
> Offer only information that is relevant to your Web visitors. Don't put your company-policy handbook on the Web just because you have one. If it doesn't serve the purpose of your message, it doesn't belong on the Web. (See Figure 3.3.) In that same vein, too much information sometimes can be a design's pitfall. Remember that anyone who has Internet access will be able to see the information on your site (unless you have it password protected). Don't put information on the Net that might jeopardize your security or your company's.

Reviewing Your Content

Now it's time to organize your content into workable sections. A good way to accomplish this is to create a flowchart or map of how and where you want your information to be organized. To do this, you first should list out headings to represent the different parts of your content and then determine the order of their importance. Distinguish the more important headings from the lesser ones. Keep in mind that the organization of your content also depends on how you intend your reader to view the information. After you map out the structure of your information, you can see more clearly what you should include or not include on your site. At this point, there will probably be more things to add and delete over the course of planning your site, so your flowchart probably will change several times more before you get it the way you want it.

Storyboarding: Bringing Ideas to Life

The process of organizing and collecting your information is crucial to your site's success. So many ideas can be going around in your mind, but if you don't take the time to write them down, an idea never has the chance to materialize. *Storyboarding* your ideas creates the visual foundation on which to build your design. It helps you plan the layout of your Web pages and organize the structure of your site.

Figure 3.3.

Your 500-page company-policy handbook does not need to be on your Web site.

Here are some general points you should tackle when storyboarding your ideas:

◆ Brainstorm. It doesn't hurt to put your ideas down on paper. It actually might help you come up with better ideas.

◆ Create a site map (or a flowchart) showing how the reader will move around in your site. Remember that the navigation on your site is not linear, so draw lines to indicate where one section will link to another.

◆ When you finish establishing the organization of your information, attack each section of information and determine whether it will be on a page with other information or on a page of its own.

The storyboarding process continues in the upcoming chapters when we go deeper into designing the user interface, page layout, graphics, and navigation of your site.

Creating a Site Map

Creating a *site map* (or a *flowchart*) helps you plan your site as well as the maintenance of your site in the future. (See Figure 3.4.) A site map can keep track of any changes or revisions during the development phase of your design. It would be pretty messy if things started to change and you didn't have a site map to show you where the changes were made. A builder needs architectural plans before he can build a house. He can't go around putting the foundation here, a wall here, and a door there, just because he thinks, "Hey, this would be a nice place to put it!" If he did, he'd end up with one very unique-looking house. It gets worse when there is more than one person working on a project. Without a plan, the whole project can turn into a complete catastrophe.

> **Tip**
>
> Mapping out your content helps you see where the flow of information is running smoothly throughout your site and where it is not. Correcting any information roadblocks early in the design process helps you avoid developing your site into a maze of dead-end links. Don't make your reader search for a piece of cheese hidden deep in the bowels of your Web site maze. Organize your information so that your reader will be able to easily access it.

Revising and Editing Your Pages

After you have everything on paper, new ideas and changes *will* pop into your mind every now and then. Nothing should stop you from implementing any changes that you feel will improve your site. At this point, the design of your site is not set in stone. Add new pages or information wherever necessary. Review how the pages flow together. Make sure that the message of your site is presented clearly and effectively. If the message is unclear, find ways to change the flow of your information to improve its presentation. This might involve not only moving the pages around but also rearranging groups of individual pages to fit the overall feel of the site. Try to do as much revising at

Figure 3.4.

A site map at Cabletron (http://www. cabletron.com/Search/SiteMap.html).

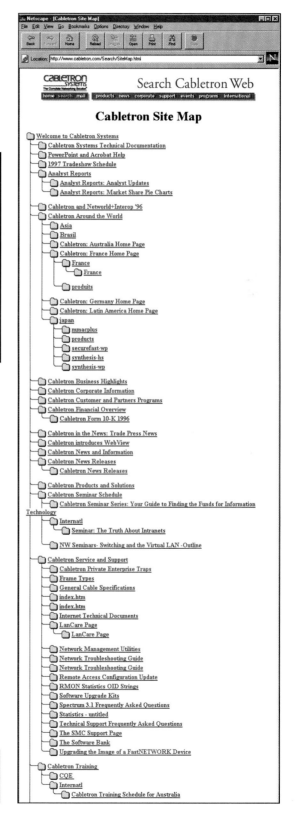

this point in the game. The planning stage is the best time to make your changes before the actual HTML work is slated to start. This method saves you time and frustration in the end. (See Figure 3.5.)

Site Map for Orange Computers

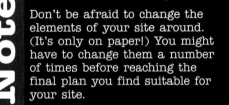

Figure 3.5.
A drawn-out site map with revisions.

> **Note**
>
> Don't be afraid to change the elements of your site around. (It's only on paper!) You might have to change them a number of times before reaching the final plan you find suitable for your site.

Form Content: What Information Do You Want From Your Audience?

A *survey form* is a marketer's dream come true. It is an excellent way to receive feedback directly from your audience. A person is more inclined to fill out an online survey than to fill out a survey at a department store or even over the phone. Don't you hate it when you get a call from someone asking you to spend a *few* minutes of your precious time to answer a *few* questions for his survey? After about 20 minutes, you silently resolve never to answer the phone again as the survey person continues on to Section 10 of his question list. People don't enjoy completing market surveys that are shoved into their faces. A survey form on the Web, however, is ideal because it gives readers the option to provide feedback only when they choose to do so.

The layout of your form is as important as the layout of your other Web pages. Your form should encourage your reader to fill it out—not to make him say "forget it" and leave. If your form is confusing and jumpy, your reader will have a difficult time trying to find the fields he is looking for. The flow of the entry fields on your form must be laid out logically and be as painless as possible for your readers to fill in. (See Figures 3.6 and 3.7.)

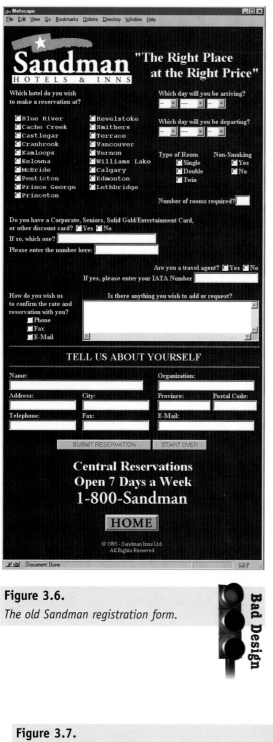

Figure 3.6.

The old Sandman registration form.

Bad Design

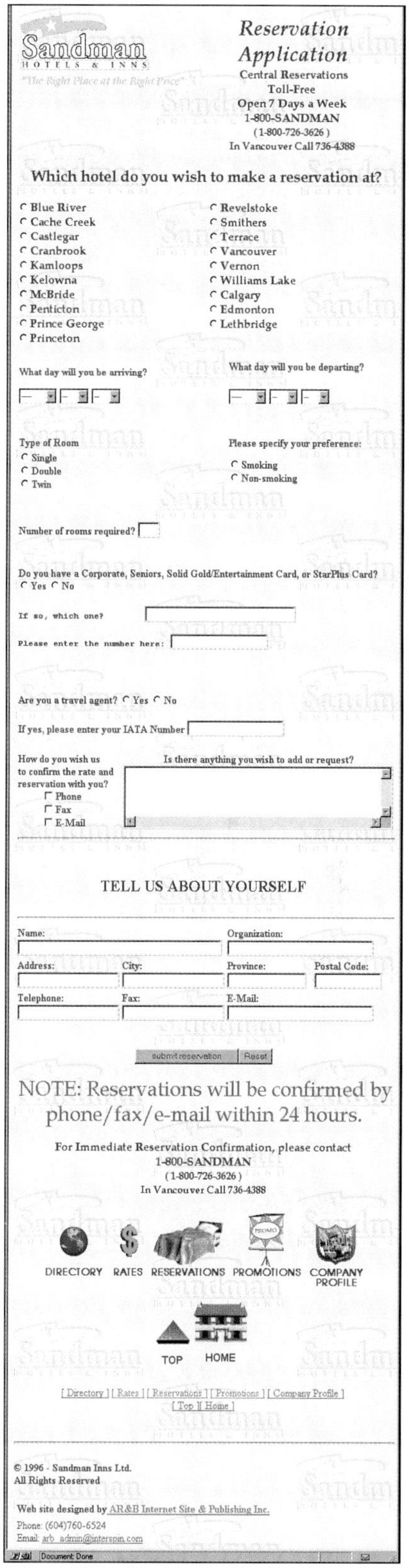

Figure 3.7.

The new and improved Sandman registration form (http://www.sandman.ca/registration.html).

Good Design

Tip

The fields on your submission form should be read from left to right, top to bottom. This provides a nice flow of information for your reader. Try to add explanatory text to help him fill out the form. You should try to provide as much information as necessary for your reader to correctly fill out the field. (This does not mean that you should include a 500-word "blurb" on the importance of capitalizing the first letter of his name.)

Feedback: Getting Other Opinions

A survey can help you learn more about your reader. You can find out where he is from, what he does for a living, what age group he is in, what hobbies he enjoys, what types of things he wants to see, what things he feels would improve your site, and so on. This information helps you determine your target audience. Knowing your audience is instrumental in designing a great Web site. You never know; a suggestion you receive might be just the concept you need to make your good page into a great page! (See Figure 3.8.)

Figure 3.8.

Feedback, both good and bad, received by the site during the design process.

Feedback on the Orange Computers Site

-It was very good, but it needed more color and flair.

-The navigational elements were very confusing.

-Too much text on home page. It needs more white space to help it flow.

-Great graphics. Good images of the monitors and printer.

-Order form is good, but it needs more text to help the user understand how to complete the purchase.

-Very good Company Profile page. Very descriptive and represents the company well.

Whether you are designing a site for commercial reasons or one just for fun, your survey form should ask questions that are quick and to the point. A wordy question can be confusing and annoying. You also should try not to ask questions that might offend your reader, like "How much do you weigh?" or "Do you have body odor?" The last thing you want to do is insult your audience. If you must ask a question that touches on a sensitive subject, try to be professional and sincere in your tone.

Allocating Tasks: Who Does What and When?

If you are the only one designing your site, poor you. You end up having to do all the work. It might be a good thing, though, because, as the lone designer, you have control over the time it takes you to design your site. You don't have to wait for some procrastinator to finish his task that was due a week ago before you can continue on to the next task (unless that procrastinator is you).

Hopefully, your site will have more than one designer. If this is the case, you can divide the work equally among the project members (unless one of you is a busybody and the other is a sloth from the bowels of the earth whose only goal in life is to do the least amount of work possible and at the same time get the most amount of credit).

When you complete your site map or project plan, set it in front of you. Assign the different tasks to your team member(s). Then start on your work ASAP! Those last-minute-at-four-in-the-morning nights usually reflect in your work. (See Figure 3.9.)

Figure 3.9.

A timeline in progress. We have given you a blank timeline for you to work with. You can find it on the CD-ROM at the back of this book.

Timeline

Person	Day	Task
GK, KY, BG, JS, AT	1 & 2	Gather content, research audience, brainstorm
GK	3	Create site map, allocate tasks
JS, AT	4	Storyboard page layout ideas
KY, BG	5	Design navigation and interface
GK, KY, BG, JS, AT	6	Test storyboards with Greg, Kyra, Bob, Jaren, and Alysa
GK, KY, BG, JS, AT	7	Revise, add, delete, restructure
GK, KY, BG, JS, AT	8	Finalize plan
GK, KY	9	Start HTML & graphics
BG, JS, AT	10	Complete navigation elements
GK, KY	11	Finish HTML for homepage
BG, JS, AT	12	Finish graphics for homepage
GK, KY	13-18	Finish HTML
BG, JS, AT	13-18	Finish graphics
GK	19-20	Test off-line
GK, KY, BG	21-23	Test on-line
GK	24-28	Get feedback
GK, KY, BG, JS, AT	29-34	Revise
GK, KY, BG	35-39	Test on-line
GK, KY, BG, JS, AT	40	Launch

Organizing Your Timeline for the Design Process

Setting deadlines for each task ensures that the work gets done. It is always good to set a timeline for yourself, even if getting the job done on time and under budget isn't your main goal. To save yourself frustration at the end, give yourself realistic deadlines. If you pace yourself, the design process won't seem so overwhelming.

If you are working with others, determine who the project manager will be. This person will oversee all the tasks and ensure that each person is meeting his deadlines. If a certain deadline cannot be met, it is up to the project manager to reallocate the time resources and stretch the deadlines accordingly. It is the responsibility of the project manager to communicate effectively with the whole team to bring the work together. If you are designing a Web site for a client, take into consideration that your deadlines might be affected by your client's ability or inability to provide you with content and graphics on a timely basis.

The more realistic your deadlines, the easier it will be for the whole project to come together at the end. (See Figure 3.10.)

Sun	Mon	Tue	Wed	Thur	Fri	Sat
1	2 ✓ finish navigation	3✓ finish home page	4✓	5✓	6✓	7✓
8	9 ✓	10✓	11✓ finish html	12 finish graphics	13	14
15	16 test site	17 test site	18 test site	19 test site	20 test site	21 test site
22	23 revise	24 revise	25 revise	26 revise	27 test site	28 test site
29 test site	30 test site					

Figure 3.10.

A calendar listing some approaching deadlines (hope they don't start on it the night before).

Summary

Now that you have learned the planning stages of Web design, let's review the major points in this chapter:

◆ Research your main audience. When determining your audience, remember to target your audience while maintaining the user-friendliness of your site for everyone else.

◆ When designing a site, you must consider the speed at which your readers can load your page. How quickly your readers can load your pages has a direct impact on the popularity of your site.

- ✦ Knowing what message and information you are trying to convey on your Web page before you begin the design process helps in the organization of your elements.
- ✦ Place only information relevant to your Web visitors on your Web page.
- ✦ Creating a site map gives you a visual foundation on which to build your design. A site map helps you plan the layout of your Web pages and organize the structure of your site.
- ✦ Don't be afraid of changing the elements of your site around. You can change the flow of your information if it improves the presentation.
- ✦ A survey form is an excellent way to receive feedback directly from your audience.
- ✦ The layout of your forms should be logical and painless for your readers to fill out.
- ✦ When you have a working copy of a site map, divide the different tasks among your team members.
- ✦ Setting realistic deadlines for each task ensures that the project will come together on time.

Q&A

Q There seems to be a lot of planning before even starting the design of the site itself. What if I don't have the time to do all this?

A Don't be frightened away by all the steps in the planning process. If you lack the time to create a comprehensive plan, you can do a quick version in a day. The better you plan your project, however, the easier it is when it comes to actually designing the site.

Q I consider myself a Web designer rather than a marketing person. The design alone will sell my site. Why should I have to target my site to a specific audience?

A Web designers who design for themselves first and their audience last sometimes can get away with not caring who their audience is. This *Rebel without a Cause* attitude might work for some people, but, unfortunately, not all of us have that natural flair for design. Overall, it is easier to design a great site when you can focus on who you are designing it for.

Challenge Yourself

The steps of planning a Web site become much easier after going through the process once or twice. To help you get hands-on practice, we are assigning you specific planning tasks for the Sharlatan Romance Novel Web site, which you will be expected to plot into a timeline. After your mission is complete, you can incorporate these tasks into your own Web designs or create your own.

Case Study

The Web design company that designed the Sharlatan Romance Novel Web site encountered a few problems in the design process that a timeline could have prevented.

Your Mission

Complete a timeline for the tasks involved in the creation of the Sharlatan Romance Novel Web site.

Required Tools

Pencil and paper

Supplied Elements

✦ A case study of Sharlatan's Web design process

✦ A calendar

Chapter 4

Planning Navigation Techniques & Building the User Interface Framework

Designing the navigation and the user interface for your Web site requires a lot of planning. In this chapter, we will show you techniques for creating an interface that is user friendly and fun to use. We will discuss using metaphors for the interface design. You also will learn about the navigational options you can use for your site.

Identify the Metaphor: Will Your Site Look Like a Book? A Building?

When a person lands on a site for the first time, he places himself in unfamiliar territory. Right off the bat, the site should be clear about its intentions or goals to avoid making the reader feel unsure of what to do or where to go. Without any guidance, a person can literally get lost at your site. So how do you design a site that doesn't require 10 pages of instructions explaining all the details of your site's navigation and user interface?

Use Yer Interface

How a reader moves around, finds information, sees things, and performs certain actions at a site depends on the design of the Web user interface. Because not every site on the Web is identical, a person surfing the Net has to learn to adjust his sense of navigation every time he lands on a different site. Whether he clicks on a hypertext link or on a hot spot on an image map, a reader learns to familiarize himself with the site's interface in order to maneuver around in it. A day of surfing the Net can take a reader to numerous sites with very different user interfaces. All in a day's surf, we visited three Web sites that used very different navigational techniques. The first site we saw simply used hypertext links for its main navigational functions. At the second site, we found ourselves automatically navigated from the home page to the Buy My Product Now! page (which was not exactly appreciated by either of us). Finally, at the last site, the navigation was not obvious to us. When we moved the mouse over a graphic to click on it, our room was suddenly filled with an ear-piercing guitar rendition of "Jingle Bell Rock" (performed by none other than the Webmaster's 15-year-old brother, no doubt). (See Figure 4.1.) Of the sites we visited, each had its own Web user interface, unique in navigation, theme, and user friendliness. The uniqueness of your Web site is key in providing your reader with an interesting experience. A reader's understanding of your site's intentions depends on the user friendliness, predictability, and consistency of the Web user interface, though.

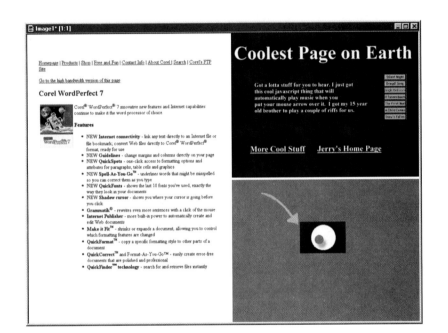

Figure 4.1.

Corel's page (`http://www.corel.ca/text/products/wordperfect/cwp7/index.htm`), *on the left, uses plain hypertext navigation. Jerry's Web site* (`http://www.sunk.com/groups/friends/jerry/`), *in the top-right corner, automatically played music when our mouse pointed over the buttons on his page. We didn't know what to do at the Sense of Art page* (`http://www.server.com/arts/artists/`), *which is in the bottom-right corner.*

An absolutely wonderful fun-and-games site can be chock full of content, graphics, and multimedia, but if a reader can't figure out how to get to the Free for All Java Game page, what's the point? (See Figure 4.2.) Make your user interface a friendly experience for your reader. The less time he spends figuring things out, the more time he has to visit your pages.

Figure 4.2.

Great stuff! But how do I get to the Free Java Game page?

Bad Design

Poetic, Ain't It?

When we think of metaphors, we usually think of poetic phrases that describe two unrelated things as being one and the same. *Her words are a dagger in my back*, for example, is a metaphor that states that *words* and *dagger* are the same, although in reality, they are not. Metaphors add meaning to things that might not be easily explained. Using metaphors to explain the unexplainable is a powerful technique by which intangible elements can be made tangible.

What Does This Have to Do with Web Design?

A *metaphor* helps represent unfamiliar elements of your Web page by substituting those elements with the description and functionality of objects that are familiar. What might be familiar to one person, however, might not be familiar to someone else. Creating the Web user interface for your site means choosing metaphors that cross computer literacy, cultural, language, and technical boundaries. A newspaper, for example, is a popular object that many people around

the world can easily identify. Using the newspaper as the metaphor for your Web page instantly gives your reader a sense of familiarity with your site. Choosing a metaphor that triggers a reader's assumptions of a task increases your site's user friendliness.

Tip

You'll notice that a lot of navigational elements on the Web use buttons to represent links. A reader will be familiar with the idea of clicking a button from his experience working with computer software. You don't have to teach your reader what to do with a button, because he will intuitively know that clicking it causes an action to occur. Again, the less time it takes for a person to understand the navigation of a site, the more likely he will stay around to check it out.

If designed well, the user interface provides readers with some predictability to help them easily navigate your site's structure. The interface also should familiarize readers with the site's elements, enabling them to navigate throughout your site with as little difficulty as possible.

Choose Your Metaphors Wisely

When choosing the metaphor for your site, consider a metaphor that will be understood by everyone (not just you, your CGI programmer, and your graphics designer). If you want your site to reach more than just techies, you shouldn't use the innards of your UNIX file server to represent the metaphor of your site (for example, "to get to the next page, take the local bus, turn left at the diode, go through the socket and over the jumpers…").

Take into consideration your reader's experience with the object used in the metaphor. If you are going to use the metaphor of a book, for example, how will you design buttons to represent flipping to the next page and back to the preceding page? Normally, a left arrow represents flipping to the preceding page and a right arrow represents flipping to the next page. You should consider whether this holds true for all your readers, though. In Western culture, this is a correct assumption, because books are read from left to right. The right page must be flipped over to get to the next page of the book. This is not the case in Chinese culture, however, where books are read from right to left, and the left page must be flipped over to get to the next page. So, you see, a reader who is used to flipping pages from left to right might become seriously confused when he clicks a left arrow to go forward and finds

himself on the preceding page. He will either assume that you made an error in the design of your buttons or that you have been reading your books backward all your life. You can see how some of your audience can become confused when their relationship to the object in your metaphor (which, in this example, is the book) is different from yours.

Try to use parts of a metaphor to represent your site. You don't have to design your entire site to be the actual metaphor. If you use an airplane as your metaphor, for example, you don't have to create the site to be the exact replication of the inside of a Boeing 777. You can use icons to represent sections of the airplane, however. You can include a Cockpit icon to represent the main content of your site, a First Class icon to represent your luxury items, a Business Class icon to represent your business products, and an Economy button to represent your discount products. (See Figure 4.3.) We can go on and on with this particular metaphor, but you probably get the picture. Try to keep your theme clear and straightforward. The main thing is to make sure that your metaphor gives your reader the feel for getting around your site without giving him a 400-page manual explaining how to do it.

Note

You will find more suggestions for possible metaphors in Appendix C, "Metaphoric Examples."

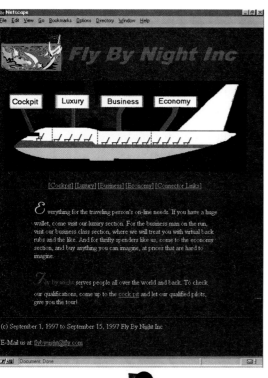

Figure 4.3.

Fly By Night's site shows you how it uses the airplane metaphor in its interface design.

Good Design

Representing the Metaphor with Graphical Symbols (Icons, Ideographs, and Mnemonic Symbols)

Representing your metaphor's graphical elements with symbols is useful when a realistic representation is impractical. Take the symbols we see every day, like the ones on the outside of public restroom doors. The symbolic representations of the male and female gender help distinguish between the two restrooms. Imagine that, one day, the President of the United States announces a law that all restroom symbols will be replaced by realistic representations of the two genders. All over the country, millions of people send in their photo portfolios to the White House in the hopes that theirs will be chosen to represent the public toilets of America. After the votes are tallied and the "man" and "woman" restroom models are chosen, the lucky couple gets whisked away to participate in the first lavatory model photo shoot in history. (Wouldn't that be a sight to see?) Eventually, after all the fanfare dies and their photos are emblazoned on every restroom door in the country, you can imagine hearing the people whisper to each other as Mr. and Ms. Restroom Model of the Year walk by, "Look! There goes the super toilet models of North America! Wow, wouldn't you love to be in their seats?" (See Figure 4.4.)

That story is pretty far-fetched, but you can imagine the types of problems a situation like that would cause if it did happen. Would the couple chosen to represent the male and female gender accurately represent the physical makeup of all men and women in the United States? More than likely, the selection of a single man and woman to represent such a diverse populace would cause a backlash from every group imaginable. (There's no way that those people with their buns of steel can represent us!) When a realistic representation is irrelevant to your metaphor, a symbolic one should suffice.

Figure 4.4.
Those pictures don't look like us at all!

Icon't Understand It Again

Symbols need to be unambiguous and clearly understandable to be functional. A single symbol can be interpreted in various ways by different people. A symbolic representation of a British police officer would be instantaneously recognizable to anyone familiar with British culture, for example, but someone unfamiliar with the culture might wonder, "Why is that man wearing a bell on his head?" (See Figure 4.5.)

Figure 4.5.
Why is that man wearing a bell on his head?

When choosing or creating an icon, the designer should strive for simplicity and clarity. Cluttering an icon can cause misinterpretation (not to mention eyestrain). The icon should be compact, but not so much that it is not easily seen or recognizable. (Don't fit a Mona Lisa into a 100×100 pixel graphic. It won't do justice to her smile.) (See Figure 4.6.)

Figure 4.6.
Where's my agent? I refuse to have my face squeezed into something so small!

Icon Consistency

Consistency in your metaphor and graphical style are major factors in determining whether your reader will be able to fully comprehend the intention of your Web page or instead will become severely confused, aimlessly wandering around your defined cyberspace with a glazed expression on his face.

You need to maintain consistency in your metaphor to maintain a unified familiarity of the whole site. A metaphor of a transit bus can have elements of a driver, a passenger, a coin box, a bus entrance, and an exit. Now would a taco stand fit in this metaphor? We think not. But if the designer absolutely had to have a taco stand on his page, he would have to reconsider the overall metaphor. In this case, he probably should change the metaphor from a transit bus to a bus terminal. There, he can place his taco stand, a newspaper stand, a bench, and anything else that might be suitable for the revised metaphor. It is natural for a person to make assumptions. A reader learns how to navigate the Web by making assumptions based on his experiences. Developing a consistency in your metaphor allows the reader to predict or assume certain things about your site. Therefore, elements that throw the metaphor out of whack also might throw your reader

out of whack. A reader will wonder how the elements relate to each other and how his own ideas of the metaphor relate to those elements that are out of place.

You need consistency in your graphical style to maintain a flow to the elements and page. If your metaphor is a zoo, and you choose to use realistic graphics as your navigational elements, you should not suddenly use cartoon drawings halfway through the page—this will throw off your readers. How consistent does a Web page look if there are realistic images of horses, ducks, and cows in the navigational bar and, suddenly, stuck in the middle of it all, is a yellow duck dressed in an olive-colored tutu sucking back a cherry cola? The contrast might add a little humor to your page, but the distracting effect it has on everything else on the page might not be worth it. (See Figure 4.7.)

Whatever type of graphical style you choose (whether realistic images, cartoons, or symbols), you always should keep the style consistent. This allows your reader to quickly become familiar with the interface and to be able to navigate your site with a minimum amount of distraction.

Figure 4.7.

Who let this duck into the photo shoot? Get him outta there!

Bad Design

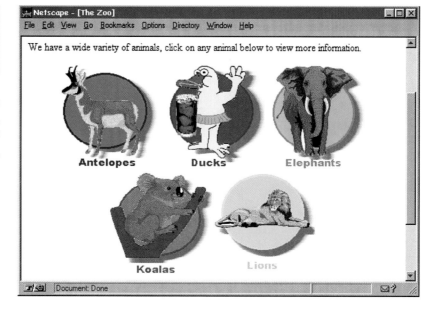

Laying Out Your Page

After you establish the metaphor you will use, you need to consider a few things. Try to keep your metaphor simple yet meaningful. Think of your reader and how he, seeing your site for the first time, might want to find the information he is looking for. It is difficult to step into a person's shoes when you've never been in them before (especially if they smell bad). It is important in the design process for people who actually use the site to participate in designing it by contributing their ideas on how your Web user interface can be improved. Make sure that your test subjects are people who will be unbiased in their opinions. (Try to choose people other than your relatives, your coworkers, or your partners.) Ask your test panel questions like, "When you arrive at a site, how do you want to find your information? What questions would you like the site to answer? How do you envision getting your information? What kinds of information are you looking for at this site?" Ask them appropriate questions as you see fit. The questions should help you envision the structure of your site and how your metaphor will work.

Suppose that we design a site with a supermarket metaphor in mind. We can design navigational elements that point to different shopping sections in our site, which can be represented by aisles (Aisle 1: Cleaning Supplies, Aisle 2: Greeting Cards, and so on). We can implement a Coupon Board section where visiting customers can find listings of discount or sale items. A customer-service desk in the metaphor can represent the *frequently asked questions* (FAQs) of our site or even our site's search engine. We can use a shopping cart in the metaphor to represent the CGI script that tallies up the items a customer chooses to purchase. Finally, we can use a

Good Design

Figure 4.8.

Using a supermarket metaphor.

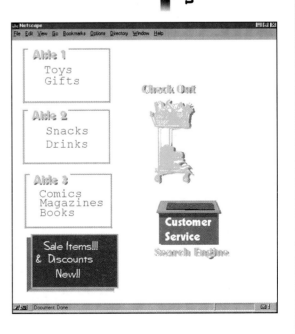

Check Out section metaphor to represent the area where a person supplies payment information and confirms the items purchased. (See Figure 4.8.)

Now that we have established the overall metaphor for the site, we can ask our test subjects what they expect to see on the home page. We can ask questions such as, "How do you expect to get to the shopping section of the site? How would you like to choose the items you want to purchase? Would you want them in a list on one page?

Or would you rather see the item separately on a page of its own and be able to add it to your shopping cart on that same page?" After we establish how our site should work, we can storyboard the ideas we have gathered. As in the old days, when advertising representatives used storyboards to help their potential clients visualize what the commercial would look like frame by frame, it's now time for us to storyboard our site page by page. After you finish the storyboarding process, you should take it back to the test panel for further testing and feedback.

To Frame or Not to Frame

Frames divide your browser screen into sections to display more than one Web page at a time. Sites that use frames are springing up all over the Web, possibly because frames give the Web designer some control over how his site will appear on his reader's browser. Frames also can give the designer control over the navigation throughout his site. A reader can click on an outside link in one frame, for example, but still have the navigational and header elements of the original site in two other frames. This effect gives the reader the impression that he has not actually left the original site. Giving the designer a sense of control over what his audience sees at his Web site can be the design solution that Web designers have dreamed of. Or is it?

Playing Web Page Roulette

At last, a designer can force his audience to move around his site in the way he intended his site to be seen. Now, let's think about that for a minute. How will a reader feel when he realizes that he has lost complete control of what is happening on his screen? Imagine this scenario… When a reader clicks on a link, frames suddenly appear from left and right. When he clicks on another link, the Web page comes up in a teeny-weenie, 400×200 pixel frame. He tries to scroll down the frame to see the information and accidentally hits another link. His page disappears and he now is looking at another frame—a bigger frame with more buttons to click. He sees a button that he recognizes as a Home button and he fervently clicks it. But instead of going back to what he thinks is the home page, he now sees something that looks like the home page in a new frame in the original set of frames. In a moment of desperation, he goes to the Back button of his browser window and clicks it over and over again, hoping that he will be transported away from this site forever. His mouth opens in dismay when he realizes that his escape plan has backfired, and he finds himself only moving backward in slow motion, through the site once again, going through frame by frame.

Click, Click, Wherever You Go, Where You Stop, Nobody Knows

Frames can be very confusing for a reader, because the basic understanding of how a Web page works gets tossed into the recycle bin. When a reader lands on a Web page with frames, he might not realize that he actually is looking at more than one Web page. If he tries to click on an outside link within a frame, it is difficult for him to know whether the Web page he now sees in the frame belongs to the same Web site, because the URL in the location bar still shows the main frame's Web site address. Even worse, if he travels around to pages he finds interesting and starts bookmarking them, when he checks his bookmarks 10 minutes later, little does he know that he has bookmarked the URL of the main frame of the site 15 times. Good luck if the reader tries printing any framed Web pages. Similar results will occur, leaving him with 15 copies of the framed main Web page in his printer tray (guess those pages go into the recycle bin, too).

Some people could say, "Hey, that's the nature of the Web! People are supposed to get confused at first. Sooner or later, everyone will get used to how frames work, and we'll all look back a few years from now and chuckle about how terrible everyone made frames out to be." Yeah, right.

Another reason why we warn you against using frames in your site is because, aesthetically speaking, frames are somewhat disruptive to the reader's sense of visual flow and proportion. They divide a reader's screen into small sections. This means that the reader's focus has to jump from one frame to the next instead of being concentrated on one single Web page. Remember that some people still view Web pages with 14-inch monitors set at 600×480 pixels. It's hard enough reading information off a monitor all day long, much less reading it squished into a narrow frame. (See Figure 4.9.)

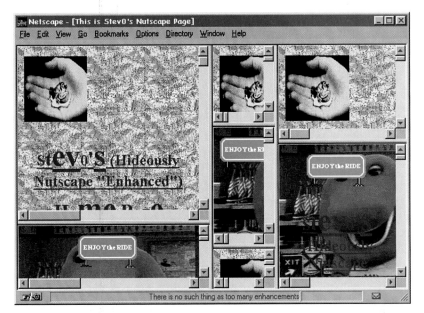

Figure 4.9.

Steve Berlin's example of a badly framed Web site at
`http://www.chaco.com/~stev0/nutscape/nutscape.html`.

Bad Design

> **Note**
>
> Not all browsers support frames. If you decide to use frames, remember to give your readers the option of viewing your site without them.

For Frame Lovers Only

So is there anything good to say about frames?

Frames are useful when your site requires one set of information to be stationary on the screen, while the information in the other frame(s) is dynamic. Sites that can benefit from using frames are ones that contain a spreadsheet, an online tutorial, or a search engine, for example. Frames can be useful when displaying a spreadsheet, when the column headings are placed in a frame at the top while the row headings and the contents of the spreadsheet are scrollable in the lower frame. When the user scrolls down the main frame, the column headings always are visible for the reader to refer to. Another site that benefits from frames is one that contains an online tutorial. The lesson can be framed on one part of the screen, while the examples of each lesson are shown in another frame. You also can use frames on sites where a submission for information is in one window while the results of the query are in another window. A search engine page, for example, can be displayed with the search engine function contained in one frame while the results of the search engine are displayed in another frame.

Frames can benefit a site in many other ways. (See Figure 4.10.) The key is to use frames only when you have a real reason to do so. Like any other element of design, use only the elements that will add to your site. Using frames just for the sake of it will more than likely take away from the functionality of your user interface instead of add to it.

Good Design

Figure 4.10.

Interspin's client page (http://www.interspin.com/service/) displays frames quite well even when viewed on a 600×480 screen.

If you decide to design your site with frames as your user interface, make sure that you use them consistently. Don't have frames appearing and disappearing all over your site. The purpose of an interface is to aid your reader, not alienate him. A lack of consistency in your interface only confuses your audience. When designing your Web pages with frames in mind, don't go frame crazy. People with smaller monitors will not appreciate having to read information in itty-bitty frames thrown all over the page. Finally, never force your reader to navigate your site by using frames. You want a site where readers will enjoy their visit. Your reader should feel in control of what's happening in his browser. If some of your readers prefer not to use frames, you should give them that option.

Parting Words

Although they can add functionality to your site when used for a specific purpose, frames go against the basic understanding of how a reader expects his browser to work. A reader's understanding of the basic functions of his browser—such as adding a bookmark, printing a page, using the Back button, scrolling a page, viewing the source, and even viewing the URL location—is thrown out of whack when he visits a site that uses frames. Perhaps, in the future, newer browsers will solve the confusion caused by the implementation of frames, but, for now, it is best to stick with the notion that a designer should use frames only when it is absolutely necessary for the site. So, if your site doesn't need frames, don't use them! The less time your reader spends trying to figure out how things work at your site, the more time he spends doing what he intended in the first place, which is visit your site. No matter how wonderfully frames control the navigation of a site, it is ultimately the reader who decides whether it is worth his while to get tossed

around in a maze of framed Web pages. Remember that if your reader can't find his way off your site, there is always the CPU's Reset button. Enough said.

Functionality and Creativity: Reaching a Pleasant Medium

Keeping the presentation of your information unique yet functional is where your design skills come into play. Unlike presentations on paper, Web pages can be interactive and dynamic. Designing quality Web pages means achieving a balance between the functionality and creativity throughout your whole site. If your site is creative but the navigation is not helpful and the site lacks any content, your site loses its appeal. If your site has a great online database of the coolest collector dolls in the state, but the main color scheme of your pages is a dreary gray and dark blue and your images look like they were scribbled out on a cocktail napkin the night before, your site—even with the power of the coolest CGI script on the Web—might get only half the reaction you expected. Finally, if you design your page haphazardly without going through the planning and testing process, your site might lack both functionality and creativity. (Trust us, we've seen tons of these sites.)

It is important to ensure that your site's user interface is functional. Your site should convey the content of your message in a clear and concise manner. The usability of the user interface is a major factor in the functionality of the site. A reader should be able to obtain the information he needs, or the site does not achieve its purpose. It might seem tempting to employ VRML in your user interface to make your site stand out from the rest. But if your site stands out like a sore thumb because your audience can't figure out how to get to your free software, what's the point? (See Figure 4.11.) Don't let creativity get in the way of functionality; don't let the creative objects and graphics get in the way of presenting the intended content of your page clearly to the reader.

Figure 4.11.

A person will have trouble finding the free software at this VRML site.

Bad Design

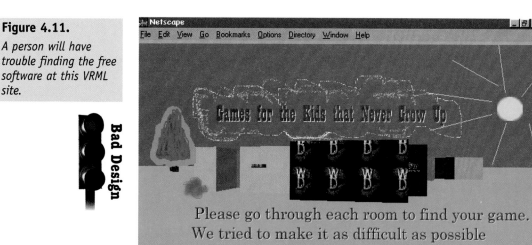

You might think it is highly creative to have embedded modules that cater to every plug-in known to man (including the Internet's first-ever virtual dance floor; join in the Macarena without even getting out of your seat!), but the price you will pay is a heavily cluttered page that takes two hours to load. Will a reader appreciate having his system burdened with 20MB of multimedia just to get to the page where your mother's recipe of homemade cherry rum balls are? Although you might want to add fireworks and cannon blasts to all your pages, sometimes the best way to convey your message is to let the content speak for itself.

Delicious and Nutritious!

It's hard to imagine that something nutritious can be delicious. (Give us a chocolate shake over carrot juice any day.) The same goes with designing Web sites. It usually is easier to focus on the strength of one aspect of a site than it is to try to balance your strengths. If we were all lucky enough to pick and choose a design team made up of the best user interface scientists, artists, and marketing experts on this planet, we might be able to come up with a site that is outstanding in both functionality and creativity. Because this is usually not the case, though, we must strive to strengthen both aspects of our site while maintaining a proper balance throughout. Imagine a group of 10 people trying to step into a lifeboat. To maintain the balance in the boat, one person must sit at one end while another person sits at the other end. As more people climb onboard, it becomes more necessary to try to keep it from tipping. It is okay if there are a few more people on one end than the other end of the boat at a time. But what happens if the rest of the group decides to join the others at the other end, and the whole boat suddenly becomes unbalanced? Let's hope that there aren't any sharks in those waters! Attaining balance in every aspect of your design means ensuring that the creativity of your site doesn't overpower the functionality of it. You don't want your reader to say, "That was a nice site, except it's too bad they wasted so much time on those huge, animated GIFs. The site would've been cool without them."

Letting Your Creativity Loose

Being creative means adding that certain flair to a page to set it apart from other pages. Creativity is difficult to define, because a creative Web site can range from subtle and classy to outrageous and twisted. (See Figures 4.12 and 4.13.) Try different ideas, techniques, and styles to present your ideas. Keep in mind that the navigational elements should be clear in where they lead your reader and consistent with your chosen metaphor. A Web page with wild-and-crazy navigational elements is fantastic until your reader becomes confused and has trouble figuring out where he's going to next. It doesn't matter how creative and powerful your Web site and user interface are if the reader wants to move around your site but is unable to do so because of the highly complex interface. It's like giving your reader a Porsche with standard transmission when he only knows how to drive an automatic.

Figure 4.12.

Porsche's Web site (`http://www2.porsche.com/home.html`) creatively uses text and typography along with nice images to present an elegant home page.

Good Design

Netscape - [Web Pages That Suck -- Lesson 1]

File Edit View Go Bookmarks Options Directory Window Help

Location: http://www.webpagesthatsuck.com/home.html

Web Pages That Suck

Learn good design by looking at bad design

Well, you've just had your first lesson in sucky web page design techniques. The first thing that sucks on the front page is the JavaScript that makes the colors fade in and out. Earlier versions of Netscape allowed you to do the same thing with multiple <BODY> tags, but Netscape fixed that around release 2.0. Now, some clever guy figured a way to get a JavaScript to recreate this very pretentious technique.

Let me re-state the last sentence. It's *going to be* very pretentious for anyone other than the original author to use this JavaScript. The original author is very talented and for him, it's OK to use this technique, but eventually *everybody* is going to start using it and then it will become pretentious. I expect by the end of October this technique will be very declassé. Well, it's past the end of October -- let's stop using this technique.

The front page features another overused web design technique that comes in two variations and I used Variation #1: *"The Animated GIF on a Black Background."* When the animation stops, you can either click on the image (mine's a textual image -- it can be a graphical image) to go to the "real" home page or if you don't click, the <META> "refresh" command automatically takes the viewer to the next page. Variation #2 is the same, but it's just a regular image or imagemap, not an animated GIF.

I'm not sure who originally created this technique, (probably *Wired* Magazine) but, like the rainbow-colored divider, it's become a cliche.

Speaking of cliches, pages with black backgrounds are a very, very popular cliche. Whenever I see a black background it's like the designer is lowering his voice and saying, "This is a cool page. I'm pretty cool, too." To be honest, I'd say maybe 5% of the sites with black backgrounds are actually cool and almost every one of those was designed by a *professional graphics artist*. If you're not a pro, black's not the way to go.

Let's go to the real home page.

Document Done

Good Design

Figure 4.13.

Web Pages That Suck (http://www.webpagesthatsuck.com/home.html) has a crazy, non-traditional theme that is effective in bringing its message across.

Consistency and Predictability: Making Your Web Site User Friendly

Creating a user-friendly site means concentrating on what the *user* considers being friendly, not the designer. The user should feel comfortable when navigating and accessing the information at your Web site.

Can You See the Strings?

A well-designed user interface should be transparent to the reader. The only thing a reader wants to see at your site is the information he is looking for. He does not care whether you are using a fancy Java script to get him where he is going. He does care, however, if the fancy Java script at your site starts causing numerous error messages to come up on his screen. As important as navigational elements are to a site, the focus of each page always should be on the content—not the navigation. When we watch a puppet show, we are aware that many people behind the scenes are holding and manipulating the strings to make the puppets' movements come to life. And yet, the action on the stage of a well-coordinated puppet show still can make us feel as though the puppets have a life of their own. When we watch a badly directed puppet show, where the audience can see the people backstage moving the strings and reciting their lines, we tend to notice that the puppets are only inanimate objects. How real would Big Bird seem to you if you could see the man inside the suit making Big Bird's mouth move? As in a puppet show, the less your reader sees what's happening behind the scenes, the better the presentation of your site. More important, your user interface should seem invisible to your reader, so don't let your strings show. (See Figure 4.14.)

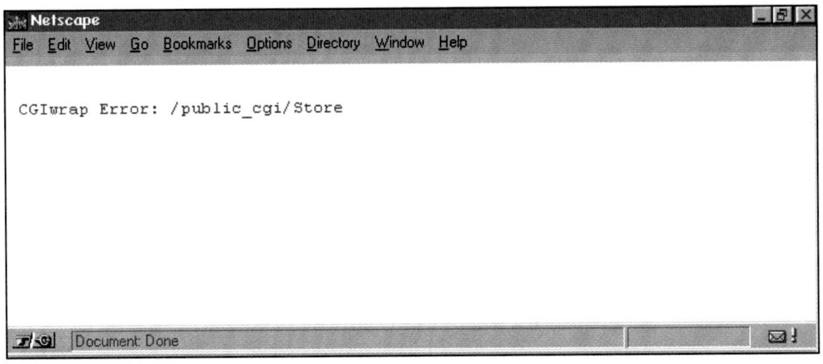

Figure 4.14.
We visited this CGI-powered Web site. Too bad we couldn't see anything.

What Is Your Web Site's Consistency?

The more a reader has to work at getting himself adjusted to the Web site environment, the more likely he will say adios, ciao, toodle-loo, or just plain bye-bye to your site in less than a heartbeat. Consistency gives your site a sense of structure and predictability. A reader who understands the structure of a site will be confident that after he clicks on something, weird or unexpected objects won't start flying at him from all directions. A reader learns how to do things by drawing from personal experience and by making logical assumptions. This basic model of predictability should be applied to your interface design. If you are designing an image map, for example, give your readers some idea where the hot spots on the image are by making the hot spot areas look like they are clickable.

Image map
An *image map* is a graphic that contains regions that are hot-linked to other Web pages or files. Image maps will be discussed in greater detail later in this chapter.

Don't assume that your reader can read your mind (unless your reader has access to the psychic 1-800-hot-line). Give your reader a sense of predictability and familiarity at your site. The more a reader accustoms himself to the environment, the more adventurous he will be in exploring the rest of your site.

TIP The user interface should facilitate what the user wants to do—not what the designer wants the interface to do. If the interface is functional to you and only you alone, your site will be one lonely place.

Navigation: How Will People Move from Page to Page?

Designing your site's navigation is a task that requires the careful cross referencing of your information while keeping your reader from becoming disoriented. In a paper medium, it is less likely that a reader will get lost. The structure of a novel, for example, allows a reader to refer to page numbers to guide him through the content of the book. On the Web, a Web designer can link a page to as many other pages as he sees fit. Providing the guiding tool to help your readers through your pages is essential in the design of your user interface.

We Don't Want a Hierarchy

A Web site should refrain from being too linear or hierarchical. A linear or hierarchical site where a reader can only move forward through the site by clicking a Next Page button to see more information is inane. If the information were only to be seen in such a rigid, sequential format, it shouldn't be on the Web. Unless the purpose of the site is to replicate the feeling of flipping through a book, you should stay away from navigational elements that say `Next Page` or `Back`. Remember that any page on your site can be seen by a reader even before he lands on your home page. The fact that search engines let readers search key words within Web pages means that your readers can link

to a particular page without having to go through the traditional home-page route. A "back" link on a page that a reader lands on directly is absolutely irrelevant to him. His last page is not necessarily the same page as what the Webmaster refers to as the "back" page. Web designers who think of their Web site navigation in their own logical terms tend to believe that their site will be navigated the way they feel it should be navigated. (After all, they designed it, didn't they?) The Web was never intended to be linear in the first place, so don't design your navigation that way.

Give It to Me Now

Give your reader the information in a quick and easy format. A reader should be able to find how to get to the information he is searching for right off the home page. Don't make him go through pages and pages of content just to find it. If one of your dinner guests asks where the bathroom is, do you first take him through the living room, into the den, around the foyer, into the kitchen, through the master bedroom, down the hall, up on the roof, down the chimney, and then into the bathroom? (If you were going to do that, you might as well tell him to do it in his pants.) The moral of the story is don't make your reader take the grand tour of your site to get him where he wants to go. Just get him there. (See Figure 4.15.)

Think about your reader when you plan the navigation of your site. The purpose of navigation is to aid him, not disorient him. If possible, keep the main navigational elements of your site displayed in a consistent location on all your pages. That way, your reader can get to a page directly without relying on the browser's Back button to lead him back to the main page.

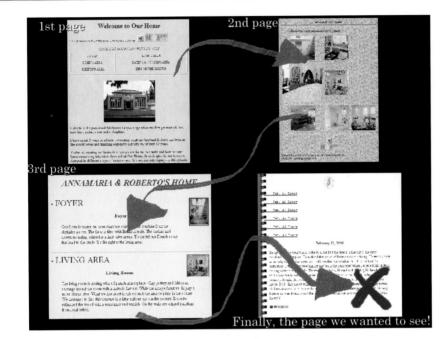

Figure 4.15.

We had the pleasure of a grand tour of this Web site before getting to the page we wanted.

1st page

2nd page

3rd page

Finally, the page we wanted to see!

Tip

The design of the user interface should allow your reader to always know where he is on your site. Don't let him get lost, wandering aimlessly in your maze of Web pages. Your reader should always have an escape hatch so that he can exit to your home page or one of the main pages on your site. If your site gives the reader the impression that he is trapped, he will create his own escape route by typing someone else's address in the URL command line.

Menus: Textual Links

Hypertext menus or *indexes* are navigational elements that give readers a quick reference to information in your site. A page that contains large amounts of information should have an index of links at the top of the page, with each link pointing to a specific subheading in the page. This way, your readers won't have to constantly scroll down your Web page to find information. (See Figure 4.16.)

When designing your menu links, try to organize them in the same order as your subheadings. Don't place the last subheading at the top of your list and your first subheading at the bottom. (This might seem obvious to you, but we've seen pages where the index list was so disorganized, we didn't bother referring to it.) Be creative with your indexes. Use pullquotes, teasers, and subheadings to give your reader an interesting and quick overview of what to expect at your site. The biggest benefit of using hypertext indexes rather than graphical indexes is the download time. If speeding up your page's download time is one of your main concerns, consider using hypertext indexes as an alternative form of navigation for your site. Hypertext might not be as pretty as graphical alternatives, but it functions the same—only faster.

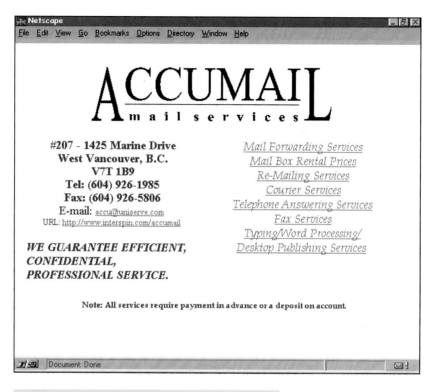

Figure 4.16.

A hypertext menu at Accumail's site
(`http://www.interspin.com/accumail`).

Image Map Hot Spots, Buttons, and Hypertext as Navigational Tools

The navigational elements people use at a Web site can include image maps, buttons, and hypertext links.

Hot Spots of the World

An *image map* is a graphical image in which certain areas contain *hot spots* linking to other Web pages, URLs, or multimedia files. Because you can place a hot spot anywhere on a graphic, image maps are useful for aligning navigational elements. You can place navigational bars in an image map, with each area on the image representing a button that links to a different page on a Web site. Image maps are not problem-free, however. The fact that a reader does not receive a visual response when he clicks on a hot spot as he does when he clicks on a hypertext link can make your interface seem unresponsive. The only way a reader can guess that he is going to another page is by looking at the browser's status bar (hopefully, the designer didn't add an annoying Java scrolling script that interferes with it) to see whether the server has contacted another URL.

> **Tip**
>
> If possible, try to keep the size of each hot spot proportionate with the other hot spots. It is understandable that you would want the link to your Nobel Peace Prize page to be more prominently displayed than the link to your Send Complaints Here page. But if you are willing to give something a link, you should give it its fair share of clickable space.

Another problem an image map creates is the reader's inability to recognize what are and are not hot spots. A designer must carefully design hot spot areas to be clearly separate from the rest of the image by making the areas look like buttons or by adding text under the hot spot areas to make them appear clickable. (See Figure 4.17.) As you can see, designing your image map requires careful thought and planning. Remember that what might be logical to you might not be logical to your reader. Just as in any part of the design process, try your image maps with your test panel. Observe what they click and what they don't click. Ask for feedback and suggestions. Don't be disappointed if you have to scrap an image map in order to design one that functions better.

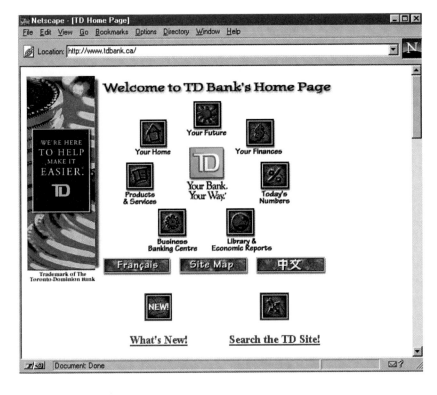

Figure 4.17.

The Toronto Dominion Bank of Canada's home page (`http://www.tdbank.ca/`) uses an image map with hot spots represented by button icons.

> **Caution**
>
> Use image maps only when necessary. The size of an image map affects your reader's download time, so try to keep the size small. The best size to use is an image that your reader can load in 30 seconds or less. Also, don't forget to provide your graphically disabled readers with alternative text links.

Buttons

Buttons are navigational elements recognized by a majority of Web surfers. Readers familiar with a Mac or Windows environment understand the basic functions of a button. Navigational buttons on your page give your readers familiar elements that they understand how to use right away. Don't design images that look like buttons but don't work like them. It is difficult enough to figure out which images are for navigational purposes and which aren't. Make it clear to your readers which images are the navigational buttons on your page by making the buttons look clickable. If you don't differentiate the buttons from the other images on your page, readers won't be able to tell the difference. Add text below or on top of your button image to help clarify where the link will take your reader. Keep your buttons proportionate with your other elements on the page. Figure out what size each button should be before designing it. The amount of text and detail you add to your button affects how you determine its width. Don't add so much text that your button becomes so wide that it almost fits the width of your screen. On the other hand, don't make your button so small that it is mistaken for a dust ball and your reader has to squint to find it on the screen. Your buttons should complement the metaphor as well as the rest of the page.

Ah, Hypertext Links, the First Form of Navigation

Hypertext links are just as functional today as they were in the days when graphically supported browsers were still a figment of Netscape's imagination. Hypertext navigation was once the only form of navigation on the Web, and it still can compete with other forms of navigation that have arrived since. (See Figure 4.18.) The benefits of hypertext links over other forms of navigation follow:

✦ Hypertext does not require extra time to download.

✦ Hypertext is supported by all graphical and non-graphical browsers.

✦ Hypertext is still a universally accepted form of navigation on the Web to this day.

When using hypertext links, try not to embed links deep within large amounts of text. It is far more beneficial to have a menu of hypertext links at the top of your Web page that guides your readers to specific sections of your page. Don't expect your readers to wade through huge paragraphs of text to get to your links. If you choose to use graphics as your navigational elements for your site, it is always a good habit to include small hypertext links at the top of your page as an alternative form of navigation for your readers who are using text-only browsers or who have disabled the graphic capability on their browsers. Finally, like all other elements on your page, hypertext links should be used only when the page requires it. Don't use hypertext links that point to places all over the same page. You don't want to confuse your reader by making him jump all over the screen. It gets pretty confusing to a reader when he clicks on a link that takes him to the middle of a page, then clicks on a link that takes him to the bottom of the page, and finally clicks on another link that brings him back to the top of the page. A person can go bug-eyed after reading a page that way. Make sure that you link your reader to sections of your site that are relevant to the topic and are in the order that makes the most sense to him.

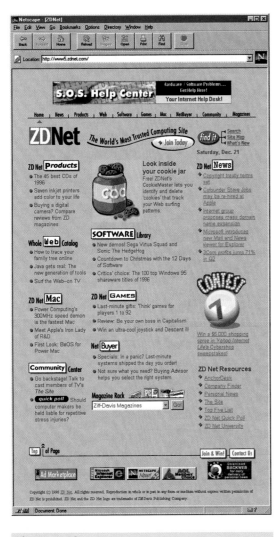

Figure 4.18.

ZD Net (http://www5.zdnet.com/) uses three forms of navigation: hypertext links, button icons, and image maps.

Site Maps: Visual Aids to the Overall Structure of the Web Site

Providing an overview of the structure of your Web site gives your reader a jump start on understanding the navigation of your site.

Honey, Why Don't We Look at the Road Map?

A *site map* is like a road map of your site. A map gives your reader a sense of how the pages of your site relate to each other. A reader can see what things your site has to offer and plan which pages he will be surfing almost at a glance. A site map is a navigational tool in itself, where the graphical representation of each Web page can be hyperlinked to the actual Web pages themselves. Functioning both as a visual guide and a navigational tool, a site map enhances your site's usability. Your site map should give your reader a clear sense of how your site is structured so that, if he knows exactly what page he wants to see, he can click a link on your site map and go straight to the page without having to go through your entire site to find it. (See Figure 4.19.) Try to make the links of your map clear. Don't let your site map become a site maze.

Give Me a Map That's Easy to Read

If the structure of the site is complicated, it can make a site map difficult to read. Try to add enough space around your links for your reader. Cramming your links too close together makes it difficult for your reader to understand which links refer to which page. Don't add extra graphical images that will clutter up the page and distract your reader's focus. Your site map should be easy to read—not give your reader a headache. If a site map is too busy, a reader will only become confused about your site's structure. And, finally, keep the links on your site map up to date. The most annoying thing when visiting a site is to see a site map that is no longer relevant to the structure of the site.

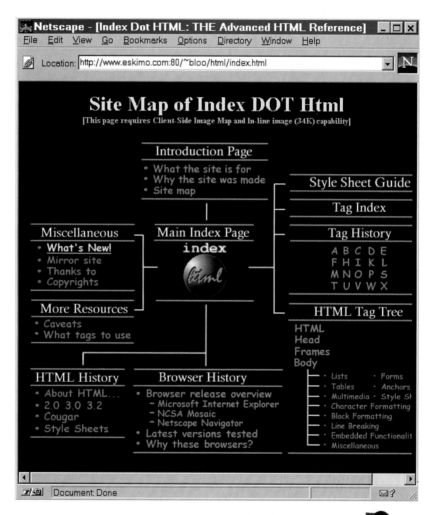

Figure 4.19.

A clear and visually appealing site map at Index DOT Html
(`http://www.eskimo.com:80/~bloo/html/index.html`).

Good Design

Giving Users a Reason to Come Back

Your Web pages might be loaded with lots of bells and whistles going off left, right, and center, with even a pink dinosaur dancing the cha-cha in the background (okay, forget the dancing dinosaur), but unless the pages are updated on a regular basis, the information will begin to grow stagnant, no matter how funky the pages are. A reader who has seen your site before probably doesn't need to see it again, unless, of course, there is a reason for him to come back. Ensuring that your reader continues to visit your site means maintaining your links, revising information that is out of date, and giving him something he'll want to come back for.

Spring Cleaning

Picture this scenario. A wife slips a brand-new pair of Odor Eater insoles into her husband's favorite ratty Doc Martin shoes. For the first month, the insoles work fabulously and his shoes go from locker-room stink to positively odor free. Everyone celebrates. But as several months go by, his shoes begin to develop their familiar aroma once again. Because personal hygiene is obviously not his top priority, he doesn't seem to realize the problem his shoes are causing until six months later. He receives a letter by registered mail from his wife and children informing him that his once-so-wonderful eaters of odor have long since lost their potency, and they aren't letting him back into the house until he changes them or invests in a new pair of shoes. The same principles of personal hygiene apply to Web site maintenance. If your site contains non-existent URL addresses referring to "upcoming events" that happened in the previous year, and the contents of your What's New page have remained the same since 1995, you definitely have a maintenance problem. (See Figure 4.20.) People often think the design of a Web site ends the day the site is launched. The truth is that Web site design is an ongoing process that continues over the span of a Web site's life cycle. Maintaining your site is essential in order to keep the quality of your site and your design at its highest. Leaving your site exactly the same way you designed it a year ago will more than likely leave a stink on the Web that your audience will certainly point out to you—if you haven't driven them away by then, that is.

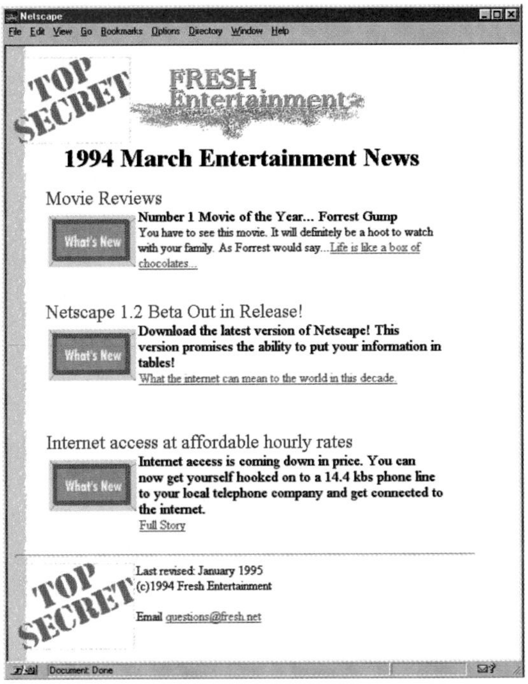

Figure 4.20.

What's new at this site?

Try to update your site at least once a month. Go through and clean up any dead links, and revise any information that has changed since the last time you maintained your site. The longer you put off the maintenance of your site, the bigger the task becomes, and the more likely you will dread doing it.

Keeping the Freshness

You can use many techniques to keep your Web pages from becoming stagnant and stale. Commercial sites can take advantage of the fact that they can update promotional information, provide current industry information, and promote new products on a monthly basis. Non-commercial sites can be more flexible in the ways they attract their readers back to their site. One interesting way to keep readers coming back is to create a game or a story that a reader can follow on a regular basis. (See Figure 4.21.) Another way is to create an ongoing dialogue with your readers that can be posted and read by others. Developing a relationship with your reader by giving him feedback on his opinions and queries can be the added feature that brings your reader back. Most important, though, is keeping the information on your Web pages constantly up to date; this maintains the freshness your site needs to draw your reader back again and again.

User Feedback

Obtaining user feedback throughout the design and implementation process of your Web site ensures that your site is designed for the people it was intended for—your users (not yourself or your design team).

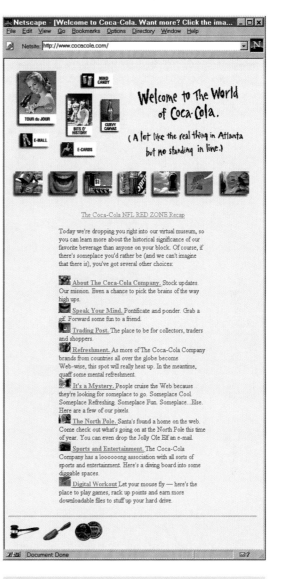

Figure 4.21.

Coca Cola (http://www.cocacola.com) uses various promotional methods to keep its readers coming back.

Good Design

Tell Me the Truth. I Can Take It.

After the user interface of your site is designed, it is time to put the site through the ringer. Testing the usability of your site allows you to see just how friendly your site really is. The best way to test your site's user interface is to get users (in this case, your test panel) to actually use it. The test panel can comment on how wonderful or how terrible the Web user interface is to move around in. (See Figure 4.22.)

Figure 4.22.
The Crash Test Dummies are out on the loose to fix cruddy sites before they find their way on the Web.

No matter how unforgiving, critical, or even cruel the test panel is, be grateful that your site design has only been seen by this handful of users and that you still have the opportunity to fix your mistakes. Don't make the Internet your testing ground for your Web design. If you publish your site without giving your site's user interface the vigorous usability test it deserves, you might later have the pleasure of receiving thousands of e-mails from people all over the world telling you why they think your animated navigation bar really sucks.

Evaluating the User Interface

Evaluating the design of your user interface is critical, primarily because this is where a user generally can spot something that the designer totally missed. A designer has the bias of knowing how the Web user interface of his site should work. (He designed it, didn't he?) Therefore, what might seem perfectly logical to him might not be so obvious to his reader. A designer knows ahead of time what to click and what not to click on his own site. A reader who has never seen the site before, however, will click on anything and everything until he gets the hang of the user interface. You will be surprised how many errors in the user interface are overlooked until Joe Blow off the street fools around with it and suddenly hits something that crashes the site.

Take It To the Test Panel

When putting your Web site through the usability test, ask your test panel specific questions on the user friendliness and the level of transparency in the Web user interface. The user interface should flow seamlessly with the entire page like a well-oiled bicycle wheel on an expensive mountain bike—not like a rusty square wheel on a container truck filled with nitroglycerin. Find out how easy it is for your test panel to familiarize themselves with the navigation of the site. Get an overall point of view of what they feel about the cohesiveness of the site. Do the pages blend together? Was it difficult to find the information they were looking for? Are the pages visually appealing? The answers to these questions and more will help you determine the effectiveness of your metaphor and the user friendliness of your Web user interface.

Go Crazy: Using Creative Interfaces

User interfaces do not need to be rigid and boring. Many sites on the Web use creative interfaces to present their information. Here are a few we have found.

A Solar System Metaphor

United Airlines (http://www.ual.com/united_bin/home_bin/home.html) uses the solar-system metaphor to represent the navigation of its page. (See Figure 4.23.) The graphic of the solar system is an image map where the planets are actual hot links to the different pages of the site. Notice that the image of the solar system is not accurately portraying the real solar system (Note: The sun is the center of the universe, not the earth.) However, the reader is able to grasp the metaphor as being a navigational aid, not an exact model of the world.

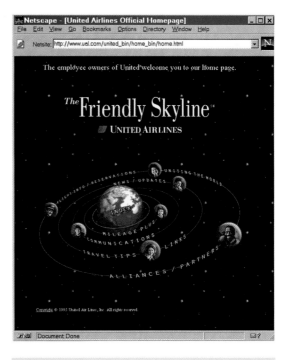

Figure 4.23.

United Airlines (http://www.ual.com/united_bin/home_bin/home.html) *uses the solar system as a metaphor for the user interface on its home page.*

A Wild 'N Wacky Interface

Fun is the main goal for the Toys "R" Us (http://www.tru.com/) home page. (See Figure 4.24.) Using wild-and-wacky cartoon images for the user interface creates a funland atmosphere for everyone. Although the navigation relies heavily on image maps to guide the reader to specific pages, the site is aimed mainly at children or kids at heart. Toys "R" Us realizes the importance of visual graphics to stimulate and entertain its main audience.

Figure 4.24.

You can find this wild-and-wacky user inter-face at the Toys "R" Us (http://www.tru.com/) home page.

An Interface Powered by Java

LookSmart is a new search engine solely powered by Java. (See Figure 4.25.) The search engine is targeted to provide accurate and quality hits rather than random ones. Surfing a site completely relying on Java for its user interface was a little eerie for us at first. We felt like our computer was being taken over by Java applets when things suddenly appeared out of nowhere. After a few minutes of getting used to the interface, though, we did manage to enjoy our experience there. The search functions and categories gave us very informative links to qual-ity sites. This site shows how traditional Web site interfaces can incor-porate more than just HTML while still relying on basic Web design principles for the main part of its design.

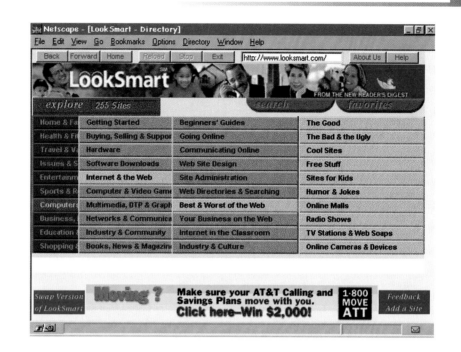

Figure 4.25.

LookSmart's (http://www.looksmart.com) *user interface is powered by Java.*

Designing an Interface for the Baud-Rate Challenged

Designing your Web user interface for the baud-rate challenged means applying minimum standards to your site design. By applying the standards to all your Web pages, your site will give a majority of your audience the capability to see it.

Viewing the Web at 14.4Kbps

You should take your audience into consideration when deciding what to implement on your Web site. Using elements that make your site slower to load could mean losing some members of your audience. Do you want to cater to those who have large bandwidths, or do you want to target a majority of the audience with a variety of bandwidth sizes? Readers with larger bandwidths can download big files without any major delays, but to someone with a smaller bandwidth, the time consumed in downloading the same elements might be too much to bear. If your reader's patience is as short as ours and your page is taking its time sucking up bandwidth while downloading onto the browser screen, we'll bet you a virtual chi-chi that he will be grumbling and cursing his way off your site before the words Document done come up in the status bar. (See Figure 4.26.)

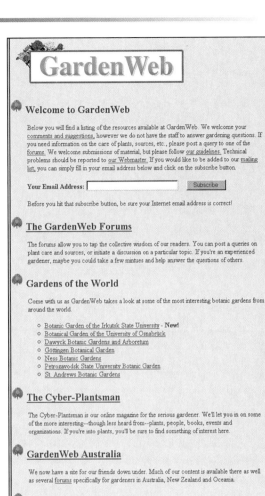

Figure 4.26.
The Garden Web (http://
www.gardenweb.com) *site
is functional and downloads
in less than one minute. This is
a good example of a pleasant,
low-bandwidth site.*

Good Design

Hypertext Solution

Remember that hypertext links do not add to your Web page's download time. Decreasing your page's download time might make it worth your while to substitute some of your graphical buttons with plain hypertext links. Even if you decide to use graphics for the navigational function of your site, add hypertext links as an option for your reader. As mentioned before, you should use hypertext links on every page that requires navigation. That way, if your reader's graphical capability is disabled, he still can navigate around your site.

Techniques to Speed Download Time

Hyperspeed modems with large bandwidth connections are still not a reality for most of us. Many people disable their graphical capability on their browser to avoid waiting a long time for images to load on a Web page. When designing your Web pages, always use the `ALT` attribute in your `<IMG SRC>` tag to describe all your graphical images. Make sure that the text you use is meaningful. A person who can't see your graphics won't understand what `graphic of header` means. Your page should be understood with or without your graphics. Displaying `graphic header` to your reader is less effective than displaying `Charo's Chit Chat Coffee Shop`. Now the reader can see the text and understand that it represents the header of your page without having to read the word `header`. You wouldn't write "This is the header of Charo's Chit Chat Coffee Shop" on a plain text document, so why do it in your ALT description? Check your Web page with your graphics disabled to see if your page makes sense. The clearer you are in the ALT attribute description, the more meaningful your whole page will be to someone who can't see all your wonderful graphics. This also ensures that the reader will know what the contents of the graphical elements are, even if he stops the page from fully loading. (See Figures 4.27 and 4.28.)

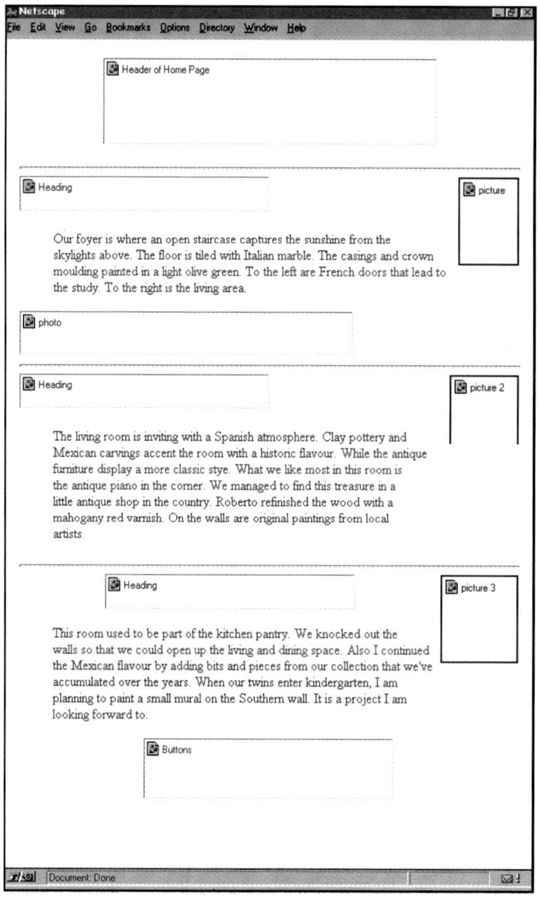

Figure 4.28.

LLS Distributors (`http://www.arnb.com/llsdist/`) *show us how* ALT *tags can be helpful for the graphically disabled.*

Good Design

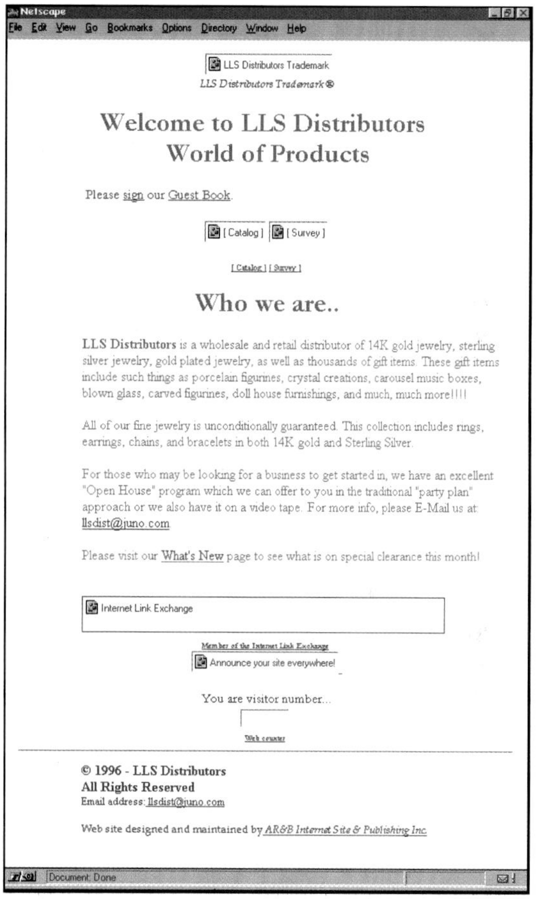

Figure 4.27.

A challenge for the graphically disabled to guess the real meaning behind these ALT *tags.*

Bad Design

Determining Your Height and Width

To help speed up the download time of your graphics, indicate the size of your graphics by using the HEIGHT and WIDTH attributes in the `<IMG SRC>` tag. This allows your browser to properly lay out your page the first time it retrieves your information from your server. This speeds the download time considerably, because a reader's browser will not have to send extra requests to the server to find out the dimensions of the graphics. Also, whenever you add JPEG images to your Web pages, indicate low-source versions of your image by using the `LOWSRC` attribute in the `<IMG SRC>` tag. This allows browsers that recognize this attribute to load lower-quality versions of your JPEG images first while the reader waits for the real image to download.

Reduce, Redo, Recycle

Reducing the number of colors in your graphics reduces the size of your images tremendously. The smaller the size of the graphic, the faster the image loads onto the browser. To reduce a graphic's size, try cropping huge graphics around the area of the image most relevant to your page. A huge, 100KB photo of you beside your car, with you and your car featured in the bottom right-hand corner of the page and the rest of the photo showing your neighbor's rundown wooden fence, is not only unflattering to your Web page but also is a big waste of time for a reader to download. Try to keep your graphics size small. Don't overuse graphical elements such as animated GIFs, bullets, icons, rulers, and banner logos. These graphics can add unnecessary baggage to your page's download time. (Now do we really need to see all those 3D, spinning, animated GIFs on your home page?) If they don't serve a functional purpose for your page, keep them away from your site.

What's Ahead?

Technology is ever changing as bandwidth and modem standards are constantly increasing and getting faster. As the baud rate for modems and the bandwidth increases, the "optimal" size for navigational elements might increase as well. So possibly those 2MB buttons that were once considered too large to be used on your page might someday become a button's accepted file size. The easier for people to obtain more bandwidth and faster modems, though, the more people might surf the Net. This actually could reduce bandwidth speed if more people surfing the Net caused huge traffic jams in cyberspace. Bigger roads don't necessarily mean less traffic jams. Perhaps bandwidth won't even be an issue one day, but, until that day arrives, it is safer to stick to keeping your Web pages as small as possible.

Summary

Now that you have become familiar with building your site's user interface and navigation, let's review the major points in this chapter:

♦ When designing your site's user interface, help readers familiarize themselves by keeping your navigation friendly and consistent.

♦ Identify a visual metaphor that a majority of your audience can associate with. Keep in mind that your metaphor should provide navigational aid to your readers, not confuse them.

♦ When designing icons or graphical symbols to represent the metaphor, strive for simplicity, clarity, and consistency.

♦ Design your site for your users, not yourself. Get feedback throughout various stages in your user interface design.

♦ Use frames for your site's user interface only when they actually serve a purpose. Otherwise, you're simply adding another level of confusion for your readers.

♦ Maintaining consistency and predictability of your user interface provides a site that is friendly to your readers.

✦ Be creative with your design but don't let your creativity get in the way of your site's functionality.

✦ Design your user interface to facilitate what the readers want to do, not what you want to do. Remember that you are designing your site for others to use.

✦ The navigation of your site should be quick and easy for your readers. They shouldn't have to go through different levels of your site before reaching the page they need.

✦ Give your readers a reason to come back to your site by updating your content on a regular basis and providing a method of interaction that your readers can participate in.

✦ Obtain feedback from your test panel throughout all the stages of your design and implementation of your Web site. This process ensures that your site is designed for your users and not for you.

Q&A

 Why would I use an image map when I can use several icons instead?

The alignment of individual graphics can become altered when viewed on different monitors. Image maps give you the capability to control the alignment of your graphical links. This is useful when the location of your hot spots is vital for your user interface's overall effect.

You mention that a site needs to be predictable. Wouldn't a predictable site be boring to visit?

When we say that the user interface should have consistency and predictability, we are not saying that you should make your site boring. When you read a book, you expect the book to have a table of contents, page numbers, and so on. The structure of the book is predictable and consistent to help the reader through the text. If the book is boring, you can blame that on the content. Similarly, if a site is boring, it is usually because of the predictability of the content, not the user interface.

Challenge
Yourself

We have divided this section into two parts. Each part should give you hands-on practice with identifying a metaphor for your site.

Part A: Creating a Metaphor

We'd like you to think of a metaphor to use for your Web site's user interface. It is easier to choose standard metaphors that already have been implemented on the Web. We've included a short list of criteria to consider when choosing the metaphor for your site. Feel free to add to the list at any time.

- ✦ Ensure that the metaphor relates to your site. If it doesn't, justify the use of it.
- ✦ Clarify the types of navigation to be used (image map, buttons, hypertext links, or a combination of all).
- ✦ Determine the images you will be using for your navigation, if any.
- ✦ Keep in mind that your site should provide consistency of navigational elements throughout.
- ✦ Determine how your site will work for people who are graphically disabled.
- ✦ Decide whether your metaphor will help your audience navigate your site.

Part B: Surfing the Net

Look for Web sites that use the same metaphor you've chosen. Decide whether the user interface of each site helps or hinders the navigation by asking yourself these questions:

- ✦ Does the metaphor actually help the user interface or take away from it?
- ✦ Are the navigational elements easy to understand and use?
- ✦ What type of navigational elements does the site use?
- ✦ How is the site structured?
- ✦ Are the intentions of the site clear to you? If not, why aren't they?

Tables, Frames, and Typography

Chapter 5

Page-Layout Techniques Using Tables & Frames

In this chapter, we will show you how to manipulate your Web page layout by using HTML tables. Because this is a design book and not an HTML tutorial, we will focus mainly on the design aspects of page layout. To get the most out of this chapter, you will have to be familiar with the HTML table tags and their attributes. John Newsom's Tables Seminar site at `http://www.ckcs.org:80/seminar/intro.htm` is a good source for learning more about HTML table tags and attributes.

Creating a Design Grid for Your Tables

The easiest way to design a table is to first plan the layout of your page on paper. Using a 600-pixel minimum, determine the pixel widths of each column. You can use percentages for your columns if the alignment of your elements is not vital to the page layout. This allows a reader with a large monitor to view the table on a full screen instead of viewing a small table that is squished up at the left of his screen. Don't get too excited yet, because there's a catch. If your page requires that the elements align properly, as in a newsletter layout, it is best to stick to exact pixel widths for your table and columns. Now, after hours of sweating over the design of your table, you finally manage to make all your text wrap nicely in your main column while maintaining the balance of all your graphics in your other column. Before you and your fellow Web designers do the Webmaster happy dance of joy, though, you'd better check it out on a larger monitor. Otherwise, you'll be yanking your hair out (if you have any left) when you find out that your gorgeous table looks more like three skinny lines at the top of the page of anyone who has the luxury of owning a bigger monitor than you. (See Figure 5.1.)

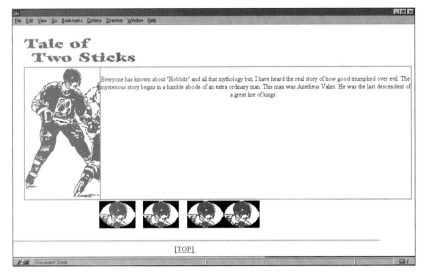

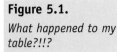

Figure 5.1.
What happened to my table?!!?

Controlling the Flow of Text and Graphics

When designing your grids, determine exactly how many rows your table will use. If you don't have too many elements to align, you probably can get away with using only one row. One row is obviously much easier to maintain and work with than many rows. All you really have to do with a one-row table is put the contents for the first column in the first <TD> tag, the contents for the second column in the second <TD> tag, and so on.

If the layout of your page requires that the elements sit on the same baseline, it is best to separate these elements into multiple rows. Each row ensures that the elements remain in the same line regardless of the length of the preceding row. This method is useful when you want to line up graphics beside textual elements. (See Figures 5.2 and 5.3.)

Aligning Elements with Images

If you want to have full control of the alignment in your table, you can set the cell-padding and cell-spacing attributes in the <TABLE> tag to zero. Removing the space between the columns and rows enables you to arrange your graphical and textual elements more closely to what you designed in your page-layout plan. Setting the cell-spacing and padding attributes to zero enables you to place an element—such as a drop cap or pullquote—butt up against the rest of the text without having an unsightly gap between them.

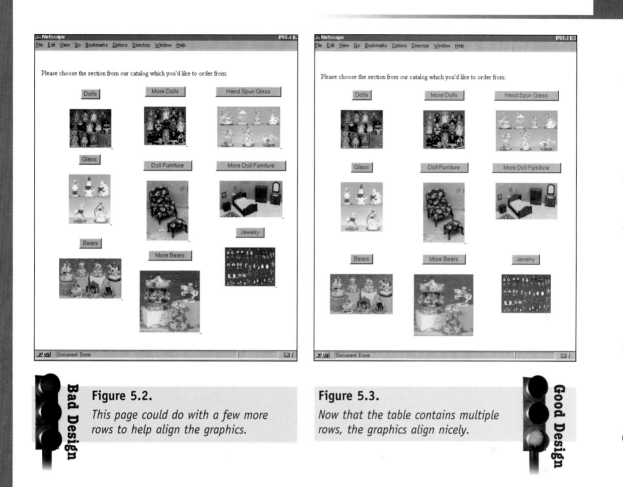

Figure 5.2.

This page could do with a few more rows to help align the graphics.

Bad Design

Figure 5.3.

Now that the table contains multiple rows, the graphics align nicely.

Good Design

Aligning Elements with the Background

With an invisible table, you can align the elements of your page with the elements in the background image. To create an interesting border on the left margin, for example, you can use a two-column table. The width of the first column should be the exact pixel width of the margin bar in your background image. The contents of the page go into the second column. When the page is displayed in a table-enabled browser, the border image appears to be running down the left of the screen beside the content. (See Figure 5.4.)

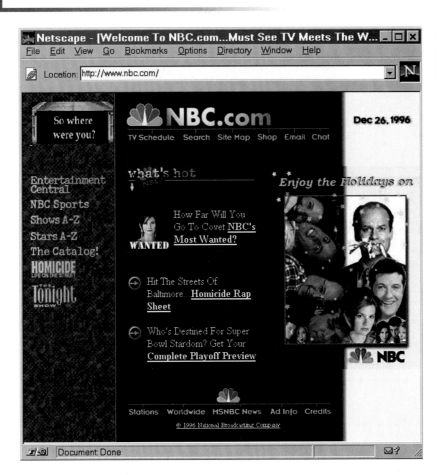

Figure 5.4.

NBC's site (`http://www.nbc.com`) uses the colored-margin effect with the help of an invisible table.

Creating Multicolumns

Designing multiple columns of text onscreen takes some work, because you have very little room to play with—especially if you are designing a table width that is 600 pixels or less.

Tools for Aligning

You can use the ALIGN and VALIGN attributes in the <TR>, <TH>, or <TD> tags to specify the alignment of elements contained in a table cell. The ALIGN attribute determines the LEFT, RIGHT, or CENTER alignment of the elements in the cell. The VALIGN attribute determines the vertical alignment of the elements in the cell using the values TOP, MIDDLE, BOTTOM, and BASELINE. The

BASELINE attribute, when used in the <TR> tag, tells the browser that all the elements in that row should be aligned vertically with the same baseline. The table tags and attributes are the tools you need to help lay out your Web pages. (See Figures 5.5. and 5.6.)

As mentioned earlier in this chapter, we will mainly be focusing on the design aspects of Web page layout using HTML tables and not teaching HTML. If you want to learn more about HTML table attributes and tags, you can visit a great HTML table tutorial on the Web: John Newsom's Tables Seminar site at `http://www.ckcs.org:80/seminar/intro.htm`.

```
Netscape - [Source of: http://pathfinder.com/@@pqzgDAUAC...]
<HTML>
<HEAD>
        <TITLE>Welcome To TIME.com</TITLE>
</HEAD>
<BODY BGCOLOR="#FFFFFF" LINK="#FD111A" VLINK="#5511CC">
<TABLE CELLSPACING=0 CELLPADDING=0 border="0">
<TR>
        <TD VALIGN=TOP WIDTH=122>
        <A HREF="http://time.com">
        <IMG SRC="/time/navimages/timelogo.g
if" ALT="TIME" WIDTH="122" HEIGHT="44" BORDER="0"></A>
        <P><BR>
        <A HREF="./daily/index.html">
        <IMG SRC="/time/navimages/a1_daily.gif" ALT="Time Daily" WIDTH="122"
        <A HREF="./magazine/index.html">
        <IMG SRC="/time/navimages/a2_mag.gi
f" ALT="Magazine" WIDTH="122" HEIGHT="28" BORDER="0"></a>
        <A HREF="./community/index.html">
        <IMG SRC="/time/navimages/a3_comm.gif" ALT="Community" WIDTH="122" H
        <A HREF="./multimedia/index.html">
        <IMG SRC="/time/navimages/a4_multi.g
if" ALT="Multimedia" WIDTH="122" HEIGHT="28" BORDER="0"></a>
        <P><BR><BR>
        <CENTER>
        <A HREF="java.html" target="_top"><FONT SIZE="2">
        <b><tt>java version</tt></b></FONT></a></center>
        </TD>
        <TD VALIGN=TOP WIDTH=480 VALIGN=TOP>
        <TABLE CELLSPACING=0 CELLPADDING=0 border="0">
                <TR>
                        <TD>
                        <IMG SRC="/time/images/hlbanner.gif" USEMAP="#banner
                        <MAP NAME="bannermap"><AREA SHAPE="RECT" COORDS="398
                        </MAP>
                        </TD>
                </TR>

                <TR>
                        <TD>
                        <TABLE border="0" CELLSPACING=0 WIDTH=464 CELLPADDING=0>
                        <TR>
                        <TD VALIGN=TOP>

                                <nobr>
                                <A TARGET="newWin" HREF="http://time.com/199
                        <IMG SRC="/time/images/magcover.gif" WIDTH="139" HEI
                        <A TARGET="newWin" HREF="bestof1996/index.html"><IMG

                        <a href="http://time.com/godcom/" target="newWin">
                        <IMG SRC="/time/images/hA5.gif" ALT="Alcoholism" ALI
                                </nobr>

                        </TD>

                        <TD VALIGN=TOP>
                        <p align="left">
                        <table border=0 CELLSPACING=0 WIDTH=199 CELLPADDING=0>
                                <TR>
                                <td valign=top>
                                <A TARGET="newWin" href="http://time.com/moy/">
                                <IMG SRC="/time/images/hA3.gif" WIDTH="199" HEIGHT="
                                </td>
                                </tr>
                        </table>
                        </TD>
                        </TR>
                        </TABLE>
                </TD>
        </TR>
<TR>
        <TD>

<NOBR>
                <A HREF="../timevista">
                <IMG SRC="/time/images/vistabutton.gif" WIDTH="58" HEIGHT="6
"></A>

<NOBR>

<!-- AdSpace -->

<link rel=pageresource href="/ng-bin/dynir/SpaceID=2326/AdID=1739/?URL=http:

<link rel=pageresource href="/ng-bin/dynir/SpaceID=2330/AdID=955/?URL=http:
<!-- /AdSpace -->

<A HREF="../adinfo/"><IMG SRC="/time/images/adinfo.gif" WIDTH="21" HEIGHT="6
</NOBR>
</TD>
</TR><TR>
<TD ALIGN=CENTER><BR><MAP NAME="../shared/images/nav/navbar.map">
                <AREA COORDS="381,10,422,26" HREF="http:
//cgi.pathfinder.com/nph-nav/navbar?op=chat">
                <AREA COORDS="261,11,378,26" HREF="http://cgi.pathfinder.com
                <AREA COORDS="228,10,278,27" HREF="http://cgi.pathfinder.com
                <AREA COORDS
="185,11,224,26" HREF="http://cgi.pathfinder.com/cgi-bin/nph-nav/navbar?op=h
                <AREA COORDS="107,10,183,26" HREF="http://cgi.pathfinder.com
                <AREA COORDS=3,10,106,27" HREF="../"></MAP>
                <A
 HREF="../shared/images/nav/navbar.map">
                <IMG SRC="/time/images/navbar.tan.gif" ALT="Pathfinder Navig
                USEMAP="#../shared/images/nav/navbar.map" ISMAP></A>
        </TD>
</TR>
</TABLE>
</TD>
</TR>
```

Figure 5.5.

TIME.com's (http://time.com) *source code for its home page. Look at all the HTML required for this seemingly simple page layout.*

Figure 5.6.

TIME.com's (http://time.com) *home page is laid out in one huge table with columns and nested tables.*

Large Animated GIFS

A trick to cut down the size of a large animated GIF is to animate only a small portion of the image and divide it into smaller graphics. Using a table, you can reconstruct the whole graphic by aligning it with the attributes in the column and row tags. The result is that, instead of downloading one huge animated GIF, the browser loads one small animated GIF along with a few small graphics. The Coca-Cola Christmas site (http://www.cocacola.com/santa/homensw.html) uses this technique to isolate one small animated section of its image map where Santa Claus waves to his viewers. (See Figures 5.7 and 5.8.)

Result

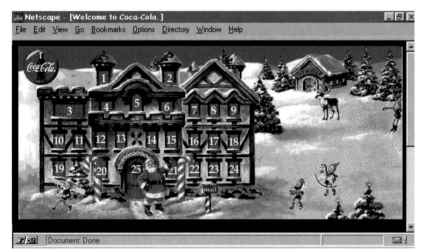

Figure 5.7.

Coca-Cola's (http://www.cocacola.com/santa/homensw.html)
*Christmas site as the graphics are loaded. The final image actually consists of
two smaller images, with a small animated GIF of Saint Nick (Hi, Santa!).*

HTML

Figure 5.8.

Here's how they did it.

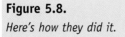

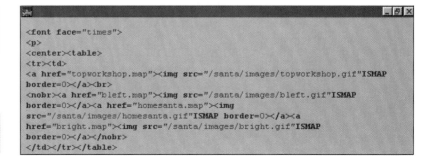

```
<font face="times">
<p>
<center><table>
<tr><td>
<a href="topworkshop.map"><img src="/santa/images/topworkshop.gif"ISMAP
border=0></a><br>
<nobr><a href="bleft.map"><img src="/santa/images/bleft.gif"ISMAP
border=0></a><a href="homesanta.map"><img
src="/santa/images/homesanta.gif"ISMAP border=0></a><a
href="bright.map"><img src="/santa/images/bright.gif"ISMAP
border=0></a></nobr>
</td></tr></table>
```

Nesting Tables to Manipulate Alignment

Sometimes, a complicated page layout requires more than a table with even-spaced columns and rows can offer. An alternative way to remedy an alignment problem is to nest smaller tables within tables. Tables in themselves are a task to master, but nesting tables within tables can be even trickier. The important rule to remember when nesting tables is to close all your tags with end tags. Although this is not necessarily specified in the HTML standards, some browsers crash when faced with nested tables within tags that have not been closed. (See Figures 5.9 and 5.10.)

Figure 5.10.

Newsom's site also provides a great example of source code for nested tables.

Figure 5.9.

John Newsom's site (`http://www.ckcs.org:80/seminar/capitol.htm`), is an excellent example of nested tables.

Stacking Tables to Control Page Layout

Consider the layout of your page as a flexible organization of your work. It is important to have some control over the flow of your text and graphics but to be aware that your reader might not be able to see your page exactly the way you designed it. Adding flexibility to your page can be as easy as using several tables instead of one huge table to organize your information.

Don't use tables if your page doesn't require them. Try to use tables only when you need help aligning parts of your page, and structural tags cannot achieve the desired layout effect. In general, most of the elements on your page probably can be aligned with structural tags. As a minimum, use structural tags within your table tags so that someone viewing your page on a non-table-supporting browser still can understand your page. Use the `ALIGN` attribute in the `<IMG SRC>` tag with all your graphics and add a `<P>` or `<BR>` tag to separate sections of text; this increases the likelihood that people using other platforms will be able to view your pages as you intended.

> **Tip**
> The best way to test the flexibility of your page is to view it on a non-table-supporting browser. Your page might not look exactly the way you intended it to; however, the strength of your design will show through if the arrangement of your elements still makes sense with or without tables.

Designing Layouts with Tables

Tables are a necessary tool to effectively control the layout of your pages. The capabilities to specify the alignment and background attributes of sections of a table, to extend your table cells into other columns or rows, to stack or nest your tables within or on top of each other, and to insert as many tables as you want on your page give you almost everything a Web designer needs to create an incredible Web page. (Pretty exciting, huh?)

Small Tables

Don't be afraid to use a small table. If you need to place a graphic with a caption below it, for example, you don't have to put your whole page into a table. The `ALIGN` attribute in the `<TABLE>` tag allows word wrapping around the table if the table is narrower than the window screen. So, if you specify the pixel width of the table as the same width of your graphic, you can just add text in a row below the graphic to create a professional-looking, captioned graphic. (See Figures 5.11 and 5.12.)

Adding Color to Your Columns

Adding color to your tables can provide effective contrasts on your page. Try using the `BGCOLOR` attribute to add color to the background of your table or column. This is handy when you want to create a contrasting background color for elements such as pull-quotes or callouts by using HTML code instead of graphics. If you still prefer to use a graphic, an interesting little trick to increase your page's download time is to match the background of the image with the background color of the column (or vice versa). This gives the impression that the column contains a graphic that is larger in size than it actually is. (See Figures 5.13 and 5.14.)

Figure 5.11.

This is the HTML source code using a small table to create a caption under our airplane graphic. We left-aligned the table so that the accompanying text wound around the graphic.

HTML

```
<TABLE ALIGN="LEFT" BGCOLOR="white" BORDER=0 CELLSPACING=0 CELLPADDING=0
WIDTH=200 VSPACE="6" HSPACE="6">

<TR><TD ALIGN="CENTER"><img src="plane.gif"></TD></TR>

<CAPTION ALIGN="BOTTOM"><FONT FACE="Book Antiqua" color="#0000FF">Bill's Private
Jet</FONT></CAPTION>
</TABLE>

<H2>Nice Guy looking<BR> for Mate</H2>
<FONT SIZE=+3>B</FONT>ill Inflates had just put on a lot of weight. You see, he spends most of his days
surfing the Net, sending nasty emails to Web masters just as a hobby, and has replied to almost every
newsgroup ever imaginable. His favorite gourmet dish is always served on a take out tray, his favorite
sound over his phone line is the beeps and static he hears right before his modem gets him connected.
His wardrobe consists of a dark blue sweat suit, where the crotch goes past his knees. He tries to
find ingenious ways to reach for things in his room without ever getting up from his chair. He's a
mighty catch you ladies out there.  If you are interested in this sexy, bristle faced stud, send him an
email at <a href=>perfectlycoolguy@snark.com</a>
```

Nice Guy looking for Mate

Bill's Private Jet

Bill Inflates had just put on a lot of weight. You see, he spends most of his days surfing the Net, sending nasty emails to Web masters just as a hobby, and has replied to almost every newsgroup ever imaginable. His favorite gourmet dish is always served on a take out tray, his favorite sound over his phone line is the beeps and static he hears right before his modem gets him connected. His wardrobe consists of a dark blue sweat suit, where the crotch goes past his knees. He tries to find ingenious ways to reach for things in his room without ever getting up from his chair. He's a mighty catch you ladies out there. If you are interested in this sexy, bristle faced stud, send him an email at perfectlycoolguy@snark.com

Figure 5.12.

This is how the small table looks on the browser screen.

Result

Caution

Don't cause your reader severe eyestrain by pouring all the shades of your color palette into every column of your table. Doing so only defeats the purpose of drawing attention to your page.

Note

Like any non-standard attribute, BGCOLOR is not supported by all browsers.

Figure 5.13.

Using the BGCOLOR *attribute to add color to your columns.*

Figure 5.14.

We played around with the colors here. The graphic's background color is the same as the BGCOLOR *attribute of the column.*

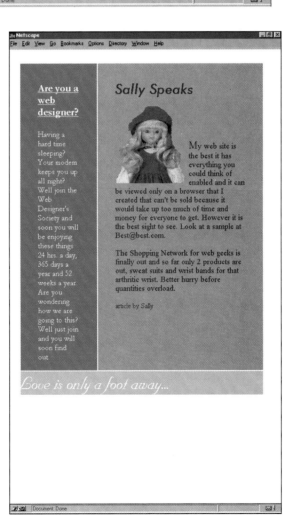

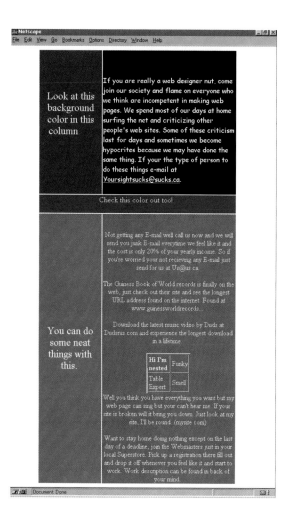

Figure 5.15.

Now, isn't this going a little overboard?

Bad Design

For All You Artsy People Out There!

Plain, boring, left-aligned pages are things of the past. With the power of tables to design any kind of page imaginable, you can set up your page any way you want and shove it up on the Web for all the world to see. Hey, but wait a minute! The whole point of page layout is planning and design. Don't throw out all the things you learned about the elements of design just because you have the tools to do almost anything you want. (See Figure 5.15.) Table alignment is just another tool to help enhance your page, not overtake it. The last thing we need to see on the Net is a page that is aligned left, right, and center with black, blue, purple, yellow, and orange stripes running through narrow columns of text; tables with borders turned on just for the heck of it; and a huge graphic divided into eight parts distributed randomly throughout the table, with a little animation of your Great Uncle Mel doing cartwheels in the left-hand corner. Of course, you can still be creative. Just do it with style.

Designing Frames: A Minimalist Point of View

If you are going to lay out your page using frames, we suggest that you make them as simple as possible. The fewer frames on your page, the better. A three-frame layout probably is the most you should use at a time.

I Never Promised You a Frame Garden

The most popular way to arrange your frames is by using the left-margin frame method. The left margin usually contains elements such as links, contact information, and navigational icons. The main frame contains the contents of the site. This setup gives readers easy access to the navigational elements at all times. (See Figure 5.16.)

Figure 5.16.

A popular left-margin frame.

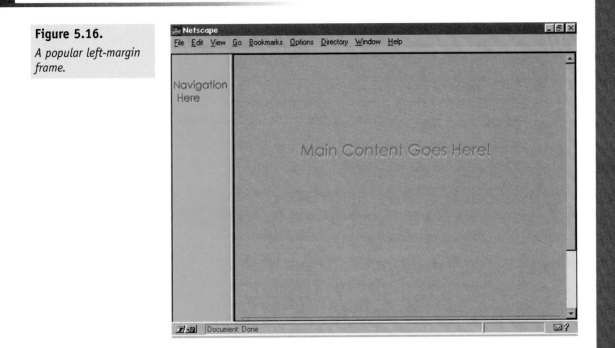

Another method of framing is exactly the same as the left-margin method except that the index frame is now on the right of the screen. Right-handed people might appreciate this structure more, because they don't have to click over so far to get to the index. Now don't start designing your frames this way just because you are right-handed. There are just as many left-handed people out there as right-handed people (well, almost).

The other way you can design two frames is by using the top- or bottom-frame method, which gives the reader a wider screen for the main content. The narrower frames generally are used for banner ads or navigational items. This method of framing seems to be growing in popularity. (See Figures 5.17 and 5.18.) Personally, we don't like being forced to see a banner ad the whole time we visit a site. If you decide to use this method of framing, you should remember to give your reader the option to resize the frame. Would you want to have the message

```
Remove embarrassing body odor, click here
```

blaring in your face for 10 minutes?

Figure 5.17.

A narrow frame at the bottom of a Web page.

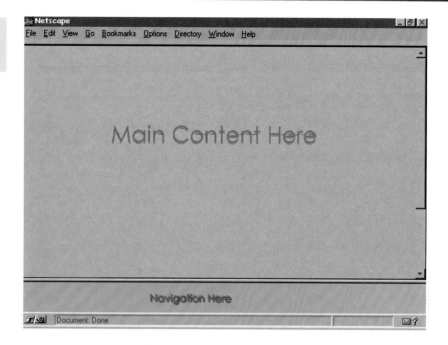

Figure 5.18.

A four-framed Web page that cuts the screen into four very small and hard-to-read sections.

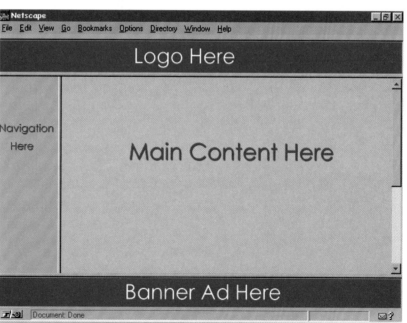

Non-Frame Alternative Navigation

This goes without saying: Always give your reader the opportunity to view your site without frames. A growing number of frame-haters positively refuse to visit a site that contains frames. Giving your readers the choice to view your site without frames is only common courtesy. If you don't think it is necessary to add a non-frames alternative to your site, don't be shocked when you find your site's URL in a list of the Top 10 Butt-Ugly Framed Sites of the Year.

Form Layout: Submission Forms, Guest Page Forms, and More

The layout of your submission forms is just as important as the rest of your pages on your site. Submission forms encourage your audience to interact with you. Organize your elements logically. You can use tables to arrange your form elements neatly on the page. Don't make the reader scroll down a whole list of checkboxes when you can lay them out in easy-to-read columns. It is less strenuous for our eyes to scan a line quickly from left to right than it is to scroll down a page. Keep the entry fields and text properly aligned with one another by placing the text and fields in separate columns. A cluttered submission form with the form fields scattered haphazardly all over the page definitely does not encourage people to fill it in. (See Figures 5.19 and 5.20.)

Figure 5.19.

What a crappy form. They didn't bother putting the entries in a table.

Bad Design

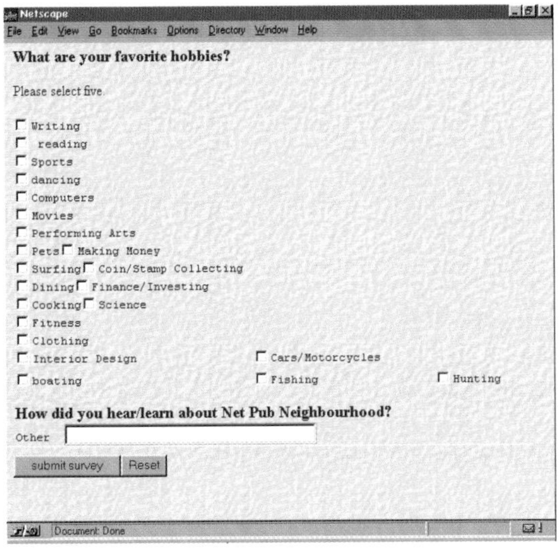

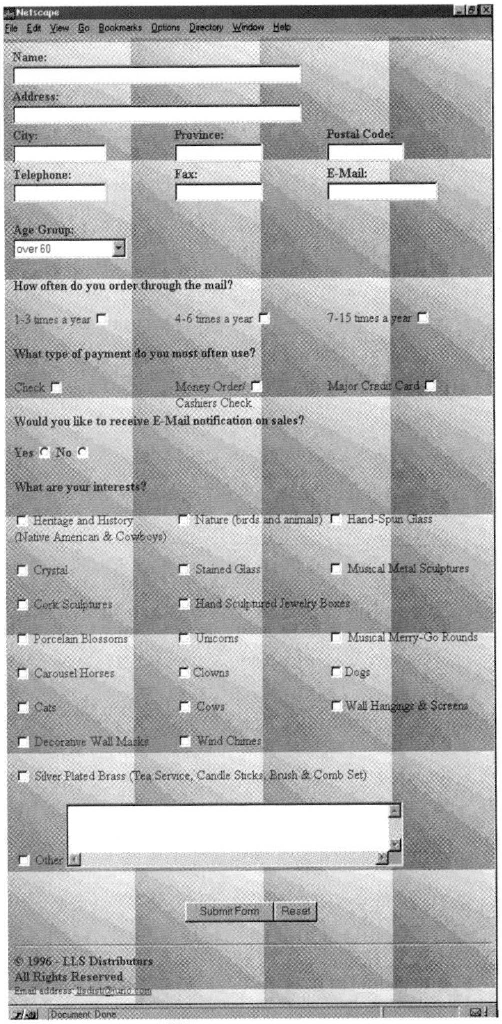

Figure 5.20.

Ah, this form is much easier to understand and read.

Good Design

Summary

Now that you have learned a bit about page layout using tables and frames, let's review the major points in this chapter:

- ✦ Remember to plan the layout of your page on paper before you start creating a table. It will make the job a lot easier for you in the end.

- ✦ Invisible tables allow you to align elements on your page discreetly.

- ✦ An alternative way to remedy an alignment problem is to nest smaller tables within tables.

- ✦ Remember to close all your tags with end tags when nesting tables within other tables.

- ✦ Try to use tables only when you need help aligning parts of your page and structural tags cannot achieve the layout effect you want.

- ✦ Test the flexibility of your page by viewing it on a non-table-supporting browser.

- ✦ Add color to your tables to provide contrast on your page.

- ✦ You can be creative with your tables, but don't forget the importance of basic design elements.

- ✦ If you are going to design frames for your site, stick with the *less is best* rule.

- ✦ The layout of your submission forms is just as important as the rest of the pages on your site. Keep the elements in order by placing them in a table.

Q&A

Q
A
Can I use tables and frames together?

Yes; you can incorporate tables on a frame-based site. Basically, the pages you see in a frame are the same as the ones in a regular HTML document. You can add as many tables to the HTML document as you want. Just be careful not to divide your page too much. Remember that your reader will have to look at that page through a very small window as opposed to his whole screen.

Q
A
Is there a better way of laying out my page? Using HTML tables seems to be quite inflexible.

Yes; the HTML 3.2 standards incorporating style sheets will give Web designers more control over their page layouts. Currently, however, style sheets are not widely supported by browsers. We do foresee that this will be changing sometime in the near future as browsers are being updated.

Chapter 5: Page-Layout Techniques Using Tables & Frames

Challenge
Yourself

Now that you have become acquainted with the different ways you can use tables, we are going to ask you to create a Web page using tables.

Case Study

Your boss has seen a really nice page layout on the cover of *Pastel Shellwork*'s magazine. He wants you to use that same page layout as a guide to design the company Web page. You are in charge of designing your own graphics and content for the page.

Your Mission

To create a Web page using a table page-layout design.

Required Tools

+ HTML software or an ASCII text notepad
+ Your computer
+ Your creativity

Supplied Elements

The page layout is located on the CD-ROM in the "Chapter 5: Challenge Yourself" section.

Chapter 6

Text & Typography: What Do They Really Mean to Web Page Design?

In this chapter, we will discuss how the design principles for text and typography can apply to Web page design. We will show you ways to improve the readability of your content just by using simple typographical techniques such as indents, columns, and pullquotes. These techniques will give your Web site the edge it needs to stand out from other Web sites.

The Importance of White Space

Currently, the capability of HTML tags to enable a Web designer to manipulate the white space on a Web page is limited. A Web page that lacks elements such as indents, margins, leading spaces, horizontal spaces, and vertical spaces can be difficult to read—especially if there is a lot of information to be displayed onscreen. In this chapter, we will show you ways to add white space to your Web pages.

Note

The *Hypertext Markup Language* (HTML) was not designed to be a typographic or Web page layout tool. As mentioned in an earlier chapter, a Web page looks and works differently on different platforms. The design examples we will show you are supported by Microsoft Internet Explorer 3.0, Netscape 3.0, and other browsers. If you are designing a site intended for an audience that uses mainly text- or audio-based browsers, some of the techniques in this chapter might hinder your audience's ability to understand your Web pages. We will try to point out alternatives to these techniques whenever possible. It is good practice to provide a text-only version of your site for the people who can't enjoy all the bells and whistles your site offers. Because this book is based on design concepts rather than cross-platform issues, though, our focus will be mainly on Web design techniques.

Using Indents to Organize Your Text

Indents are elements used to indicate to your reader the beginning of a new paragraph. Unlike a desktop-published document, where spaces between text affect the amount of white space on a page, browsers translate consecutive spaces in an HTML file as only one space. That means that no matter how many spaces you put between two words or text, the reader sees only one space on his screen. You can arrange your HTML source code for better readability by adding spaces in your HTML document without altering the appearance of your Web page on a browser screen. On a design level, though, the inability to add more than one space between elements forces you to find alternative ways to add white space to your page. Because no HTML tag exists to enable a designer to produce an indent or tab, we will show you several alternative ways to achieve this effect.

Using Non-Breaking Spaces

You can use several non-breaking spaces ( ) in a row to achieve an indent in a line of text. Each   code specifies one character space. If you use five   codes in a row, your browser should display five character spaces, for example. (See Figures 6.1 and 6.2.)

            I click to the bottom I go back to the top of the site.
When I stop and I turn and I go for a ride.
Till I click to the bottom and see the top of the page again.
Do you, don't you want me to use you.
I'm downloading fast but I'm miles from you.
Tell me tell me tell me come on tell me you browser.
You may be Netscape but you ain't no browser.

Do you, don't you want me to use you.
I'm downloading fast but I'm miles from you.
Tell me tell me tell me come on tell me you browser.
You may be Netscape but you ain't no browser.

Browser browser browser browser...
Browser browser...

Figure 6.1.

The source code for the Freeland Web page, showing how to use the   code.

HTML

Figure 6.2.

This is how the Web page looks on our browser. Notice how the   code produces a nice little indent right before the word I.

Result

The purpose of the   code is to force a non-breaking space on a Web page. You can use this code any time you need to create one or more character spaces on your page.

> **Caution**
>
> Not all browsers support the   code. Instead of translating the code into spaces, some browsers actually display the text . This can make your page look pretty strange when viewed on these particular browsers. (See Figure 6.3.)

Figure 6.3.

"Why does this guy have gibberish in front of sections of his text?" The   *code as seen on Netscape 1.0.*

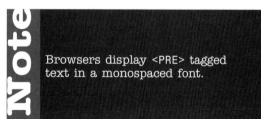

            I click to the bottom I go back to the top of the site. When I stop and I turn and I go for a ride. Till I click to the bottom and see the top of the page again. Do you, don't you want me to use you. I'm downloading fast but I'm miles from you. Tell me tell me tell me come on tell me you browser. You may be Netscape but you ain't no browser. Do you, don't you want me to use you. I'm downloading fast but I'm miles from you. Tell me tell me tell me come on tell me you browser. You may be Netscape but you ain't no browser. Browser browser browser browser... Browser browser...

Pre-Tag This, Please

The <PRE> tag is a structural tag that enables the Web designer to display formatted text, such as computer code, exactly the way it was typed originally. Usually, browsers won't recognize line spacing or character spacing, but, within the <PRE> tag, the character and line spacing is preserved.

You can use the <PRE> tag to produce an indent by creating multiple character spaces in a line. This is a primitive way to create an indent, but the effect is understood across different platforms. (See Figure 6.4.)

> **Note**
>
> Browsers display <PRE> tagged text in a monospaced font.

Using the <PRE> tag does prevent the automatic wrapping of your text at the end of each line, though. To get the word-wrapping effect, you have to press Enter at the spot you assume to be the narrowest browser width. That's pretty tricky, because different monitors have different screen widths. Some people use the 70-character-maximum rule to determine when they should break the line of text. In our example, the words wrapped nicely on a 600×480 screen. (See Figure 6.5.) When the same page is viewed on a larger screen width, though, the forced end-of-line break gives the text the appearance of being squished up beside the graphic. (See Figure 6.6.)

HTML

```
<font size="4">

<img src="legs.gif" alt="Hairy Legs?" align="left" vspace="0" hspace="0" valign="top">

<PRE>                              Removing unwanted hair from your
legs is the focus of our next topic. Men and women have tried various methods to remove leg hair. Waxes, depilatories, and
razors are the traditional methods used in this century.
</PRE>

</font>
```

Figure 6.4.

The source code for creating a five-space indent using the <PRE> tag.

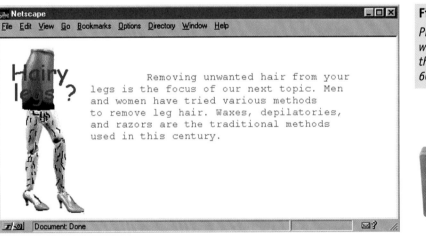

Figure 6.5.

Pressing Enter to force word wrapping within the <PRE> tag on a 600×480 screen.

Result

Figure 6.6.

Viewing the same Web page on a 1,024×768 screen.

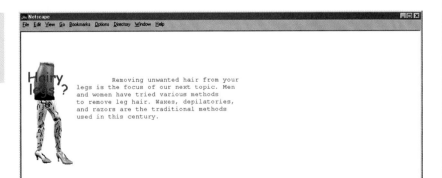

The Spacer GIF

The *spacer GIF* is a creative way to produce an indent by creating a GIF image, which you can make approximately 80 pixels wide and 2 pixels high. All you have to do now is insert the image right before the text you want to indent. (See Figure 6.7.)

HTML

```
<img src="spacer.gif" alt="">     Illiterate? Email us for free information and we
          will send you our 300 page pamphlet that will explain to you in great detail
          the techniques of reading. We will teach you how to read in a matter of hours!
          Just send us a check for $500, and you can download a zipped version of
          our reading secrets once we cash your check.
```

Figure 6.7.

The HTML source code for a Web page that uses a GIF image to create an indent on the first line of text.

Note

Make sure that the GIF image is the same color as the background. If you are using a patterned background, you should use a transparent GIF image to ensure that the spacer GIF is not visible on your page.

Creating transparent GIFs is discussed in greater detail in Chapter 9, "Manipulating Your Graphics."

In our example, we made the GIF image a different color from the background color of the Web page to show you how the GIF image creates the indent effect on a browser screen. (See Figure 6.8.) Of course, when creating your GIF images, you should make your GIF image the same color as your background image.

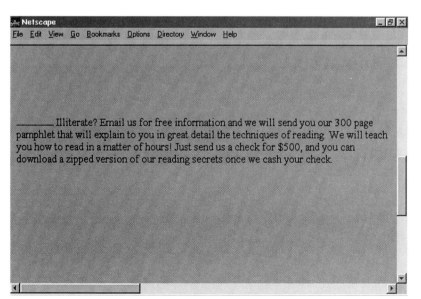

_____ Illiterate? Email us for free information and we will send you our 300 page pamphlet that will explain to you in great detail the techniques of reading. We will teach you how to read in a matter of hours! Just send us a check for $500, and you can download a zipped version of our reading secrets once we cash your check.

Figure 6.8.

We used a GIF image—or spacer GIF, as it is more commonly known—to produce the indent effect on this Web page.

Result

Chapter 6: Text & Typography: What Do They Really Mean to Web Page Design?

Controlling Horizontal Spacing with Blockquotes

The `<BLOCKQUOTE>` tag is a quick way to add margin space to your document. You can wrap sections of text with the `<BLOCKQUOTE>` tag to force a browser to add margin space to the left and right of the section of text. (See Figures 6.9. through 6.11.)

To increase the margin widths of your Web page, all you need to do is add another set of `<BLOCKQUOTE>` tags around the first set of tags. (See Figures 6.12 and 6.13.)

Figure 6.9.

This text is difficult to read because of the lack of margin space on this Web page.

```
Netscape                                                    _ 8 X
File  Edit  View  Go  Bookmarks  Options  Directory  Window  Help
```

Once upon a time, in a land not far away, lived a little flea named Ferdinand. He was a very lonely flea since none of the other fleas wanted to play with him. He didn't know why they didn't like him. He wasn't a bad looking flea. Actually he thought he was a pretty good looking little guy. Every morning, he would stand in front of his mirror, marveling at just how wonderful he looked that day.

```
Document: Done
```

HTML

```
<BLOCKQUOTE>
```

Once upon a time, in a land not far away, lived a little flea named Ferdinand. He was a very lonely flea since none of the other fleas wanted to play with him. He didn't know why they didn't like him. He wasn't a bad looking flea. Actually he thought he was a pretty good looking little guy. Every morning, he would stand in front of his mirror, marveling at just how wonderful he looked that day.

```
</BLOCKQUOTE>
```

Figure 6.10.

The source code shows where to place the `<BLOCKQUOTE>` tags around a section of text to create left and right margins.

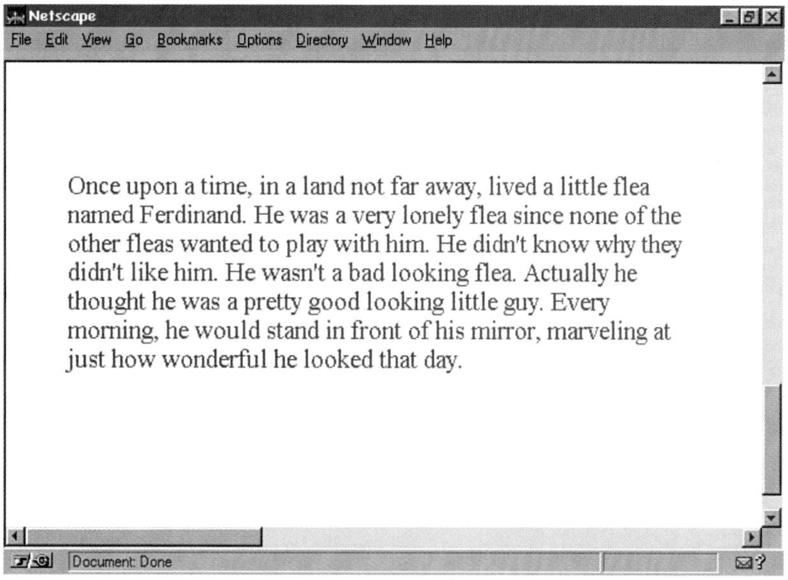

Figure 6.11.

Here is what the text looks like with the <BLOCKQUOTE> *tags added.*

Result

> Once upon a time, in a land not far away, lived a little flea named Ferdinand. He was a very lonely flea since none of the other fleas wanted to play with him. He didn't know why they didn't like him. He wasn't a bad looking flea. Actually he thought he was a pretty good looking little guy. Every morning, he would stand in front of his mirror, marveling at just how wonderful he looked that day.

```
<BLOCKQUOTE><BLOCKQUOTE>
```

> Once upon a time, in a land not far away, lived a little flea named Ferdinand. He was a very lonely flea since none of the other fleas wanted to play with him. He didn't know why they didn't like him. He wasn't a bad looking flea. Actually he thought he was a pretty good looking little guy. Every morning, he would stand in front of his mirror, marveling at just how wonderful he looked that day.

```
</BLOCKQUOTE></BLOCKQUOTE>
```

Figure 6.12.

Adding another set of <BLOCKQUOTE> *tags to increase your margin widths.*

HTML

Result

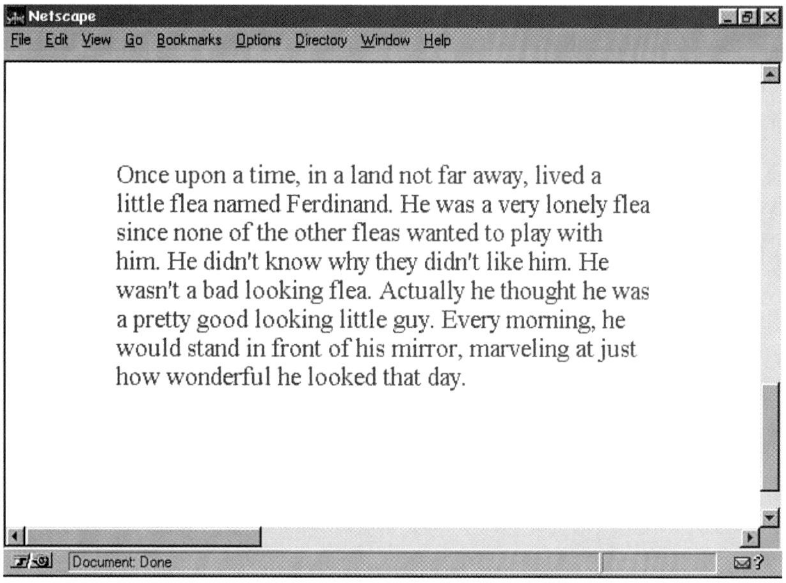

> Once upon a time, in a land not far away, lived a little flea named Ferdinand. He was a very lonely flea since none of the other fleas wanted to play with him. He didn't know why they didn't like him. He wasn't a bad looking flea. Actually he thought he was a pretty good looking little guy. Every morning, he would stand in front of his mirror, marveling at just how wonderful he looked that day.

Figure 6.13.

Using the double <BLOCKQUOTE> *tags doubles the margin widths of the Web page.*

Chapter 6: Text & Typography: What Do They Really Mean to Web Page Design?

The text is much easier to read with a sufficient amount of white space around it. The `<BLOCKQUOTE>` tag makes adding margin space fast and easy. The margin effect works in Netscape 2.0 and higher, as well as in Microsoft Internet Explorer 2 and higher.

Not all browsers render the `<BLOCKQUOTE>` tag the same way. Some browsers translate the text within this tag into a different font or, worse, into italics. The reason for the difference is because the `<BLOCKQUOTE>` tag was created to separate quoted text from regular text on a page. Use the `<BLOCKQUOTE>` tag around text for quick margins only when the width of the margin space is not absolutely vital to the page layout. When you need to create a specific margin space, it is better to use tables.

Adding Margins to Increase Legibility

Adding margins to your Web page increases the legibility of your page and adds contrast to it, especially when you have a lot of information to display. Left margins provide space for index links, headers, callouts, notes, pullquotes, graphics, contact information, and other elements.

Style sheets probably will be the most reliable way to add margins to your Web pages, but they currently are supported only by a handful of browsers. Until style sheets are implemented by a majority of browsers, tables are the next best method to use to create margin space.

You can use tables in several ways to create margin space, depending on how you want the information on your page to be displayed.

A simple way to create margins is to put your text in a centered, one-column table that is 75 percent of the width of the browser screen. This makes your table narrower than the actual browser screen, allowing your text to wrap within the table column cell. (See Figures 6.14 and 6.15.) We left the table borders on to show you how the table creates margin space. When designing your tables, make sure that the BORDER attribute is 0 so that the table borders are not visible onscreen.

```
<CENTER>
<TABLE WIDTH=75% BORDER=1>
<TR>
<TD>

        In the Ruley Land of Ryan lived men in peace. These men of peace were in pieces. None of them knew
        where they were or where they were going. They did nothing all day but sit around living in peace.

        However, this peace was soon going to be destroyed by a group of Keuheus. The Keuheus
        were a bunch of nomadic people who wanted to settle in a prosperous land like the Ruley
        Land of Ryan. To achieve this goal, their leader, Achoo, gathered all his men and started
        toward the Ruley Land of Ryan.

        As usual, the people of Ryan sat around doing nothing. They were sitting around when a
        huge, wet piece of Kleenex flew out over the blue sky and on top of the land.

</TD>

</TR>
</TABLE>
</CENTER>
```

Figure 6.14.

Achieving margin space by using a one-column table set at 75 percent of the width of the browser screen.

HTML

Figure 6.15.

We set the table border to 1 to show you how the table adds even margin spaces to the left and right of the body of text.

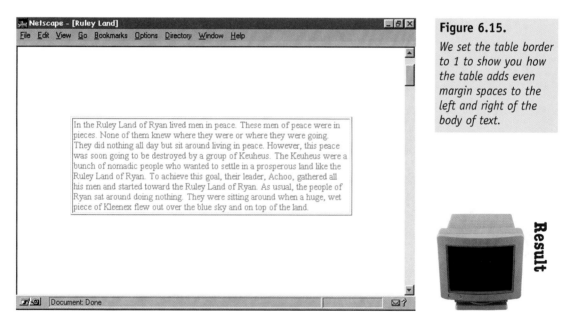

Result

The one-column table is a fast way to create white space around your text. If you are setting the table width with a percentage, however, the body of text might be stretched across the screens of larger monitors. If your layout relies on the proper alignment of your elements, you can specify the exact pixel width of the table to be 450 pixels (when designing for a 600-pixel-width screen).

> **Caution**
>
> You might notice that some people use the definition list tags (`<DL>` and `<DD>`) to add margin space around their text. Although these tags do produce the desired indentation effect on some browsers, the actual function of the definition list tag is to give structural meaning to items in a definition list. Therefore, not all browsers indent the information within the definition tag.

Overcoming HTML Limitations

Structural tags enable many browser types to understand the structural meaning of the text on a Web page. Tags—such as `<H1>` for a level 1 heading, `<EM>` for emphasis, and `<STRONG>` for more emphasis—are specified by HTML 2.0 and 3.0 standards to give Web page textual elements specific structural importance. These tags enable users with special needs, search-engine robots, text-based browsers, and so on to understand the structural importance of text within the tag. (A visually impaired user can understand the emphasis of content within an `<EM>` tag as opposed to a `<FONT SIZE=+3>` tag, for example.) Structural tags do not give a Web designer much flexibility to format a Web page, which gives the other members of his audience a visually unpleasant experience.

We try not to advocate breaking the HTML rules as specified in HTML 2.0 standards, but, sometimes, it just can't be helped. We have to work with what we have, and what we have right now isn't much for a designer to work with. As we said before, it is difficult to please everybody. The only options we have are to design a site that adheres strictly to the HTML 2.0 standards and to create a lukewarm site that works well on all platforms, or to create a great site that breaks some rules but compensates for that by including reasonable equivalents of any unsupported elements. The better alternative perhaps is to design two versions of your site so that people can choose which way they want to view it.

Incorporating Columns

You can create visual contrast and help control the alignment of your elements on your page by placing them into columns.

Two-Column Tables

But how do you put elements such as an index list into the margin? You can use a two-column table to place elements in the left margin of your Web page. To do this, you have to create a two-column table specifying the widths of both columns. The left column should be narrower than the right column, because it will be the left margin of your page. Indicate the pixel width of both columns by using the `WIDTH` attribute in the `<TD>` (table data cell) tags. Place the contents of the left margin within the first `<TD>` tag. Place the main contents of your page in the second `<TD>` tag. The final result of your two-column table creation will be a nice-looking Web page separated into two columns. You can enhance this effect with a background image of a contrasting color on the left part of the image. (See Figures 6.16 and 6.17.)

Figure 6.16.

The HTML code for a two-column table.

```
<TABLE WIDTH=600 BORDER=1>
<TR>
<TD WIDTH=100>
<CENTER><img src="ruleynew.gif" alt=""><BR>
<small><a href=>Tired?</a><BR>
<a href=>Happiness</a><BR>
<a href=>Html Land</a><BR>
<a href=>Where?</a><BR>
<a href=>Jump</a><BR>
<a href=>Home</a><BR></small></CENTER>
</TD>
<TD WIDTH=400>
         In the Ruley Land of Ryan lived men in peace. These men of peace were in pieces. None of them knew
         where they were or where they were going. They did nothing all day but sit around living in peace.

         However, this peace was soon going to be destroyed by a group of Keuheus. The Keuheus
         were a bunch of nomadic people who wanted to settle in a prosperous land like the Ruley
         Land of Ryan. To achieve this goal, their leader, Achoo, gathered all his men and started
         toward the Ruley Land of Ryan.

         As usual, the people of Ryan sat around doing nothing. They were sitting around the day when a
         huge, wet piece of Kleenex flew out over the blue sky on top of the land.

</TD>

</TR>
</TABLE>
```

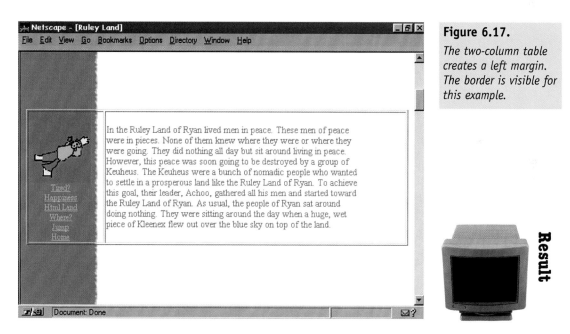

Figure 6.17.

The two-column table creates a left margin. The border is visible for this example.

Result

Three-Column Tables

If you want to create a right margin on your page, simply insert a transparent spacer GIF into a third column of your table. Indicate the width of the spacer GIF by using the WIDTH attribute in the <IMG> tag. The other option is to create a spacer GIF with the pixel width you need for the margin. You always can use the third column to insert more elements into the page. Be careful not to make very narrow columns. Narrow columns are hard to read and are not very pleasant to view. (See Figure 6.18.)

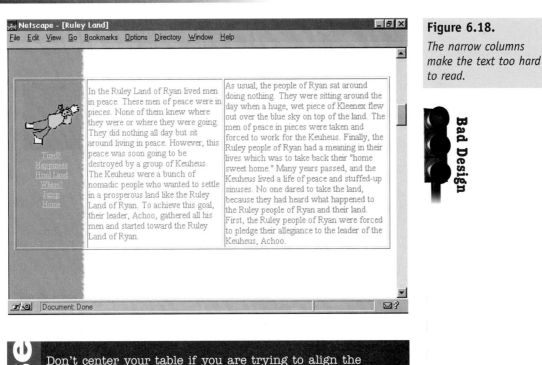

Figure 6.18.

The narrow columns make the text too hard to read.

Bad Design

Don't center your table if you are trying to align the elements in your left margin with the background image. A centered table on a larger screen causes the information to become misaligned. (See Figure 6.19.) If you want the information in your table to align with your background image, keep the table left aligned and your column widths at a fixed size.

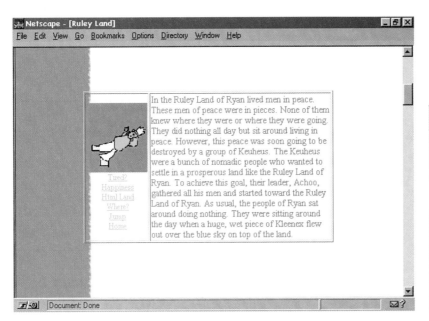

Bad Design

Figure 6.19.

A centered table causes misalignment of the table elements when viewed on a larger screen.

Controlling Column Height & Width

Various column widths and lengths are used in magazine and newspaper page layouts to create visually exciting pages of information. A Web designer can use this same technique by creatively arranging his information in columns of varied lengths and widths. You should refrain from using too many column lengths and widths on your page. Remember that too much clutter makes for a messy Web page.

Spanning Your Columns

Manipulating the column widths of your page takes a little creativity, a lot of patience, and the magic of the COLSPAN tag, the COLSTART tag, and the table cell's WIDTH attribute. Before you begin any HTML for your columns, you should have the layout of your page already drawn out on a grid for easy reference. Determine the width of your table and calculate the widths of each column. When you are creating your HTML code, make sure that you also include the empty table data (<TD>) cells in each row (<TR>) tag. This might seem like unnecessary work, but the more accurate you are with your table tags, the easier it will be to achieve your desired page layout—not to mention the easier it will be for browsers to figure out what your page is trying to do. (See Figures 6.20 and 6.21.)

```
<TABLE WIDTH=600 BORDER=0>
<TR>
<TD WIDTH="100" VALIGN="TOP" COLSTART="1" COLSPAN="1">
<CENTER><img src="ruleynew.gif" alt=""><BR>
<small><a href=>Tired?</a><BR>
<a href=>Happiness</a><BR>
<a href=>Html Land</a><BR>
<a href=>Where?</a><BR>
<a href=>Jump</a><BR>
<a href=>Home</a><BR></small></CENTER>
</TD>
<TD WIDTH="400" COLSTART="2" COLSPAN="1">
        <BLOCKQUOTE>         

    <FONT SIZE=6>I</FONT>n the Ruley Land of Ryan lived men in peace. These men of peace
    were in pieces. None of them knew where they were or where they were going. They
    did nothing all day but sit around living in peace.
```

HTML

Figure 6.20.

Some of the source code for a page layout that uses the COLSPAN tag and WIDTH attribute to control the alignment of the page. The entire HTML source code is located on the CD-ROM at the back of this book.

Figure 6.21.

This is how the browser interprets the COLSPAN tag and WIDTH attribute.

Result

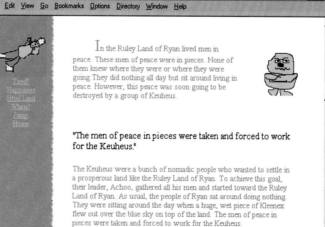

Controlling Column Heights

The simplest way to control the height of your columns is to break your content into rows by using the `<TR>` tag. If you need the content of a cell to expand into another row, you need to add the `ROWSPAN` attribute to your table data (`<TD>`) cell.

Controlling Word Spacing

At times, one character space just isn't enough. Textual elements, such as capitalized headers, sometimes require more than one space between two words. There are only a few techniques to create space between words. The fastest way is to use six or seven occurrences of ` ` (non-breaking spaces) wherever a bigger space between two textual elements is required.

Another way is to create a transparent spacer GIF with the exact pixel width of the space required. If you're too lazy to create another spacer GIF image, you can create one 1×1 pixel, transparent spacer GIF and use the `WIDTH` attribute in the `<IMG>` tag to control the size of the space. (See Figure 6.22.)

The most common way to control the space between two words is to create an actual graphic of the textual element. Using a graphic to control the appearance of your textual element ensures that your reader sees the element the way you intended it to be seen.

Leading: Controlling Vertical Line Spacing

The space between lines of text and graphics is called *leading*. The amount of white space above and below an element can help make your Web page more readable. With HTML, though, the line spacing between lines of text that wrap automatically can be controlled only with style sheets (which, as we mentioned earlier, are not supported by many browsers yet), and there are only two tags that control the vertical-line spacing between blocks of information. The `<P>` (paragraph) and `<BR>` (line break) tags add vertical space between elements. Unfortunately, the tags do not allow you to control the actual height of the space. Depending on what browser you use, the spacing created by the tags can vary.

Controlling Vertical Space

You can create a table with one row and insert it between two sections of your page where you want to control the vertical spacing. (See Figures 6.23 and 6.24.) When you indicate the pixel height with the `HEIGHT` attribute in the `<TD>` (table data) tag, the height of the empty column simulates several vertical spaces. In our example, we have left the border visible to show you how the table creates the appearance of vertical spacing. It is good to include two `<BR>` tags within the empty `<TD>` tag so that a reader with a browser that does not support tables still can see a space between the two sections of information.

```
<!--spacer.gif-->

<FONT SIZE=6>Returning <IMG SRC="spacer.gif" alt="" WIDTH="90" HEIGHT="10"> Ryan</FONT>
```

Figure 6.22.
Controlling the space size by using the attributes in the `<IMG>` tag.

Figure 6.23.

Using the HEIGHT attribute to create vertical space between two sections of text.

HTML

Many years passed, and the Keuheus lived a life of peace and stuffed-up sinuses. No one dared to take the land, because they had heard what happened to the Ruley people of Ryan and their land. First, the Ruley people of Ryan were forced to pledge their allegiance to the leader of the Keuheus, Achoo. Achoo forced all of them to work for him for the rest of their lives. This included their offspring! The land itself was still peaceful, but all the beautiful trees were knocked down to grow cotton bushes in order to produce more Kleenex. Although this was happening to the former people of the Ruley Land of Ryan, the believers of redemption hoped for a doctor to mix them a cold medicine to wipe out the Keuheus. They found a doctor, and his name was Andraw First.

```
<table border=1>
<tr><td height=150><br><BR></td></tr>
</table>
```

Andraw First compiled many elixirs, but none of them did the right job; none of the Keuheus were freed from their colds. One little boy told Doctor First that he should use the old chicken soup on the Keuheus. He said that his mother always gave him some if he was sick. Doctor Andraw First ignored the child's comment and continued to mix cough drops and syrup. After many times at the drawing board, Doctor First actually decided to give the Keuheus chicken soup. He told the Ruley people of Ryan that they would soon be saved from the coughs and sneezes of the Keuheus and that he was the one to save them.

Figure 6.24.

This is how the code looks in our browser. We made the border of the table visible for example purposes only.

Result

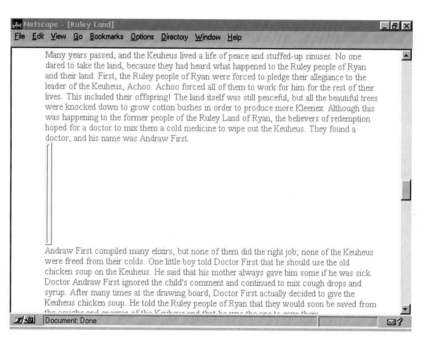

Using Images to Control Vertical Line Space

The easiest way to control the vertical space between two elements is to create a transparent spacer GIF. You can specify the size of the space you need by using the WIDTH and HEIGHT attributes within the <IMG> tag. If you are picky about your graphics, you can create your spacer GIF image to be the exact height and width of the space you need.

Using Fonts to Convey Your Message with Style

Different font styles on your page can add style to your Web pages. No longer must we read everything in our default font. When used carefully, the type of font you use can bring life to your pages. On the other hand, an inappropriate font can destroy the legibility of your Web page.

> **Note**
>
> When you do not specify a font for your text, the reader sees your Web page with the browser's default font or one that he has chosen himself.

Serifing the Net

A *serif* font generally is used for the body section of a document, because it improves the readability of the text. (See Figure 6.25.) The specific wedge-like shapes at the ends of each character help the eye move from one letter to the next. There are several types of serif fonts, but it is better not to waste your time using fonts that are exclusive to your computer. The less people who have that particular font, the less people will be able to see it.

Serif Fonts

This is MS Serif.

This is an example of Garamond.

This is an example of Book Antiqua.

This is an example of Times New Roman.

This is Century Schoolbook.

Sans Serif Fonts

This is Futura Bk BT.

This is Futura MD BT.

This is MS Sans Serif.

This is Arial.

Figure 6.25.
Examples of serif and sans serif fonts.

Fonts without Serifs

Sans serif fonts do not have the wedge-shaped ends. In a body of text, sans serif fonts often are difficult to read. Sans serif fonts are used mainly in headers, titles, and logos. They generally are thicker and taller than serif fonts.

Font Text Versus Graphical Text

You can control the appearance of an element, such as a heading, by using plain HTML text or by creating a graphical image. You can use a graphical image to control the color, texture, size, and letter spacing of your heading elements. Of course, if you have too many graphical headings on your page, the increased download time of your page might cause your reader to leave your site even before he sees your fancy graphical headings. If you want to achieve creative typographical effects without adding to the download time of your Web page, you should use plain HTML text with the <FONT> tag. If that doesn't satisfy your design needs, consider using a combination of graphical headings and HTML text headings on your page. (See Figure 6.26.)

Figure 6.26.
Graphical text and font text working together.

Text Size: Sizing Up Your Characters

The size of your text can increase or decrease readability on a Web page. Not every browser renders font size the same way. In some browsers, the reader can determine the size of text on his screen. No matter how picky you are with the font sizes of your text, don't be shocked when you discover that the way it looks on your screen is totally different on someone else's screen. So why bother worrying about your choice of font sizes? In general, different sizes are used to specify the importance of one element compared to another, to create rhythm and visual contrast in your text, and to give your page an overall style that you can't achieve just by using one font size. (See Figure 6.27.)

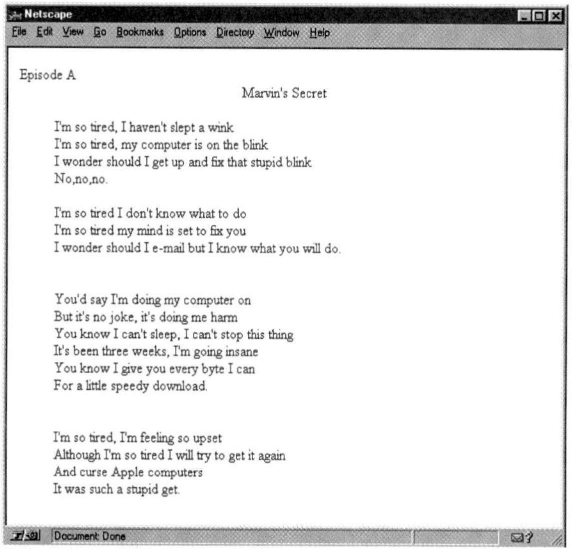

Bad Design

Figure 6.27.
This page is functional but looks pretty plain.

Creating Initial Caps and Drop Caps

An *initial cap* is a typographical technique used to help a reader find the beginning of a section of text. This is done by making the first letter of the section larger than the size of the main body of text.

Initial Caps

You can create a simple initial cap relatively easily by using the <FONT> tag and the SIZE attribute. Insert the first letter of the body of text within a <FONT> tag and determine the size of your initial cap by specifying a number in the SIZE attribute. To add more visual contrast, use an interesting font or add the bold (<B>) tag around the initial cap.

Note

You should use structural tags (such as <BIG>, <SMALL>, and <B>) to determine the size and importance of certain textual elements. The <FONT> tag gives you more flexibility in controlling your text size, though.

Yes, It Can Be Done: Drop Caps in HTML

A *drop cap* is an initial cap around which the body of text wraps. Decorative drop caps are an easy way to add contrast to a large section of text. You can create a drop cap in HTML in two ways. One way is to create a drop cap by using a one-column table. To get the drop

Tip

When creating your initial cap, make sure that it is large enough to distinguish it from the body text. A wimpy-sized initial cap can weaken the appearance of your page. Also, don't be tempted to use initial caps all over your document. Overusing this technique can make your page read like a bowl of alphabet soup.

cap effect, you have to enclose the initial cap within the table. Align your table to the left by using the `ALIGN` attribute in the `<TABLE>` tag. Now right align the `<TD>` tag so that your drop cap sits right beside the body text. Insert a `<FONT>` tag in the table cell and choose a large font size. (We chose the font size 10.) Insert the character into the cell. Finally, place a break (`<BR>`) tag after the table to align the body text with the top of the drop cap and insert the rest of the body text after it. (See Figures 6.28 and 6.29.)

HTML

```
<table align=left valign=middle cellpadding=0 cellspacing=0 border=0>
<tr><td align=right valign=middle cellpadding=0 cellspacing=0 border=0>
<font size=12 face="Arial" color=#004080><b>D</b></font></td></tr></table>
```

octor Andraw First went to the Keuheus' leader, Achoo, and gave him some chicken soup. He told the king that he made the best viruses ever made just by drinking this soup. Falling for the doctor's trick, the king and all the Keuheus were given some of this new "drink," and all of them drank it. They noticed that their sinuses were clearing and that they did not feel mean anymore. They actually felt good about themselves for the first time and joined the Ruley people of Ryan, wiping out the rest of the Keuheus.

Figure 6.28.
Creating a drop cap with HTML.

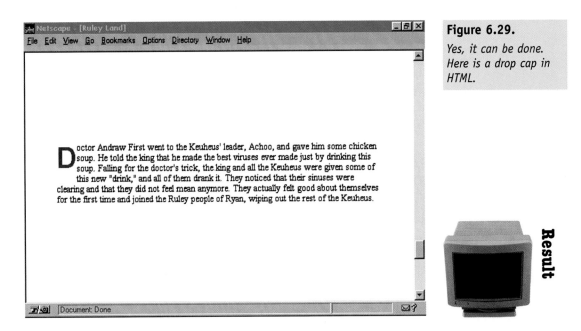

Figure 6.29.

Yes, it can be done. Here is a drop cap in HTML.

Result

Graphical Drop Caps

Of course, the alternative to creating an initial cap or drop cap is to do it graphically. You have much more choice with the appearance of the initial cap and its background. Be creative with your initial caps without making them difficult to read. (See Figure 6.30.)

Figure 6.30.
A graphical drop cap.

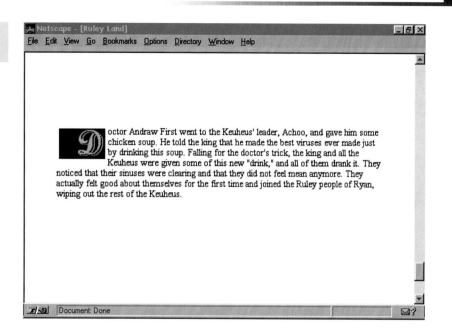

Creating Vanishing Text

Vanishing text is actually a silly effect we thought we'd throw in here to help liven things up. The only real purpose of using vanishing text is maybe to give your audience a subliminal message right before they see the actual page. Don't overdo it, though. It can get real old, real quick.

Yeah, Yeah, Just Tell Me How To Do It Already

This little effect works only if the background color or BGCOLOR attribute in the body (<BODY>) tag contrasts with the color of the background image. Next, choose a line of text you want your reader to see first, and make it the same color as your background image by specifying the color in the COLOR attribute of the <FONT> tag. Place this line right after the <BODY> tag. Now the content of your page goes below the first line of text. Make sure that the color of the text in this section is the same color as the BGCOLOR attribute. While the graphics are being loaded, the reader sees your first line

of text on top of the background color. After the background image loads, the first line seemingly disappears while, in actuality, it is blending in with the color of the image. The second line of text should be visible after the background image loads. The vanishing-text effect works only if it takes a while for your Web page to load on your reader's browser.

Creating Vanishing Text with GIF Animation

Now, if you thought that was funky, let's show you how to do it with a GIF animation. This is actually a simpler way to do it. Create a small graphic with the background the same color as the background image of your Web page. Insert the text on which you want to use the vanishing technique. Make sure that the color contrasts with the background. Then create 10 versions of your image, making the color of your text lighter and lighter until it blends in with the background color. Create a GIF animation with the images you have created by using GIF animator software (you can find a shareware version of the GIF Construction Kit by

Alchemy on the accompanying CD-ROM). Make sure that you don't use the looping effect in the GIF animation; otherwise, your text will disappear and reappear over and over again (unless, of course, that's the effect you're trying to achieve). Now stick that graphic animation on your Web page and—ta-da! You should have vanishing text!

Arranging Text Elements

Some people assume that only graphics have the power to add excitement and life to a Web page (ask our graphics designer). Not so, little grasshopper. Using typographic techniques to arrange your textual elements can in fact bring more life to your Web page than three or four cool graphics. Now that you have learned all about the different textual elements in Web design, you can think of interesting ways to add variety to your Web pages by adding elements such as pullquotes, headers, teasers, and other textual elements. You can add visual contrast to your page just by ensuring that your textual elements have sufficient breathing room or white space around them. You can draw attention to important sections of your page by starting your main topics with drop caps or initial caps. Create a nice visual effect by changing the alignment of your marginal information. (See Figure 6.31.)

As a designer, you must envision blocks of textual elements as the tools to create a visually stimulating Web page. The shape and size of each element either adds to or takes away from the overall visual look of your page.

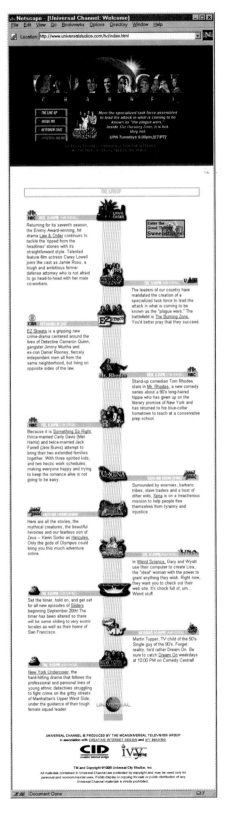

Figure 6.31.

A visually stimulating page that uses both graphics and creative typography at Universal Studio's (`http://www.universalstudios.com/tv/index.html`*) site.*

Good Design

A Web page that is completely left-aligned, with text running from the left to the right edges of the browser screen, with huge <H1> headers blaring titles at you like there is no tomorrow, with the navigational links all neatly placed in bulleted lists, and with the text of the page consistently the same size is pretty boring to look at. (See Figure 6.32.) Sure, the pages are functional, and, yes, they follow every nook and cranny of the HTML 2.0 and 3.0 standards. But what's the point if a reader finds it difficult to read and also the most boring experience of his life? If there weren't designers out there who took it upon themselves to add visual life to the Web, the Internet would be a collection of ugly sites.

Tombstones & Ladders (Not the Board Game)

Tombstones and *ladders* occur in columns where a picture or heading lines up on the same line beside another picture or heading in an adjacent column; this causes a bar effect across the Web page. (See Figure 6.33.)

When this occurs more than once on the same page, the rows of graphics give the appearance of ladder rungs going across the page (*ladders*). You should not place your heading elements beside each other; this detracts from their individual impact. A reader will have trouble determining where one heading ends and another begins. Also, for visual contrast, it is best to avoid lining up headings and graphics beside each other. Insert white space or even pullquotes between these elements to separate them.

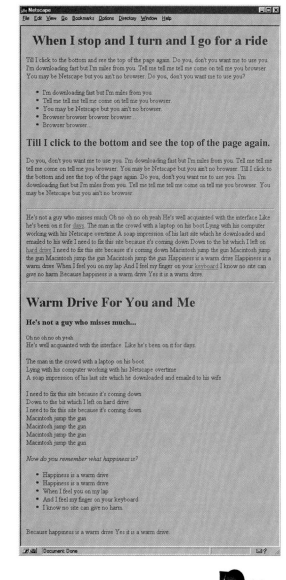

Figure 6.32.
This page could use a face lift.

Bad Design

Figure 6.33.

Tombstones and ladders make this page look unprofessional.

Bad Design

Widows and Orphans

As you probably know by now, it is quite difficult to control how the text on the page arranges itself on other browsers and monitors. You can run into problems such as your text stretching across someone's huge monitor after all the time you painstakingly tried to align your textual elements. But it is not something to fret about. Although frustrating at times, the fact that Web pages are not entities that you can create and completely control makes the task of designing for the Web more challenging and fun. In this section, we will point out some typographical design errors that you can't prevent when your work is viewed on different platforms.

Widows

A *widow* is a line of text consisting of two words or less that is isolated at the bottom of a block of text. A widow makes the page seem unbalanced, with a huge element resting on a smaller element. Widows usually are typographical no-nos in print media. On the Web, however, there isn't much you can do to prevent widows.

Orphans

An *orphan* is the opposite of a widow; an orphan is a line of text consisting of two words or less that is isolated at the top of a block of text. Orphans can occur if column widths are too narrow and the first word is the only element that can fit on the first line of the column. An orphan also can occur when you have columns, and the last word of a paragraph is inserted at the top of a new column and is followed by a <BR> or <P> tag to separate that paragraph from a new paragraph. To commit this design error, someone must consciously insert the last word of a <TD> tag into the next <TD> tag. We don't know why anyone would do that, but just in case someone out there is thinking about it, we want to make people aware of it. (See Figure 6.34.)

Figure 6.34.

The orphan text is red, and the widow text is blue.

> Flew in
> from Mosquito beach BOAC Didn't get to bed last night On my way laptop was on my knee Man I had a dreadful flight I'm back into HTML It is just too bad I can't spell I'm back into HTML.
>
> I've been
> surfing so long I hardly knew the place Gee it's good to be back on home page Leave it to tomorrow to unpack me laptop case Don't disconnect the phone I'm back into HTML It is just too bad I can't spell I'm back into HTML.
>
> Fox site
> really knocks me out Leaves Adam West's page behind And the MTV site makes me sing and shout That a site from Georgia's always on my mind. I'm back into HTML It is just too bad I can't spell back into HTML.

Headings: The Initial Impact

Headings aren't just tools to draw attention to your page; they should make a statement to your reader when he views your page. The alignment, font, and point size affect the impact of the statement you are trying to make. You can create headings by using structural heading tags, font tags, and graphical images.

Textual Headings

The easy way to create headings is to simply use the HTML structural tags, such as <H1>, <H2>, <H3>, <H4>, and so on. Aesthetically speaking, though, the tags create loud, screaming headlines that are annoying to read. (See Figure 6.35.)

Wonderful stories by my imaginary friend

Joey Jo-Jo Jim Bob was a kind man. He did everything that normal people in their right minds did. He had a family, went to work, and went home every day.

A little insight on Jo jo's enemy....

Everyone liked Joey Jo-Jo Bob; he had no enemies. Except for the ones who envied his gift of being loved by everyone. Not really "the ones," but one man named Boey Bo-Bo Job. This guy was the total opposite of Joey Jo-Jo Bob. He was as mean as anyone in the world, and he hated everything. That is why he wanted to know Joey Jo-Jo Bob's secret.

Figure 6.35.

Ugly heading tags. Stop screaming, already! We heard you the first time!

Bad Design

An alternative is to use the SIZE, COLOR, and FACE attributes in the <FONT> tag. You can create attractive heading elements by combining a large initial cap with a large point size, sans serif font, and text color that contrasts with the color of the body text.

Graphical Headings

You have more flexibility to create wonderful headings by using graphical images. You can choose the font and size without having to worry that a specific font won't be supported by the computers of all your readers. You can add texture, color, logos, images, or anything your heart desires (like a picture of your mother-in-law, for example—NOT!) to your graphical heading. Just remember to make the heading proportionate with the rest of your page. Don't make your heading so huge that your reader is blinded by the words. Also, try to keep the letter spacing close together to keep it from looking too loose. Use sans serif fonts whenever possible. The fonts should provide an effective contrast with the body text. Use colors that complement the page. Don't use colors that will overpower the other elements on the page. If you are taking the time to make a graphical heading, do it properly. A bright, lime-green heading on a page that uses sandy brown tones certainly will be the focus of your Web page. Everyone will be busy commenting on the lack of color coordination on this page. Finally, keep your headings concise and to the point. Headings should grab a reader's attention at a glance. (See Figure 6.36.)

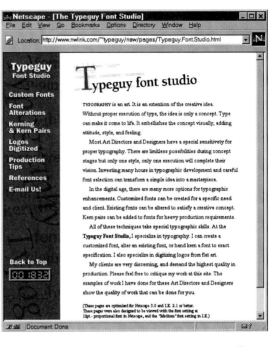

Figure 6.36.

A really nice graphical heading from the Typeguy Font Studio (`http://www.nwlink.com/~typeguy/new/pages/Typeguy.Font.Studio.html`) site.

Good Design

Pullquotes That Grab You

Pullquotes can make your page more fun and exciting. You can add flair to your pullquotes by placing them in a graphic and adding a contrasting background color to it. Create more contrast by adding an initial cap or a drop cap. Add style by enhancing your pullquote with decorative accents. A pullquote should be fun and draw your reader's attention without overshadowing your heading elements. To keep the consistency of your page, however, make sure that the font of your pullquotes is the same as your headings.

You can achieve the pullquote effect by using a two-column table in which the first column contains the pullquote and the second column contains the main body of text. Use the <FONT> tag to control the font, color, and point size of your pullquote. (See Figures 6.37 and 6.38.)

Figure 6.37.

Here is how we used a table to create a pullquote.

HTML

```
<TABLE WIDTH=100% BORDER=0>
<TR>
<TD WIDTH=180 VALIGN="TOP" vspace="40" hspace="40">
<font size=5 face="arial" color=blue><BR><BR>
"Boey Bo-Bo Job spied on Joey Jo-Jo Bob every day"</TD>

<TD WIDTH=380 vspace="40" hspace="40"><font face=courier size=3>
<font size=+3 color=blue>E</font>veryone liked Joey Jo-Jo Bob. He had no enemies. Except
for the one guy who envied his popularity. This one man was named Boey Bo-Bo Job. This guy was
Joey Jo-Jo Bob's total opposite, because he was meaner than anyone in the world. He hated everything
he ever saw. He hated Joey Jo-Jo Bob the most, because everyone liked him even when he didn't do
a thing! Boey Bo-Bo Job spied on Joey Jo-Jo Bob every day until he found out as much as possible,
but he could not find out his secret.


<BR><BR><BR><BR>


So he dressed up as a door-to-door salesman and asked if Joey Jo-Jo Bob could tell him a secret that
he could sell to the whole entire world. Joey Jo-Jo Bob said that he had a secret and it was to brush
and shower every day. Boey Bo-Bo Job was confused but tried it out anyway. For the first time ever,
he felt nice. This soon wore off, because Boey Bo-Bo Job did not like baths and they were too much
for his hydro bill. So again he went to Joey Jo-Jo Bob's house and asked him the same question.
Joey Jo-Jo Bob told him that he should be himself and shouldn't try to know his secret. Boey Bo-Bo Job
ran off and lived in a different land and tried the suggestion, and for the first time in his life,
he had a long-term relationship with someone.
</font>
</TD></TR></table>
```

Figure 6.38.

Viewing the pullquote in our browser.

Result

Netscape - [Headings]

File Edit View Go Bookmarks Options Directory Window Help

"Boey Bo-Bo Job spied on Joey Jo-Jo Bob every day "

Everyone liked Joey Jo-Jo Bob. He had no enemies. Except for the one guy who envied his popularity. This one man was named Boey Bo-Bo Job. This guy was Joey Jo-Jo Bob's total opposite, because he was meaner than anyone in the world. He hated everything he ever saw. He hated Joey Jo-Jo Bob the most, because everyone liked him even when he didn't do a thing! Boey Bo-Bo Job spied on Joey Jo-Jo Bob every day until he found out as much as possible, but he could not find out his secret.

So he dressed up as a door-to-door salesman and asked if Joey Jo-Jo Bob could tell him a secret that he could sell to the whole entire world. Joey Jo-Jo Bob said that he had a secret and it was to brush and shower every day. Boey Bo-Bo Job was confused but tried it out anyway. For the first time ever, he felt nice. This soon wore off, because Boey Bo-Bo Job did not like baths and they were too much for his hydro bill. So again he went to Joey Jo-Jo Bob's house and asked him the same question. Joey Jo-Jo Bob told him that he should be himself and shouldn't try to know his secret. Boey Bo-Bo Job ran off and lived in a different land

Document: Done

Chapter 6: Text & Typography: What Do They Really Mean to Web Page Design?

Readability: Keep an Eye on Your Line Length

When placing large amounts of body text on a Web page, consider breaking up sections of your page with columns. Columns reduce the length of a line, making it easier for a reader to find the beginning of the next line. If you do not want to use columns on your page, try increasing the margin space of your document by placing it into a three-column table. You should use the first and third columns only to hold transparent spacer GIFs, and the middle column should contain your text. Make sure that the table border is set to zero so that it won't be visible to your reader.

> **Tip**
>
> Try to keep the widths of your columns proportionate with the rest of the page. Too many columns can create very narrow line lengths, making the text on a page extremely hard to read.

Even or Uneven Lines

Controlling the evenness or the unevenness of your line lengths is almost, but not completely, impossible in HTML. You could force a break at the end of the line by using the `<BR>` or `<P>` tag, but that would cause too much vertical white space between two lines. The best way to control line length is to place your text in columns. Make sure that the column widths are wide enough for your text to flow easily. If your columns are too narrow, you could be defeating their purpose. Narrow columns can give the effect of a very ragged right edge, which makes the page very difficult to read. Style sheets probably are the most reliable way to control line lengths, but, as mentioned earlier, until they are supported by more browsers, it is best not to incorporate style sheets yet.

Using Appropriate Page Lengths

Have you ever landed on a site where the whole site was contained all on the home page? Lengthy Web pages with huge amounts of information are difficult to read, not to mention annoying as heck to scroll through. A reader who has to navigate his way through a lengthy page can get mighty confused when he clicks on a link that points to a section of a page, clicks on another link to go to another section that takes him further down, clicks on another link that takes him part way up, and then clicks on another link that takes him back to the top again. (See Figure 6.39.)

On the other hand, a Web site that is chopped up into wee little sections of three or four lines of information on each page is just as annoying. A person doesn't have the patience to bounce around your site from page to page just to see only blobs of information. A person who takes the time to download your page demands to see content on the page. Don't tease your reader by enticing him to visit a page that is void of information.

Don't feel that you have to create a Web page for each topic you are presenting. If you have numerous amounts of short, informative sections, try putting them together on one page and separating them by subheadings. The rule of thumb that some sites use is to not allow more than two scrolls down a page (using the 600×480 screen as the minimum standard). There is no right and wrong as to what the length of Web pages should be, but if you can justify making a person scroll all the way to the bottom of an extremely long page or making him load a short, insignificant page, the option is yours to use.

Stuck in a site trying to get out.

Stuck in a site trying to get out. Come on Come on Make it easy Make it easy I have nothing to hide except for me and my web browser. Deeper you go the more you get lost. The more you get lost the deeper you go. Come on Come on Make it easy Make it easy I have nothing to hide except for me and my web browser. Your home page is in and your destination out. Your destination in and your home page out Come on Come on Make it easy Make it easy I have nothing to hide except for me and my web browser.

[Block of repeated placeholder text continues throughout the browser window, with repeated headings "Stuck in a site trying to get out." and a bulleted list:]

- Come on
- Come on
- Make it easy
- Make it easy
- I have nothing to hide except for me and my web browser.

Stuck in a site trying to get out.

Figure 6.39.
Whoa! When does this page end?

Breaking the Rules: Limiting Your Horizontal Rules

A *horizontal rule* is a line or bar that is handy to use when separating sections of text, such as the footer section, from the rest of the page. People have gone to great lengths to add the horizontal rule all over their Web pages, though, sometimes resulting in distracting graphical bars or annoying animation. Disrupting the overall rhythm and appearance of the page disturbs the reader's sense of flow and takes his attention away from the information. It is best to keep horizontal rules to a minimum unless you want to give your reader the *climb-down-my-horizontal-rule* ladder effect.

Undermining the Underline

The underline <UL> tag's main purpose is to give emphasis to a particular word on a Web page. Unfortunately, this tag only creates confusion, because hypertext links also use the underline to distinguish clickable hypertext elements from the other elements. A reader who sees an underlined word automatically would assume that it is a clickable link. How frustrating would it be for him to click on something that looked like a link but wasn't one? Maybe frustrating enough for him to leave your site, because he figures that because this link didn't work, probably none of the others will either. (See Figure 6.40.)

Figure 6.40.
This link doesn't work. Ciao, baby.

You should not underline sections of text if hypertext does not exist for them. (You can underline text on a bibliography page to indicate a title of a published document, as long as you point that out to the reader at the top of the page.)

Blink, Italics, and Other Overused Formatting

Blinking text, italics, underlining, borders, rules, scrolling Java scripts, bulleted icons, animated banners, and other wonderfully useless and distracting gizmos can brutalize even the best-designed Web page. These elements are used for enhancement purposes only, but they sometimes become the key focus on Web pages. We once visited a site that had a huge heading that blinked the words `WELCOME to Cement Week` with big, honking, animated bars and bullets spinning out of control. The main body of the document was in italicized red type, and an unending Java script scrolled across the status bar. A site like this can drive anyone absolutely batty. It's hard enough to keep a Web page balanced, consistent, and visually appealing. Don't rely on these non-enhancing elements to add zest to your page. Your readers will thank you for your restraint. (See Figure 6.41.)

The good, the bad and the Webly

By Mary Elizabeth Williams
Illustration by Christian Clayton

SO it came to pass that the newfangled thingie they called "the Web" rose from a neat-o concept to full-on stardom in the mid-'90s. And lo, the history books would later write, it was in 1996 that it became apparent at last to all that the Web was no mere flash in the pan, no Macarena of text and image.

Remember, just two years ago, when Hotwired wasn't just the hottest thing, it was pretty much the only thing? Remember last year, when if you didn't have a domain name, you were as pathetically out of date as Ann Landers' hairstyle?

This year, the honeymoon was over. Even as pundits proclaimed the Web had crested and was on the downswing, ever more individuals and corporations stampeded to carve out a virtual room of their own. In other words, like every other medium before it, the Web settled in, made itself at home in our lives, and observed with amusement reports of its demise. Because whether it's entertaining, informing, or boring the crap out of us, it's not going anywhere.

Herewith a few highlights and low points to store on the server of your memory.

+ + + + + + + + + + + + + + + +

THE CDA TOOK MY BABY AWAY

The bad news was that the Communications Decency Act passed. The good news for all of us was that it was challenged and shot down faster than a Clinton cabinet nominee. The Web responded to the threat against free expression with the highly visible blue ribbon campaign, articulate and impassioned reports from the trenches, and a flurry of grassroots consciousness raising that demonstrated powerfully the commitment those who've found a home on the Web have to keeping their words and ideas on it intact.

+ + + + + + + + + + + + + + +

BUT WHAT I REALLY WANT TO DO IS ACT:
THE SITE/C|NET/NETIZEN TV

By now, every television network has its own Web site, plus there's a bucketload of hit shows that have more fan pages devoted to them than David Duchovny has panting groupies. But this was the

Figure 6.41.

Salon's (`http://www.salon1999.com/dec96/webyear961223.html`) *site shows you what simple text and typography can contribute to a document.*

Good Design

Summary

Now that you have become familiar with the text and typography of Web design, let's review the major points of this chapter:

- ✦ A Web page that lacks elements such as indents, margins, leading spaces, horizontal spaces, and vertical spaces can be difficult to read.

- ✦ You can use several non-breaking spaces (` `) in a row to place an indent in a line of text.

- ✦ The `<BLOCKQUOTE>` tag makes adding margin space fast and easy. The tag might be rendered differently on various browsers, though.

- ✦ Sometimes it's difficult to strictly adhere to HTML standards and still design a nicely laid-out site. It is always a good habit to give your reader two versions of your site that he can choose from.

- ✦ The simplest way to control the height of your columns is to break your content into rows by using the `<TR>` tag.

- ✦ The easiest way to control the vertical space between two elements is to create a transparent spacer GIF. You can specify the size of the space you need by using the `WIDTH` and `HEIGHT` attributes within the `<IMG>` tag.

- ✦ Serif fonts generally are used for the body section of a document, whereas sans serif fonts are used for headings.

◆ When creating an initial cap, make sure that you make it large enough to distinguish it from the other text. An initial cap that is too small will look insignificant.

◆ Using typographic techniques to arrange your textual elements can bring more life to your Web page than three or four cool graphics.

◆ As a designer, you must envision blocks of textual elements as being the tools to create a visually stimulating Web page.

◆ You should not place your headings and graphical elements beside each other; this detracts from their individual impact.

◆ Lengthy Web pages with huge amounts of information are difficult to read. Keep your page lengths to two screen scrolls at the most.

◆ Don't underline your text! A reader will not appreciate it when he clicks on a word that looks like a hypertext link but then discovers that it really isn't.

◆ Don't rely on non-enhancing elements, such as blinking text, animated rules, and crazy bullets, to add zest to your page.

Q&A

Q **You mentioned that HTML is not meant to be a typographical tool. When will style sheets be accepted as the standard?**

A Style sheets are being written into the HTML standards as you read this. No one is quite sure when style sheets will be set in stone, though. Currently, only Microsoft has incorporated style sheets into the latest version of its browser.

Q **Will all these techniques I am learning become obsolete in future versions of HTML?**

A As we mentioned earlier, style sheets might be the layout tool Web designers have been waiting for. A lot of issues still have to be discussed regarding the implementation of these standards across all platforms, though. The Web is always changing, but it is safe to say that, for now, it will still be a while before the HTML 3.0 standards are supported by all browsers.

Challenge
Yourself

In this section, we are going to let you apply the techniques and concepts you have learned about typography.

Case Study

Lucas Times wants you to add its developer's review for the month of January onto its Web site. They would like the page to be laid out similar to a newspaper article, in which the content is divided into columns.

Your Mission

To increase the legibility and presentation of an HTML document by using the typographical elements you learned about in this chapter, such as columns, drop caps, white space, and so on.

Required Tools

- ✦ HTML software or an ASCII text notepad
- ✦ Your computer
- ✦ Your creativity

Supplied Elements

A large body of ASCII text saved in an HTML document is supplied on the CD-ROM in "Chapter 6: Challenge Yourself."

Colors and Spicy Graphics

Chapter 7

Splashing on the Color: Effective Color Schemes for Your Web Site

In this chapter, we are going to teach you everything you need to know about color in Web designing. You will learn about how color functions on a Web page, using loud and soft colors, blending foreground colors with background colors, choosing appropriate color combinations for your designs, and optimizing the bit size of your color palette. By the time you get through this chapter, we're going to make you a Web color expert. So get ready to begin your tour through the exciting world of color!

The Psychology of Color 101

Color is an integral part of our lives. We look at and react to different colors, tints, and shades countless times every second of our waking hours. How can we not? The world we live in is the ultimate Technicolor movie.

We rely on color to convey meanings for many things—from traffic lights to file folders. Countless books and courses discuss how color impacts us emotionally and psychologically. One thing is certain: We all react in varying degrees to different colors, shades, and tones. Pink might be considered a gentle color, for example. But suppose that, as a child, you were chased by a big bully named Egor who, just for laughs, shoved wads and wads of pink bubble gum into your hair until your head looked like one huge Hubba Bubba hot-air balloon. In that case, the word *gentle* might not be the first thing to come to mind when you see a shade of pink. Certainly colors do capture our attention and cause us to react consciously or subconsciously based on our own experiences and beliefs. As a designer, you should familiarize yourself with the deeper meanings of color and tap into the power that color provides. The more conscious you are about the statements the proper use of color can make, the greater impact you will have on your reader.

Colorful Meaning

We rely heavily on certain colors to give meaning to certain things. When we were young, for example, we always associated fire engines with the color red. When we moved out of our old neighborhood in the city to a newly developed suburb across town, we were astonished to discover that the fire engines were a ghastly yellow! We thought we were on a different planet. Just the difference in color affected our whole sense of reality. (That couldn't be a real fire engine. Aren't fire engines supposed to be red?!) (See Figure 7.1.)

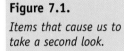

Figure 7.1.

Items that cause us to take a second look.

Red is associated with the words *hot, passion,* and *stop.*
Green is associated with the words *envy, nature,* and *go.*
Blue is associated with the words *cold, sad,* and *sky.*
Yellow is associated with the words *warm, coward,* and *caution.*
Brown is associated with the words *dirty* and *earth.*
White is associated with the words *innocent, clean,* and *good.*
Black is associated with the words *evil, fear,* and *death.*

In other cultures, colors take on totally different meanings. In the Chinese culture, for example, black is associated with happy and joyful events, whereas in North America, it is associated with death. On the other side of the coin, we consider white to be a sign of purity and birth, which is symbolized in many weddings to this day, where the bride traditionally wears a white gown. In the Chinese culture, however, a woman would not wear white at her wedding, because white represents bad luck and death.

The Purpose of Color

Color can control the look and feel of your site. Just mix in a few clashing colors and your whole site is thrown into the abyss of ugly Web sites. Slapping a few random colors onto your Web page is definitely not the approach you should take. Use color to your advantage. The color combination at your site shouldn't scream **LOOK AT ME!**

LOOK AT ME! LOOK AT ME! Nor should it whisper please ignore my color scheme. my page is bare because i do not proclaim myself as being a color expert. Get a life! Anyone designing a Web page should be thinking about the ways he can help his reader enjoy his experience at his site instead of using color to measure the loudness (or softness) of his own ego.

Bring This Color to My Attention

Bright colors are good attention grabbers, because they are loud and obvious. But if every color on your page is bright, the page just becomes an eyesore. (See Figure 7.2.) Creative color schemes are exciting, but make sure that they add to the readability of your content. Overstimulating a reader's eyes should be a concern only for the designers of the *Sports Illustrated* Swimsuit site.

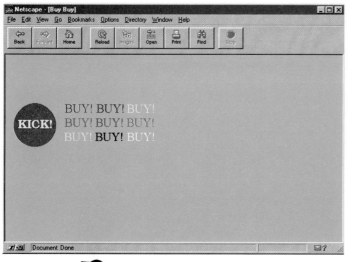

Figure 7.2.

Using too many colors to grab attention.

Bad Design

We know that color has a powerful effect on how we associate things. Colors can give a reader predefined feelings and prejudices toward a Web page even before he sees the content. Take a look at big companies. Marketing departments take color very seriously. They know that, in order to get people to associate certain colors with their company, they must be consistent in the way they splash their colors all over their promotional materials, correspondence, commercial packaging, signs, and so on. As a designer, you have to take some of that mentality and add it to your Web design. Consistent color schemes give your site a sense of familiarity and professionalism that a reader can recognize right away. (See Figure 7.3.)

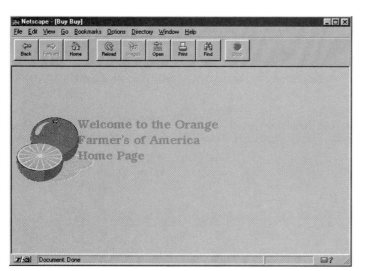

Figure 7.3.

Using the appropriate color for a site.

Good Design

No, I'm Sorry: We're All Out of Bug Spray

Colors help create an aesthetically pleasing atmosphere in which a reader can navigate. The colors in your site should correspond to the overall mood and feel of the message you are conveying. Color should only enhance your content. Your reader is here to see your information—not your color scheme. Having said that, poor choice and application of colors certainly can diminish the effectiveness and aesthetics of your page, which, in the end, can repel readers from your page as quickly as bug spray in a cloud of mosquitoes. (See Figure 7.4.)

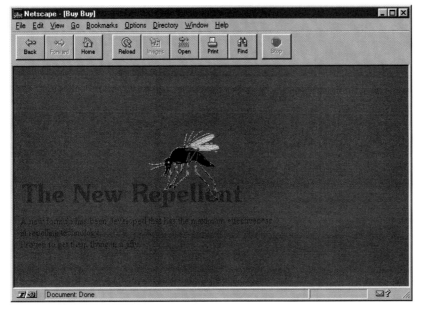

Figure 7.4.

Repelling a reader from your page through poor color selection.

Bad Design

The Functions of Color

The art of choosing colors for a color scheme includes a variety of techniques, from *close-my-eyes-and-choose* to *ooo, that looks good with that*, all the way to *after applying the formula and finding the square root of it to the nth degree...* Luckily, there is a method to the madness in choosing the colors for your site. You first have to understand how colors function and relate to each other. After you understand how colors work, the color selection process becomes much easier.

Displaying Color

Colors come in an infinite number of shades and hues, but unless someone out there is aware of some alien technology that can display every color known to man on a screen, there are currently only three major display types used by most color enthusiasts worldwide:

✦ *True-color display* stores 24 bits per pixel. This allows a true-color display to present 16,777,216 colors.

◆ *High-color display* stores 15 or 16 bits per pixel. This allows a high-color display to present 32,768 colors with 15 bits per pixel and 65,536 colors with 16 bits per pixel.

◆ *256-color display* stores 8 bits per pixel. This allows a 256-color display to present any one of 256 colors in the palette. The palette can contain any of a few million colors, but it can show only 256 of the colors at any one time.

A true graphics junkie would give his right pinky finger (okay, maybe only his nail) for a true-color display. Although many new computers can display true color, we still must take into consideration the group of people who can only view it as 256 colors. Many computers with true-color display can use true color only at the lowest resolutions. But many users would rather give up that capacity to run at a higher pixel resolution. Another consideration is all those millions of older computers using the Web today—some of which aren't capable of displaying more than 256 colors. Therefore, when using color, you must choose between catering to true color or going with the lowest common denominator (256 color).

Figure 7.5.
An RGB color cube.

Identifying Color Systems

You have allowed your five-year-old child to play with some magic markers. Little do you know that he has been using them to redecorate your wife's newly painted kitchen wall. Realizing that she will be home any minute, you call up your brother and beg him to bring over a can of light blue paint from the paint store near his house. When he arrives, both of you rush to paint over the fresh markings of your little future Van Gogh. Just as you begin to feel a sense of relief that you have finally outsmarted your wife, she arrives home, and, before two words come from your lips, she asks, "Honey, why does that wall have a lighter shade of blue than the other one?"

Light blue to you most likely means another shade of blue to someone else. Describing a color by its name is workable only when there is a limited selection of colors to choose from. We know that colors are not limited to two or three shades, though. Fortunately, there is a uniform system of rating the values of a color. When you add a shade of color to a Web page, that shade is interpreted exactly the same way by all browsers. Three major systems are used to describe colors.

The RGB Color System

The RGB color system matches a color by the specific amount of red, green, and blue elements that go into the color. (See Figure 7.5.) On computers, each element has a value between 0 and 255. The RGB color system is used when describing color in HTML.

The HSV Color System

The HSV color system uses three attributes to specify a color on a color wheel. (See Figure 7.6.)

Hue distinguishes one color from another by showing the position of the hue on the color wheel. This value is expressed as an angle between 0 and 360 degrees, with red at 0 degrees.

Figure 7.6.
An HSV color wheel.

Saturation refers to the intensity of the color. On computers, this element has a range between 0 and 255, with 255 being the highest value. The higher the value of saturation, the more vivid the color.

Value (also called *lightness* or *brightness*) refers to the relative light or dark quality of the color. On computers, this element has a range of 0 to 255, with 255 the lightest and 0 the darkest.

CMYK Color

The CMYK color system describes colors by the specific percentage of *cyan*, *magenta*, *yellow*, and *black*. (See Figure 7.7.) In print, many of the values for each color are expressed in percentages. On computers, each element has a value between 0 and 255.

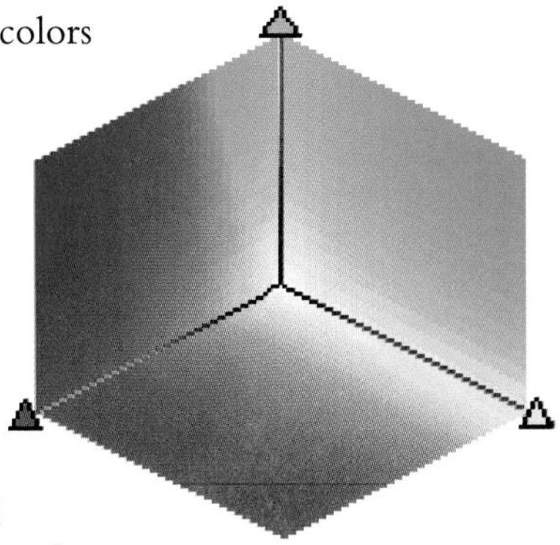

Figure 7.7.
A CMYK color cube.

Throughout the rest of this book, we will refer to the RGB and HSV color systems. With a precise number system in hand, colors can be described with more accuracy.

Don't Dither Me Now

You scan a very flattering picture of yourself with the intent of placing it on the Web for the world to admire. After painstakingly ensuring that your new computer has adjusted the tones and color scheme perfectly, you FTP it to your site. Amazingly, your picture is as stunning on the Web as it was when you saw it from your hard drive. The next day, after asking your friend in Australia to check out the latest photo of yourself, you receive an e-mail saying, "I hope you're feeling okay, mate. I looked at your picture on my 386

and, well... I hope those spots on your face go away real soon."

You, my friend, have just been dithered.

Have you ever created or scanned a great graphic and put it on the Web only to find that dithering has made it look disgusting? Or have you placed what you thought was a perfectly fine background on your Web page only to find it impossible to read because of all the little dots behind the text? Well, if you have, you have been dithered.

It is important to know about the dithering disease, because many people are connected to the Web with older computers that only support 16 colors, and still other people have newer computers and prefer to use the 256-color display. Unless you choose to cater only to the 24-bit crowd and ignore the millions of people still using 8-bit displays, understanding how dithering works will help you learn how to create great graphics that both crowds can enjoy. Consider this inoculating your graphics against the dithering disease.

Usually, when a computer is set at 256 colors, it still attempts to display any images that are 16 bits or more. Even though the computer is not capable of producing all the actual colors, it will try to reproduce the graphic as true to the original as possible. This effect is called *dithering*. Dithering is used to fool the human eye into thinking that there are more colors than are actually onscreen. The process involves the computer picking two or more colors from the existing 256-color palette and positioning them in close proximity to produce an illusion of a color that isn't actually in the palette. From a distance, the colors might look just as good as in the original graphic. It's when we get up close that we can see the effects dithering has on images. (See Figures 7.8 through 7.11.)

Figure 7.9.
This a nice picture of Mount Rushmore.

Figure 7.10.
The image of Mount Rushmore after dithering.

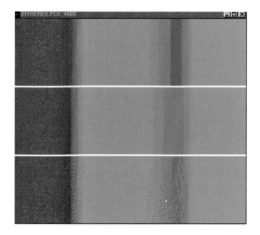

Figure 7.8.
The bar at the top is the undithered image. The middle bar is created with the nearest color replacement. The third bar is dithered.

Figure 7.11.
A close-up view of the effects of dithering.

The only time dithering does not take place is when all the colors in the image are in the 256-color palette. Images that use flat-colored areas and graphics that don't have an abundance of gradual changes in colors are prime examples of graphics that are not dithered. (See Figure 7.12.)

Dithering will take place until the day the last computer that uses a 256-color display is put to rest. Until that time, taking a few moments to review your graphics with the dithering effect in mind will allow the maximum number of people to enjoy the vividness of your work. To get those really sharp colors of your image to show up, don't use too many colors. Limit yourself to the colors in the 256-color cube. This will eliminate or minimize the effects of dithering on your images.

A Six-Sided Cube

To be able to create images that don't dither, you need to know which palette the browser is using. Fortunately, browsers such as Netscape and Internet Explorer stick to a prechosen palette. Images that are to be reduced in the number of colors are crunched through this palette.

This prechosen palette is contained in a 6×6×6 color cube. This cube is a combination of equally spaced colors in the RGB color system. The value for each element of the color—red, green, and blue—will always be one of these:

0, 51, 102, 153, 204, or 255 in decimal

or

00, 33, 66, 99, CC, or FF in hexadecimal

This cube produces 216 colors. (See Figure 7.13.)

This cube crosses the PC/Mac boundary and the Netscape/Internet Explorer boundary. It is a platform-independent color palette. "But

Figure 7.12.
A graphic that will not be dithered.

why only 216 colors?" you ask. The other 40 colors will show up on a 256-color Macintosh system, but, in PCs, a certain number of colors are taken up by the Windows system for its own use. Those 40 colors on the PC therefore might not match the colors on the Macintosh. If those colors are applied and are not found on the other platform's palette, some cross-platform dithering might occur. Because we want to be cross-platform ditherproofed, it is safer to stick with the predefined 216 colors.

Any images with all their colors contained in the palette will not be dithered; any images to be reduced to 216 colors that contain a color not in the cube will be dithered. But with this equal spacing between colors in the color palette, any colors that need to be dithered will not have to look far to find a combination that will closely match the requested color.

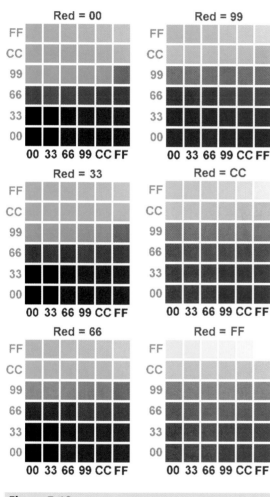

Figure 7.13.
The entire palette of the 6×6×6 color cube.

At Last: The Ditherproof Color Wheel

Yes, we know that there is a color cube with all 216 nonditherable colors, but *why do we need to know all of this, and what's the next step*? As you can probably appreciate, color can greatly enhance the appearance and feel of your home page. Color is as much a part of the overall communication of your Web as your textual content. If you know how to use color effectively, you can grab a reader's attention and hold it while he is absorbing the content. A color wheel shows you the full range of visual hues. It shows you the basis of how colors relate to one another, and it is an excellent tool to help you decide which colors to select to best portray your page.

We have gathered a selection of colors and placed them in our color wheel; however, not all 216 colors have been used. ("And why is that?" you might ask.) The human eye is quite sensitive, but slight changes in color sometimes can go undetected. (See Figure 7.14.)

How many colors can you see in section A? In section B? In section C? In section D? As you might notice, in sections A and C, the changes in the tones are almost unnoticeable. This tells us that it is more difficult to distinguish changes in darker tones than in lighter tones. All the colors in Figure 7.14 are included in the color cube. So, even if the colors are provided, only a certain number of them are actually useful. Therefore, in creating this ditherproof color wheel, many of the colors that seemed redundant have been removed. The color selection reflects the majority of the hues and tones of the entire color cube.

Figure 7.14.
A color-distinguishing test.

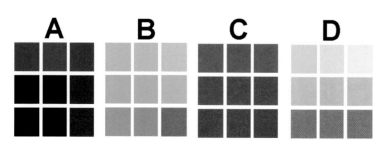

Note

If you want to use the colors that are not contained in the ditherproof color wheel but are in the color cube, all you have to do is look for the colors you want in Figures 7.15 and 7.16 or find them in the palette image in Appendix B, "Color Reference Guide," or a GIF image on the CD-ROM at the back of this book.

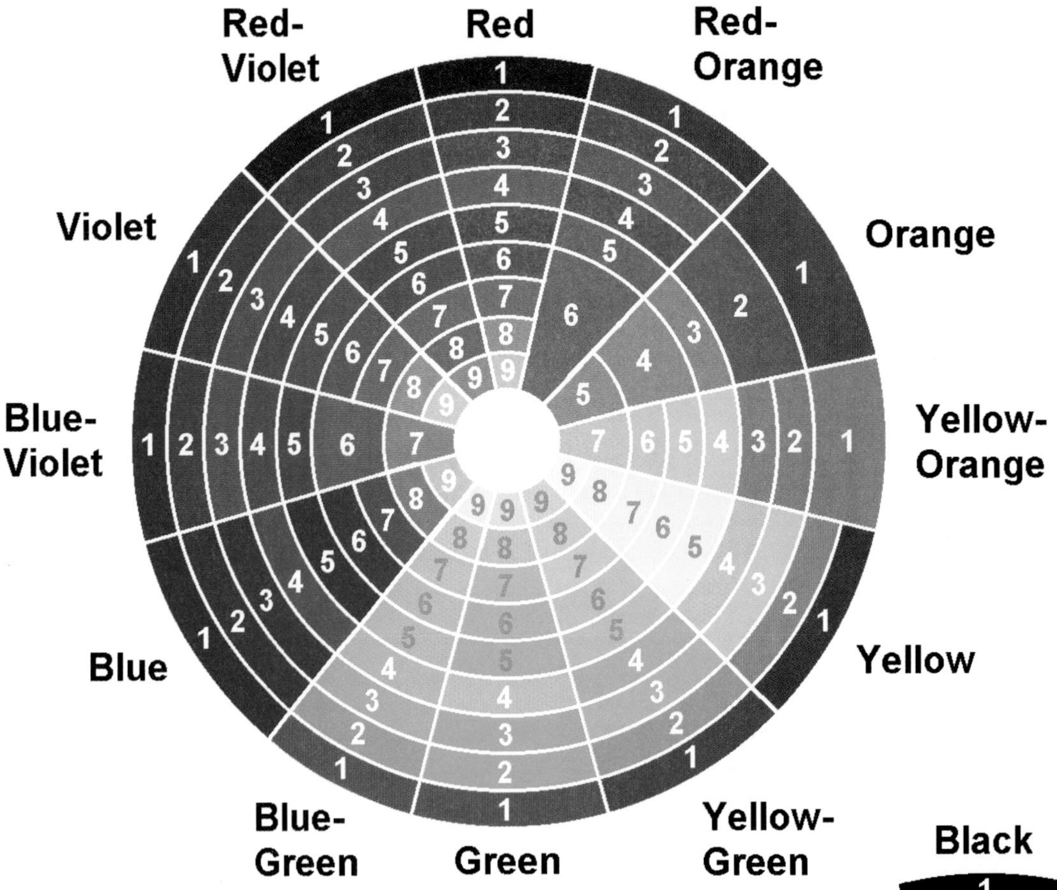

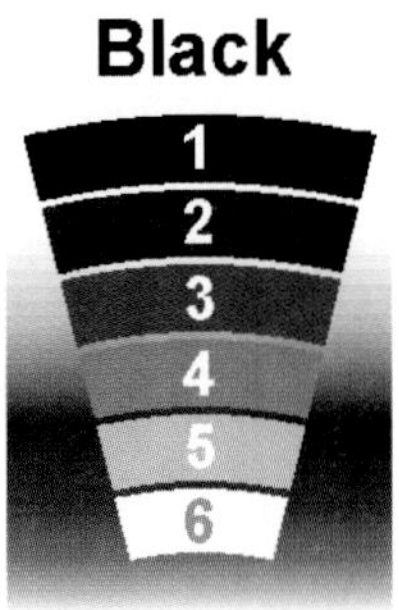

Figure 7.15.
The ditherproof color wheel.

Figure 7.16.

A list of all the RGB color values for the ditherproof color wheel.

Red
1		660000
2		993333
3		CC3333
4		CC6666
5		FF0000
6		FF3333
7		FF6666
8		FF9999
9		FFCCCC

Red-Orange
1		993300
2		CC3300
3		CC6600
4		FF3300
5		FF6600
6		FF6633

Orange
1		996633
2		CC6633
3		FF9900
4		FF9933
5		FF9966

Yellow-Orange
1		CC9966
2		CC9933
3		CC9900
4		FFCC00
5		FFCC33
6		FFCC66
7		FFCC99

Yellow
1		666600
2		999900
3		CCCC00
4		CCCC99
5		FFFF00
6		FFFF33
7		FFFF66
8		FFFF99
9		FFFFCC

Yellow-Green
1		336600
2		339933
3		66CC00
4		33FF00
5		99FF00
6		99FF66
7		CCFF00
8		CCFF66
9		CCFF99

Green
1		006600
2		009900
3		00CC00
4		99CC99
5		00FF00
6		33FF33
7		66FF66
8		99FF99
9		CCFFCC

Blue-Green
1		006600
2		339999
3		00CC99
4		66CCCC
5		00FFCC
6		33FFCC
7		66FFCC
8		99FFCC
9		CCFFFF

Blue
1		000099
2		333399
3		3333CC
4		6666CC
5		0000FF
6		3333FF
7		6666FF
8		9999FF
9		CCCCFF

Blue-Violet
1		660099
2		9933CC
3		9966CC
4		CC33FF
5		CC00FF
6		CC66FF
7		CC99FF

Violet
1		663366
2		993399
3		996699
4		CC33CC
5		FF00FF
6		FF33FF
7		FF66FF
8		FF99FF
9		FFCCFF

Red-Violet
1		660033
2		993366
3		CC3399
4		CC6699
5		FF0099
6		FF00CC
7		FF6699
8		FF66CC
9		FF99CC

Black
1		000000
2		333333
3		666666
4		999999
5		CCCCCC
6		FFFFFF

Relationships Between Colors

Now that you have the color wheel, you can explore the relationships between the colors. This will help you understand the process of selecting colors for your Web pages. The *primary* hues are red, yellow, and blue. All other hues are derived from these hues. (See Figure 7.17.)

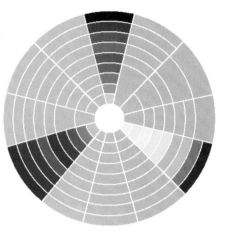

Figure 7.17.
The primary hues.

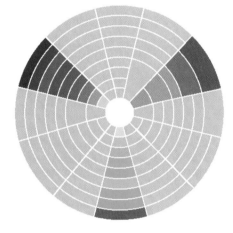

The three *secondary* hues are orange, violet, and green. These are between the primary hues at even intervals. A secondary hue is composed by equally combining the two adjacent primary hues. (See Figure 7.18.)

Figure 7.18.
The secondary hues.

Between the primary and secondary colors are the *intermediate* colors, which are red-orange, yellow-orange, yellow-green, blue-green, blue-violet, and red-violet. Like the secondary colors, they are the result of evenly mixing the hues beside them. They sometimes are referred to as *tertiary colors*. (See Figure 7.19.)

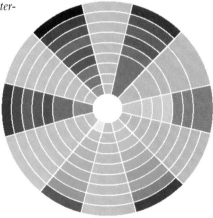

Figure 7.19.
The intermediate colors.

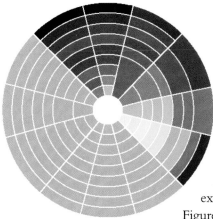

The colors ranging from red-violet to yellow are referred to as *warm* colors. Orange is considered the extreme of warm. Warm colors are vibrant and active. (See Figure 7.20.)

The colors ranging from violet to green-yellow are referred to as *cool* colors. Blue is considered the extreme of cool. Cool colors are relaxed and subdued. Creative color selection starts with a few basic color schemes. (See Figure 7.21.)

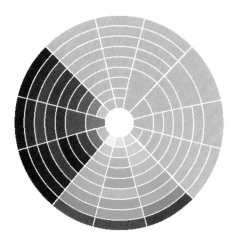

Figure 7.21.
The cool colors.

Analogous colors are any three consecutive color segments on the color wheel. Analogous colors produce a palette that blends well together and gives a feeling of harmony. (See Figure 7.22.)

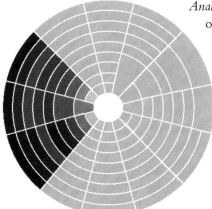

Figure 7.22.

This wheel uses blue, blue-violet, and violet segments as examples of analogous colors.

Chapter 7: Splashing on the Color: Effective Color Schemes for Your Web Site

Complementary colors use two hues that are directly opposite. Their strength can sometimes also be their weakness. This color selection is very powerful and provides high contrast, but it sometimes can be quite jarring and hard to view over long periods of time. (See Figure 7.23.)

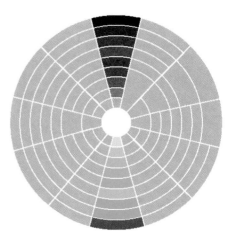

Figure 7.23.

This wheel uses the red and green segments as an example of complementary colors.

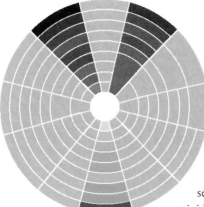

Figure 7.24.

This wheel uses the green, red-violet, and red-orange segments as an example of split complementary colors.

Split complementary colors are made of one hue and the two segments adjacent to its complement. This color scheme is vivid and not too overpowering. (See Figure 7.24.)

Monochromatic colors use all the hues of one color segment. A monochromatic color scheme conveys harmony through gradual tone changes in the single hue segment. (See Figure 7.25.)

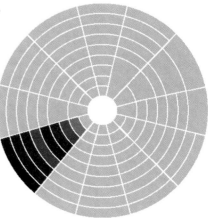

Figure 7.25.

This wheel uses the blue segment as an example of monochromatic colors.

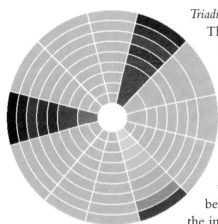

Triadic colors use three colors equidistant from each other. This can include the primary, secondary, and intermediate colors. This color scheme gives a sense of balance between the colors. (See Figure 7.26.)

Using LOUD & soft Colors Effectively

Colors are an effective way to convey a feel and tone throughout your page. Sometimes, you might want to bellow out your message so that your reader understands the importance of an item or element. At other times, you might want to give your reader a soothing, lulling effect to gently guide him through your content. You can do this by properly selecting your colors.

The use of vivid colors and high contrasts is central for a wacky site to entertain Generation Xers and other members of its audience. You can produce a high-powered page in a variety of ways. A main source for vibrant and energetic colors is the warm-color set. Warm colors give a hyper type of feel to the page. What more could a wacky site need? You should be careful when designing such a page, though. A high-energy page is fine, but if it becomes too high strung, the colors might overpower the reader and cause him to have a true psychedelic headache. Careful selection and use of warm colors can create a high-powered page that could wake up even the dead. (See Figure 7.27.)

Figure 7.26.

This wheel uses the blue-violet, red-orange, and yellow-green segments as an example of triadic colors.

Figure 7.27.

A wacky site for a wacky guy. Weird Al Yankovic's site (http://www.allamermusic.com) uses warm colors.

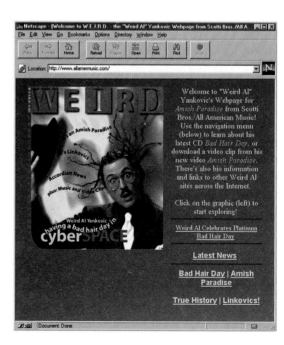

For those mellow, soothing pages, using cool colors is the way to go. Because cool colors have a certain subtle quality about them, they lend themselves well to being used with the monochromatic and analogous color schemes. Even though you might want that blended, low-key feeling for your page, make sure that you have enough contrast on the page when using these color schemes; otherwise, it might be difficult for your reader to read the text. It is great to blend mellow colors together, but if the content is impossible to read, you will put to sleep even the most chronic insomniacs. (See Figure 7.28.)

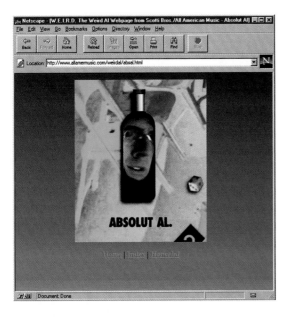

Figure 7.28.
More weirdness. Weird Al Yankovic's subtle page using cool colors.

You can create loud and soft sites by selecting proper color schemes. High-energy sites use many warm colors, whereas subtle sites use a selection of cool colors.

Background/Foreground Blending

Color selection is very important when designing the foreground and background of a Web page. An important design issue is to create the background and foreground with enough contrast to make the content legible. Be sure that the colors and tone do not match too closely; otherwise, your text will vanish into the background. You should also make sure that the colors do not contrast too severely unless you enjoy having your reader go bug-eyed.

Colors that are close together on the color wheel are good to use when designing items that need subtle changes. Using them as a foreground/background color scheme isn't wise, however. Unless specifically designed to fade into the background, images should at least be noticeable against the background. (If you are going to all that trouble to not show it, why have it there in the first place?) (See Figure 7.29.)

Colors that are complements on the color wheel have a very vibrant feel when used together. You need to keep an eye on them when you put one next to the other—especially when you use them as a background/foreground color. A high contrast might be exciting and attention grabbing, but its overuse can cause severe monitor damage. (See Figure 7.30.)

The color combination used is very important when dealing with backgrounds and foregrounds. Complements might be too powerful. Analogous and monochromatic might be too subtle. Achieving balance in color is vital in order to properly convey the contents of your page without injuring the reader's eyes.

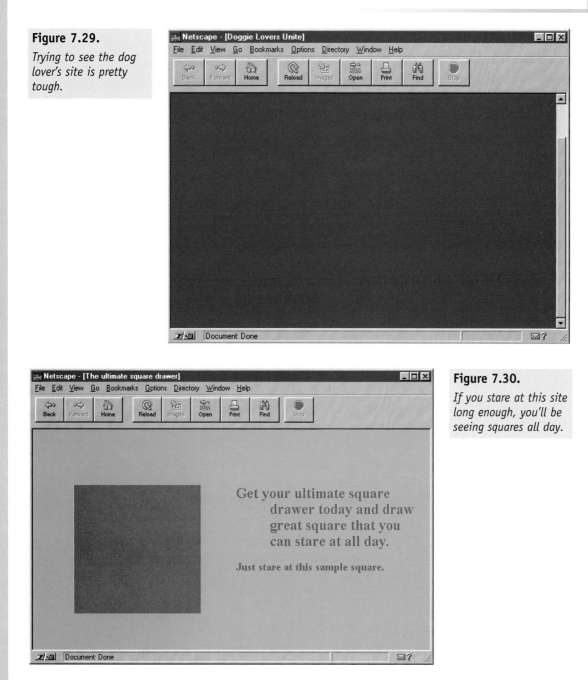

Figure 7.29.
Trying to see the dog lover's site is pretty tough.

Figure 7.30.
If you stare at this site long enough, you'll be seeing squares all day.

Text & Links: Colors That Enhance Legibility

The colors for your text and links are an important consideration when ensuring that your site is legible. You must make sure that the colors you choose balance well with the background. As described in the preceding section, foreground/background color combinations are crucial in making your site legible.

Do not choose colors that are complements to the background. (See Figure 7.31.) Text in this color scheme is legible for the first few lines, but after reading a few lines of text, it might become quite painful to continue. This is not a good color selection for your Web site (unless you cater to optical masochists). Again, don't choose colors that will be difficult to read or might even disappear into the background. Don't make your reader go treasure hunting for your text. (See Figure 7.32.)

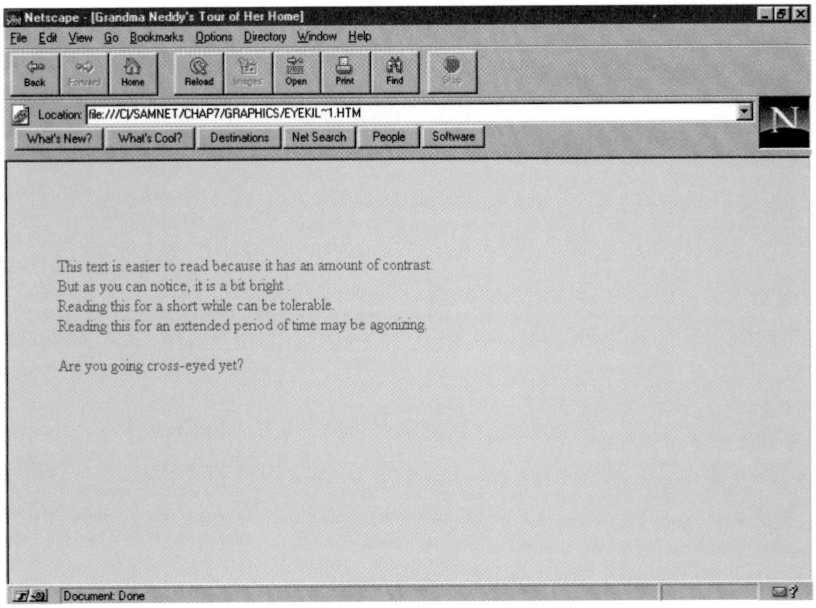

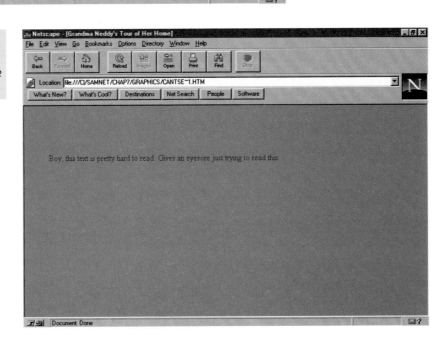

Figure 7.31.

Text and background colors that are complements.

Figure 7.32.

The color combination on this page makes the text difficult to read.

Links should be distinguishable from the body text, even after it has been clicked. Try not to select colors that match the body text around the link. Take the visited link color into consideration as well. Make sure that after the link has been visited, the link color does not turn into the surrounding text color or blend into the background. (See Figure 7.33.)

Figure 7.33.
Not knowing which is a link and which is text.

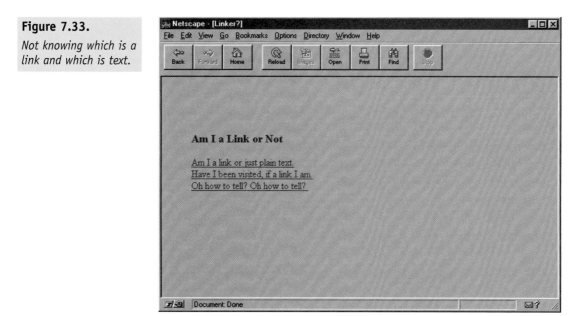

Using Color to Give Meaning to Your Images

The color of images helps convey visual continuity and contrast. Selecting the proper color scheme from the color wheel is an important step in creating effective graphics. Care should be taken when designing your graphics for maximum impact. You can use the ditherproof color wheel when designing flat-colored illustrations, or the wheel can be a good starting point when selecting colors for a more complicated color palette. (See Figure 7.34.)

Contrasting color combinations can attract and guide the reader's eyes to a specific area on the page. If the entire page is a soft color and you have a bright red logo to place on

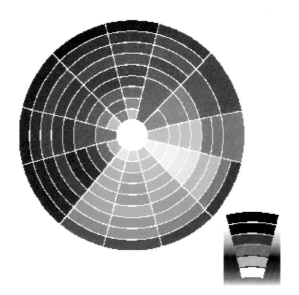

Figure 7.34.
The color wheel in action.

the page, no matter where it goes, it most likely will attract the reader's attention first. When multiple images in a site have similar color schemes, they give a sense of continuity to the entire site. This allows the reader to become accustomed to the elements of your site. This holds true especially for navigational elements. Color also can convey an association with the image that is not inherently there. (The color green, for example, can be associated with nature and the environment.)

Color Trends in Graphic Design

As you are reading this, fashion-color professionals are trying to reach a consensus on what the trendy colors for the next five-year period will be. Many industries—such as advertising, marketing, graphics design, fashion, interior design, car manufacturing, industrial design, and more—take color combinations very seriously. A good combination can make them millions or make them go bankrupt. (See Figure 7.35.)

Figure 7.35.
The new color trend for vehicles in the 90s brings flashbacks of trendy colored vehicles of the 70s.

What does this have to do with Web page design? Trendy colors change over years, and what might be hot one year might be the hue of ugliness the next. By knowing what the current or future trendy color schemes will be, a Web designer can create sites that will be attractive and in style for many years. (An attractive site can mean a visited site.)

Finished! Bob completes a new site for a client marketing the newest, hippest line of espresso makers aimed at the trendiest crowd in the state. Every photo was researched for its impact and placed in the most effective areas on the page. A few months after launching the site, Bob receives only one positive e-mail, which says, "Hey, I love the color scheme you've chosen for your site. It brings me right back to the 60s. Peace, man."

Keeping up with color trends is important, because you wouldn't want someone to comment that your site has a good "retro" look when you are aiming for a fresh, new 90s look.

> **Tip**
>
> Great sources for finding the latest color schemes are magazines. Magazines generally are quite recent and up to date with the latest color coordination. Some magazine types to look at are fashion magazines, interior design magazines, magazines aimed at teenagers, and automotive magazines.

Designing with Basic Color Schemes

In "Relationships Between Colors," you saw basic color relationships between different color segments. Using the techniques and suggested color segment combinations gives you a great start in choosing different colors that blend, contrast, and harmonize with each other.

The best way to find the most attractive color combinations is to try them in various site situations. Another way to find good color combinations is to surf the Net to see whether any color combinations catch your eye. Figures 7.36 through 7.38 illustrate some of the techniques and theories just discussed.

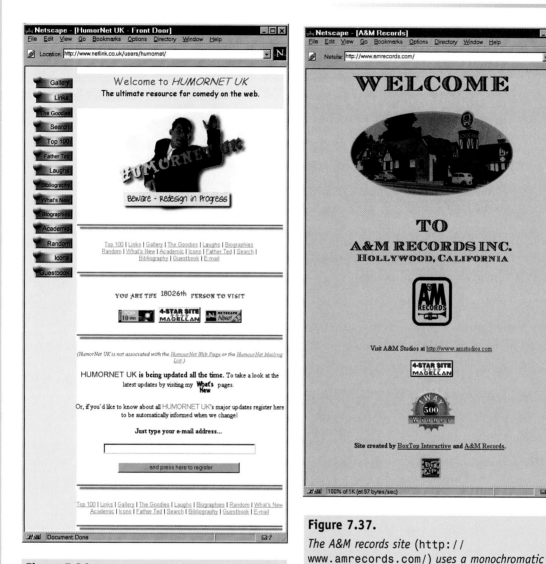

Figure 7.36.

The Humornet UK page (http://
www.netlink.co.uk/users/humornet/) *uses
warm colors quite effectively.*

Figure 7.37.

The A&M records site (http://
www.amrecords.com/) *uses a monochromatic
color scheme to achieve quite a mood.*

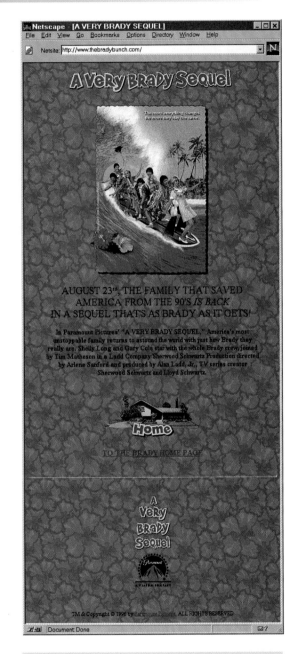

Figure 7.38.

The Brady Bunch Sequel page (http://www.thebradybunch.com/) shows how an analogous background with cool colors gives a soothing effect. Notice the use of the complementary color of yellow in the header to make it stand out.

Creative Color Combinations

The color wheel is a good source for colors and their related combinations when preparing images within the color-cube restraints. You can choose your color combinations by adhering strictly to what we have suggested, or you can determine your color combos by pinning the color wheel on the wall and throwing darts at it. However you want to experiment with different color combinations, just remember that there are thousands upon thousands of color combinations out there just waiting for you to sample them.

Those of you who don't care about the color-cube restraints have the luxury of choosing from countless numbers of colors to create many more color combinations. The color wheel is a handy starting point for those who dare to dive into the world of 24-bit color.

Note

Appendix B contains a list of useful color combinations. It is a good starting point, but it is by no means complete. We suggest that you try using the color wheel to explore and create your own colorful combinations.

8-Bit or 24-Bit Palettes: When Should You Use Them?

The choice between using an 8-bit palette and a 24-bit palette is one that must be taken into consideration when preparing images for the Web. You need to decide whether you want to cater to the masses or to work with the highest possible quality and allow the pixels to fall where they may. You need to select which option is best for you, depending on the situation. (See Figure 7.39.)

Figure 7.39.

The color palettes you can expect to see when you work with 8-bit colors (left) and 24-bit colors (right).

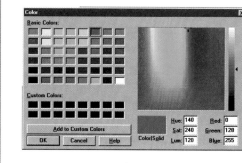

The GIF format uses an 8-bit palette. GIFs are useful for illustrations that contain flat-colored areas that need a small number of colors. The advantage of the 8-bit palette is that all the ditherproof colors are known and can be applied to the image. This means that what you see is what someone else will see.

The JPEG format was designed specifically with 24-bit photographic images in mind. An image that contains more than 256 colors is better saved at the 24-bit level. You should choose the JPEG format when working with photographic images.

palette. Using these colors contained in the color cube for your images allows them to become dither-resistant.

If you have a ready-made GIF image, the colors in the graphic should be compared to the colors in the ditherproof palette. If possible, try to change all the colors in the existing GIF that are not in the ditherproof palette to ones contained in the palette. If you run your existing GIFs through the ditherproof palette, it should reward you with images that are as dither-resistant as possible.

> **Note**
>
> We go into more detail about GIF and JPEG formats in Chapter 8, "Creating Graphics to Spice Up Your Page."

8-Bit Graphics Preparation

If you are designing 8-bit artwork to be saved in the GIF format, the best thing to begin with is to load up the ditherproof

Optimizing the Bit Size of Your Palette: GIF versus JPEG

With GIFs, the main way to optimize your images is to ditherproof them by using the ditherproof palette. Try to limit the number of colors the GIF image uses. The fewer number of colors an image has, the more compact the graphic will be. An easy way to lower the number of colors is to use only the colors on the ditherproof color wheel.

It is hard to choose and limit the number of colors when dealing with JPEG images. If you are designing with only 24-bit color in mind, your images will be dithered on a 256-color display. You can take certain steps to try to minimize the effects of dithering. Filling in flat-colored portions of the image with a dither-resistant color ensures that at least that portion of the image will not be affected.

Summary

Now that we have shown you ways to incorporate color into your designs, let's review the major points in this chapter:

- Consistent color schemes give your site a sense of familiarity and professionalism that a reader can recognize right away.

- When using color, you must choose between catering to true color or going with the lowest common denominator (256 color).

- Taking a little extra time to review your graphics with the dithering effect in mind gives the maximum number of people the enjoyment of experiencing the vividness of your work.

- For mellow, soothing colored Web pages, cool colors are the way to go.

- For wild-and-wacky Web pages, use warm colors.

- Colors that are close together on the color wheel are good to use when designing items that need subtle changes. Make sure that the text is set in a contrasting color, though; otherwise, the text will become difficult to read.

- You can use the ditherproof color wheel when designing flat-colored illustrations, or you can use the wheel as a starting point when selecting colors for a more complicated color palette.

- With GIFs, the main way to optimize your images is to ditherproof them by using the ditherproof palette. Try to limit the number of colors the GIF image uses.

- Fill in flat-colored portions of JPEG images with dither-resistant colors to ensure that at least those portions of the images will not be affected.

Q&A

What happens to the ditherproof color wheel when all the displays are finally converted to 24-bit displays?

The theory and basis behind the color wheel still holds true no matter how many colors are added to the palette. Although the number of colors might increase from 103 to millions, the techniques for selecting proper and useful color combinations will remain the same.

Why do certain color segments have fewer colors in them?

If you look at the color chart (refer to Figure 7.13), you will notice that the color distribution is weighted toward the cool colors. Within the warm colors, the predominant colors are hues with a mixture of red in them. In this situation, you can choose from a wide number of colors when selecting colors that contain blue or red. When creating the color wheel, we had to work within these constraints. Sometimes, we could not find enough colors in a segment of the spectrum to have an even distribution. Therefore, we distributed the colors on the basis of their hue values and not as to whether they would make an even circle.

Challenge Yourself

In this section, you will explore the color schemes and techniques discussed in this chapter.

Case Study

Cartoonland Inc. has asked you to colorize some cartoon graphics they need for an upcoming ad campaign.

Your Mission

Load the ditherproof color wheel and some of the uncolored graphics into your graphics program. Using the color wheel and techniques in this chapter, select appropriate color schemes to color them in. Don't be afraid to experiment. You will always have a clean copy of the graphic on the CD-ROM to start fresh from.

If you get tired of the graphics from the disk, you can create your own. You can use the ditherproof color wheel for any number of graphics you create.

Required Tools

+ Your computer
+ A graphics editor
+ A ditherproof color wheel

Supplied Elements

The ditherproof color wheel and graphics are on the accompanying CD-ROM.

Chapter 8

Creating Graphics to Spice Up Your Page

Now it's time for the fun stuff you've all been waiting for. We are going to show you different ways to create great graphics to improve your Web site. You might have visited a killer site and asked yourself, "How *did* they do that?" In this chapter, we'll reveal those secrets and more! So stay tuned...

Background Image Sizes: Speed and Image-Tiling Issues

When the curtains first open at the beginning of a play or musical, there is usually a short moment, right before the actors come on, for people in the audience to have a quick glance at the background scenery and props on the stage. An elaborate stage set can give the audience the feel of the time period or location of where the story is taking place. The background elements of the stage can make the performance seem almost real. This is not to say that simple background sets cannot produce the same kind of magic. A simple set is actually more difficult to design, because there are fewer elements for the designer to work with. A stage designer who can create a set that is subtle in its simplicity, yet powerful in the overall message to the audience, has accomplished just as much as, if not more than, a designer of an elaborate set. Although a show is only as good as the performance, the time and effort spent in creating a wonderful background can only add to the overall performance. As in a play or a musical, the background is what you should see as the stage of your Web page. If used properly, a background image or color conveys the overall feel of your site and provides the elements that bring your Web pages to life.

Gray Used to Be My Background

The simplest way to add color to your pages is to specify the RGB color in the BGCOLOR attribute in the <BODY> tag. If the color of your text and links balances well with the background color, you can have a very appealing page without the use of graphical images. Without the use of background images, your reader won't have to wait for your background images to load onto your Web page.

Another way to apply background color is to create a 1×1 pixel graphic of the color you want to use and insert the image filename in the BACKGROUND attribute in the <BODY> tag. When viewed in a browser supporting the BACKGROUND attribute, the image is tiled over and over again until it fills the screen completely, giving the reader the impression that the background is one solid color. This same technique is great to use when you want to add images or patterns to your background.

Tip

When using a background image, set the BGCOLOR attribute to the closest color of the background image. That way, there will be less visual transition from a colored background to a graphical background. Also, this ensures that the text on your page will be visible against the colored background while the background image loads.

Speeding It Up

The background image should be one of the first things to be loaded onto your page, because it sets the overall mood of your site. As you know, the larger the image you use for your background, the longer it takes for someone to load your page. It is a royal pain in the you-know-where when you start reading text halfway through a Web page and the background image suddenly appears from behind the text, startling you enough to lose your place on the page. If you were watching a show, you wouldn't expect to see the background scenery wheeled in from stage right in the middle of an actor's dramatic monologue. Remember: The less the audience sees what's going on behind the scenes, the better it is for them to concentrate on what's happening on the page. The smaller the size of your background image, the quicker it loads onto your page, which means that your reader will have the chance to see the background image before reading your text.

Background Tiling

The number of times your background pattern tiles on your page depends on what pixel setting your reader has his monitor set to and the size of the graphic. If your reader has a 640×480 pixel setting and you have a 160×120 graphic, the background image repeats 16 times on his screen. If your reader's monitor is set at 800×600 pixels, the image repeats 25 times, and so on. Be careful not to add too much detail to your graphic. Even though it might look great in a 640×480 pixel setting, it might be utterly intolerable in a 1,280×960 pixel setting. Figures 8.1 through 8.4 show examples of how different tile sizes show up.

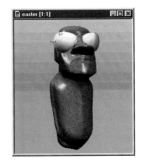

Figure 8.1.

The tile used in the background examples.

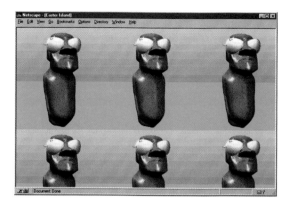

Figure 8.2.

Using a 270×300 pixel image as a background tile.

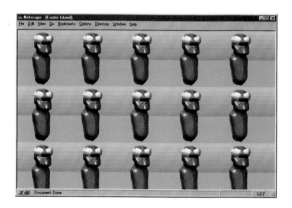

Figure 8.3.

Using a 150×166 pixel image as a background tile.

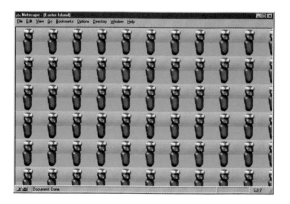

Figure 8.4.

Using a 75×83 pixel image as a background tile.

Interlacing Background Images: A Big No-No

When watching an interlaced graphic load onto a page, you will notice that the graphic first appears blurry and, after a few seconds (or minutes, in some cases), it eventually becomes a clear image. An *interlaced graphic* generally is used to display a low-quality version of a graphic for a reader to see while he is waiting for the browser to finish transferring the entire version of the graphic onto the screen. Never use interlaced or transparent GIFs for your background images. Downloading an interlaced background image causes your reader's browser to go into spasms of slow-motion dithering right before his eyes. Remember that a background image is tiled repeatedly on a screen. A browser has to work extra hard to display each tiled image little by little on your page. This could cause some browsers to stall, giving your reader the impression that his browser has crashed. Now you don't want to make your reader experience that, do you?

As for using transparent GIFs for background images, all we can ask is *why?* Transparent GIFs are meant to make a graphic transparent so that the edges of the image blend in with the background image. What is the purpose of making a background image transparent? We suppose that some people want to make the `BGCOLOR` visible behind the background image. None of the browsers we know support this technique, and we don't see why they should when all you have to do to get this effect is set the background image at the same color as your `BGCOLOR`. For whatever reasons, some people out there will still insist on using transparent GIFs for their background images. All we can say is, if they have the time to waste creating an effect that no one else can see in the end, cheers to them.

Tiled or Seamless Backgrounds: Which to Use?

If you take a close look at an expensive party dress in a designer store, more than likely, the seamstress has done a darn good job hiding all the seams, giving the illusion that this dress was created from only one piece of material. A background image tiled on a screen can appear tiled or seamless, depending on how you create your background graphic. A *seam* appears when the image is tiled and the borders of the image are noticeable. (See Figure 8.5.)

Tiling sometimes is used to create a grid-like pattern on a page. The effect is similar to the repetitive pattern of bathroom or kitchen tiles on a wall—henceforth the term *tiling*. If you are creative, you can design an interesting tiled background.

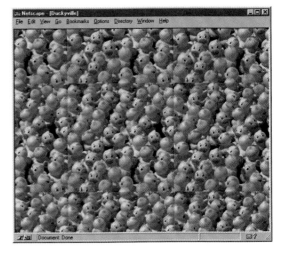

Figure 8.5.
Seams in a ducky background.

More likely than not, you probably will want to design a seamless background. A seamless background gives continuity to a Web page. Unsightly seams on some pages can ruin a continuous flow of images (like crummy wallpapering in a house). A well-designed background image is one in which no one can see the seams on your page.

How Unseemly: Creating Seamless Backgrounds

An easy way to avoid seams in your background image is to ensure that there are equal amounts of border space around the image. Centering the image within a graphic with a uniform border color ensures that the tiling effect is invisible when viewed on the browser. (See Figure 8.6.)

Figure 8.6.
A background graphic with a uniform border color.

If the detail of your graphic runs off the edge, it is a little bit trickier to make your seams "seem" invisible.

It All Seems So Seamless: Removing the Seams from a Background Image

Some graphics software packages offer an offset filter, which rearranges the outside borders of a graphic to the opposite sides and creates a seamless outside border. This filter produces a cross-hair seam in the image, which allows you to immediately see any seams that your graphic will create when it is tiled. If you don't have an offset filter, you still can create an offset of your graphic by cutting and pasting portions of the graphic into a new graphic.

> **Tip**
>
> Some software programs, such as Paint Shop Pro 4.0, give you a filter that automatically creates a seamless background for your image. This is useful when you are creating a seamless background from a pattern. When you use photographic images with this effect, though, the outcome of the seamless background is not as impressive.

Creating an offset manually means that you have to divide the graphic into four equal sections. The first step is to create a new graphic with the identical dimensions of the graphic you are working with. Rearrange the four sections within the new graphic in the order shown in Figure 8.7. This gives your graphic the same effect that an offset filter automatically creates. (See Figures 8.8 through 8.10.)

Before Offset   After Offset

Figure 8.7.

Rearranging the numbered sections from the original graphic to match the numbered sections of the offset graphic.

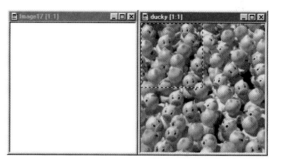

Figure 8.8.

After you create a new, identically sized blank graphic, select section 1 from the original graphic.

Figure 8.9.

Paste section 1 into the proper position in the new graphic.

After the offset graphic is created, you should be able to see the seams in your graphic. Next, you have to remove the seams in the graphic. You can use a variety of techniques to accomplish this. We will show you three techniques with our example of the duck-pond graphic.

Figure 8.10.

Continue to select and paste sections from the old graphic into the proper positions in the new graphic until an offset image is created.

The Clone Brush is very effective in copying segments from a graphic from one section to another. Use the Clone Brush to copy parts of your graphic over the seam.

If you prefer not to use the Clone Brush, you can select a section of the graphic and paste it over the seam. This produces results similar to the Clone Brush technique. If the two areas are quite similar in color and contrast, you can try smudging the seam until it becomes less distinguishable. (See Figures 8.11 and 8.12.)

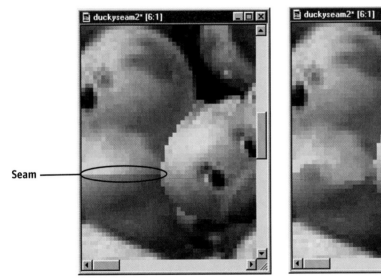

Seam

Figure 8.11.
You can still clearly see this seam.

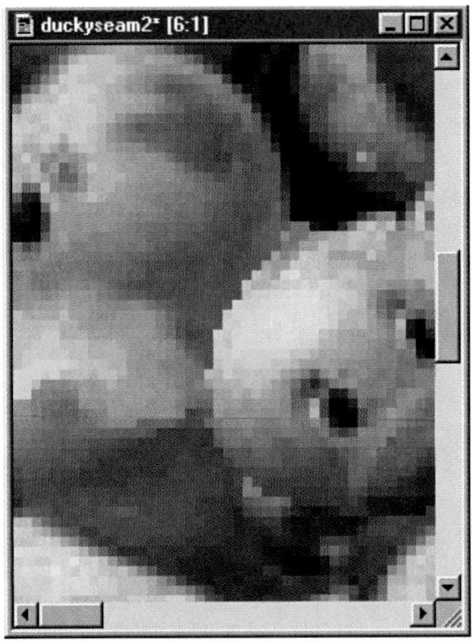

Figure 8.12.
Now the seam is blended into the image of the duck above it.

After using any or all of these technique to clean up all the seams, the final product you should have is a seamless background image. (See Figure 8.13.)

Look at the difference between the background image with seams (Figure 8.5) and the background image without seams (Figure 8.13). Figure 8.14 shows the background with seams on the left and the

Figure 8.13.

There we have it! A seamless background.

Figure 8.14.

A background with the seams intact and a background with the seams removed.

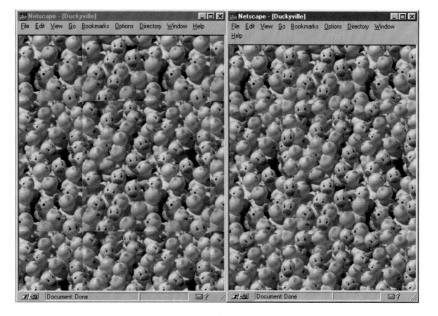

background without seams on the right. Notice that the image on the right gives the impression that the whole background is one continuous image.

Making Text Legible on Top of Your Background

If the background of your Web page overrides the readability of your text, you know your page has a legibility problem. If the color of your text is similar to the background color, your text fades into the background, giving your reader the challenging task of figuring out what your text is trying to say. Add a busy background pattern to your page, and you will create the infamous camouflaged text effect. Both ways cause severe eyestrain and make your page very difficult to read. Readability of your page always should be your main focus, so you must ensure that you add a proper amount of contrast between your text and background colors.

Pleasant Blending

To create a seamless background that didn't overpower our text, we took a logo and converted it into the background image of our page. We reduced the contrast by lightening the graphic until the background color and the image blended together while still remaining visible on the page. (See Figure 8.15.)

Figure 8.15.

The logo to be used as the background.

Figure 8.16 shows the image we used to create the faded background logo technique. We lightened the image by adding brightness.

Then we added the background color. (See Figure 8.17.) Even after brightening this graphic, we realized that it was still too busy to be a background image. Our next step was to make the image even lighter.

Figure 8.16.

Brightening the logo.

We chose colors that were lighter and blended closer together. The idea was to lower the contrast of all the parts in our graphic. After we achieved a good blend of color, we changed the colors of the image to lower the contrast. (See Figure 8.18.)

Figure 8.17.

The background logo with a background color added.

After we lowered the contrast of the background image, we viewed our Web page using our new background. In Figure 8.19, you can see the difference the softening of the colors makes to the legibility of the text on top of each background.

Figure 8.18.

In this image, we filled the areas with lighter colors.

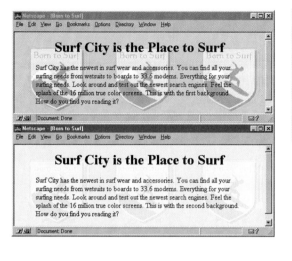

Figure 8.19.

The top window contains the darker background, and the bottom window contains the lighter background. Which one is easier to read?

Text for Success

The choice of text color is crucial in making your page pleasant yet readable. Don't choose colors that match closely with elements of your background, unless you want whole sections of text to disappear from your page.

> **Tip**
> To avoid overpowering the reader with awful color combinations, try applying the color combination techniques you learned in Chapter 7, "Splashing on the Color: Effective Color Schemes for Your Web Site." If you work with the ditherproof color wheel in Chapter 7, you can achieve effective text and background contrasts in color.

Working with Light Background and Dark Type

The best color combinations for legibility are white text on a black background, and black text on a white background. If all our Web pages were created with these two combinations alone, however, the Web would become a dull collection of checkerboard pages.

A good level of contrast is the key in making text colors stand out from the background. The contrast can be a combination of a light background with a darker text color or a dark background with a lighter text color. You will see that most sites on the Web use a light background with dark text. The type of Web site you are designing can affect the lightness and darkness of your background. An artsy site might use more dark backgrounds and lighter text than a commercial banking site, for example. It really depends on what type of mood you want to create for your pages. Don't let examples from other Web sites stifle your creativity. Experiment with your colors and have fun choosing different combinations. Just remember to test the colors of your site with your test panel before finalizing your color choices.

Working with Dark Background and Light Type

Working with a dark background is more difficult than working with a light background, because it is easier to read dark text on a lighter background. That is why most paper media—such as books, newspapers, and magazines—basically use dark text on white or off-white paper. It probably is best to use dark backgrounds with light type on banners, logos, or graphics when you want to create an effective mood or style. Again, the thing to remember is *contrast*. Always make sure that the text is light enough to be readable against the dark background.

When selecting colors to use as the background/foreground combination, a good color-selection technique is to pick dark and light shades of the same hue. You can add continuity to your graphics when you use a subtle but substantial contrast with your background and foreground colors, especially if the entire site uses only a select set of shades of similar hues. (See Figure 8.20.)

Note

A good starting point in selecting the background and text colors is to use the ditherproof color wheel introduced in Chapter 7.

Creating Stylish Graphical Banners, Headers, and Logos

A banner or header does not have to be an ordinary, run-of-the mill text bar. Good design technique and a little artistic flair can turn that text bar into an eye-catching work of art that accents the overall look of your page.

Figure 8.20.
This page uses a light text type on a dark background.

Like any other graphical element on your Web page, the size of the graphic is always an issue. Always make sure that the graphics you design are compact in file size. This doesn't mean that you have to create skimpy, understated banner or logo graphics. With the use of color selection, 3D effects, graphical filters, and continuity, you can create your own professional-looking banner or header. (See Figure 8.21.)

Tip

When working with a banner, header, or logo in GIF format, try to stick with the colors provided in the ditherproof color wheel. This ensures that the masterpiece you create will not be marred by unsightly dithering.

To create our Gold Nugget logo, we created a new image that was 500×140 pixels. The RGB values we used for the color palette were R:223; G:142; B:15 for the foreground color. We left the background color white at this point. With a hollowed font type, we added the words `Goldnugget Jewelers` to our image. (See Figure 8.22.)

> **Note**
> We are using Paint Shop Pro 4.0 to demonstrate our graphical design techniques. You can find a shareware version on the CD-ROM at the back of this book. If you choose to use your own graphical software program, the filter names referred to in this book might differ or might not apply, depending on the software program you use.

Figure 8.21.
We created the Goldnugget Jewelers logo by using simple graphical techniques.

Figure 8.22.
We added the text to our image using a hollow font.

We filled in the outline of each letter from top to bottom with a line gradient fill with the colors going from dark to light. For the inside of the text, we used the same fill technique, except that, from top to bottom, the colors went from light to dark. (See Figures 8.23 and 8.24.)

Figure 8.23.
We filled in the outline of the text with a line gradient fill.

Figure 8.24.
We also filled in the inside of the text with a line gradient fill, except that, from top to bottom, the colors went from light to dark.

We added a hot-wax coating to our text using our foreground color. This gave our text an embossed effect. (See Figure 8.25.)

Figure 8.25.
Our logo after applying a Hot-Wax Coating filter.

Now, to make our logo look more like a gold bar, we increased the brightness by 24 percent and the contrast by 9 percent. We did this by choosing Colors|Adjust|Brightness/Contrast. (See Figure 8.26.)

Our graphic just needed a little more touching up to make it look really good. We changed the background RGB values to R:255; G:231; B:127. We then applied a line gradient fill to the background. (See Figure 8.27.)

Figure 8.26.

Our logo after increasing the brightness and contrast.

Figure 8.27.

We applied a gradient fill to the background of the graphic to add some contrast.

Finally, to give our logo a 3D effect, we outlined the graphic with the Photo Retouching Brushes tool. We darkened the right and bottom edge, and we lightened the left and top edge. (See Figure 8.28.)

Figure 8.28.

The final outcome of our logo after applying the 3D effect.

Showing Off Your Font Collection with Text Images

You can spice up the text on your page in many ways. The textual content on your page does not have to consist only of HTML text. Using graphical images containing textual elements is a very useful and powerful way to manipulate font types and colors to suit any mood or feeling you want to portray on your page.

After text is moved out of the HTML textual dungeon into the graphical realm, the possibilities for manipulating and molding textual elements into a perfect visual stimulus for a Web page are limited only by your imagination. Basically, you can do almost anything with graphical text. You can use any font type in your font collection, create 3D fonts, add color to any letter or character, apply filters to your text, and do anything else you can imagine. (See Figures 8.29 through 8.33.)

Figure 8.29.

We created the Notsosoft button.

Figure 8.30.

An Edscape header we created.

Figure 8.31.

We created a Yoohoo logo.

Figure 8.32.

The exciting logo we designed.

Creating Text Images

Before creating your text images, it is important to choose the RGB values for your background and foreground colors first.

Stop! You Can't Edscape!

For our Edscape logo, we chose the background RGB values to be R:175; G:111; B: 47 and the foreground RGB values to be R:255; G:175; B: 32. Next, we created a new image and specified the dimensions for an image to be 400×300 pixels. We chose our background color to be automatically filled into the graphic. Depending on what you are designing, you can choose any color in the background color drop-down box to be the background color of your graphic. Make sure that you create your image in 16.7 million colors first; otherwise, you might not be able to use all the enhancing functions in your graphical software program. We will reduce the number of colors used after the graphic is complete.

Figure 8.33.

We created a gold name plate for Ivannah Tinkle.

We added the word `Edscape` to our graphic, choosing Kidnap as our font type and 72 as our point size for the first letter, `E`. For the remaining letters, we used 36 as the point size. (See Figure 8.34.)

Figure 8.34.
Adding our text to the graphic.

 We used the Freehand Selection tool (the icon with the picture of the lasso on it) to select the area we wanted to use for our enhancements. With the selection tool, we went around the textual element in a wavy fashion to give the illusion that the word `Edscape` had been ripped out of a magazine article. We applied the Hot-Wax Coating filter (which you can specify by choosing Image|Special Effects|Hot Wax Coating) to the area we selected. (See Figure 8.35.)

Figure 8.35.
We added hot wax to our text and got this neat effect.

We found the colors to be a little on the dark side, so we made the graphic brighter by choosing Colors|Adjust|Brightness/Contrast. We added 38 percent brightness and 38 percent contrast to our graphic. (See Figure 8.36.)

Finally, to make the word `Edscape` stand out from the graphic, we made the outline of the text

Figure 8.36.
Brightening the graphic makes the text easier to read.

sharper by using the Edge Enhance filter. We did this by choosing Image|Edge Filters|Edge Enhance. (See Figure 8.37.)

Figure 8.37.
The final Edscape logo.

Yoohoo! We're Over Here!

For our Yoohoo text, we chose the background RGB values to be R:95; G:120; B:112 and the foreground RGB values to be R:255; G:91; B:91.

Figure 8.38.
Outlining the word Yoohoo.

Next, we created a new image and specified the dimensions for the image to be 400×300 pixels. We added the letter Y to our graphic first using the font type FZ Warped 4 and point size 72. We wanted to create an outline around the Y, so, while the letter Y was still highlighted, we applied the Feather filter. We did this by choosing Selections | Modify | Feather. Then, we adjusted the hue, saturation, and luminance by choosing Colors | Adjust | Hue/Saturation/Luminance and choosing a hue of −21 percent, a saturation of −26 percent, and a luminance of −4 percent. We decided to use negative values to decrease the hue, saturation, and luminance of our graphic.

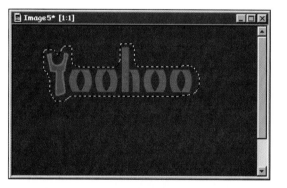

For the rest of the word Yoohoo, we chose the font type Kino MT bold and a point size of 48 to give the textual element some contrast. We lightened the background color and used the Freehand Selection tool to lasso around the text. We then chose Selections | Invert and pressed Delete. We lassoed the text again, this time adding a brightness of 20 percent and a contrast of 4 percent. To top it off, we added the Edge Enhance filter to give the textual elements more detail. (See Figures 8.38 through 8.40.)

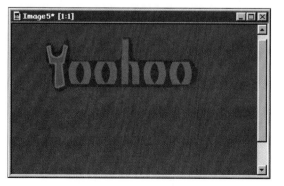

Figure 8.39.
After lightening the background, we used the Invert filter.

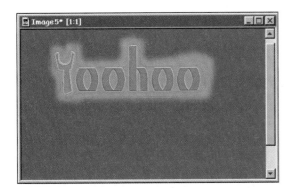

Figure 8.40.

Adding brightness and contrast around the word Yoohoo *to get a halo effect.*

Crazy Text

With our Ivannah Tinkle graphic, we used the RGB values R:127; G:0; B:63 for the foreground and R:255; G:128; B:0 for the background. We chose the FZ Lucida Handwriting font to create the letter I. While the letter I was still highlighted, we added the chisel effect to it by choosing Image|Special Effects|Chisel. We pressed Delete to remove the color inside the letter I. Then, we added a brightness of 22 percent and a contrast of −3 percent to lighten up the graphic. (See Figures 8.41 and 8.42.)

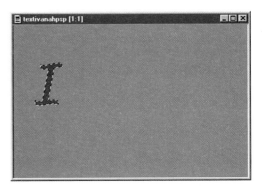

Figure 8.41.
We added the letter I *in the graphic.*

For the rest of the text, we used the Garamond font type and point size 48. We decided to put the word Tinkle below the first word to give the textual element a unique shape. We applied the Freehand Selection tool to lasso around the text and adjusted the brightness to 11 percent and the contrast to −7 percent. While the text was still highlighted, we added a drop shadow by choosing Special Effects|Drop Shadow. For the drop-shadow effect, we set the blur value to 17. We changed the drop shadow's offset to have a vertical setting of 8 pixels and a horizontal setting of 15 pixels. Then, we changed the foreground color to the background color and added texture to the graphic by using the paintbrush. We chose Lava for the paper texture and used it to paint between the letters of text. (See Figure 8.43.)

Figure 8.42.

We added the chisel effect to the letter I *and deleted the inside color.*

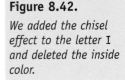 We used the Geometric Selection tool (the icon with the broken-line rectangle) to select around our text. Then we applied the Buttonize filter by choosing Image| Special Effects|Buttonize.

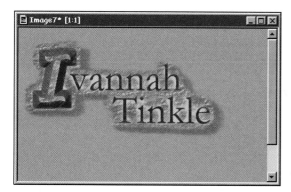

Figure 8.43.

After applying a drop shadow, we used the paintbrush with the Lava filter.

Finally, we lightened the foreground to a color close to gold, and then we used the Paintbrush tool again with the Paper Texture option set to Daze to paint in the background of the graphic. This gave the background of the graphic a grid-like effect. (See Figures 8.44 and 8.45.)

Figure 8.44.

The graphic after being buttonized.

Figure 8.45.

As a final touch, we painted the background of the graphic with the paintbrush and the Daze filter.

Exciting, Ain't It?

For our `exciting` graphic, we chose the foreground RGB values of R:238; G:47; B:0 and background RGB values of R:239; G:255; B:240.

Figure 8.46.

The exciting *graphic after applying the sunburst radiant to the text and adding a brick effect to the background.*

For the font type, we used FZ Script 25 with bold italic and a 36 point size. After darkening the foreground color to R:5; G:165; B:89, we added the text to the graphic and added a sunburst radiant fill. As an added touch, we painted in bricks with the Paintbrush tool using the Medium Bricks Paper texture. We changed the luminance and increased the hue to make the page look chrome green. Finally, we applied a coat of hot wax and edge enhanced the text to give us our final image. (See Figures 8.46 and 8.47.)

Figure 8.47.

We applied a coat of hot wax and edge enhanced the text to give us our final graphic.

Don't Shoot Blanks: Creative Bullet Designs

In this section, we will show you several techniques to create simple but effective bullets.

Creating Bullets

When you create bullets, it is best to start with a large graphic and reduce it to a smaller size when the graphic is completed. You have to remember, though, that the details of the image might disappear when it is resized. We created a new graphic at 200×200. Our foreground color RGB values were R:204; G:204; B:255, and the background colors were R:0; G:0; B153.

We filled the graphic sphere by using the Fill tool with the Fill style set to Sunburst Gradient and the Tolerance level set at a value of 20. We set the options of the gradient fill to 65 percent vertical and 35 percent horizontal. This gave our graphic the appearance that the light source for the bullet was coming from the upper-left corner.

In the color palette, we changed the background color to white so that, when we used the Circle effect, it would make the background color of the image white. Doing this made it easier for us to apply a transparent background later. We then chose Image|Deformations|Circle to create a sphere. We increased our white space by choosing Image|Enlarge Canvas to enlarge our canvas. In the Enlarge Canvas dialog box, we increased the dimensions of the graphic to 250×250 pixels and selected the Center Image option.

To create a drop-shadow effect, we chose Image|Special Effects|Add Drop Shadow. We adjusted the shadow to be 17 pixels vertically and 20 pixels horizontally away from our cir-

Figure 8.48.

The bullet after applying the Circle filter.

cle. We now had our completed 3D sphere. At this stage, the sphere was way too large for what we needed, so we resized the image down to bullet size, which we chose to be 30×30 pixels. (See Figures 8.48 through 8.50.)

Figure 8.49.

The final sphere image.

Figure 8.50.

The bullet size after shrinking it to 30×30 pixels.

Figure 8.51.

The first step in creating our concave icon is to make a double ring.

Concave 3D Icons

You can use the concave 3D icon technique to create neat bullets, icons, and buttons. We first created a smaller circle within a larger circle. (See Figure 8.51.) Of course, you can choose whatever shape you want to use for your bullet or icon.

We chose RGB values of R:255; G:227; B:255 for the foreground and R:145; G:0; B:145 for the background. We used the Linear Gradient Fill tool. Then, in the Flood Fill dialog box, we clicked the Options button and chose 135 degrees in the Gradient Fill Direction dialog box to create a diagonal gradient fill. We filled the outside ring by using the Fill tool and clicking the left mouse button. The gradient fill produced a lightness-to-darkness effect from the top-left corner to the bottom-right corner of the image. (See Figure 8.52.)

Figure 8.52.

Filling the first ring with a gradient.

Then we removed the inner circle by changing the Fill tool selection to Solid Color, and we changed the foreground color to white so that it matched the white background of the image. When we filled the inner ring, the line disappeared into the white background. (See Figures 8.53 and 8.54.)

Figure 8.53.

This inner ring must be removed.

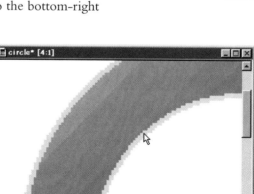

We then changed the foreground color back to its original color. We also changed the Fill tool selection back to Linear Gradient. Next, we filled in the inner circle by clicking the right mouse button. This produced a darkness-to-lightness effect from the top-left corner to the bottom-right corner of the image. The contrast between both rings gave the concave effect we wanted. (See Figure 8.55.)

Figure 8.54.
Removing the inner ring by filling in the line with the background color.

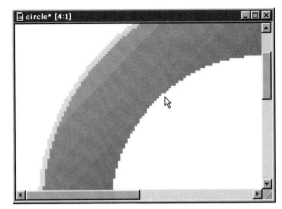

3D Arrows

For our 3D arrows, we used the RGB values R:207; G:255; B:159 for the foreground and R:0; G:152; B:0 for the background colors. We wanted to have the light source appear from the upper left of our graphic, so we drew the left and top half of our arrow in our foreground color, and the right and lower half of our arrow in the background color. (See Figure 8.56.)

Figure 8.55.
Our finished concave icon.

Next, we had to fix the corners where the foreground and the background colors met. We filled in the pixels from the inside edge to the outside edge with our Paintbrush tool. This created a straight diagonal line from one edge to the other. (See Figures 8.57 through 8.60.)

To give the corners of the arrow a 3D effect, we added a contrasting diagonal line from one edge of the corner to the other. (See Figures 8.61 and 8.62.)

We filled the inside of the arrow with a sunburst gradient. As a finishing touch, we selected our completed image with the Freehand Selection tool and added a drop shadow. (See Figures 8.63 and 8.64.)

Figure 8.56.
The outline of our arrow.

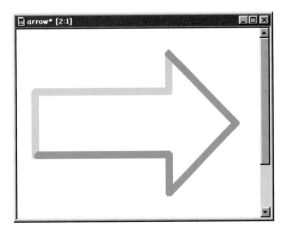

Figure 8.57.
This corner needs to be cleaned up.

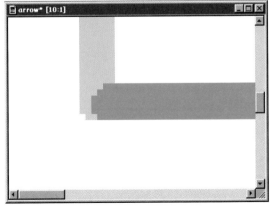

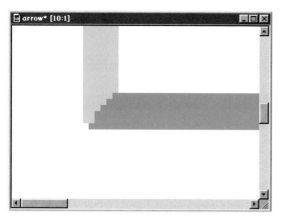

Figure 8.58.
Cleaning up the corner.

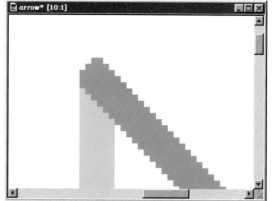

Figure 8.59.
Another corner before it is cleaned up.

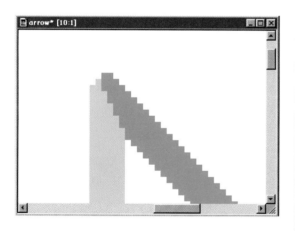

Figure 8.60.
The corner after it is cleaned up.

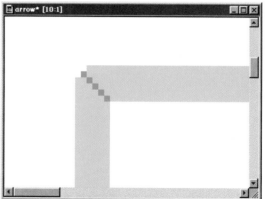

Figure 8.61.
A solid-colored corner after adding a contrasting line.

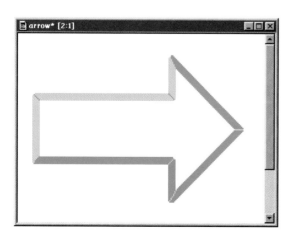

Figure 8.62.
All the corners after being cleaned up and edited.

Figure 8.63.

The arrow after a gradient fill.

Figure 8.64.

The arrow after selecting it and adding a drop shadow.

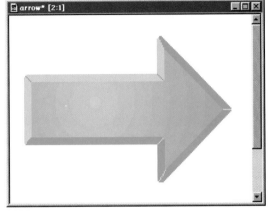

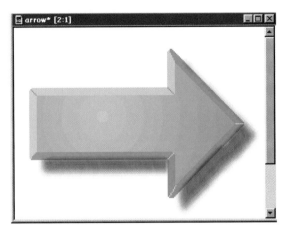

Animated, 3D, and Illustrated Bullets

Animated bullets might seem cute, but too much animation can make a bullet more distracting than helpful. Bullets should help draw the reader's eye to certain points in a list of information. If an animated bullet does a somersault, the reader's eyes might find it difficult to focus on the content of the page, especially when his eyes keep trying to look over and see what animated move the bullet will do next. Animated bullets that never stop moving also can be quite annoying after a while, so keep the movement in your animation subtle. Keeping the animation small adds variety to your page without distracting your readers. (See Figure 8.65.) We will discuss in greater detail the process of creating an animated image in Chapter 10, "Animating Your Web Pages."

Figure 8.65.

Two frames we created of an animated GIF with a little taxi bouncing around as if it were moving.

> **Tip**
>
> You can import plug-in filters to your graphical software program to add exciting effects to your images. Figure 8.66 shows you samples of bullets created with the spheroid designer by Metatools Kai's Power Tools Package. You can download a trial version from the Metatools Inc. site at http://www.metatools.com.

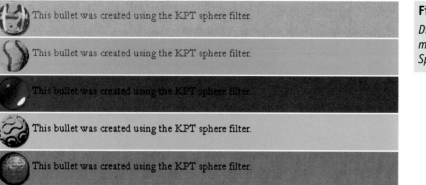

Figure 8.66.

Different bullets we made using the KPT Sphere filter.

Horizontal Rules: More Than Just a Line

You can create horizontal rules in many ways. The easiest way to make a horizontal rule is to create a 600×100 pixel rectangle and fill it with a gradient or any combination of colors you want to use. BORING! Or, you can be creative and design horizontal rules that represent your metaphor.

If we were designing a Dental Hygiene Web site, for example, we would choose items used in the dental industry. We could use a string of dental floss or even a row of teeth. (See Figure 8.67.)

Figure 8.67.

A creative horizontal rule.

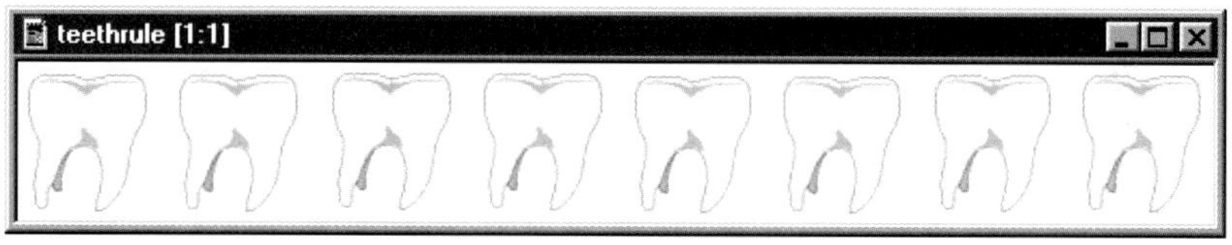

Or, we could take our metaphor a step further and use a toothbrush and toothpaste to create our horizontal rule. "How would I create a horizontal rule with a toothbrush?" you might ask. Well, stick around, and we'll show you.

Toothpaste Rules!

We first pulled up an illustration of a toothbrush and a tube of toothpaste from our selection of clipart. (See Figure 8.68.) We created a 600×75 pixel rectangle and placed the toothbrush image on one end and the tube of toothpaste at the opposite end.

Figure 8.68.

The toothbrush and toothpaste image we used for our graphic.

Instead of using normal white toothpaste for our horizontal line, we decided to use blue gel instead. The RGB values we used were R:102; G:153; B:255 for the foreground, and we left the background white for now. For the next step, we had to be a little creative to try to simulate the toothpaste oozing out of a tube. First, we created a straight line with the foreground color and added a simulated toothpaste swirl to connect the line to the top of the toothbrush. It took us several tries until we attained the perfect oozing effect. (See Figure 8.69.)

Figure 8.69.
Let the gel toothpaste ooze.

To give the toothpaste some dimension, we selected a lighter shade of blue for the foreground and a darker shade for the background. We outlined anything to the top or left side of the string of toothpaste with a light shade of blue. On the bottom of the string of toothpaste, we used the darker background color. And as a famous pig would say, "Th-th-th-th that's all, folks!" We now have a cool and original horizontal rule. (If we wanted to be even more creative, we could have designed a tricolor string of toothpaste, but we'll leave that for another book…)

Too Many Rules: Using Horizontal Rules Sparingly

Some Web designers have incorporated the horizontal rule as a decorative element for their Web pages. Unfortunately, the horizontal rule is overused on many Web pages, which makes them look tacky with candy-like graphics chopping up the content. People who use the horizontal rule to separate sections of information should use white space to achieve more effect. Of course, it is wonderful to be innovative and original with your horizontal rules. Just remember to keep them consistent throughout your site and to use them only when you absolutely need them.

Compressibility Versus Quality of Graphical Image

You can design your Web graphics in different formats, but you must save them as a GIF or JPEG file.

GIF Compression

The *Graphics Interchange Format*, or what we commonly refer to as *GIF*, contains a maximum of 256 colors and is suited for flat-colored illustrations. The size of a GIF image is determined by the number of times a pixel color changes along each horizontal line in an image. When you save an image in a GIF format, the compression occurs when the same pixel colors are continuous on the horizontal line. Therefore, if you have many different pixel colors along the same horizontal line, the

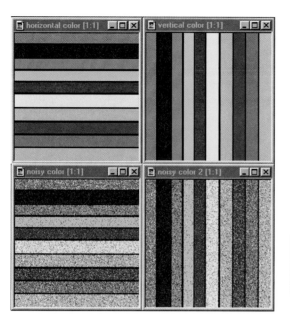

compression of the line will be less than it would be if the horizontal line contained only one or only a few solid colors.

Figure 8.70 shows four images of identical pixel sizes that we saved in GIF format. We saved the same images using the JPEG format with various compression values. In Figure 8.71, you can see that the graphics with the horizontal stripes of color are smaller in file size than the graphics with the vertical stripes of color.

Figure 8.70.

Four graphics saved in a variety of formats.

	Horizontal Lines	Vertical Lines	Horizontal Lines with Noise	Vertical Lines with Noise
Gif	1.92 k	4.16 k	26.1 k	32.2 k
Jpeg - minimum compression	6.67 k	7.03 k	25.2 k	25.6 k
- low compression	5.82 k	6.28 k	18.4 k	19.6 k
- mid compression	4.64 k	5.14 k	12.3 k	12.8 k
- high compression	3.53 k	4.22 k	6.92 k	7.62 k
- maximum compression	2.12 k	2.21 k	1.92 k	2.16 k

Figure 8.71.

A table showing the file sizes of the four graphics in a variety of graphical formats.

Note

The graphics in Figure 8.72 are saved in various file formats. The top-left graphic is in a GIF optimal palette format. The lower-left graphic is in a GIF dithered format. The top-right graphic is in a JPEG low-compression format, and the bottom-right graphic is in a JPEG high-compression format.

Figure 8.72.

Four saved versions of a photo image.

Notice that the GIF file size increased when the Noise filter was added to each graphic. The increase of color changes within the horizontal lines of the graphics caused the files to balloon in size.

Use the GIF format with graphics that contain flat-colored surfaces. Graphics that contain millions of colors, such as photographic images, are reduced to a maximum of 256 colors when saved in GIF format. This means that a photograph containing millions of colors would be dithered down to a lower-quality version of the original photograph. (See Figure 8.72.) Photographic images do not compress well in the GIF format primarily because of the constant color changes in the photographic image, though.

Figure 8.73.

A table showing the file sizes of the four saved photo graphics.

	Orange
Gif - Standard Palette, Dithered	15.6 k
Gif - Optimized Palette, Nearest Color	24.9 k
Jpeg - low compression	9.28 k
Jpeg - high compression	4.55 k

JPEG Compression

The *Joint Photographic Experts Group* (JPEG) graphics format can contain up to 16 million colors. The JPEG format was designed specifically for compressing photographic images or images that contain subtle changes in color (See Figure 8.74.) Looking at the table in Figure 8.75, you can see that the graphics with solid colors compressed better in GIF format than in JPEG. But when you look at the table in Figure 8.73 of the graphics containing many speckles of different colors (Figure 8.72), you can see that the JPEG format compresses these images better than when they were saved in the GIF format, even at the minimal compression setting.

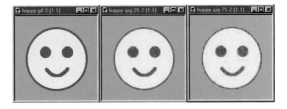

Figure 8.74.

Three happy faces saved in different file formats.

	Happy Face
Gif	2.15 k
Jpeg - low compression	5.35 k
- high compression	2.88 k

Figure 8.75.

This table lists the file sizes of the three saved versions of the happy face.

Tip

You can see that both graphical formats have their strengths and weaknesses. If you are trying to decide which format to save your graphic in, remember this rule of thumb: If it's an illustration with a lot of flat-colored areas, just GIF it. If it's a photograph or image with many subtle color changes, just JPEG it. This not only gives you the best-quality images for the Web, but it also gives you the best compression possible.

 **Note**

It is interesting to note that JPEG compression also adds small amounts of noise whenever an area of solid color occurs or areas with big changes between colors occur. (See Figures 8.76 through 8.78.)

Figure 8.76.

A close-up of the happy face graphic saved in GIF format.

Figure 8.77.

A close-up of the happy face graphic saved in JPEG format with low compression.

Figure 8.78.

A close-up of the happy face graphic saved in JPEG format with high compression.

Scanned Graphics: A Picture Is Worth a Thousand Words

Pictures can convey information very quickly and can be much more stimulating than a page full of text. Owning a scanner allows you to take images from paper and use them to create graphical images for the Web. One way you can use a scanner is to create sketches on paper and transfer them to computer graphical images where you can manipulate and edit them to your heart's content. If you don't have a digital camera, a scanner is great for using your own photos and scanning them into graphical images for the Web. (See Figure 8.79.)

Figure 8.79.
Caught in the act!

> **Note**
>
> After you scan a graphic, you still might need to clean up the image. We discuss how to clean up a scanned graphic in Chapter 9, "Manipulating Your Graphics."

Shortening Download Time with Thumbnail Images

If you are designing a Web page that will contain a number of large graphics, you should consider using thumbnail images to give your reader a preview of what graphical images your page offers. This speeds up the time it takes for your reader to download your page, and it also gives him the option of viewing only the graphics he really wants to download. Creating thumbnail graphical images simply means resizing your original images into smaller graphics.

> **Tip**
>
> To link your thumbnail image to the full-sized image, just add `<A HREF="large.gif">` around your `<IMG SRC>` tag. Also remember that it is not always obvious to your reader whether a thumbnail image is clickable, especially if the border is disabled from the image source tag. Don't forget to add hypertext links below or beside the thumbnail image to help your reader distinguish your clickable thumbnail images from your other graphics. (See Figure 8.80.)

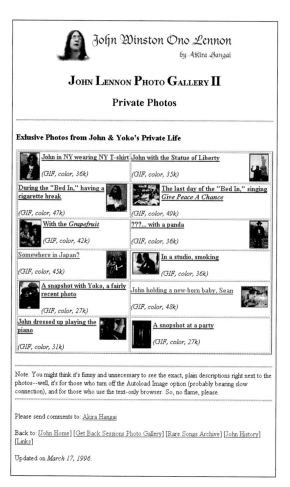

Figure 8.81.

This man is rendering his thoughts about the world of 3D.

To 3D or Not to 3D

You can use many techniques and effects to give an image a 3D effect. You saw a few of them earlier in this chapter. Drop shadowing is a simple, effective way to give your image that instant 3D effect. Using shadows along with gradient fills can give any button, bullet, or banner the perception of being three dimensional. This is all fine and dandy when designing little bullets or icons, but if you want to dip into real 3D graphics design, you have to step into another world: *The World of Ray Tracing…* (See Figure 8.81.)

To create *ray-traced* images, the computer has to go through a series of mathematical equations to determine the relationships between objects in virtual space. Although we're not here to discuss 3D theory, we will give you a simple explanation of how ray tracing works. The minimum three elements used when creating ray-traced images are the object, camera, and light. As in a photo shoot, the light element shines on the object element. To capture the element, the camera takes a picture of the object. The biggest difference between a real camera and a virtual camera is that a real camera captures the image automatically. With the virtual camera, the computer has to calculate mathematically to re-create the image. After the computer completes its calculations, it re-creates a 3D picture of the image, pixel by pixel. The process of creating the 3D image is called *rendering*.

Even though there is nothing wrong with using 3D images all over your Web page, how much 3D is too much? A 3D image can be as simple as a gradient-filled illustration or as complicated as a colorful photograph. Remember that each image is still a graphic, and the more complicated the graphic, the bigger the size. You must consider the size of the 3D graphic along with all the other graphics when putting together a Web page.

3D graphics can be extremely huge in size because of the number of shades and colors required to simulate the 3D effect.

Say It Again, Sam. Say It Again, Sam.

We have said this before (and, no, this is not déjà vu), but you have to ask yourself, "Will the 3D graphic really add to my page, or am I using it just because I made it?" Like a long strand of hair growing between your eyebrows, if it doesn't add to your page, yank that sucker out!

Setting Up 3D Rendering

Before you can start creating 3D graphics, you must get your hands on a good ray-tracing program. With the aid of 3D graphical software, you can create three-dimensional objects, manipulate them in a scene, render them, and produce an amazing 3D graphic. (See Figure 8.82.)

Figure 8.82.
A creative explosion in progress!

For those who want to enter the world of 3D, do not fear. Creating ray-traced images is not as painful as it once was. Creating graphics with 3D programs used to mean agonizingly typing commands in the 3D software's very own programming language. But now, with the creation of drag-and-drop 3D graphical packages, 3D rendering is much easier.

Note

Simple 3D software packages are now affordable for the average user and can be purchased at many software retail stores.

A big factor in creating your own 3D-rendered image is whether the power of the computer and the software package you use can withstand the heavy-duty nature of ray tracing. Ray tracing a scene takes a lot of computing power. The more powerful the machine, the less time it takes to render a scene. How much time does it take for a computer to ray trace an image? Depending on how complicated the objects in the scene are, it can take anywhere from a few seconds to a few hours (or even days!). So if you have a single computer that's just getting you by, you might want to consider upgrading your hardware before you take on the world of 3D ray tracing.

Summary

Now that we have shown you ways to create interesting graphics for your Web site, let's review the major points in this chapter:

✦ Keep the file size of your background image small to give your reader the chance to see the background image before reading the text on your page.

✦ Never use interlaced or transparent GIFs for your background images. Doing this slows the download time of your page and can cause browsers to stall while downloading.

✦ Well-designed background images have no visible seams.

✦ The choice of text color is crucial in making your page pleasant and readable. Don't choose colors that match closely with elements of your background. A good level of contrast is the key to making text colors stand out from the background.

✦ Use dark backgrounds with light type on banners, logos, graphics, or whenever you want to create an effective mood or style.

✦ Using graphical images containing textual elements is a very useful and powerful way to manipulate font types and colors to suit any mood or feeling you want to portray on your page.

✦ When using animated GIFs for bullets, icons, or banners, try to keep the animation small to add variety to your page without distracting the reader.

✦ Be creative when creating horizontal rules. For continuity of your user interface, try to design horizontal rules with the metaphor of your site in mind.

✦ Avoid overusing horizontal rule images throughout your page. Too many rules make your Web page look choppy.

✦ For graphics with mainly flat-colored areas, GIF it. For photographs or images with many subtle color changes, JPEG it.

✦ If you don't have a digital camera, a scanner is great for scanning your photos into graphical images for the Web.

Q&A

Q **Is there an easier way to create bullets? I am not a graphics designer, but I would like to be able to make my own bullets; however, I don't want to start from scratch.**

A Fortunately, you can use filters with your graphical software program that allow you to create nice bullets with a click of a button. Metatools, Inc. has a great package of filters called Kai's Power Tools; this contains interesting filters that can add instant professional effects to your images. (You can find a demo version of KPT filters at `http://www.metatools.com`.)

 Is there an easier way to make seamless backgrounds?

Again, you can use special filters that automatically create seamless backgrounds from your images. The resulting graphic, however, might not produce a professional-looking background image, depending on the number of details in the image you use. Also, if you surf the Net, you can find tons of Web sites that offer free graphical libraries of bullets and seamless backgrounds.

Challenge Yourself

Challenge Yourself

In this section, we are going to let you create your own graphics by applying the techniques you learned in this chapter.

Case Study

Welcome to the Snake Charmers Society Web site. Currently, it looks pretty boring and the members know it. They need something more visually appealing to attract new membership.

Your Mission

Spice up the Snake Charmers Society Web page by completing the following tasks:

- ◆ Add a background on which text is legible.
- ◆ Upgrade the bullets with fancier ones.
- ◆ Re-create the Snake Charmers Society's header banner into something more visually catchy.
- ◆ Redesign the horizontal rules to be much more interesting than just straight lines.

These are some suggestions you can use to create an interesting background:

- ◆ Apply a seamless snake background.
- ◆ Use the Snake Charmers Society's logo as a tiled background.
- ◆ Create a dark background and choose an appropriate text color for the content of the page.

Here are some alternatives you might want to consider for the banner and header graphic:

- ◆ Create a plaque header graphic.
- ◆ Use drop-shadowed text.
- ◆ Add illustrations as part of the text.

Here are some suggestions to consider when creating the bullets:

✦ Create color-coordinated, 3D bullets.

✦ Shrink various snake images and use them as bullets.

Here are some suggestions to consider for creating horizontal rules:

✦ Create a horizontal rule as a single-lined snake.

✦ Use various illustrations tiled together to form a horizontal rule.

Required Tools

✦ Your computer

✦ A graphics editor

Supplied Elements

In the "Chapter 8: Challenge Yourself" section on the CD-ROM, you will find a variety of illustrations and clipart the society uses in its literature. Feel free to use your own clipart.

Designing Graphics and Animation

Chapter 9

Manipulating Your Graphics

Have you ever seen a site on the Web and wondered how the Web designers got their graphics to look so good? When you look at a photo in a magazine, more likely than not, that photo has been touched up in some shape or form. In this chapter, we're going to show you how to manipulate your graphics just like the pros do! You'll learn about appropriate graphics sizes, editing, cropping, dithering, anti-aliasing, image-map editing, graphics filters, and many more ways to improve your graphical designs.

What Size Should Your Graphics Be?

When talking about graphics size, we are focusing on the file size of the graphic, not the dimensions of the graphic itself. As you saw in the last chapter, two graphics with the same dimensions can vary greatly in file size. To keep the download time of the Web page manageable, your graphics should be as compact as possible. A good rule of thumb is to aim for the entire Web page to be loaded in no more than 30 seconds with a 28.8Kbps modem connection.

> **Tip**
>
> It is better to have a number of smaller graphics for your reader to download than one enormous graphic. Waiting for one huge graphic to load is sometimes a little too much for a reader to endure. Even though the total file sizes of smaller graphics might equal the huge graphic, it is better to spread out the downloading between the smaller graphics.

Low/High-Resolution Graphics: Allowing a Smoother Download

The LOWSRC attribute is a Netscapism that allows a browser to fetch a lower-quality version of an image and display it onscreen while it completes the transfer of the real image. The LOWSRC image can be loaded quickly, giving the reader an idea of what the graphic looks like before the real graphics are completely loaded. This gives the reader the option to wait for the high-resolution images to load or to continue through the site.

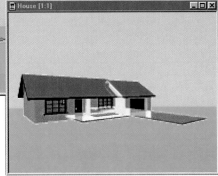

Figure 9.1.

The low-resolution graphic is just 2.72KB, while the original, high-resolution graphic is 28KB.

Cropping Your Images for Maximum Effect

Cropping your images can reduce the graphic's file size and bring focus to specific areas in your image. It is a wonderful technique to use when cleaning up your scanned images or even manipulating your artwork illustrations.

 By using your Select Area tool in your graphics paint program (which usually is shown as an icon with a broken-line rectangle or lasso), select the area you want to crop. Then copy the cropped image by choosing Edit | Copy. Next, paste the

image into a new window by choosing Edit | Paste | As New Image. Your image appears in its own window. (See Figure 9.2.)

Figure 9.2.

Cropping the lobster adds more focus to the image. We cropped the lobster twice to show you the difference that cropping can make to a photograph.

Editing Images to Remove Distractions

When editing your images, try to remove any distracting elements, such as unnecessary items in the background or foreground, reflections off elements in the image, areas with poor lighting, and so on. You can do this by cutting out or painting over the distracting areas in a graphic. (See Figure 9.3.)

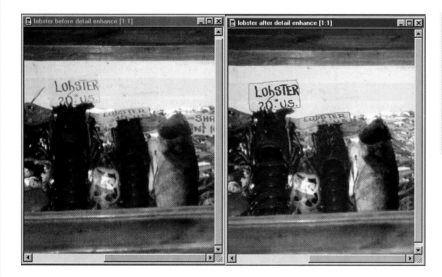

Figure 9.3.

The left image is the original image. In the right image, the shrimp sign and shrimps on the right edge were removed, and the tin foil background was copied over.

Fixing Details in Photographic Images

With graphics-editing tools, you can do just about anything to a photograph. Never again do you have to worry about pimples or dark shadows under someone's eyes. If you had to, you could shave inches off someone's butt in no time, or even remove all the hair from a person's head. Not only can you remove things, but you also can add things to an image. If something is missing from your photo, why not add it in? To fix the details in a photo, you just need some imagination, a steady hand, and lots of patience.

We were given the job of cleaning up a photo of a seafood freezer section. We lassoed the images of the lobsters, tomatoes, and green peppers and added more brightness and contrast with the Brightness/Contrast filter. We also cleaned up the image by bright-

ening the lobster sign and redrawing the letters with a darker shade of gray.

For another client, we were asked to add a boat to one of their scenic ocean shots. They gave us a photo of the boat they wanted and a photo of the scene they wanted the boat to be in. We cropped the boat from the photo and added it to the scenic picture. (See Figure 9.4.)

Figure 9.4.

We added the boat, which we cropped from another photo, into our scenic picture.

Shedding Light on the Picture: Brightening Where Needed

After some photographic images are scanned, they tend to come out a little bit on the dark side. By using the Brightness/Contrast Filter (choose Image | Color | Brightness and Contrast in Corel Photo Paint or Colors | Adjust | Brightness | Contrast in Paint Shop Pro), you can make the colors in your images more vivid. (See Figure 9.5.)

Figure 9.5.

The images in the original graphics on the left were too dark to see, so we brightened the images with our graphics paint program's Brightness/Contrast filter.

Take What You Need and Trash the Rest

Don't be kind to your graphics. Apply the techniques of brightening, cropping, softening, and colorizing to edit an image wherever necessary. A good thing to remember when cleaning up your graphics is to keep copies of your edited image throughout the various stages of the editing process. You never know when you might have to salvage details from these previous images to re-edit or retouch an image you are working on. Most important, you don't want to be left without anything to go back to if you somehow make an irrecoverable mistake with the graphic you are working on.

Adding Effective Text and Illustration to Graphics

With your graphics paint program, you can add exciting text to your images with any font you have on your computer, in any color you choose from your color palette. By applying the concepts of design you learned earlier in this book, you can transform your photo into a professional-looking advertisement.

You also can mix illustrations with photographic images. You will notice this effect used more commonly in graphical advertising or banner logos. (See Figure 9.6.)

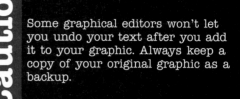

Some graphical editors won't let you undo your text after you add it to your graphic. Always keep a copy of your original graphic as a backup.

Matching Image Background Color with Background Color

When an image is displayed on a browser, you usually can see the edges of the image when it is displayed on top of a contrasting background color. To create a transparency effect without actually converting a graphic into a transparent GIF, you can match the background color of your image with the background color of your Web page. By matching these colors, you can effectively display images with irregular shapes without having to use the transparency process. In Figure 9.7, we filled in the Disco King's background color to match the background color of the Web page. In the Netscape window, the image on the left has the same background color as the Web page, giving it the illusion of a transparent border. The dancer on the right looks silly with his white border against the contrasting blue background of the Web page.

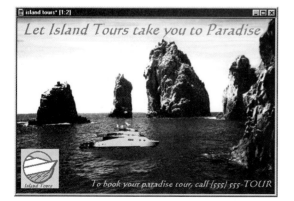

Figure 9.6.

We designed our Island Tours logo in a separate window. After adding text to our photo, we copied and pasted the logo into the left-hand corner of our image.

Figure 9.7.

Filling in the Disco King's background color to match the background color of the Web page.

Dithering Your Image

The background and sign were touched up

JPEG, with its 16-million-color capability, is the best format to use when working with photographic images. When interlacing an image or making it transparent, though, you eventually need to convert it into the 256-color palette. Doing this causes some dithering to appear on your image. To minimize the effect, you should make a copy of the image beforehand and use the copied image to test the dithering effect. After applying the filter, look for areas in the image where the dithering effect might not have been too kind to the image. You can touch up your original graphic by adding solid colors to the areas where the dithering destroyed your image. Then save your image under a new filename. (See Figure 9.8.)

Figure 9.8.

The original graphic is in the left window. The middle window shows our lobster after the effects of dithering. The lobster on the right has some dithered areas cleaned up.

Interlaced Images

The advantage of an interlaced GIF is that the reader can get an idea of what the image looks like before the image actually finishes loading onto a page. (See Figure 9.9.)

Interlaced and transparent GIFs are supported by the GIF89a format and not the older GIF87 format.

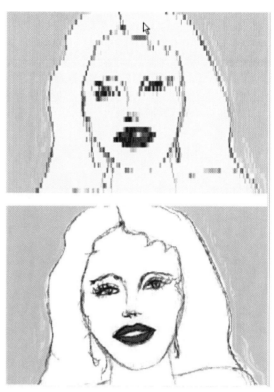

Transparent GIFs: Now You See Them, Now You Don't

When your Web page contains background images, the only way to remove the border around your graphic is to save it as a transparent GIF. Transparent GIFs are useful when working with irregularly shaped images.

Making the Background Invisible

To make the background of your image transparent, you first have to fill in the background of your image with a uniform color. Make sure that the color is not contained in the image itself. The color you choose to be transparent also will make any region in your graphic with that same color transparent. The graphic utility therefore might interpret the colors in the image to be part of the background, which could cause an undesirable effect.

Figure 9.9.

The image on the top is a non-interlaced graphic. The image on the bottom was saved as an interlaced GIF.

The Halo Effect: Anti-Aliasing and Transparency Just Don't Mix

Anti-aliasing an image means removing the rough edges around elements in the graphic with your graphics program's Soften tool. The anti-alias effect is accomplished by softening the edges with gradual shading. This effect smoothens jagged edges around your images; it usually is a good thing, except when you are saving your image as a transparent GIF. The colors of the anti-aliased edges around the image are composed of subtle blends of the edge color and the background color. This means that when the solid background color of the image is made transparent, the subtle colors are ignored; this gives the image a halo effect when shown over a different-colored background. (See Figures 9.10 and 9.11.)

Figure 9.10.

The man in the left window shows what anti-aliasing looks like from a distance, whereas the window on the right shows the effect up close.

> **Note**
>
> The methods for creating the transparent color for an image may differ, depending on what graphics editor or utility you are using. In most cases, you can select the transparent color with an Eyedropper tool, or the transparent color is set automatically to the graphics utility's background color of the color palette.

Creating Illustrated Images with Transparent Backgrounds

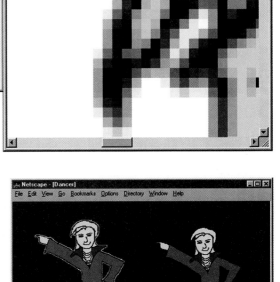

When preparing to make an illustration transparent, make sure that the image is not anti-aliased (unless you actually want the halo effect). Clean up the pixels in the background of the image to make it one uniform color, and make sure that the color is not being used in the image itself. When the background of the image is ready to become transparent, you will have to open your image in a graphics editor or graphics utility that creates transparent backgrounds. We used LView Pro and Paint Shop Pro for the transparent GIFs we created in this book.

To select a transparent background in LView Pro, choose Options | Background Color. In the Select Color Palette Entry dialog box, you can select the transparent color by choosing it from the color palette or by using the Eyedropper tool to click on the background color of your image. (See Figure 9.12.)

Figure 9.11.

The left Disco King will not get many dancing partners if he looks like he just stepped out of a nuclear reactor. The right Disco King is not anti-aliased.

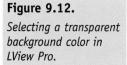

Figure 9.12.

Selecting a transparent background color in LView Pro.

Creating Photographic Images with Transparent Backgrounds

To create a photographic image with a transparent background, you use the same techniques that you use for illustrated graphics, except that you need to prepare the image more before you can make it transparent. To give you an example, we used a boat from a photograph. To cut out the boat, we first isolated it by using the Lasso tool in Paint Shop Pro. (See Figure 9.13.)

 We brought up a new graphics window and filled the background with a color that was not contained in the boat (in this case, we chose red). We then pasted the boat into the new graphics window. To tidy up the edges on the image, we magnified it until we could see the darker pixels around the edge. We removed the dark pixels by using the Pen tool to color in the red background. Then we saved the image as a transparent GIF with the transparent color set to red. (See Figures 9.14 and 9.15.)

Figure 9.13.

We used the Lasso tool to select the boat in the original photographic image.

Figure 9.14.

We pasted the boat into a new graphics window. Notice that the background color is red so that, when it becomes transparent, the boat will not be affected.

Figure 9.15.

Our transparent GIF as seen in our browser.

Hot Spot to the Rescue! Incorporating Client-Side Image Maps

Figure 9.16.

The button bar is a hot spot image map with the button regions hot linked to other pages.

An image map can contain a number of links to other pages in a site or even off the site. Image maps have become very popular as navigational tools because of their capability to manipulate your graphical images to almost any graphical interface imaginable. You can create a button bar with one image instead of creating four or five separate button images, for example. In the image, you then can hot link the button region to the appropriate Web page. Another advantage of hot spot image mapping is the fact that your image and hot-spot region are not restricted to one shape or size. (See Figure 9.16.)

Identifying Image-Map Components

Before creating an image map, you must determine which regions need to be linked to other Web pages. This example will show you the steps for designing an effective image map.

We will be hot spotting a number of dolls from the graphic in Figure 9.17.

Many image-mapping tools are available on the Web. We are using a wonderful image-map editor called Web Hotspots World Wide Web Image Map Editor, by Automata. You can find a shareware version on the CD-ROM at the back of this book, or you can visit Automata at

http://www.concentric.net/ ~automata/support

Figure 9.17.

Our doll graphic in the Web Hotspots image-map editor.

Creating Appropriate Images for Hot Spotting

The graphics you use for creating image maps should be clear and uncluttered. One thing to keep in mind when designing your image map is to make the hot-linked regions large enough for users to easily click. An itsy-bitsy hot-spotted region can be difficult for your reader to click on, especially if he has bad aim or a shaky hand. Also, make the clickable areas on your image map obvious. Don't make the reader guess which areas contain the hot links. If necessary, provide short, detailed instructions that list the specific items the user can click.

Note

If you are using image maps for the navigation on your page, remember to always include text links on your page as an option for your reader.

Defining Effective Hot-Spot Regions on an Image

Using our image-map editor, we will create a new image map to hot link to our doll gallery graphic. (Refer to Figure 9.17.)

Next, we selected a region by using the Polygon tool. This tool allows you to hot spot irregular shapes. We then added the URL path for the Web page we wanted the hot spot to link to. (See Figure 9.18.)

After all the regions on the image were hot linked, we saved the information to an HTML file. We saved the host entry with the image-map coordinates by specifying the image-map name, image comment, and image URL. Although this is not necessary, it is extremely useful when it comes to maintaining your HTML documents later. After saving the HTML file, our image map was complete. (See Figure 9.19.)

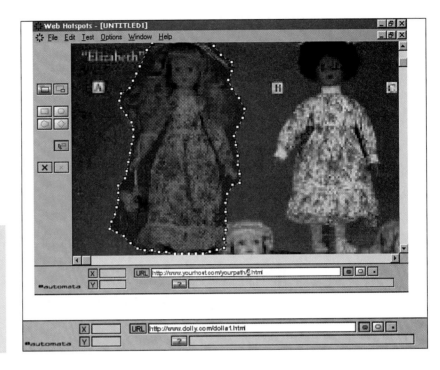

Figure 9.18.

We selected a region around the first doll with the Polygon tool. We then specified the URL path we wanted the doll image to link to.

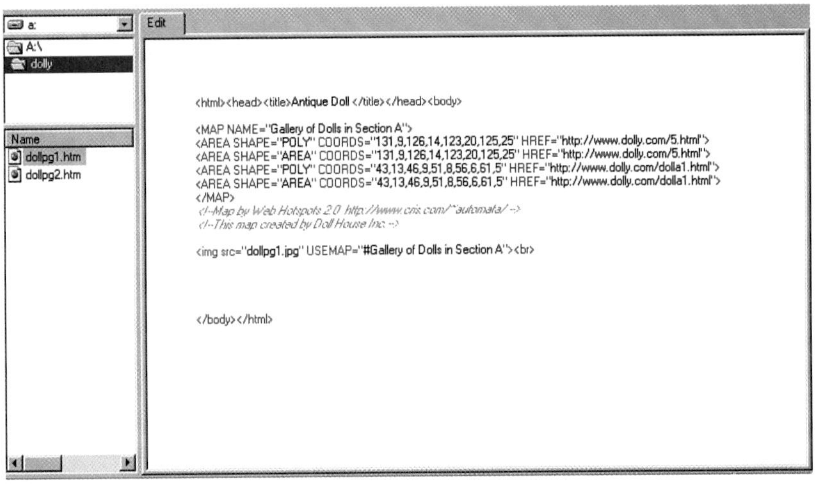

Figure 9.19.

The final source code produced by the image-map editor after the file was saved.

Adding Borders to Your Images

Borders around photographic images can add variety to your photographs. You can give an image a certain look and feel by choosing the correct border. The border around an image is like an accessory on a person. People wear jewelry, hats, scarves, watches, and hair clips to help accessorize their attire. A border around an image can be the finishing touch for a graphic.

You can create your borders from scratch or purchase them with a clipart package. If you are using premade borders, you need to cut out and copy the correct size and shape of the image and paste it within the border. (See the left image in Figure 9.20.) Another way

Figure 9.20.

Borders, borders, borders.

to create borders is to add a blurring effect around the edges of the image itself. (See the middle image in Figure 9.20.) Another technique is to use colored shapes and paste them around the edges of your image. In our example, we used a heart shape to paste around our image on the far right.

Of course, you can be creative when designing the borders for your images. Experiment by adding different filter effects, colors, shapes, and sizes around your images.

Note

The border you add to your image should be related to the image or the rest of the design elements. Don't add clashing borders that will diminish the value of the image. Also, don't add borders unless your image really needs one. Too many borders around your images can give your page a bout of *boxitis*—or, in layman's terms, too many boxes on one page.

Resizing/Resampling

You can use the Resizing/Resampling tool to change an image's size. To get the best results, you can choose from a variety of formats in which to resample the graphic. The most useful formats enable you to anti-alias or stretch the image.

you can look at the details and fix the image if necessary. By using this method, you ensure that the image is resized by the designer and not placed at the mercy of the browser. (See Figure 9.21.)

Figure 9.21.

Resizing our boat three different ways.

When an image is bigger than you need, you can resize it to make it the size you want. Shrinking the graphic's size also has the advantage of shrinking the file size of the graphic.

When you need an image that is bigger than what you currently have, you can use the Resizing/Resampling tool to increase the size of your image. This is a useful capability because, after you resize the image,

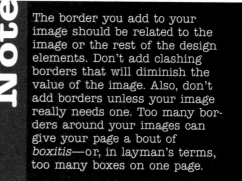

Removing Hard Edges by Anti-Aliasing

Despite how we harp on not using anti-aliasing when creating transparent GIFs, anti-aliasing does have a place in a graphics designer's toolbox. Some graphics need a softer look to give them a better effect. Anti-aliasing is great for creating softer edges, because it gives the edges of an image a less jagged look. (See Figure 9.22.)

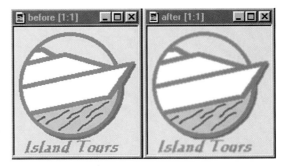

Figure 9.22.
Anti-aliasing smoothes the lines of the Island Tours graphic on the right.

Enhancing Your Graphics with Filters

Filters are great for adding different effects to your images. Sometimes you need to use a filter to create an effect for your graphic that you couldn't create otherwise. To demonstrate the effect (good or bad) filters have on different graphical types, the filters in this section were applied to three types of graphics: photographic, text, and flat-colored illustrations.

> **Note**
>
> The examples in this chapter are here only to demonstrate filter effects. We do not necessarily recommend that you apply filters to all your graphics. We only want to show you ways to alter your graphics when needed. In our examples, we applied our selection of filters to a photo image, a textual image, and an illustration to show you the different effects filters create on different types of graphics.

Add Noise

You can use the Add Noise filter (choose Effects | Noise in Corel Photo Paint or Image | Special Filters in Paint Shop Pro) to add a speckled effect to your images. (See Figure 9.23.)

The Noise filter, when applied without rhyme or reason, distorts your image and gives it an unpleasant appearance.

> **Tip**
>
> Use the Noise filter when you want to add texture to a solid color in your image. Suppose that we don't want the shirt of our Disco King image to be a solid purple color. To add texture to his shirt, we can apply the Noise filter to the shirt area alone. This certainly gives our Disco King a really groovy-looking shirt.

Figure 9.23.

The Add Noise filter did just that. It added noise to all the images, giving them a grainy look.

Blur

The Blur filter removes the fine detail from an image to make it appear blurred. (See Figure 9.24.) You can use this filter to blur an image to the point where it looks like an unfocused version of the original image. (You can create a good number of "authentic" Bigfoot photos this way.) You can access the Blur filter by choosing Image | Normal Filters in Paint Shop Pro.

Figure 9.24.

The Blur filter made each of our images blurry and removed fine detail.

Another way to use the Blur filter is to help bring focus to the main content of an image by blurring the elements in the background. This is especially useful when the background contains a distracting element that is interfering with the quality of the content in the picture. We once had a photo of the outside of one of our client's buildings, for example. Unfortunately, the photo also

Note

Different graphics packages may have different filters. We selected only a few that are more or less available in the majority of graphics packages in one form or another.

captured a St. Bernard wandering into the scene beside the building. We selected the area around the building in the photo and applied the Blur filter to remove the distraction.

Contour

You can use the Contour filter (or the Trace Contour filter, as it is called in Paint Shop Pro) to outline the edges of your image. As you can see in Figure 9.25, we added the Contour filter to our graphical images. The filter made the photo image appear cartoon-like, whereas the filter outlined the text in the text image and hollowed out the inside. The filter basically reduced the illustrated image to line art.

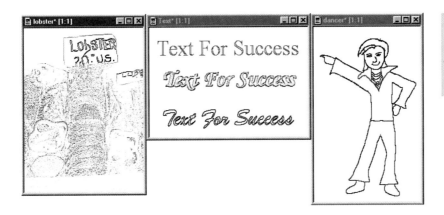

Figure 9.25.

We applied the Contour filter to our three graphics to get these results.

Cutout

A *cutout* on an image is like taking a pair of scissors and cutting out little pieces of a picture in a magazine. In Paint Shop Pro, you can access the Cutout filter by choosing Image | Special Effects | Cutout. For this filter to take effect, an area must be selected from the image. This filter creates a cool cutout effect in the image. Cutouts can create great funny effects, because you can cut out any portion of a graphic. In the Disco King image, for example, we could have inserted a photo of someone's head into the cutout area just for fun.

> **Tip**
>
> The Contour filter is very useful when you need to create a line-art version of your illustrated images or text. It does not work as well with the photographic image because of all the different colors the image contains.

Despeckle

You can use the Despeckle filter to give your image a blurred effect, making it seem like someone dabbed a cotton ball all over the image while the paint was still wet. You can access this filter by choosing Effects | Jaggy Despeckle in Corel Photo Paint and Image | Special Filters | Despeckle in Paint Shop Pro. (See Figure 9.26.)

Figure 9.26.
We added the Despeckle effect to our graphical images.

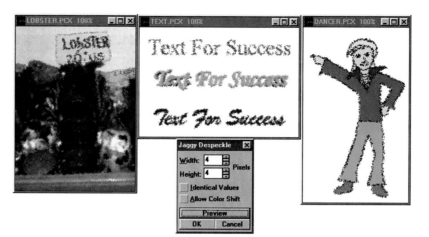

We applied the Despeckle effect to our graphical images. The filter makes the photo image of our lobster look like certain sections of the color had mini-explosions. With the variety of colors and gradual tones, the effect on the photo image gives it a nice speckled look. The Despeckle effect makes the text and Disco King images look like their molecular cohesiveness has completely deteriorated. This interesting effect makes it look like the image is separating molecule by molecule.

Edge Detect

You can use the Edge Detect filter (or Find Edge filter, as it is called in Paint Shop Pro) to add different outline effects to a picture. As you can see in Figure 9.27, we used the filter with the same graphical images, which gave the photo image somewhat of a negative look. With our middle image, the filter created an interesting hollow effect on our text. For the illustration image on the far right, the filter gave our Disco King a cool neon look. This filter is useful when you want to create a neat neon-looking image or text that stands out. If you've seen sharp-looking logos on the Web, the graphics designer probably used the Edge Detect filter to sharpen up the edges of the text in the logo.

Edge Emphasis

You can use the Edge Emphasis filter (or Edge Enhance, as it is called in Paint Shop Pro) to highlight edges around the areas of different colors and shades in your image. We experimented with this filter to see what effects they would produce on different types of images.

We noticed that the Edge Emphasis filter washed out the photo image of the lobsters. It had no real effect on the regular text. With the 3D text, though, the filter highlighted the edge. The filter had the best effect on the illustrated image; it gave the Disco King a uniform edge.

Embossing

You can use the Embossing filter to add a 3D effect to flat images.

You also can use the Embossing filter to transform an image into a background image. You might need to fiddle with the colors in your image after embossing it to make the text in your image more readable. You can use a subtle embossed image to make impressive background images. (See Figure 9.28.)

Figure 9.27.

We applied the Edge Detect filter to our three images to produce these results.

Tip

When you need to darken the outline of an illustrated image, you should use the Edge Emphasis filter.

Note

In Corel's Photo Paint 4.0, you can determine the direction in which the light hits your image by clicking on a directional arrow.

Figure 9.28.

We applied the Emboss filter to our images to get these results.

We applied the Emboss filter to our three graphical images. This filter gives a nice effect to the photo image by giving it depth. With the flat text, the filter created a 3D effect. With the Disco King illustration, the filter produced an interesting outline; however, it still requires major touching up.

Impressionism

You can use the Impressionism filter (choose Effects | Artistic in Corel Photo Paint 4.0) to make your image look like it was painted by a great artist with wild brushstrokes and

Note

Sometimes, embossing can make your text illegible. See Chapter 8, "Creating Graphics To Spice Up Your Page," for more details on the importance of legibility of text on background images.

blends of colors. You can alter the brushstroke length and direction to suit your taste. This artsy-type filter gives the best effects when the image has a wide variety of colors and color changes. That is why the photographic image was transformed into a very pleasant-looking image, but the other two did not fare as well. (See Figure 9.29.)

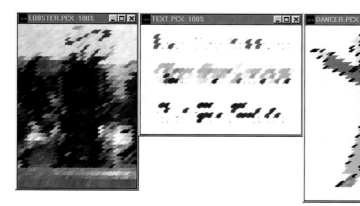

Figure 9.29.

Impressionism converts all three images into simulated oil paintings. Who needs Picasso when we have Impressionism?

Invert

You use the Invert filter (choose Effects | Invert in Corel Photo Paint or Colors | Negative Image in Paint Shop Pro) to turn images into simulated photograph negatives.

We applied the Invert filter to our three graphical images. As you can see in Figure 9.30, the filter creates a negative of each of the images. For the text and illustration, the entire effect was merely a change in color. In the photographic image, the effect was much more impressive; the photo has a type of X-ray feel. Inverting may be best suited for photographic images, because it has a much better effect than it does on mere solid-colored images. If you were designing a hip, new age, or alternative type of Web site, you could use the Invert filter to make your images look really funky.

Figure 9.30.

The Invert filter creates a negative of each of our images.

Mosaic

You can access the Mosaic filter by choosing Image | Special Filters in Paint Shop Pro. This filter creates a tiling effect in an image that produces the same effect as the Pixelate filter in Corel Photo Paint. (See Figure 9.31.)

You can create lower-resolution images by using the Mosaic filter. This is useful when you want to create JPEG images for the `<LOWSRC>` tag.

Figure 9.31.

The Mosaic filter gave an unfocused effect to each of our images.

Motion Blur

The Motion Blur filter (choose Effects | Motion Blur in Corel Photo Paint and Image | Normal Filters | Blur in Paint Shop Pro) is similar to the Blurring filter, except that you can determine the direction of the blur. The blurring effect adds a sense of motion and speed to an image. (See Figure 9.32.)

The Motion Blur filter gave all our images a pulled look. The effect it created for our text images reminds us of the days when we smudged the fresh ink from a page just printed from our bubble-jet printer.

Like the name suggests, the Motion Blur filter gives an image a sense of motion by pulling some of the image's color at a certain angle away from the image. This effect is useful when you want a blurred image to appear

to be dynamic or in motion. This filter produces the effect that the image is moving from a certain spot to another. This pulling effect is especially useful when you want to guide the reader's eyes toward a certain direction on the page.

Outline

With the Outline filter, elements in your image that contain solid colors are outlined. The inside of objects and the background areas of the picture are filled with a gray color.

Notice in Figure 9.33 that the Outline filter doesn't impact our photo image on the far left very much, because with all the different colors in the image, it is difficult to find a clear edge. The filter works well with our

Figure 9.32.
Using the Motion Blur filter to stretch our graphical images.

text that was saved in GIF format, but notice that the 3D text, which was saved as a JPEG file, did not receive the same effect. The noise in the 3D image is not noticeable to the naked eye, but the Outline filter picked it up and outlined it as well. The filter gave a nice colored outline to the illustrated image.

Pixelate

You can use the Pixelate filter in Corel Photo Paint (or Mosaic, as it is called in Paint Shop Pro) to give a tiled-like effect to your images. In Corel Photo Paint, you can access this filter by choosing Effects | Pixelate. (See Figure 9.34.)

Figure 9.33.
The Outline filter and the effects it created on our three images. There was not much impact on the photographic image, but the text and illustration had good results.

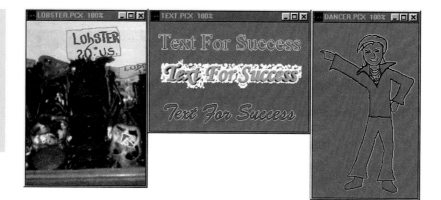

Tip

The Outline filter removes solid colors from your illustrated images. Use the Outline filter when you want your illustrated images to be reduced to line art. Depending on the solid colors on the edges, the effect can produce a very interesting colored version of line art.

Figure 9.34.

The Pixelate filter gave all our images a tiled effect.

Tip

The Pixelate filter is useful for creating fade-in animation. To do this, just copy the image a number of times while reducing the intensity of the pixel effect in each frame. After you put the frames together, the animation appears to fade in, with the first frame being fuzzy and the subsequent frames becoming sharper.

and the colors in the graphics. We applied the Pointillism filter to our three graphics. (See Figure 9.35.) We noticed that the filter gave a nice effect to the photo image but was completely hideous in the textual images. The effect on the illustration image was not as pleasant as it was in the photo image, but we probably could use it if we were trying to give an artsy feel to our Web page.

Pointillism

You can use the Pointillism filter (choose Effects | Artistic in Corel Photo Paint 4.0) to give your image a dot-like effect. The effects can vary, depending on the size of the dots

Posterize

You use the Posterize filter (choose Effects | Posterize in Corel Photo Paint or Colors | Posterize in Paint Shop Pro) to combine gradual colors into solid colors in an image, which gives it a poster-like effect.

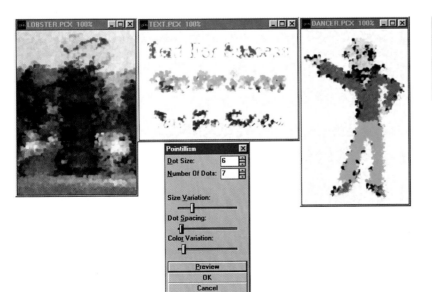

Figure 9.35.

Here is how our three images looked after a dose of the Pointillism filter.

We applied the Posterize filter to our three graphical images. (See Figure 9.36.) The filter didn't affect the Disco King or our text images very much because they consist of solid colors, but it had good results on the photographic image. By making the gradient colors one solid color, the filter made our lobster look more like a poster. You can use this filter to make your photographic images look like posters.

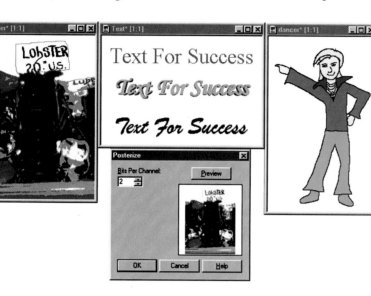

Figure 9.36.
We applied the Posterize filter to our graphical images.

Psychedelic

You can use the Psychedelic filter (choose Effect | Psychedelic in Corel Photo Paint) to create radical color changes in an image and give it a psychedelic effect.

We added the Psychedelic filter to our graphical images. (See Figure 9.37.) The filter had a pronounced effect on the photographic image. In the text and illustration, the effects were more like a color change.

Psychedelic images are great to use for those weird-and-wacky pages when you want to give your image a radical, Technicolor metamorphosis. Although the effect is not as pronounced on illustrated and text images, it can produce a shocking color shift and edge modification to photographic images.

Figure 9.37.
All the leaves are brown, and the sky is gray.

Sharpen

You can find the Sharpen filter by choosing Image | Sharpen in Corel Photo Paint and Image | Normal Filters | Sharpen in Paint Shop Pro. You use the Sharpen filter to remove some of the gradient colors in an image and also to sharpen lines.

We added the Sharpen filter to our graphics for comparison purposes. The filter did not have much effect on the text or illustration images, because the edges of the images already were sharp. The effect on the photographic image was more noticeable because of all the gradual colors the graphic contains.

The Sharpen filter had a minimal effect on our solid-colored illustrated image. Solid-colored images do not usually need this filter, because the borders around the solid-colored shapes are quite sharp, and using this filter would only be redundant. This filter is very useful when a fuzzy image needs to be made clearer and the outline of the image needs to stand out. Usually, you'll want to apply this filter to photographic images or illustrated images that have been dithered.

Soften, Diffuse, & Blend

In Corel Photo Paint, the Soften, Diffuse, and Blend filters all basically give a soft blurring effect to an image. These filters are the most effective when two very different colors line up together in your image. These filters give the edges of an image a nice anti-aliasing effect. For photographic images in which there is a gradual color change, the effects are not as noticeable. You can access these filters by choosing Image | Smooth in Corel Photo Paint or Image | Normal Filters for the Soften filter in Paint Shop Pro.

These filters smooth jagged lines by softening the color change between two colors. They are useful when jagged line art, illustrated images, or text needs to be smoothed out to give it a softer appearance.

Solarize

You can use the Solarize filter to make your image look like a photographic negative by inverting colors over a certain threshold in your graphic. The difference between this filter and the Invert filter is that you can control the negativity of your image by setting the threshold of the colors in the image. You can access this filter by choosing Effects | Solarize in Corel Photo Paint and Colors | Solarize in Paint Shop Pro. (See Figure 9.38.)

Figure 9.38.

Your X-rays are ready, sir. With the threshold set at 10, all the images begin to look quite like the negatives of the original images.

The Solarize filter is a great filter to use in place of the Invert filter when you want a varying degree of inversion instead of complete inversion. As with the inverted images, the images produced by the Solarize filter can be quite interesting to work with. Now that you have control over the amount of inversion applied to the image, you can experiment and create new images with a suitable look and feel for your site.

Summary

Now that we have shown you ways to create interesting graphics for your Web site, let's review the major points in this chapter:

- ✦ A good rule of thumb is to aim for the entire Web page to be loaded in no more than 30 seconds with a medium-speed connection.

- ✦ Cropping your image brings focus to your graphic and also can reduce the file size.

- ✦ When editing your graphics, try to edit out any distracting elements, fix up any details in photographic images, and brighten where needed.

- ✦ Always keep copies of the images you are working with at various stages of the editing process. You never know when you might need them.

- ✦ If the Web page background is a solid color, it is easier to give an irregularly shaped image the same background color than to make it transparent.

◆ You should interlace only images that are large. Interlacing small images has no effect, because the image is loaded quickly.

◆ When creating a transparent GIF, make sure that the image is not anti-aliased.

◆ Use an image map only when there is more than one element to link or if the element is an irregular shape.

◆ Anti-alias an irregularly shaped image only when the Web page background is a solid color. Make sure that the anti-aliasing is done with the same background color.

◆ Don't be afraid to experiment with filters. They might surprise you by giving you an effect that you never thought was possible.

Q&A

 There are many other types of filters and many other plug-ins. Why didn't you give examples of those, too?

 Well, if we could have added another 65 pages to this book, we might have been able to include a portion of all the filters available on the market today. But, alas, we have limited space. Therefore, we decided to focus on filters that were more or less universally available in the majority of graphics packages. There are many great filters out there that we haven't even talked about. That doesn't mean that you shouldn't try them. Go ahead and experiment with different filters. You might find something you will like.

Q **If I want to add a few elements from different photographic images together, what can I do before or during the process to make sure that the elements look like they belong together?**

A For photographic images, you should keep a few things in mind. Make sure that the elements are proportionate to what they would be in real life. Check the shading of the objects. Sometimes your objects have the light coming from the left, and other objects have their light coming from the right. Also, make sure that the shadows in the edited image fall in the same direction. Make sure that you get rid of all the background when selecting an image. It usually is better to cut into the image than to have a background halo effect. These are some of the basics you should consider when making sure the various elements work well together.

Challenge Yourself

In this section, you will manipulate and alter graphics by applying the techniques you learned in this chapter to develop graphics that stand out and are appropriate for a Web site.

Case Study

"Can you help us out?" you hear over the phone, "We need your expertise."

Island Tours needs a Web site developed for them, and they want you to do it. They have a logo, some photographs, some text, and an idea of what they want their Web site to look like.

Your Mission

To use some or all of the material provided to create a wondrous Web site that draws thousands of people to this tour of a lifetime.

Island Tours is offering a special new tour to Mexico, and they want a splashy promotional Web page. Here are some of their requirements:

✦ They know they want "one of them fancy-dancy image map things" as their main navigation.

✦ They want their boat, the Los Lostos, to be placed in some of the scenic photographs.

✦ They want their logo and name to be inconspicuously placed on each photographic image used in the site.

✦ They want to hit a younger crowd so that some special visual effect also will go a long way.

Required Tools

✦ Your computer

✦ A graphics editor

✦ An image map editor

✦ An HTML editor

✦ The Island Tour graphics and text

Supplied Elements

In the "Chapter 9: Challenge Yourself" section on the CD-ROM, you will find a number of photographic images of various qualities. Also included are the Island Tours logo and text about the special new tour.

Chapter 10

Animating Your Web Pages

Adding animated GIFs to your site can enhance your Web page. Without proper design and control, however, an animated GIF can quickly become annoying. In this chapter, you'll find out the best ways to incorporate animated GIFs into your Web page. You'll learn a variety of tips and techniques, such as stretching and squashing, choosing the proper cast, and planning a scene; these techniques will improve the effectiveness of your animation. Get ready to move into the realm of animation!

Using Animated GIFs

Using multiple-block or animated GIFs is a popular way to add moving graphics to a Web page. The popularity of these GIFs stems from the fact that animated GIFs are fairly simple to make, do not require special plug-in features to view, are quicker to download than other animation formats, are supported by most popular browsers, and can be created with inexpensive software tools. So, with a good GIF animation tool, anyone can create fun, animated GIFs.

An *animated GIF* is simply a series of multiple images contained in one GIF image. When seen on a browser that supports this format, the images in the animated GIF are streamed consecutively onto the screen, giving your reader a frame-by-frame slide show of your images.

> **Note**
>
> You can find a number of commercial and shareware GIF animation tools on the Web or at computer retail stores. For the purposes of showing animation design techniques, we are using Alchemy's GIF Construction Set. You can find a shareware version on the CD-ROM at the back of this book or visit Alchemy Mind Works' Web site at
>
> http://www.mindworkshop.com

3D Rendering or 2D Illustration

You can design an animation using traditional two-dimensional images, or you can be daring and design exciting animation with three-dimensional images.

Using Illustration for Animation

Creating animation with flat or 2D images can be fairly simple when the animation is limited to a small area of the image. By using illustrated images or line art, you can keep the size of your animated GIF small. You can design an effective 2D animation using a few frames without losing the smoothness of the transition between images. (See Figure 10.1.)

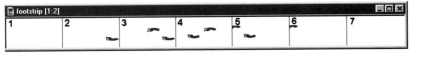

Figure 10.1.

We created a little footprint animation using a 2D graphic.

Using 3D Images for Animation

If you want to add dimension to your animation, why not use 3D graphics? To make a 3D animation, you need to obtain or create the images in a 3D ray-tracing graphics program and then convert your images into GIFs to be used for your animated GIF. Be aware of the file size of your animated GIF when using 3D images for animation. Because of the detail needed to simulate dimension, 3D images are comparatively bigger in size than line art or illustrations. In addition, 3D animated GIFs usually require more frames to make the transition between images smooth. Still, if you compress the animation properly, you can reduce 3D animated GIFs to a reasonable size for use on the Web. (See Figure 10.2.)

Figure 10.2.

We created 3D text for our spinning-text animation.

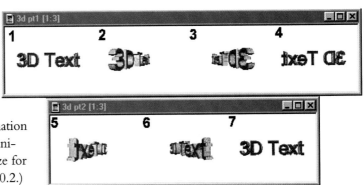

Note

Some 3D ray-tracing programs can create animation and convert the animation into separate graphics or, even better, straight into an animated GIF. You might have to pay a price for this type of software, but if you plan on creating a lot of 3D animation, it might be worth your while to check it out.

Motion Animation or Changing Images

The first step in designing an animation is to create the series of images needed to simulate a movement or action. You can use a graphic or artwork that already exists, or you can design your own. From one image, you can alter sections of an area to create the other images for your animation.

To add realism to your animation, consider changes that occur to the density of the object when you change its shape or form to convey action or movement within the image. Solid objects, such as boats, are very dense; you do not need to edit their shapes much to reflect the motion in the image. On the other hand, flexible objects, such as balloons, are less dense and can be stretched and squashed, depending on what effect or motion you are trying to achieve. Adding these little details to your images adds realism to your animation and makes your animated GIFs stand out from the rest.

To show you how speed lines and shape changes give the illusion of motion in a graphic, we created Figure 10.3. We started with a circle and elongated it in different directions. To further enhance the speed and direction of our object, we added speed lines. The first two frames show that you can add a few lines around an object to create a shaking effect. The last four images show how you can convey the direction of motion by using speed lines and elongating the object.

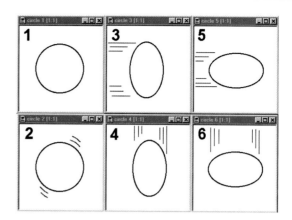

Figure 10.3.

We simulated motion in our graphic by adding speed lines and elongating the shape of our circle.

Selecting Area Size

When selecting the area size of your animation, you have to consider the desired movement or action of your object within the graphic. If the graphic is too narrow, you restrict the movement of your animation. Restricting the movement of your animation is useful when you only want a very small part of your animation to move. If your animation requires an object to move across an area, however, such as a banner animation, you must determine the width of the animation. To ensure the compactness of your file size, select only the area size necessary for your animation. Remember that small animated GIFs are much faster to download than large ones. (See Figure 10.4.)

Tip

You can use certain tricks to give your image a sense of motion. You can add speed lines, for example, to simulate the movement of an object in a certain direction. (See Figure 10.3.)

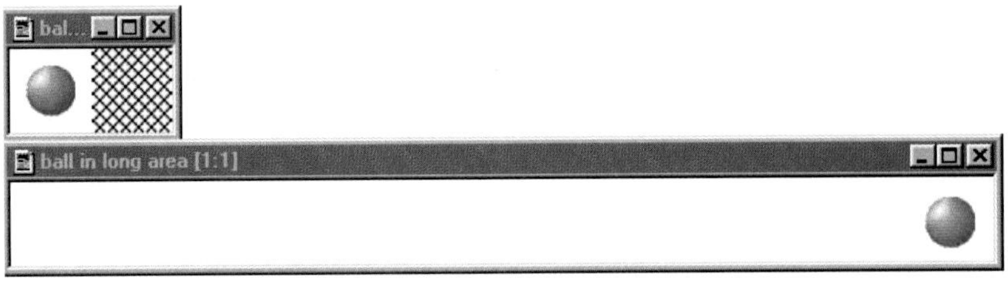

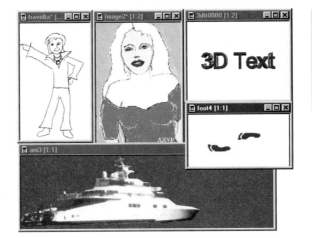

Figure 10.4.

In the top window, our ball animation will support only a small amount of movement. In the bottom window, our ball will travel toward the left.

Selecting Your Cast of Objects or Characters

Choosing the characters or objects in your animation is just as important as picking the proper cast members for a motion-picture movie. Your animation requires academy award-winning star material—not talentless no-names. After all, your animation may be seen by people all over the world. If you start with an ugly graphic, don't even bother trying to animate it. The last thing your Web page needs is an ugly animated graphic to annoy your reader (unless you want a B-rated animation).

If you are not artistically inclined, you should consider hiring a professional artist to draw the frame-by-frame illustration for your animation. If that isn't possible, another option is to use premade clipart for the first frame of your animation. You then can apply movement to your image by manipulating sections of the image. Figure 10.5 displays the cast of objects and characters we designed for our animation examples.

Figure 10.5.

Introducing the cast of our show: Neil Travelta, Desiree May, 3D Text, Dirty Feet, and the Love Boat!

Illustration Animation

Graphical illustrations are flexible and easy to manipulate. With your graphics paint software, you can edit elements, apply filters, rotate objects, remove details, and perform any other tasks your graphics software supports.

Figure 10.6.

We cut out a photographic image of a boat and moved it from frame to frame on a solid-colored background.

Photographic Animation

A fun way to capture real-life images in an animated GIF is to take several consecutive photos of a moving object and scan them into your graphics paint program. Another way to create photographic animation is to scan a single object and move the whole object or parts of the object from frame to frame. (See Figure 10.6.)

Video Animation

The other option you have to capture real-life animation is to film your moving objects with a video camera and import individual frames from the video into individual graphics via a video-capture card. To reduce the size of the animated GIF, you can remove any frames that show only very slight movements of the object.

Figure 10.7.

With our boat image, we chose blue colors for our background to represent the ocean. In the animation, the boat appears to sail across the ocean.

Selecting an Effective Background

Avoid adding a noisy background to your animation. Remember that adding noise can cause your file to balloon in size. Try to imagine waiting for a 20-frame animation with a background image of colorful speckles, dots, and tiles to download. (Talk about waiting 'til the cows come home!) Using solid background colors for your images helps reduce the file size of your animations. (See Figure 10.7.)

If you plan to do a lot of real-life animation, it might be wise to invest in a digital camera. That way, you can work on your photos immediately without having to wait for them to be developed.

Transparent Background: Floating Animation

To add transparency to your animated GIF, you must individually save each frame of your animation with a transparent background using your graphics animation utility to select the transparency color. Adding transparency to the background of your animated GIFs gives you more control over how your animation appears against the background of your Web page.

> **Tip**
>
> You can do so many neat things with transparent animation. You can have a snail appear from a hole and start sliming its way across your Web page, for example. The transparency effect gives the illusion that the snail is actually on top of your Web page, as opposed to being just an inline, animated image. (See Figure 10.8.)

Figure 10.8.

The background comes through when we make the background transparent for the Snail Trail animated GIF.

Obvious Screen: Viewing Objects on a Mini TV

Creating a slide-show animation or an animation within a bordered area is an interesting and easy effect. Simply create each frame of your animated images in a border. Voilà! You now have a cool animation created in less than 10 minutes. This effect is great for displaying a variety of assorted images.

> **Note**
>
> The GIF Construction Set enables you to offset your image from the margin. In the TV animated GIF, the second image in the television screen was offset by 12 pixels from the left and 8 pixels from the top of the image. In the bottom-right corner of each edit window, you can see the edited image. (See Figure 10.9.)

Figure 10.9.

The second image contains the offset graphic. (This animation was designed by Interspin Web Design.)

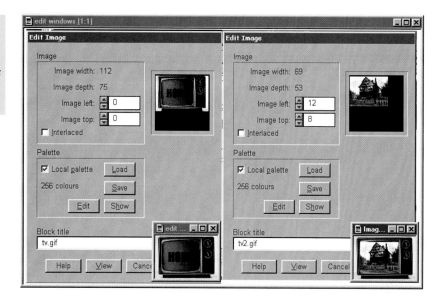

Planning the Image Sequence

Planning the movement of your object makes creating the images in your animation much easier. The best way to plan the sequence of images for your animation is to actually simulate the movement in real life to give you an idea of how to design your graphics. To simulate a human action, for example, you can get a friend to act out the movement for you. If you are talented with your pencil, you can sketch his movements directly onto a piece of paper for later reference. For those of you who are not so artistically inclined, another option is to use a camera to capture the action on film, and then to trace the actual movement from the photos onto paper.

Planning the Path of Objects

Planning the path of objects can be a fun-filled event. For our example, we wanted to simulate the action of a water-filled balloon being flung from one side of the graphic to the other. To get an idea of how this should be drawn, we actually got a balloon and filled it with water. We got someone to go across the room to catch it. With our camcorder in hand to capture the event, we threw the water balloon across the room toward him. The unexpected result was the balloon landing smack dab on his head. (It wasn't a pretty sight.) Capturing the event on video tape provided us with a wonderful basis to sketch out the path of objects for our water balloon animated GIF (and also gave us a few good chuckles).

To create our first image, we drew a slingshot and balloon. We made the elastic of the slingshot appear to be stretched to the point where it would almost snap. In the second frame, we used the stretch-and-squash effect to distort the image of the balloon, which made it look like it was accelerating across the room. Once the balloon was in motion, we made the shape of the balloon warp to exaggerate the illusion of the speed at which it was flying. In the third frame, the balloon sails through the air, homing in on its target. We elongated the shape of our object to further enhance the illusion of speed. To keep the angle perspective consistent in all the frames, we added a little reflection on the left side of the balloon image in every frame. In image 4, as the balloon impacts the target, we tried to make it look like it splattered against Bob's face. Notice again that the reflection is still in the same spot on the balloon. Now, in the fifth frame, we created the illusion that Bob's face is hidden behind the impact of the water explosion by drawing blue and black water lines completely covering his features. In the final frame, we depicted the expression on Bob's face after being soaked with the water bomb. (See Figure 10.10.)

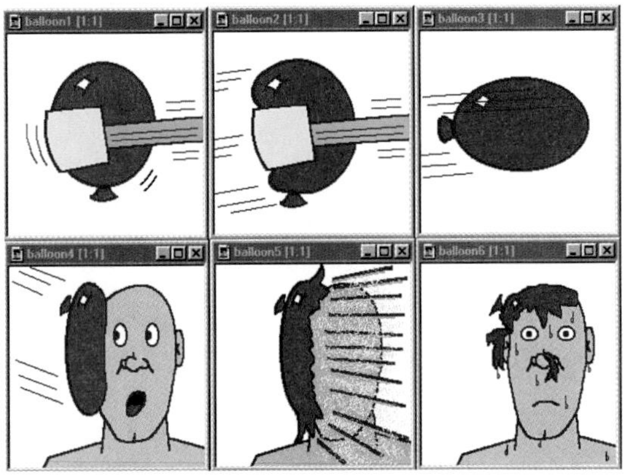

More Frames = Bigger Size

Large, animated GIFs consume enormous amounts of bandwidth and can cause some browsers to crash. The more frames you use in your animation, the larger the size of the file. Keep your animated GIFs small by keeping the number of frames for your animated GIFs to seven frames or less. (See Figure 10.11.)

> **Tip**
>
> If you decide to use a larger graphic animation, consider animating a small section of the image while keeping the rest of the image static. Make the static section of your image a regular GIF. Cut out and create an animated GIF with the section you want to animate. To incorporate this into your HTML document, place the images in a table so that the animated GIF appears to be connected to the regular GIF image.

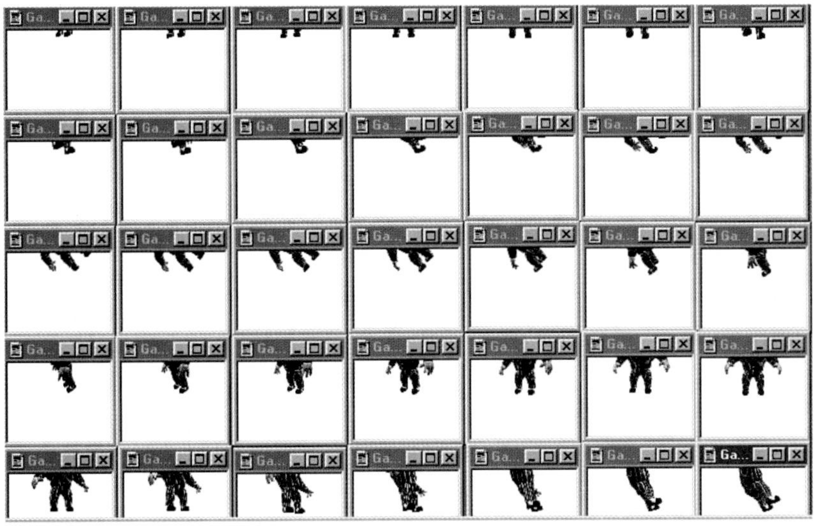

Figure 10.10.

Bob's mobile shower service strikes again.

Figure 10.11.

This figure shows only a portion of a cool, 3D animation of a man falling out of the sky. There is a total of 72 frames, which is a little too much to put on the Web as an animated GIF.

Looping, Looping, Looping, Looping...

If you have an animation with a wide range of motion, it can become very distracting (not to mention annoying) to have the animation repeat on the screen over and over and over again. It is best to restrict an animation to loop to two or three times at most. Constant repetition of a motion can cause even a great animated GIF to grow stale. Never-ending animated GIFs only distract your reader from the content of your page.

tip

If you want your animation to continue looping, we suggest that you provide a break or a pause between the last frame and the first frame of the loop by increasing the delay in the last frame. If you want your animation to loop two times before the delay, copy the first set of frames and control blocks, and then insert them at the end of your animation. This allows your animation to loop twice. Finally, increase the delay in the last frame to create a break in the animation before it loops back to the beginning.

Draw It Yourself and Scan

Sketching out your own images and scanning them yourself gives your animation the originality that you just can't get from free clipart. Although you don't have to be a great artist to draw images for your animation, you still have to be careful with detail. Be consistent with the movement between images, and use real-life models to simulate the action for you. Remember that the movement in your animation does not have to be huge. For this example, we took our Disco King cartoon and used it to create an animated GIF. By moving his hip and his arm in each frame, we created a cute and original animation. (See Figure 10.12.)

Figure 10.12.
The three images we used to create our Disco King animated GIF.

Editing Images in Sequence

Creating animation can be a little time consuming, but attention to detail rewards you with the best effects. To show you an example of editing images in a sequence, we drew a picture of a woman and scanned it into a graphical image. We made a copy of the graphic and named it GIRLFANIM1.GIF. To give the graphic in image 2 a windy effect, we added some fullness to the woman's hair. With a paintbrush tool, we added the color white over the outline of her hair. After adding the illusion of fullness to her hair, we re-drew the outline of her hair with the same paintbrush tool and the original color of the outline. (We saved this frame as GIRLFANIM2.GIF.) In the third frame, we edited the movement of the wisps of her hair to make it appear that it was being blown away from her face. (We saved this frame as GIRLFANIM3.GIF.)

In the fourth frame, we colored in her eyes to make it appear that she was about to blink. (We saved this frame as GIRLFANIM4.GIF.)

In the fifth frame, we completely colored in her eyes and removed her eyelashes to complete the blinking effect. We also edited her lips to make it appear that she was closing her mouth slightly. (We named this frame GIRLFAN-IM5.GIF.) (See Figure 10.13.)

In the sixth frame, we used the first original image and saved it as GIRLANIM6.GIF. The last image is identical to the first image, because we wanted to control the length of time the last image was displayed onscreen before looping to the beginning of the animation. (See Figure 10.14.)

Figure 10.13.
With our paintbrush tool, we colored in her eyes completely, removed her eyelashes, and added fullness to her lips.

Figure 10.14.
The six images that make up our animated GIF.

Frame-by-Frame Creation

You might want to incorporate the effect of an object moving across the screen. This kind of animation requires you to create six or seven new graphics of the same dimensions. We took a boat and created an animation by just moving the placement of the object in one frame to the next.

For the animation, the boat was to enter from the left side, travel along the frame, and exit off the right side. With this in mind, we created five frames for the animation, filling the background of each with a solid red. We intended to make the background transparent. This color was selected because the boat image did not contain the color red.

To show that the boat was entering the scene, we left the first frame blank. We then pasted the boat in various locations along the path. The first location showed only a portion on the boat entering from the left side. (See Figure 10.15.)

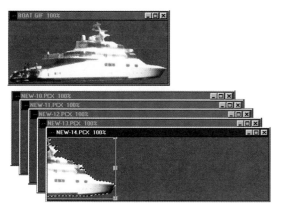

Figure 10.15.

To give the impression that the boat was entering the scene, we only showed half of it in the second frame.

After the boat entered the scene, we used two frames to give it movement across the scene.

We then showed only half of the boat leaving the scene in the final frame. This gave the illusion that the boat was floating right off the page.

Although we only used five frames, by adding enough delay time between frames and carefully placing the boat, we gave the impression that the boat actually was moving across the screen.

Putting the Frames Together

Putting the frames of your animation together does not require too much brain work. Your trusty GIF animation utility is the tool that transforms your sequence of cool images into one awesome animated GIF. In our example, we used the GIF Construction Set by Alchemy Mindworks, Inc. to show you how a graphic utility merges your frames into a single GIF file. It is easy to add new images, loop information, control information, comments, and plain text by clicking the Insert button. (See Figure 10.16.)

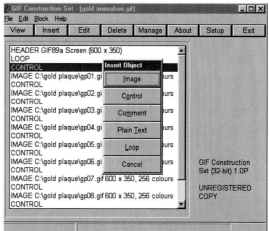

Figure 10.16.

Inserting an item is as easy as clicking a button.

After the frames are in place, you can view the animation by clicking the View button. In View mode, each frame of the animation is played out onscreen. At this time, you can make changes to and edit the animation file before you save the entire animation.

You use the control block to manage the look and feel of each frame in the animation. It helps you perform tasks such as choosing a transparent background color, adding a user input delay, setting the delay between frames, and specifying how each frame in the animation is displayed and replaced.

> A graphics animation utility is a great tool that makes creating animated GIFs headache and hassle free. You can find a shareware version of the GIF Construction Set on the CD-ROM at the back of this book.

Timing Between Frames

You should keep some things in mind when designing your animated GIFs. Be sure to add enough delay between images. Refrain from letting the animation loop too many times. If the delay between images is too short, your animated GIF loses its clarity. If you add an endless loop to that same animated GIF, the result is an animation that is as annoying as a fly landing in your soup. Like any other design element, your animated GIFs should add to your reader's enjoyment of visiting your Web page, not irritate the heck out of him.

> You can control the speed of your animation by adding a proper delay time between frames. The GIF Construction Set graphics animation utility enables you to edit the delay between each frame.

> A trick to make a few frames of animation appear to have more motion is to increase the delay between the frames. An animation of a ball bouncing in 10 frames looks just as good in four frames if you add enough delay between the frames.

Applying Animation Techniques

This section gives you some examples of animation techniques we applied to images used in previous chapters.

Headers and Logos

An effective way to add animation to a header or logo graphic is to change the lighting effects in the image.

In our example, we selected the Goldnugget Jewelers' header that you saw in Chapter 8. We took a subtle approach to the animation by adding a sparkle to the corner of the image. The original image was a JPEG image with gradient-filled areas; we converted this image to a GIF format. After the conversion, the surrounding edge of the image had to be redrawn. We cleaned up the graphic until the final image had the feel and look of the original graphic. (See Figure 10.17.)

Figure 10.17.

The left image was the original JPEG. The right image is after we reduced the number of colors to 256.

The little sparkle appears in the upper-right corner in each of our five frames. Figure 10.18 shows each frame of the animated sparkle. When the sparkle was at its brightest in the animation, we had to create a way to allow the sparkle to dim before disappearing. For the dimming effect, we used the same set of frames and added them to the animation in reverse order. This enabled us to give our animation a dimming effect without having to create new graphics. We added a loop to make the animation repeat several times.

Figure 10.18.

A close-up of the sparkle on the header graphic.

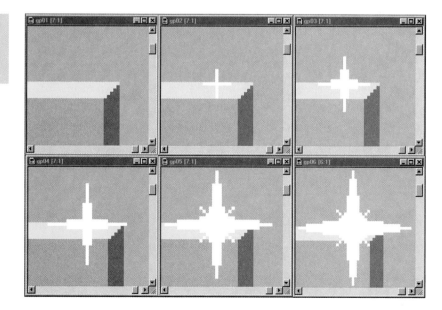

Photographic Images

We created a photographic image animation using the Love Boat and coast scenery photos from Chapter 9. We wanted the boat to appear as though it were traveling behind the rocks across the scene. The first thing we did was to convert the boat and the scene from JPEG to GIF format. By using an adaptive palette, our scenery came out quite well. (See Figure 10.19.)

Figure 10.19.

Converting the scenery to GIF.

Next, we made a few copies of the scene. We added a portion of the boat to the background of the second frame. It looked all right, except that the boat covered a portion of the rock. To fix this, we took a portion of the rock from the original photo and placed it on top of the boat. Doing this effectively hid the boat behind the rock. (See Figure 10.20.)

Figure 10.20.

Copying portions from the original scenery photograph helped us touch up the boat image.

We applied the same technique to each frame of the animation. The result was a groovy, five-frame animation showing a boat traveling behind scenic rocks. (See Figure 10.21.)

Figure 10.21.

The five frames of the traveling boat animation.

Text Images

We chose to animate the word HOWDY by using a number of individual text images. Each letter in the word HOWDY is a graphic itself. For each graphic, we skewed and rotated the letters in various directions. (See Figure 10.22.)

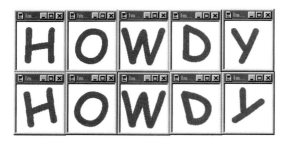

Figure 10.22.

Wiggle it, just a little bit.

We then saved each letter as a separate animated GIF. To give the effect of separate motion to each letter, we set the delay for each letter to a different value. When we viewed the completed animated GIF, the result was that each moving letter gave the word HOWDY a dancing text effect.

> **Tip**
>
> Like any other effect, overusing dancing text can become annoying. Have fun playing around with different animation effects, but restrain yourself from using too many kinds of effects on one site.

Horizontal Rules

You can create an interesting horizontal rule by adding a little animation. For our example, we used the toothbrush and toothpaste horizontal rule from Chapter 8. We wanted to get the effect of the toothpaste being squeezed out of the tube across the screen.

To create the animation, we created a number of blank graphics of the same dimensions. In the first graphic, we pasted the toothpaste tube close to the toothbrush. In each of the other graphics, we copied and pasted the toothpaste tube in the appropriate location in each graphic. Next, we added sections of the toothpaste to each graphic. In

Figure 10.23, you can see what path the string of toothpaste takes to get from one end of the graphic to the other.

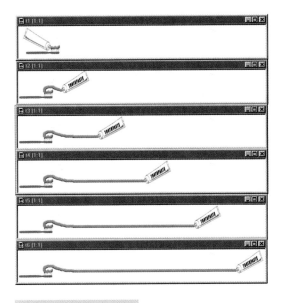

Figure 10.23.
Look Ma, no cavities!

An animated horizontal rule can become distracting, so we set our toothpaste rule animation to loop once every 60 seconds.

Bullets

In this example, we wanted to create a button that looked and acted like a stoplight. With a simple color change, we achieved the effect we wanted. First, we created the outline of a stoplight by placing three circles inside a rectangular box. We then filled the box with a darker color. We filled each circle with the corresponding stoplight color. We darkened the color of each circle to give the impression that all the lights were off. We copied the unlit stoplight graphic three times. In each of the graphics, we replaced one of the darker shades of light with a brighter shade. After we completed all the frames, we reduced the graphics down to

25×25 pixels and placed them in an animated sequence. We then set the delay between light changes to three seconds each. Figure 10.24 shows the step-by-step creation of the bullet.

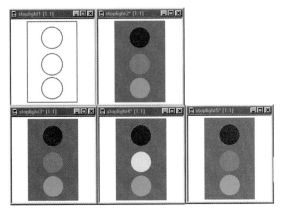

Figure 10.24.
Shall I stop, or shall I go?

Summary

Now that we have shown you some ways to design animated GIFs, let's review the major points in this chapter:

✦ An animated GIF is the best way to incorporate animation into your Web page. Animated GIFs are easy to create, do not require special plug-in features to view, are quicker to download than other animation formats, are supported by most popular browsers, and can be created with inexpensive software tools.

✦ When creating illustrated animation, techniques like stretching, squashing, and adding speed lines can contribute to the dynamic effectiveness of the animation.

✦ When selecting the area size of your animation, consider the amount of movement the object(s) will have.

- Choose characters and objects that reflect the feel and purpose of your animation. The improper selection of objects might throw off your reader.

- Avoid noisy backgrounds in your animation. Unnecessary colors in the background increase the size of your file.

- A transparent background can add realism to an animated GIF. Transparency can give the illusion that the animation is actually a real object on your page.

- Planning the movement of your image makes it easier for you to create the sequence of frames for your animation.

- Don't have the animation loop forever, loop forever, loop forever… An animated GIF that just keeps on going can be as annoying as the dreaded `<BLINK>` tag.

- Allow enough delay time between your frames to prevent your animation from going into hypermode.

Q&A

Q What type of material would be considered good reference material for illustrated animation? Is there a good source that has examples of the stretch and squash, speed lines, and other animation techniques?

A Great resources for learning about dynamics, viewing angles, and speed lines are comic books. Yup, those old comic books tucked away in a box in the basement are a great resource for learning about dynamic illustrations. Of course, you can find tons of resource and reference material at your local library, but it probably won't be as fun as going to your local comic book shop and flipping through a really great comic book.

Q **What about using Java to create Web animation?**

A You can create animation in other ways, but we decided to concentrate on a technique that was affordable, flexible, and easy to learn. We also wanted something a person can use almost immediately without getting too technical. Animated GIFs already are supported by most browsers and do not require any plug-ins. You can create animation with Java if you know how to program in Java. With Java, you not only need to create most of the frames for the animation, but you also have to write a Java applet to run the animation. That can involve quite a few lines of code. You then need to rely on the user to have a Java-enabled browser. With animated GIFs, all you need to do is create all the animation frames and put them together with an animated GIF utility. No programming is required here. As you can see, animated GIFs have many advantages over other forms of animation. Also, designing animated GIFs gives you a great foundation to learn more about the world of Web animation.

Challenge
Yourself

In this section, you will design your own animated GIFs using the tips and techniques you learned in this chapter.

Case Study

An established company, Keep It Moving, Inc., wants to expand its collection of animated clipart. They are searching for new talent. You have been asked to submit a Web page portfolio.

Your Mission

To design a few cool animations and place them on the Web for Keep It Moving, Inc. to view. You should provide a home page that links to each animation individually. The company has given you a list of animations they would like to see for their products. Many of these products are in their developmental stage; therefore, you should be sure that each of your animations conveys creativity and individual style. You need to design the following animations:

- ✦ An animated header for a product called Hydrofoam Shaving Gel.
- ✦ An illustrated or photographic animation of an animal for a pet store company.
- ✦ A single, animated bullet or a series of related animated bullets pertaining to a new cereal named Puffy Stuff.
- ✦ An animated horizontal rule that conveys the metaphor of rush-hour traffic.

Required Tools

- ✦ Your computer
- ✦ A graphics editor
- ✦ Animation GIF software
- ✦ An HTML editor

Putting It All Together

Chapter 11

Completing the Core Web Site: Implementing the User Interface

Now that you have all the components in place to create a great Web site, the next action-packed step is actually putting the site together. You now know that you can't just throw things together and expect a good, effective Web site to be hatched. This chapter focuses on helping you choose the correct elements to put on your page. You will learn how to choose the metaphor, color scheme, and navigational elements. You'll also pick up some tips on how to make the site as user friendly as possible to ensure that people will return to your page.

Designing Graphics to Represent a Metaphor

Implementing the user interface is the best part in the Web design process. Here, you can show your creative powers and put your ideas into action. In this chapter, we will show you, step by step, the design process of a user interface.

We were given the task of designing the Web site for Ade Meringue's Really Used Car Mall. With the black-and-white brochures containing its logo, a couple of car photos, and illustrations given to us, we set out to design the graphical elements for the site. We chose the car lot metaphor to bring focus to the design of our user interface.

After meeting with our client, we decided to go with a 1950s feel for the site. When we first walked onto the car lot, we were greeted by a waving man in a brown, checkered jacket and dark, polyester slacks. Seeing this man smiling and waving at us gave us our first real idea of how to design our Web site.

For our first graphical element, we used the idea of a smiling and waving salesman to create our first animated GIF. From that initial graphic, we came up with the idea that the animation should convey some information about the page the reader is currently on. After we developed this idea, we created a cast of car salesmen to display on subsequent pages of the site. The top graphics in Figure 11.1 are the original sequence for the animated waving salesman. The bottom graphics are the redesigned animated images for the informative salesman.

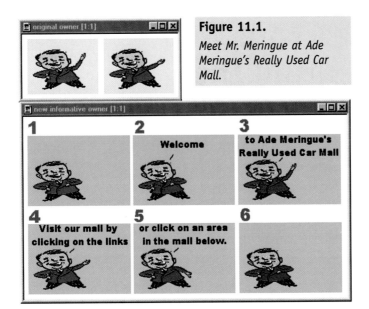

Figure 11.1.

Meet Mr. Meringue at Ade Meringue's Really Used Car Mall.

Using Color Schemes That Complement Your Metaphor

We determined the color combinations for our Web pages by researching the fashion trend during the 1950s. We were lucky that we had an actual period of time to focus our design colors on.

Because Ade Meringue's Really Used Car Mall deals with used and collector cars, we decided to go with a real retro-looking color scheme. We chose light blue and green for the predominant colors of the site. We scanned the Ade Meringue logo from his brochure and added blue to the lettering. We added a reddish shade to the word Really. Finally, to complete the logo, we added a blue ring and a drop shadow to enhance the effect of the new color scheme. (See Figure 11.2.) The top graphic is Ade Meringue's original text logo. The bottom graphic shows

Figure 11.2.

Splashing on the color from the 1950s.

how we added a retro feel to the logo just by adding our 1950s color combinations.

tip

Appendix B, "Color Reference Guide," contains some useful color combinations and is a good place to start looking into color schemes for your site.

Designing Images to Make Navigation Easy

We wanted to further use the car lot metaphor to create the navigation for the site. We decided to use an image map for the main part of the navigational user interface.

We used a 3D line drawing of the mall for the basis of the navigation on the main home page. (See Figure 11.3.) We decided that we would later add hot links to sections of the image map to link to other pages on the site.

Creating Buttons

The next step in designing the user interface was to add navigational buttons to our image map. We wanted to give our site a car lot feel, so we used the map of Ade Meringue's car lot from the back of his brochure as the basis for the navigation on the home page. We wanted the areas on the map to be represented by hot-spot areas that would be consistent with the other navigational elements throughout the site. We decided to use button images to distinguish the clickable areas on the map. Also, to continue the 1950s theme, we used 1950s-style cartoon illustrations on top of the buttons.

The five main areas we had to link to were the Car Lot, Car Parts, Customer Service, Service Center, and Tires sections. We created a template for our button images using an oval background button. We then added an image related to the page the button represented and a textual reference to the page. (See Figure 11.4.)

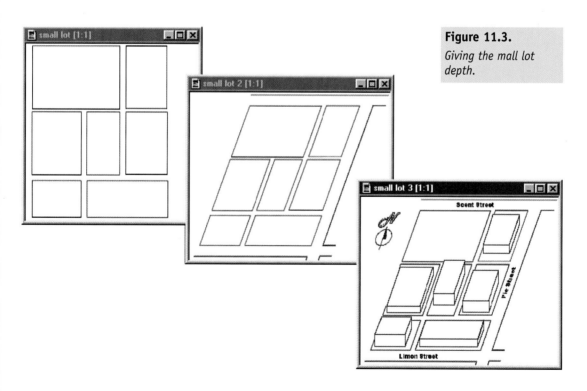

Figure 11.3.
Giving the mall lot depth.

Figure 11.4.
Creating five buttons for the home page.

Using Illustration Techniques to Make Navigation Easy

We had some fun choosing the illustrations for the site. We used a variety of interesting sketch images from our graphics collection.

We chose a few selected illustrations for the navigational elements of our page. We wanted to use illustrations of classical cars and people to help give the site an overall feel of the time period. With all the images we chose, we altered the color scheme to ensure that the images blended in with our theme. We did this by using the Paint Fill tool in our graphics editor to colorize the images in the areas we wanted to change. For the base of our buttons, we created different-colored oval shapes. We wanted the base of our buttons to be consistent throughout the site. We felt that consistency in the button shape would help users recognize the clickable elements at this site. To finish the images, we added our graphical illustrations and text on top of the buttons. (See Figure 11.5.)

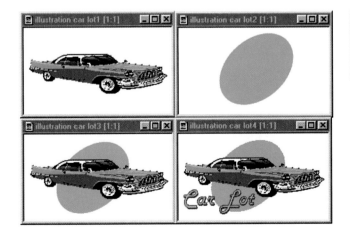

Figure 11.5.

Creating the illustration for the Car Lot button.

After we established our metaphor, color scheme, cast of characters, and buttons, we had all the pieces we needed to assemble the Ade Meringue's Really Used Car Mall site. Figures 11.6 through 11.8 show the home page, Car Lot page, and Car Parts page of the site.

Figure 11.6.

The retro-looking home page for Ade Meringue's Really Used Car Mall.

Figure 11.7.

This is the Car Lot page where all the cars travel through to get sold.

Figure 11.8.
All the new parts are featured in the Car Parts page.

Using Photographic Images to Make Navigation Easy

Photographic images give a sense of realism to the navigational elements. Photographic images are more difficult to manipulate than illustrated images. When designing graphics with photographic images, try to isolate the portion of the image you want to focus on. This might require removing the background or editing out unwanted items in the photo.

We used a few photos to represent the navigational elements of our site. We prepared each photo by removing the background and isolating the desired image. We used an oval shape as a base for our button images. We placed the images onto the oval-shaped buttons and touched up the graphics by removing any unwanted edges. After we finished editing each image, we applied a drop shadow to the entire button image. We finished the button by adding the text. (See Figures 11.9 and 11.10.)

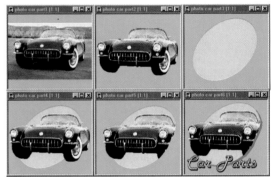

Figure 11.9.
Creating the photographic Car Parts button.

Figure 11.10.
Creating the set of five photographic buttons for the site.

Creating Effective 3D Navigational Graphics

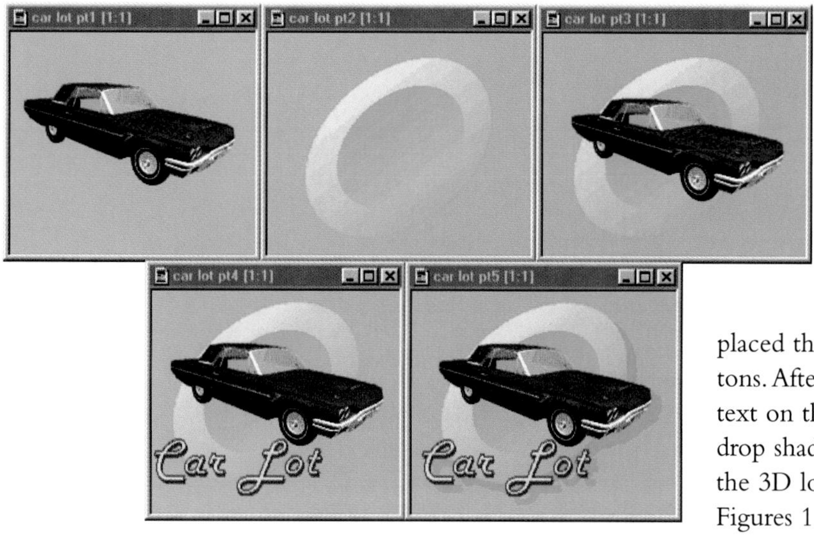

Figure 11.11.

Creating the 3D Car Lot button.

We decided to try something different and see what 3D navigational graphics would look like on our site. We thought 3D images might add a sense of sophistication to the site.

We created a few 3D images for our navigational button images. This time, we made oval-button templates using a 3D concave button. We used 3D rendered images and placed them on top of the buttons. After placing the images and text on the buttons, we added drop shadows to further enhance the 3D look of our images. (See Figures 11.11 and 11.12.)

Using Hypertext Links as Navigational Tools

For our home page, we made sure to include hypertext links near the top of the page. We placed these links right below the logo so that people could refer to them quickly without having to wait for all the graphics to download. (See Figure 11.13.)

Figure 11.12.

We wanted to see how 3D buttons might enhance our site.

At the completion of the first stage of our design, we decided to stick with using cartoon illustrations for all our graphics. We found that the drawings established the feel of the 1950s more than the photographic or 3D images we had created.

There was another good reason why we decided to stay with our cartoon illustrations. When you go to a car lot, how many times are you approached by one or more salesmen as you walk through their department? The last time we visited a car lot was when we had to pick up some spark plugs for our car. Before we reached the parts counter, at least three car salesmen came up to ask whether they could help us. By having the illustrations of car salesmen welcoming customers to the Web pages, we felt that we would be giving our Web site visitors that same experience of being welcomed to an actual car lot.

Reviewing the Aesthetics of Your Page

When designing the Car Parts page of our site, we noticed that something was not aesthetically correct on the page. After careful scrutiny, we decided to remove the illustration of the salesman in the Car Parts page graphic, because we were using the same illustration in our animated GIF right below it. We initially wanted to make the Car Parts page graphic consistent with the hot-linked graphic on our image map as we had done with our other pages. Aesthetics won over consistency in this part of our design process, though. (See Figure 11.14.) The original Car Parts page had one design error that was destroying the aesthetics of the page. In the right window, you can see that by removing the redundant car salesman illustration, we brought back the focus of the page.

Figure 11.14.

Now you see him, now you don't.

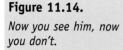

Maximizing Your White Space

Again, after looking at our Car Parts page even more closely, we noticed that we were not maximizing the amount of white space we could have used. The graphical elements seemed to be crammed toward the top of the page. We also noticed that the table of car parts did not have any breathing room around it. We decided to increase the white space on our page by adding <BR> between sections and narrowing the width of our table. By adding white space, we increased the readability and gave some balance to the page. (See Figure 11.15.)

Figure 11.15.

The original Car Parts page looked pretty cramped. A bit of white space made the page more readable and pleasant to the eye.

Ensuring the Continuity of Your Elements

We wanted to maintain a strong sense of continuity throughout Ade Meringue's Web site. We created a standard for all our graphical designs and stuck to it.

By using a few elements, such as the header elements, buttons, animated GIFs, and color schemes, we maintained the continuity of the site. We designed each of the buttons on the home page's image map to contain the same graphic on the Web page to which each was hot linked. We wanted the reader to recognize the graphic when he landed on the hot-linked page. Another element that connected the Web pages was the color scheme. We maintained the same color combinations on every page of the site. Finally, to complete the continuity, we included the same navigational buttons on every subsequent page that was linked to the home page to help the reader become familiar with the navigational images. (See Figure 11.16.)

Figure 11.16.

These three pages maintain a continuity of the elements from one page to another.

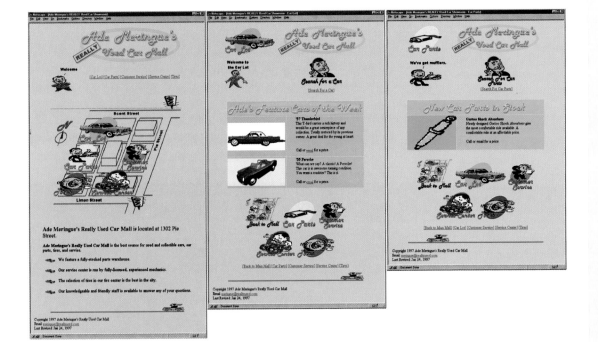

Ensuring Coherence Between Graphics and Text

Maintaining the coherence between our graphics and text was a problem for us at the beginning of our design, because of the retro color combination used for the main part of our site. We had to be careful to make the text clear enough against the background color of the page and the images themselves.

We found it difficult to read the text on the hot-linked graphics in our image map, because the white color of the text seemed to disappear into the background of the graphic. Also, the choice of the font we used added to the poor readability of our text. Because we wanted to make the text consistent with the Ade Meringue's Really Used Car Mall logo, we decided to refrain from changing the font type. To solve our dilemma, we added a darker shade of blue to the inside of the text. (See Figure 11.17.)

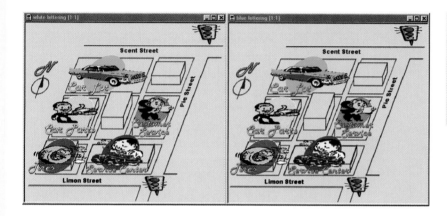

Figure 11.17.

The white lettering in the left image does not stand out. The blue lettering in the right image is much easier to see.

Placing Graphics Strategically

We were very careful with the strategic placement of the graphical elements for our site. We wanted to make the pages fun and inviting while still maintaining consistency.

We structured our Web pages first by dividing each of the pages into separate sections. We designated the top section to be the header section, which would contain the logo of the page and the Car Mall logo beside it. The middle section of each page contained information on the page itself—whether about the Car Mall or a car for sale. We included a section below the middle for the graphical and hypertext navigational elements. For the final section, we divided the copyright and e-mail information for the site using an animated horizontal rule.

By breaking down and defining each section of our pages, we found adding the graphics to be stress free. We made sure that the structure of all our pages did not leave too much room for the graphics to be accidentally misplaced. (See Figure 11.18.)

Figure 11.18.
We divided each page into the Header, Information, Navigational, and Footer sections.

Getting Your Message Across

When we finished the design of the Ade Meringue's Really Used Car Mall Web site, we made sure that every page delivered the message that this site is a great place to buy a car. We wanted to communicate to the reader that Ade Meringue's car lot is a fun, one-stop car shop for all auto-related needs. We incorporated little animated salesmen on every page to introduce the reader to the section of the car mall to which the page referred. (See Figures 11.19 and 11.20.) We created cute, animated, horizontal-rule images of cars racing across the page to add some humor. (See Figure 11.21.) Most important, we ensured that the content of each section was precise and straight to the point.

Figure 11.19.
The animated Car Lot salesman greets the reader.

Figure 11.20.

The animated Car Part salesman uses examples of car parts to help sell his page.

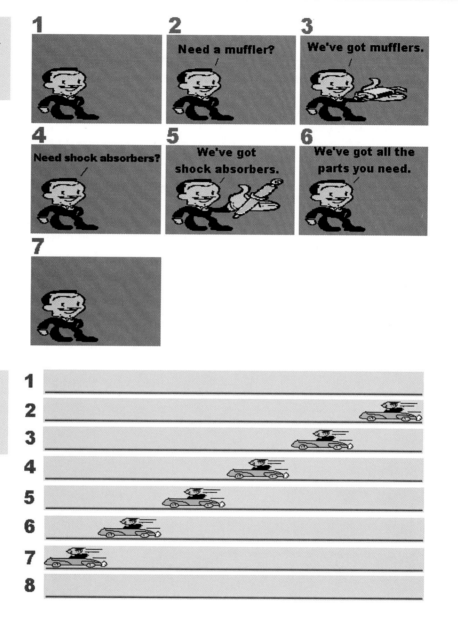

Figure 11.21.

This is a happy test driver traveling down the horizontal-rule road.

Testing Your User Interface

It is important to test the intuitiveness of the user interface before putting your site up on the Web. We asked a group of people to freely use and abuse Ade Meringue's newly designed Web site. We wanted our test subjects to be thorough and to show no mercy when going through each Web page. We wanted them to catch any inconsistencies we might have overlooked or missed. Before we presented the site to our client, we made sure that Ade Meringue's site went through the most rigorous testing our group could put it through.

Summary

Now that we have gone through and created the core of our Web site, let's review the major points in this chapter:

- ✦ When choosing elements to place on your site, try to stick closely to the metaphor while allowing your creativity to flow.

- ✦ Decide on a color scheme that best represents the site.

- ✦ Try to create navigational elements that belong within the metaphor.

- ✦ No matter how graphically intense your page is, always remember to add hypertext links.

- ✦ Review the aesthetics of your site. Try to look for elements that might clash, and add sufficient white space around your elements.

- ✦ Plan the location of your graphics. If you create a strong structure for your pages, it will be easier to add your graphics later.

Q&A

Q How can I know when to use illustrated, photographic, or 3D graphics as navigational elements?

A When choosing what type of navigational element to use, you first should have an overall feel of the site. If you are designing for a client, try to talk to the owner or employees. Look at their brochures to get an idea of what type of images they already use. If you're designing a site from scratch without any references, try to imagine what type of image you want to portray. Generally, illustrated images are good for general purposes or even a cartoon-like feel. Photographic images add a sense of realism to a page. 3D images can add a sense of realism, along with a technical feel, to a page.

Q Can I mix different graphical image types on the same Web page? If I have a 3D graphic, for example, is it OK to put it on a page with illustrated images?

A You have the freedom to add whatever type of graphics you want to your pages. You must keep some things in mind when mixing graphic types. You must make sure that all the graphics are related to the metaphor. You must review all the graphics to make sure that no graphics distract or detract from the other graphics on the page. Try not to have any graphics that stick out like a sore thumb (unless you want aching fingers on your page). Try to make sure that there is a balanced number of the different types of graphics and that no graphical types become lonely on your page. Surrounding a single photographic image with a sea of illustrated images may mean it's time to rescue that little photographic image and change its graphical type. You can place any type of graphic you want on your page, but the bottom line is to make sure that all the graphics work together as one to present your content in the best light possible.

Challenge
Yourself

In this section, we are going to get you to design a Web site from start to finish. We would like you to apply the tips and techniques shown here in this chapter.

Case Study

Ade Meringue asks you to design a test site for Ade Meringue's Really Used Car Mall. It is now your turn to test your design skills.

Your Mission

To create Ade's Car Lot page, Car Parts page, Customer Service page, Service Center page, and Tires page. You are free to choose the metaphor and to design the graphics you need to complete this section. The specific instructions for each page follow:

- ✦ Create two car images to be featured on the Car Lot page.
- ✦ Create two new stock items to be featured on the Car Parts page.
- ✦ Create a Customer Service page with this phone number: (555) CAR-MALL/(555) 227-6255.
- ✦ For the Service Center page, create a listing of the hours (8 a.m.–5 p.m., Monday through Friday) and a short listing of available services.
- ✦ Create a promotional page for Ade's new Laba Tires.

Required Tools

- ✦ Your computer
- ✦ A graphics editor
- ✦ Animated GIF software
- ✦ An HTML editor
- ✦ Your imagination and creativity

Supplied Elements

A copy of Ade Meringue's Really Used Car Mall logo on the accompanying CD-ROM.

Chapter 12

Quick Ways to Improve Your Future Designs

As you get into the stride of creating Web pages, you can use a few techniques to improve and speed up any future designs. By using graphics repertoires, style sheets, and templates, creating new Web sites can be as easy as picking relevant elements and plugging them into a Web page. We'll also show you a variety of design felonies to teach you how to keep yourself from falling into the same traps.

Creating Your Graphics Repertoire

Keeping a collection of your best graphics gives you the starting point you need for your future Web designs.

Illustrations, Photographs, and 3D Images

A good collection of illustrations, photographic images, and 3D images provides you with great reference material when it is time for you to design new graphics. Great ideas for designs often are inspired by other designs. Try to organize your graphical images in a directory where you easily can access them for future inspiration. (See Figure 12.1.)

Figure 12.1.

A collection of some of the graphical photos, 3D images, and illustrations used on our Web sites for this book.

Tip

Always save your original image at the largest size possible. Use a copy of the image for your designs, and reduce the size of the copied image after the design is complete. It is best to save your images in the highest quality possible until the graphic is completely ready for resizing. Unlike resizing a small graphic to a large one, resizing a large graphic to a small graphic helps maintain the quality of the image.

Bullets, Horizontal Rules, Icons, Symbols, and Navigational Buttons

Bullets, horizontal rules, icons, and navigational buttons are great to collect, because you can reuse them in many different designs. Always keep a copy of a template version of your buttons and navigational icons. This will save you from starting from scratch when you need to add another button to your Web page. (See Figure 12.2.)

Figure 12.2.

A collection of the bullets, icons, horizontal rules, and navigational button images we gathered from our Web designs.

Background Images

Images used for the background usually are generalized enough to use again for future sites. A textured background or one with a simple bar going down the left side is easy to modify to suit the needs of a new Web page. Specifically designed backgrounds, such as background logos, will not be appropriate for other Web sites. Keeping these backgrounds for visual reference gives you a useful guide for future background graphical designs, however. (See Figure 12.3.)

Figure 12.3.

A small collection of background images we used for our Web designs.

GIF Animations

An existing animation gives you the basic framework you can refer to when designing an animated GIF. You can determine the amount of delay, loops, and frames to use for future designs by looking at your current animated GIFs. You are more likely to improve your skills in creating animated GIFs by revamping your current collection. (See Figure 12.4.)

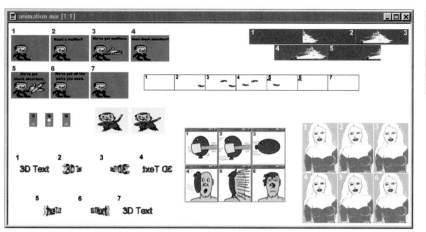

Creating Templates for Page Layouts

After you design a few Web sites of your own, you will notice a sense of style coming out in your designs. A good way to get your future designs off the ground is to create Web page templates by gathering together your best Web page designs.

To help you get started, we have put together a collection of Web page styles that you can use as a basis for future Web designs.

Web page templates give you a head start on your Web designs. This section presents some basic design ideas to help you create your own template pages.

A Two-Column Web Page Template

You can design a two-column Web page in several ways. We used table columns, rows, and the `BGCOLOR` attribute to arrange the elements on our page. (See Figures 12.5 and 12.6.) We placed our graphical elements in the first column of our page and the text in the second column. Of course, when you design your page, you can place the elements of your choice in either column. The top row spans two columns and contains our header graphic. The bottom row spans two columns and contains our navigational bar, complete with hypertext links.

Figure 12.5.

This two-column page layout is flexible and easy to maintain.

Result

```
<HTML>
<HEAD>
<TITLE>2 column</TITLE>
</HEAD>

<BODY BGPROPERTIES="FIXED" BACKGROUND="" BGCOLOR="#ffffff5" TEXT="#000000" LINK="#FF73EF"
VLINK="#72a8a1">

<P>

<!--Two column table begins here-->

<TABLE BORDER=0 CELLPADDING=0 CELLSPACING=0>
<TR><TD COLSPAN=3><CENTER><IMG SRC="header.gif" WIDTH=600 HEIGHT=140
BORDER=0></CENTER></TD></TR>

<!--Start column one-->

<TR><TD VALIGN="TOP" WIDTH=220 bgcolor="#FFDEFF">
<P>
<BR><BR>
<I>
Matt Martian has some wonderful stories to tell! Come visit his planet.
</I><CENTER><IMG SRC="man.gif" ALT=""></CENTER>
<P>
<P>
<CENTER><IMG SRC="dog.gif" ALT=""></CENTER>
<CENTER><I>
Did anyone say toys?</I>
</CENTER>
<IMG SRC="pink.gif" WIDTH=19 HEIGHT=15 BORDER=0>
</TD>
```

Figure 12.6.

The HTML source code for colomn 1 of our two-column page layout. You can find the entire HTML file on the CD-ROM in the section "Chapter 12: Quick Ways to Improve Your Future Designs."

HTML

Note

You are welcome to use the HTML templates on our CD-ROM by cutting and pasting your own Web page elements into the current placeholders on the page. Remember that these are only templates, though; we encourage you to revise or expand the design to suit your needs.

A Magazine Page Layout Template

We tried to simulate a magazine or newspaper layout for our magazine template. (See Figures 12.7 and 12.8.) The header consists of four separate graphics. We designed it this way so that parts of the header could be altered individually when needed. For the content of the page, we used columns. In the left margin, we placed our pullquotes or photos for our site. The middle column was reserved for our teaser material, with snippets of our page's main articles. The heading in this section links the reader to the page that contains the feature article. The footer section contains our copyright and contact information. We placed the graphical navigational bar at the bottom of the page. We also included hypertext links below the graphic and in the third column at the top of the page for our graphically challenged readers. We placed graphics and icons in certain columns to help break up our text.

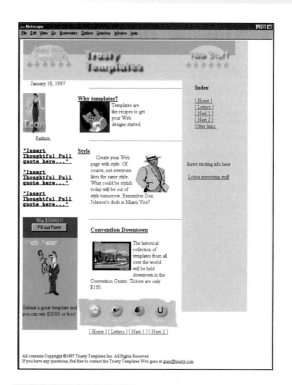

Figure 12.7.

This template can help you start a future Web page with a magazine page layout.

Result

Figure 12.8.

The first part of the HTML source code for our magazine page layout template. You can find the entire HTML file in the Chapter 12 section on the CD-ROM.

```
<HTML>
<HEAD>
<TITLE>Magazine template</TITLE>

<BODY background="background2.gif" bgcolor="#FFFFFF" vlink="#0066cc" text="#000066" link="#3333cc"
alink="#ffcc00">

<!--We have incorporated tables within tables to get the magazine feel for our page-->

<TABLE BORDER=0 cellpadding=0 cellspacing=0 width=600 align="center">
<TR valign=top align=left>
<TD valign=top align=left> <!--Insert 1st table-->

<TABLE width=122 border=0 cellpadding=0 cellspacing=0>
<TR><TD COLSPAN=2 VALIGN=TOP ALIGN=LEFT bgcolor="#EFDE9C">
<IMG SRC="line.gif" ALIGN=TOP VSPACE=0 HSPACE=0 BORDER=0 WIDTH="20" HEIGHT="20"></TD></TR>

<TR><TD COLSPAN=2 VALIGN=TOP ALIGN=LEFT bgcolor="#EFDE9C">
<IMG SRC="leftlogo.gif" ALIGN=TOP WIDTH="168" HEIGHT="87"></TD></TR>

<TR><TD COLSPAN=2 VALIGN=TOP ALIGN=LEFT HEIGHT=36>      January 18,
1997<br><br></TD></TR>

<TR><TD COLSPAN=1 VALIGN=MIDDLE ALIGN=LEFT HEIGHT=44><IMG SRC="woman.gif" VSPACE=0 HSPACE=0
BORDER=0 ALIGN=TOP WIDTH="70" HEIGHT="120"></TD>

<TD COLSPAN=1 VALIGN=MIDDLE ALIGN=LEFT HEIGHT=44></TD></TR>

<TR><TD COLSPAN=2 VALIGN=MIDDLE ALIGN=LEFT HEIGHT=44><a href=""><font size=2><BLOCKQUOTE>Fashion
</BLOCKQUOTE></a></TD></TR>
```

HTML

A Submission Form Template

Our submission form was organized by using the basic elements of design, such as the header, body, and footer. (See Figures 12.9 and 12.10.) We arranged the input fields inside a small table. We placed the navigational buttons below the form along with the hypertext links. We wanted readers to have an option to leave this page if they decided to not fill out the form.

Win a really used car from Ed Meringue's Car Lot

Application Form

Name:

Address:

City: Province: Postal Code:

Telephone: Fax: E-Mail:

Submit Application   Reset

showroom   tires

service   customer

[tires] [customer service] [showroom] [service center]
[Top][Home]

© 1997 - Meringue Ltd.
All Rights Reserved

Web site designed by http://www.yourcompany.com

Email: yourcompany@interspin.com

Document Done

Result

Figure 12.9.

A simple, basic Web page with a submission form.

Figure 12.10.

The first part of the HTML source code for Ed Meringue's submission form. You can find the entire HTML file in the Chapter 12 section on the CD-ROM.

```
<HTML>
<HEAD>
<TITLE>Submission Forms</TITLE></HEAD>

<BODY BGCOLOR="#42F7D6" BACKGROUND="" TEXT=#0000A0 LINK=#FF0000 VLINK=#008080>


<A NAME=top></A>

<TABLE BORDER=0 WIDTH=100%>
<TR>
<TD ALIGN=LEFT VALIGN=TOP>
<IMG SRC="header.gif" BORDER=0 vspace=0 hspace=0 alt="">
</TD>
</TR>
</TABLE>


<CENTER><B><I>
<FONT SIZE=+3 Color="#0000A0" FACE="Arial">
Application Form</FONT></I>
</B>
</CENTER>

<form action="/cgi-bin/cgiwrap/yourcompany/cgiscript" method="POST">
<INPUT TYPE="hidden" name="recipient" value="email@yourcompany.com">
<INPUT TYPE="hidden" name="redirect" value="http://www.yourcompany.com">

<center>

<TABLE CELLPADDING=0 CELLSPACING=1 WIDTH="600">
<TR><TH COLSPAN=3><H3><HR></H3></TH></TR>
<TR><TD COLSPAN=3><B>Name:<BR><INPUT TYPE=text NAME="NAME" SIZE="50" MAXLENGTH="50"></TD></TR>
<TR><TD COLSPAN=3><B>Address:<BR><INPUT TYPE=text NAME="ADDRESS" SIZE="50"
MAXLENGTH="55"></TD></TR>
<TR><TD><B>City:<BR><INPUT TYPE=text NAME="CITY" SIZE="15" MAXLENGTH="33"></TD>
<TD><B>Province:<BR><INPUT TYPE=text NAME="STATE/PROVINCE" SIZE="14" MAXLENGTH="33"></TD>
```

HTML

A Catalog Page Template

We designed our Sleek Models page using a three-column table for our template. (See Figures 12.11 and 12.12.) We placed the hypertext links of each model's name in a row above the graphic so that the graphics and text would line up evenly. The header logo is an image map containing the page's navigational links.

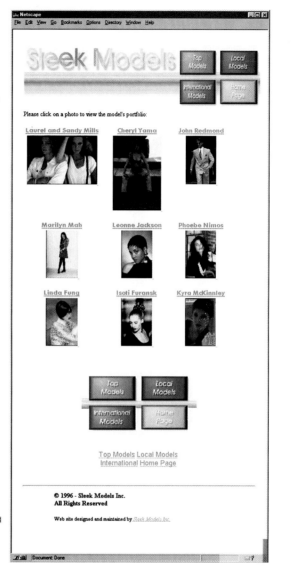

Result

Figure 12.11.

Our Sleek Models Web page uses a three-column table to display the models in the catalog.

```
<HTML>
<HEAD>
<TITLE>Catalog Template</TITLE>
</HEAD>

<BODY BGCOLOR=#FFFFFF TEXT=#000000 LINK=#FF732F VLINK=#F9A22D ALINK=#

<img src="sleek.jpg" vspace=0 hspace=0>
```

Please click on a photo to view the model's portfolio:
```
<BR><BR>

<CENTER> <!--Insert Catalog page-->
<TABLE BORDER=0 WIDTH=100% align=center>
<TR>
<TD WIDTH=33.3% ALIGN="CENTER">
<font color="#F9A22D" face="Futura MD BT"><A HREF=""> Laurel and Sandy Mills </A></font>
</TD>

<TD WIDTH=33.3% ALIGN="CENTER">
<font color="#F9A22D" face="Futura MD BT"><A HREF=""> Cheryl Yama </A></font>
</TD>

<TD WIDTH=33.3% ALIGN="CENTER">
<font color="#F9A22D" face="Futura MD BT"><A HREF=""> John Redmond </A></font>
</TD>
</TR>

<TR>
<TD WIDTH=33.3% ALIGN="CENTER" VALIGN="TOP" VALIGN="TOP">
<A HREF="">
<img src="mod1.jpg" alt="" border="0">
</A>
<BR><BR>
</TD>
```

HTML

Figure 12.12.

The first part of the HTML source code for our catalog page layout template. You can find the entire HTML file in the Chapter 12 section on the CD-ROM.

A Chart Template

Charts are wonderful for displaying large
amounts of information. We have provided
you with a six-column chart template. We
used the **BGCOLOR** attribute in the table cells
to give you an idea of how you can use
color to differentiate sections of your chart.
(See Figures 12.13 and 12.14.)

Figure 12.13.

*Bernard's Web page
uses a chart to display
its Top 10 hits.*

```
<html>

<head>

<title>Chart Template</title>
</HEAD>

<BODY BGCOLOR="#FFFFFF" text="#295252" link="#76BABA" vlink="#4D9999">

<CENTER><IMG SRC="header.jpg" WIDTH=400 HEIGHT=90 BORDER=0 alt="">
</CENTER>


<center>
<table border=2 cellpadding=1 cellspacing=1 width=100%>

<tr>

<th bgcolor=#FFC0A2>This<br>week</th>

<th bgcolor=#FFC0A2>Last<br>week</th>

<th bgcolor=#FFC0A2 align=center>Song</th>

<th bgcolor=#FFC0A2 align=center>Singer</th>

<th bgcolor=#FFC0A2 align=center>Song writer</th>

<th bgcolor=#FFC0A2 align=center>Weeks<br>on chart</th>


</tr>
<tr>

<td bgcolor=#D2A6A6 align=center>    01    </td>

<td bgcolor=#D2A6A6 align=center>    12    </td>

<td bgcolor=#D2A6A6>    Gotta Stick in My Hand    </td>

<td bgcolor=#D2A6A6>    Tanya Hardy    </td>

<td bgcolor=#D2A6A6 align=center>    Baby Drool    </td>

<td bgcolor=#D2A6A6 align=center>    100    </td>


</tr>
<tr>

<td bgcolor=#D2A6A6 align=center>    02    </td>

<td bgcolor=#D2A6A6 align=center>    67    </td>

<td bgcolor=#D2A6A6>    Bubble gum in my hair    </td>

<td bgcolor=#D2A6A6>    Shaved Head    </td>

<td bgcolor=#D2A6A6 align=center>    Barrie Maninlaw    </td>

<td bgcolor=#D2A6A6 align=center>    30    </td>


</tr>
<tr>

<td bgcolor=#D2A6A6 align=center>    03    </td>

<td bgcolor=#D2A6A6 align=center>    66    </td>

<td bgcolor=#D2A6A6>    Up in my Hot Air Balloon    </td>

<td bgcolor=#D2A6A6>    Head Cheese    </td>

<td bgcolor=#D2A6A6 align=center>    Cheryl Crone    </td>

<td bgcolor=#D2A6A6 align=center>    50    </td>


</tr>
<tr>
```

Figure 12.14.

*The first part of the
HTML source code
for our chart tem-
plate. You can find
the entire HTML file
in the Chapter 12
section on the
CD-ROM.*

Creating Templates for Frame Layouts

Designing a frame-based Web page can be a bit tricky. To help you get a good head start with your designs, we have included a couple of frame templates. We designed a basic two-column and three-row frame template. (See Figures 12.15 through 12.18.)

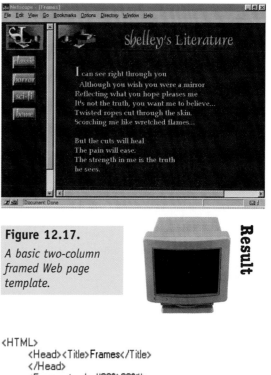

Figure 12.17.

A basic two-column framed Web page template.

Figure 12.15.

The Shelley's Literature page uses a three-row frame template.

```
<html>
<head>
<title>frame template 1</title></head>

<frameset rows="105,*,50">

    <frame name="banner" scrolling="no"
        noresize src="banner.html">

    <frame name="content" scrolling="yes"
        noresize src="content.html">

    <frame scrolling="no" noresize src="toolbar.html">

</frameset>
</html>
```

```
<HTML>
    <Head><Title>Frames</Title>
    </Head>
    <Frameset cols="20%,80%">
    <frame src="frame1.html" scrolling="auto"
    frame name="Directory" marginheight=3 marginwidth=3>
    <frame src="frame2.html" scrolling="auto"
    frame name="Contents" marginheight=3 marginwidth=3>
    </Frameset>
    <Noframes>
    Your browser does not support frames...this is where the
    <A HREF="noframes.html">non-frames version</A> of
    Internet Resources is available.
    </Noframes>
</HTML>
```

Figure 12.18.

The HTML source code for the frame page of our two-column frame template. You can find the complete HTML files in the Chapter 12 section on the CD-ROM.

Figure 12.16.

The HTML source code for the frame page of our three-row frame template. You can find the complete HTML files in the Chapter 12 section on the CD-ROM.

Developing a Standard for Your Web Designs

You always should determine the standard at which you design your sites. You can apply our basic rules of thumb for Web designing to your own sites. Here are some of the standards we apply to our designs:

- ◆ Keep your graphical and other elements to less than 100KB.
- ◆ You can make your graphics size smaller by reducing the number of colors in your graphic's color palette.
- ◆ Use thumbnail graphics on pages that use extensive graphics.
- ◆ Don't let your animated GIFs loop endlessly.
- ◆ Try not to use more than 10 frames in your animation to keep the file size down.
- ◆ When dividing up sections of information, try to use white space instead of horizontal rules.
- ◆ Don't design your site around plug-ins.
- ◆ Make your navigational elements easy for your reader to understand.
- ◆ Be consistent in all aspects of your design.

You probably will come up with more specific standard requirements that you would like to apply to your Web designs. It is a good idea to keep a checklist of your own standards to refer to later.

Great Combinations! Font Types, Sizes, and Colors

You can put together great font combinations by being consistent with your font types and sizes on your page. The effect of a delicately handwritten font type is utterly destroyed when placed beside text displayed in a bizarre, jagged type. (See Figure 12.19.)

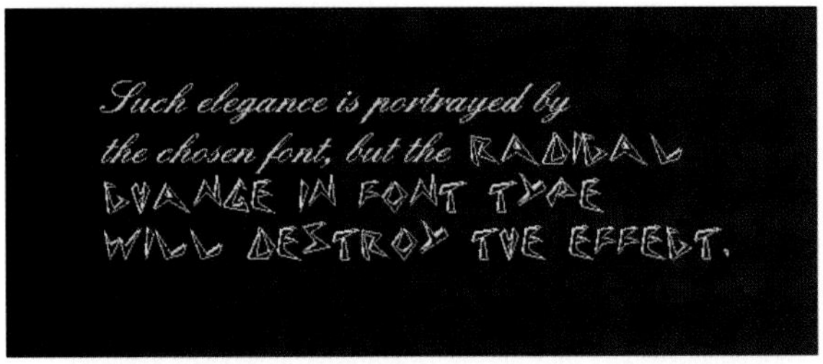

Figure 12.19.
A nice, quaint, handwritten message blown away by a bizarre-looking new font.

You can use varying sizes of the same font type when you need a larger font for headings. You also can slightly increase the size of words that you want to emphasize. Try to use only a small selection of font types and text on your page. (See Figure 12.20.)

Fortunately, text color is not limited to black and white. Your text can be displayed in all the colors of the rainbow. In addition, you can create a nice, subtle effect by making the background and text different shades of the same color. A light blue background with dark blue text gives a Web page a very pleasant look, for example. (See Figure 12.21.)

Figure 12.20.

Using the same font type effectively in different sizes.

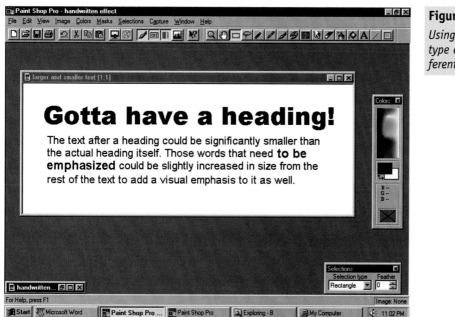

Figure 12.21.

Subtly matching the color of your text and background elements.

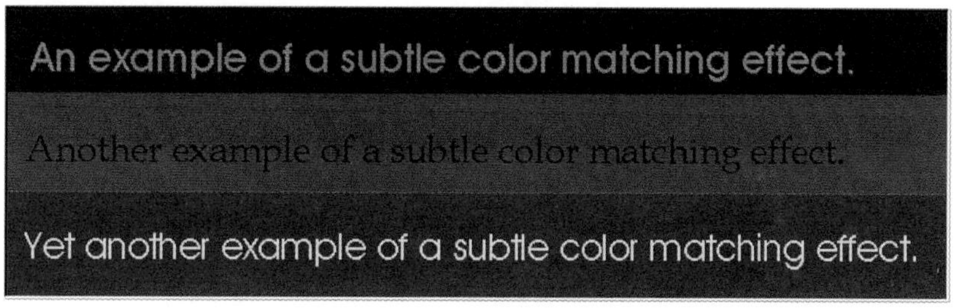

An example of a subtle color matching effect.

Another example of a subtle color matching effect.

Yet another example of a subtle color matching effect.

Caution

Remember that you can show different fonts in two ways: with the HTML <FONT> tag and with a graphical text format. As mentioned in Chapter 1, "Web Page Elements: What Design Elements Go into a Web Page?," fonts defined with your HTML <FONT> tag might not be seen by your reader if he does not have the same font on his computer. Try to avoid using any obscure fonts that you find on sale at the bottom of the bargain bin.

Design Felonies

The Web can be an ugly and murky place to surf when faced with Web designs that should be prosecuted for visual injustice. Here are a few of the famous design errors that should put a Web page in jail.

Mixing Your Types

Consistency of font types and sizes might not seem like a huge issue, but you'd be surprised at how the inconsistency of font types can destroy the aesthetics of a Web page. Determine the most effective font size for your headings by sizing the font from largest to smallest, depending on the heading's importance on the page. Keep your headings consistent throughout your site. Likewise, keep the font type and size for your body text the same on all your Web pages. Applying these simple tips adds to the quality of your Web designs. (See Figures 12.22 and 12.23.)

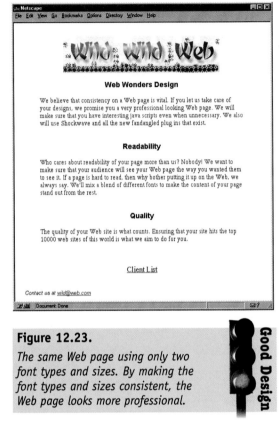

Figure 12.23.

The same Web page using only two font types and sizes. By making the font types and sizes consistent, the Web page looks more professional.

Good Design

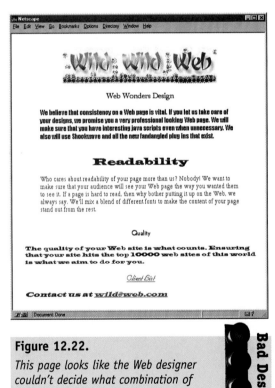

Figure 12.22.

This page looks like the Web designer couldn't decide what combination of font types and sizes to use.

Bad Design

Graphics Life Sentences

Clipart should be used only as an embellishment to your graphics designs. What we see most commonly on the Net is the overuse of clipart on a single Web page. Even worse, some sites use a combination of free clipart with free, crappy, animated GIFs. Free clipart usually has a distinct flavor that most readers can pinpoint a mile away. Which would you prefer—a bowl of your grandma's homemade soup or something that crawled out of a can? An original graphic gives your site more impact than a graphic that has been used all over the Net. (See Figure 12.24.)

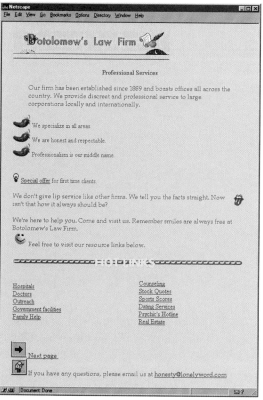

Bad Design

Figure 12.24.

Now can everyone say the word cheesy? This Web page would have been better off without using any graphics.

Bad Design

Figure 12.25.

You'll need a bottle of aspirin to help you get through this site.

Color Injustice: What's Black, Red, and White All Over?

Some color combinations on the Web are absolutely nauseating to look at. We recently visited a site that had a puke-green, textured background with red text and brown graphics splashed all over the page. If the designers were trying to make their audience sick, they most certainly achieved their goal. It is amazing to count the number of awful color combinations out there on the Web. We counted at least 20 sites in one day. Fortunately, you can avoid any color injustice at your site by carefully choosing effective color combinations with the help of the color wheel. You can find the color wheel in Appendix B, "Color Reference Guide." (See Figure 12.25.)

Capital Crime

Capitalization of words and phrases might seem like a legitimate way to bring emphasis to your text. In reality, however, capitalized text is as annoying as never-ending animated

GIFs. Capitalized words can make readers feel like they are being shouted at. EVEN WHEN IT IS NOT INTENDED TO, CAPITALIZED TEXT CAN MAKE ANY WORD OR PHRASE SEEM LIKE YOU ARE SHOUTING. Instead of adding emphasis to the word or phrase, capitalized text only alienates or annoys your readers. GET THE PICTURE?

The Never-Ending Story

It is easy to get off track when putting the content into your Web designs. Many Webmasters add personal, irrelevant things to their Web page just because they happen to be the Webmaster. If your site is a professional site, we don't want to see pictures of your pet parakeet or a list of your favorite TV shows right smack dab in the middle of it all. If the content is not relevant to the overall message of the site, it doesn't belong there. Try to avoid adding personal opinions and comments to your home page. Many sites these days seem to contain long, exhausting explanations of why the Webmaster added this or that to a Web page. Although it might be interesting to some people, not all members of your audience want to see your life story on the home page. The best thing to do in this situation is to keep comments or personal opinions on a separate page altogether.

Summary

Now that we have shown you quick ways to improve your future Web designs, let's review the major points in this chapter:

- Keep a collection of your best graphics in one easily accessible file. You never know when you will need some inspiration to help you design new graphics.

- After you design a few Web sites of your own, you will notice a sense of style coming out in your designs. It is always wise to keep templates of your best Web designs stashed away for future use.

- Keep your font type, color, and size consistent throughout your site. A little consistency goes a long way.

- Don't use color combinations that will blow your reader away. Concentrate on making the color combinations of your site pleasant to the eye.

- Never capitalize your text to emphasize a word or a phrase. Capitalizing words is the same as shouting them to your reader.

- When designing your Web site, remember to stick to the point. Don't add irrelevant information, personal comments, or opinions to your home page.

Q&A

Q **Won't saving all my graphics and HTML files use up all the space on my hard drive? How can I keep all my templates and graphics?**

A We suggest that you back up as much as you can on tapes or disks. Keep everything you think you might need again. Keep graphics that can give you a good starting point for future graphical designs. If you don't have much space in which to store your files, reduce your collection only to the very best of your Web designs. For items that are borderline on the to-keep list, it might be sufficient to keep a paper copy of the element that you can file away for future reference.

Q If I use templates for my designs, isn't that cheating? Also, won't my Web page end up looking like a cookie-cutter design?

A First of all, you should use a template only as a basis for a Web design. You should use templates as a foundation for the design of your Web page. After the foundation is established, you can improvise, revise, and expand the Web page to suit your purposes. In answer to the second question, a cookie-cutter Web page design will occur only if you completely rely on the template without letting your creativity evolve from it.

Challenge Yourself

Now it's time for you to collect all the Web site elements you worked on in the "Challenge Yourself" sections of this book. With the items you designed for your projects, you will build your own graphics repertoire and collection of templates.

Your Graphics Repertoire

Organize your graphics into categories (such as backgrounds, illustrations, photos, bullets, horizontal rules, buttons, and so on). If you have a lot of items to organize, you might want to break down the major categories into smaller sections, such as dog photos, car illustrations, circle bullets, and rectangular buttons. The more precise you are, the easier it will be for you to find a particular image in the future.

Your HTML Templates

Organize your HTML templates into categories (such as frames templates, chart templates, magazine templates, and so on). If necessary, create subdirectories for your templates (such as fancy frames, two-column layouts, creative magazine layouts, and so on). The more styles of Web pages you collect, the easier it will be for you to come up with ideas for future designs.

Multimedia and What the Future Holds

Interactivity: Making Your Web Site Come Alive with Multimedia

In this chapter, we will discuss ways to add interactivity to your Web page with audio and video files. You'll learn how to optimize your audio and video techniques to give the greatest impact to your pages. We will show you a few current technologies that allow a higher level of interactivity to be added to your Web sites. You'll learn about each of these technologies and which ones might be the best choices for you.

Incorporating Video into Your Web Pages

The Web is an exciting medium where people can obtain and publish information. Because larger bandwidths now are available, other mediums are finding their place on the Web. A reader now can download video right off the Net, for example. This opens up many possibilities for professional and amateur video producers alike. The capability for any Joe off the street to broadcast video over the Net is a very frightening thought indeed. Important design issues must be addressed when developing appropriate video files for the Web; we will discuss these issues briefly in this chapter.

Considering Video-Compression Types

A few different video formats are popular on the Web. Choosing the right format for your video is the first step when incorporating video into your pages.

QuickTime

QuickTime is a popular video file format for the Mac and Windows; it was developed by Apple Computer. QuickTime is a great tool for developing video because of its cross-platform capability. You can download QuickTime from

```
http://quicktime.apple.com
```

QuickTime is available for both the Mac and Windows.

AVI

Audio Video Interleave (AVI) is a format supported by Video for Windows. The disadvantage of the AVI format is that it must be converted to a suitable format when viewed on a Mac.

MPEG

The *Motion Picture Experts Group* (MPEG) is a standard developed specifically for video compression. The major disadvantage of this format is that the video and audio portions of an MPEG video are split into two separate files. Because the information is in two separate files, proper sequencing must be attained in order for the files to be displayed properly. Another disadvantage of using MPEG is that designers need dedicated MPEG-encoding hardware to create MPEG videos. The average cost of an encoder is about $1,000, which the average designer might not be willing to dish out.

Tips on Movie Editing for the Web

Editing and producing digital videos are definitely not trivial tasks. Reducing the file size of a digital video for acceptability on the Web can mean destroying the quality of the video itself. Therefore, you must be careful when editing the number of frames in your video to provide the best results.

Less Is More

The size of the frame that displays the video is measured in pixels. The smaller the frame size, the smaller the size of the file. File size is crucial when developing video for the Web, so the goal is to reduce the size of the frame as much as possible. A standard size for a Web-based video is 160×120 pixels. A smaller-sized video frame drops the file size to a point where it makes the video more bearable to download. In Figure 13.1, we show you two video files. The larger file is set at 320×240 pixels, whereas the smaller video file is set at 160×120 pixels. Each video contains five frames per second, with a total of three seconds per video. When the video clip was produced in AVI file format, the size of

Figure 13.1.

The left video window is 320×240 pixels and is 274KB. The right video window is 160×120 pixels and is 85KB.

the large video clip was 274KB. When we reduced the size of the frame around the video, the file size shrunk to 85KB.

Your Frames Are Numbered

When designing for the Web, you also have to consider the number of frames in a video file. Normally, full-motion videos run at 30 frames per second. For Web purposes, you can reduce the number of frames to anywhere from 1 to 15 frames per second. You determine the number of frames to reduce by considering the content, frame size, and length of the original video.

Controlling the manageability of a video's file size means comparing the frame size to the number of frames in the video. If you cannot reduce the frame size any more, reduce the number of frames in the video.

For Clarity, Label It

To incorporate a link to your video file in your HTML document, simply use the `<A HREF>` tag and point it to the location of your video file. (See Figure 13.2.) After the reader clicks on the reference link, the browser downloads the video for viewing.

Tip

You can remove more frames without losing much of the content when the movement in the video is slow and minute. A video of a cruise ship going across the water only has the motion of the boat moving forward, for example. You can reduce the file size of the video by chopping out frames that show only a small change in movement. To get the best results, view the video a number of times in various frame sizes and frame counts. To keep the file size small, you might have to sacrifice some element of the video, whether it be the frame size or frame count.

Go ahead, `<A HREF="video.wav">play my video file.</A>`

Go ahead, play my video file.

HTML

Figure 13.2.
Linking your video in HTML.

Give your reader an opportunity to decide whether downloading your video will be worth his while. You can do this by indicating the content, file size, and format of your video on your Web page. (See Figure 13.3.) It isn't funny for a reader to find out after the fact that the 8MB video he waited 30 minutes to download is actually a video of the Webmaster doing his aerobic workout.

```
<A HREF="video.wav">A video clip of my new rock video</A>
<BR>
Format: 160x 120 .AVI
<BR>
Length: 20 seconds
<BR>
File Size: 632 K
<BR>
```

A video clip of my new rock video
Format: 160x 120 .AVI
Length: 20 seconds
File Size: 632 K

HTML

Figure 13.3.
A link that is much more informative for the reader.

Tips for Making Web-Based Audio Files

Audio on the Web is constantly changing and evolving. At present, only a few standard audio formats are supported on the Web. Unfortunately, audio files still have the similar size-restraint problems that plague video files on the Web. When creating your audio file, try to keep the file size down so that it does not take forever to download.

Audio File Formats

Here are the popular audio file formats and the platforms that support them:

It is always a good idea to save your audio file in multiple formats so that more people will be able to download and enjoy it.

- ✦ Audio Interchange File Format (.AIFF) for Macintosh systems
- ✦ Windows Wave format (.WAV) for Windows systems
- ✦ Sun Audio (.AU) for UNIX systems

Downloaded Versus Streamed Files

A *downloaded* audio file can be played only after it is selected and transferred in its entirety to the user's computer. The user does not have the option of listening to anything prior to downloading the entire file, so a silent lag time exists between the start of transfer and the playing of the file. The amount of time it takes to download an audio file depends on the audio file size and the modem speed of the user's computer.

Streamed audio refers to a continuous stream of uninterrupted audio fed to and played by the user's computer in small, manageable chunks. No download time exists other than a few brief seconds of initial buffering. Streamed audio is great for lengthy audio and real-time broadcasting. On the downside, it might take more than just having a link to the audio file to play a streamed audio file. A Web server might need to run the required software to stream the audio over the Net.

Choosing the Quality Best Suited for Your File

Digitally recorded sound basically is composed of sample rate, bit depth, and number of channels.

- ✦ *Sample rate* is the rate at which the audio is recorded in kilohertz. The four rates commonly used are 44.1KHz (CD quality), 22.05KHz (FM radio quality), 11KHz (AM radio quality), and 8KHz (low quality).
- ✦ *Bit depth* is the range between the loudest and softest sounds. A digitally recorded sound can be 8-bit or 16-bit in depth.

◆ *Number of channels* refers to mono or stereo recording. An audio file that has only one channel of recording is called *mono*, and an audio file with two separate channels for left and right is called *stereo*.

When deciding which rate to make an audio file for a Web page, you should consider a few design issues. Of course, the main concern is the file size of the audio file.

You can select a sample rate and bit depth that will produce the best-quality sound for your audio file. A music audio file requires a higher sample rate and bit depth to obtain the best quality possible for the range of sounds. For audio files that contain mainly dialogue, a lower sample rate and bit depth are acceptable, because the range of sounds is not as wide. Each step down in the quality reduces the audio file size by half. You won't find too many 44KHz, 16-bit stereo (CD quality) audio files on the Web unless they are very short in length.

Ultimately, your desired file size will help determine the quality of audio file you use. You must anticipate the length of time your audience will want to wait for the file to download. If your audio file is a bootleg version of Bryan Adams' latest CD, your user might consider waiting the 30 minutes for it to download. There is a trade-off in quality versus length. If you want a high-quality audio, you must keep it short. If you want to keep it long, you have to sacrifice the quality.

Note

Stereo uses two channels recorded simultaneously to give depth to the audio. Mono records only one channel. An audio file recorded in mono therefore needs only half the space that a stereo audio file needs.

Designing a User-Friendly Audio File Link

As with video files, each audio file should be clearly labeled on the Web page with the description of the content, file extension, total time of the clip, clip size, and recording information (sample rate, bit depth, and number of channels—mono or stereo). This information helps the reader select the files that are compatible with his hardware and software. To link your audio file from an HTML file, simply use the <A HREF> tag. (See Figure 13.4.)

```
<A HREF="audio.wav">An audio clip from my new rock CD</A>
<BR>
Format: .WAV
<BR>
Length: 20 seconds
<BR>
Sampled at 22.05 kHz, 16 bit Stereo
<BR>
File Size:  1.7 MB
<BR>
```

An audio clip from my new rock CD
Format: .WAV
Length: 20 seconds
Sampled at 22.05 kHz, 16 bit Stereo
File Size: 1.7 MB

Figure 13.4.
An audio link on a Web page.

Play It Again, MIDI

Musical Instrument Digital Interface (MIDI) is a popular standard for musicians. It is also an up-and-coming format for playing music over the Web. MIDI (.MID) files save the instructions for playing a certain piece of music instead of the sample sounds themselves; the .WAV format saves the sounds. Speaking metaphorically, a .WAV file can be compared to an actual audio tape of the music, whereas a .MID file would be the sheet music or instructions to play the music.

HTML

With a .MID file, the instructions are downloaded to the reader's computer, translated, and played back by the sound card. Because a .MID file only contains the instructions for playing a musical score, the file is quite compact. This makes .MID files great for delivering music over the Internet. A one-minute .MID file is usually about 10KB. Compare this to a one-minute .WAV file, which can run from 1MB to 10MB or more, depending on the audio quality you choose. You can quickly see that unless the reader has a gigantic amount of patience and hard-drive space, he would prefer to download the smaller .MID file instead of the huge .WAV file.

Note

Unlike .WAV files, which capture the actual sample of a sound, a .MID file's playback quality depends on the quality of the reader's sound card. As better sound cards become more and more affordable, the quality of these .MID files definitely will improve. The one major drawback of .MID files versus .WAV files is that, because .MID files only contain instructions and not samples of music, a MIDI player cannot play any sound outside the set number of sounds that the sound card contains. Because .WAV files are an actual sample of the sound, they can contain anything from unique tribal instruments to a singer's actual voice.

Designing Audio Files with RealAudio

The biggest difference between RealAudio files and other audio formats is the capability to stream the files over the Internet instead of downloading them. This means that larger audio files can be played over the Net without having to be downloaded.

Progressive Networks provides streaming technology on the Web via its RealAudio software. The sound quality of streamed audio is comparable to that of AM radio. The RealAudio format requires a RealAudio plug-in to hear the files. Progressive Networks provides three software components with RealAudio: the RealAudio Player, RealAudio Encoder, and RealAudio Server. (See Figure 13.5.)

Figure 13.6 shows how the streaming works with RealAudio. It follows this process:

1. The user requests the URL from the Web server.
2. The server sends the URL of the file back to the user's computer.
3. The RealAudio Player is launched.
4. The RealAudio Player requests the audio file from the RealAudio Server.
5. The audio file is streamed back to the user's RealAudio Player.
6. The user hears the audio file on his computer.

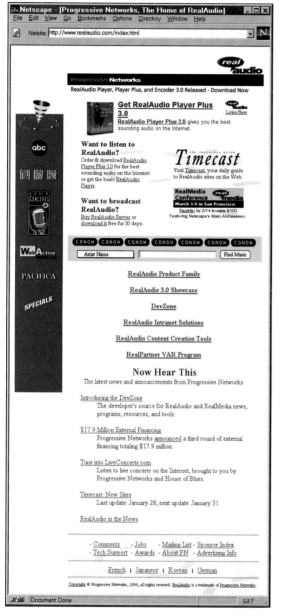

Figure 13.5.

You can find more information about RealAudio at Progressive Networks' Web page at `http://www.realaudio.com/index.html`.

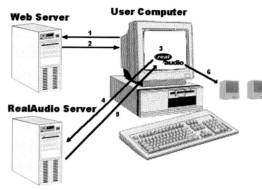

Figure 13.6.

The steps in getting the audio file to stream to the user's computer using RealAudio.

To create and play a RealAudio file, you need the RealAudio Encoder and Player. Transforming sound files into the RealAudio format is as easy as starting the RealAudio Encoder, loading up the audio file, picking the desired compression, and clicking the Start Encoding button. The Encoder converts the file into an .ra file that can be played with the RealAudio Player. (See Figure 13.7.)

RealAudio or .ra files can only be heard when using the RealAudio Player. RealAudio is becoming popular because of its capability to play live, streamed audio broadcasts over the Net. RealAudio is useful for people who want to broadcast live, online talk shows and interviews over the Net.

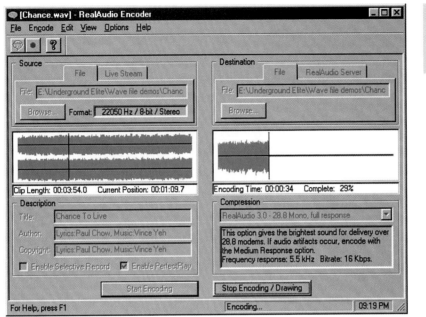

Figure 13.7.

The RealAudio Encoder hard at work churning out our audio file.

Putting the Metafiles in the HTML

To place the reference to the RealAudio file into the HTML of the Web page, you must create a metafile that contains the URL address of the RealAudio sound file. The extension for this file would be .RAM, which stands for *RealAudio metafile*. To broadcast a RealAudio file, you have to store your sound files on a RealAudio Server in order for the sound to be streamed over the Internet. The protocol in the URL for the RealAudio Server must start with `pnm://`. Therefore, a reference to the RealAudio sound file would look like this:

```
pnm://realaudioserver/pathname/
audiofilename.ra
```

This file would be saved with the RealAudio metafile extension (.RAM).

To place your sound file onto the Web page, simply add an `<A HREF>` tag pointing to the metafile URL address. An HTML line with a link to a metafile, for example, might look like this:

```
<A HREF="http://realaudioserver/
myaccount/chance.ram">Play the File</A>
```

That's it. Readers now can listen to your streamed audio files. (See Figure 13.8.)

Interacting with CGI

Common Gateway Interface (CGI) enables the user to interact with the Web site. A user sends a request using the CGI's interface, which then sends the request to the server. The server then comes up with a response and sends it back to the reader. A variety of interactive tasks can be developed using CGI, such as a search engine for a site, data retrieval from an online database, and on-the-fly Web pages containing unique content tailored by the reader's requests.

An advantage of CGI is that it can be written in any language capable of understanding standard input, output, and environmental variables. The languages can range from interpreted script languages such as Perl

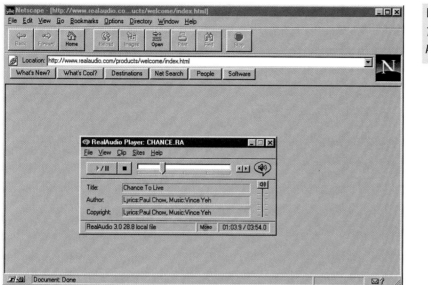

Figure 13.8.
The RealAudio Player playing a favorite tune.

(*Practical Extraction and Reporting Language*) to compiled languages such as Pascal and C++. This gives the programmer the flexibility to choose a language that he is already familiar with.

A Web designer who wants to develop CGI files has to know a programming language that can be used to program CGI files. If the designer does not know anything about computer programming, he could still add premade CGI scripts to his sites. Many sites out on the Web have CGI scripts available. All the designer has to do is search the Web for free CGI scripts or CGI that can be purchased, and then install it in the CGI bin of his Web server. (See Figure 13.9.)

Stirring Things Up with Java

Java is a programming language developed by Sun Microsystems specifically for the Web. Java allows you to add dynamic interaction to your Web page by running small programs called *applets* on your hard drive.

Although Java is a very dynamic and robust programming language, it is still that: a programming language. If an average Web designer has never programmed in Java and wants to quickly throw together a Java applet or two, he should at least have a basic understanding of a computer programming language such as C++. This basic background is recommended before it truly becomes viable to dive straight into Java programming. If a designer doesn't have any programming knowledge but wants to spend the time to learn, Java is a great starting point for Web-related programming.

If programming is still not on the Web designer's list of the most important things to learn, he can purchase and/or download Java applets to use on his sites. He then can configure the Java applet as he wants.

Although a majority of browsers are Java-enabled, some readers disable their Java capabilities for security reasons. It is important to ensure that the elements on your Web page are not Java-script dependent. (See Figure 13.10.)

Figure 13.9.

Many Web sites on the Net feature collections of CGI scripts. This page containing free CGI scripts is called Dave's Perl/CGI page and can be found at http://www.upstatepress.com/dave/perl.shtml.

Figure 13.10.

You can download the latest Java Development Kit at http://www.javasoft.com/products/JDK/1.1/.

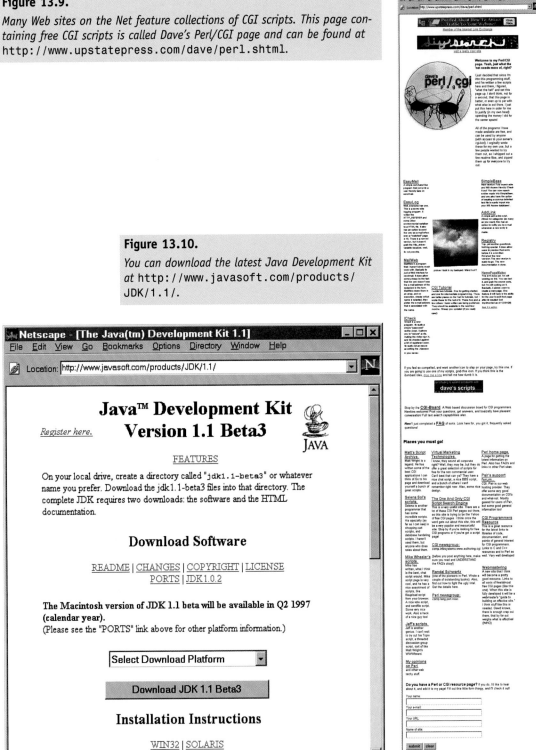

Applying Design Principles to VRML Design

With *Virtual Reality Modeling Language* (VRML), a designer can create an entire three-dimensional virtual world of his own. The designer can build whatever he wants, limited only by his imagination. He can even link objects within the virtual worlds, thereby enabling him to send a reader through an endless maze of 3D landscapes.

You can design VRML worlds by learning the VRML language and typing the language into an editor, or by using software that allows you to intuitively create a world. The route of typing the language code is best saved for the most diehard graphics programmer. The quicker and easier route is to spend the money and pick up a VRML editor.

VRML is very cool and fascinating, but even it cannot escape design principles. You must justify having a VRML world on your site. Does it add to the overall content of the site, or is it there just because it's so cool? Some sites go with the "because it's so cool" answer. These sites with VRML usually make the reader wait expectantly as time slowly ticks while the VRML world loads into his browser. After the download completes, the reader is totally disappointed to find only the company's logo, which he already saw on the home page, floating in the middle of dark cyberspace.

If VRML is an absolute necessity on your Web site, make sure that you keep an eye on the size of the graphic. A reader might want to wander your 256 hectares of Martian canyons, but if it takes 10 minutes to load, it will put off even the most enthusiastic interplanetary explorer. (See Figure 13.11.)

ActiveX?

ActiveX, which was developed by Microsoft, is a technology that allows interactive objects, called *ActiveX controls*, and non-HTML documents, called *ActiveX documents*, to be embedded on Web pages. An ActiveX-enabled browser allows ActiveX controls to run and provides interactive and user-controllable functions. ActiveX documents allow the reader to view non-HMTL documents through an ActiveX-enabled browser.

Figure 13.11.

VRMLSite Magazine is located at
`http://www.vrmlsite.com/.`

A programmer can use a wide assortment of programming languages and tools to develop ActiveX controls. If the designer is familiar with developing *object linking and embedding* (OLE) applications, his knowledge and skills easily can be transferred to ActiveX development. If he does not have OLE programming knowledge, there are thousands of companies out there that do, so he easily can obtain ActiveX controls.

Because an ActiveX control can be as involved and complex as a mini-program, size might be an issue in low-bandwidth situations. This technology is still being developed, so designers who want to make their Web pages ActiveX-enabled should keep an eye on new developments in the ActiveX field. (See Figure 13.12.)

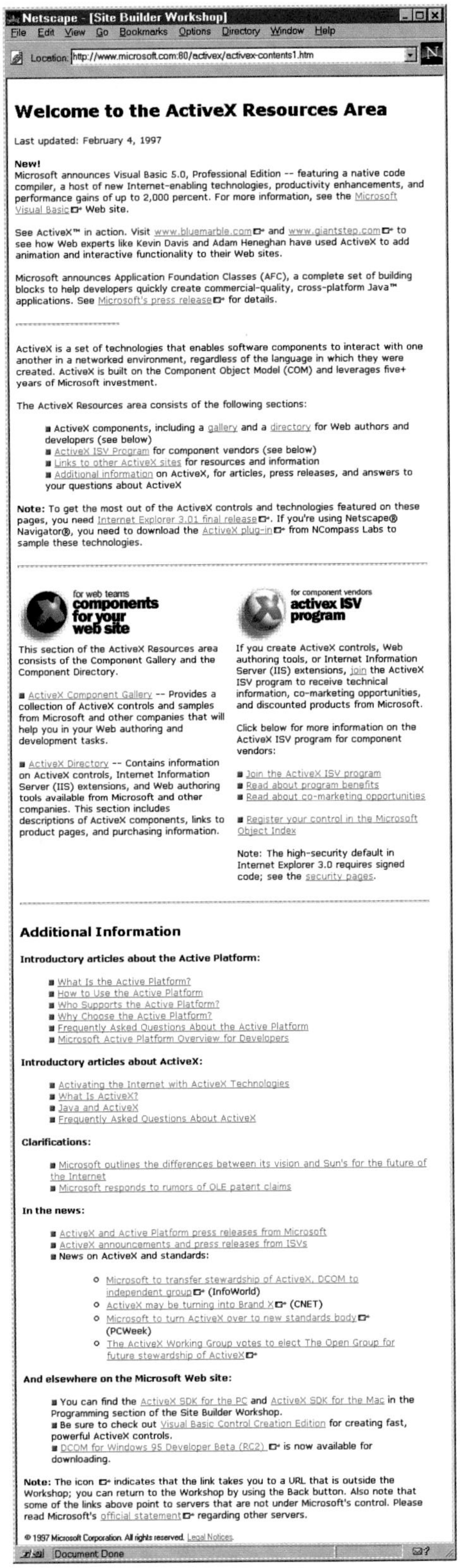

Figure 13.12.

This ActiveX resource page by Microsoft is at `http://www. microsoft.com:80/activex/activex-contents1.htm`.

Shockwave: Designing with Multimedia Director

Macromedia is a leading provider of multimedia authoring tools. Shockwave is the Web-enabling add-on to its popular multimedia applications. Shockwave comes in three flavors of plug-ins: Shockwave for Director, Shockwave for Authorware, and Shockwave for Freehand. With the appropriate plug-in loaded on a browser, a reader can download and view multimedia files on Shocked Web pages. The type of multimedia files can range from visual tutorials to games. Shockwave enables you to add a new type of multimedia interactivity to your Web page.

For the Shockwave developer, a second necessary component in the Shockwave technology is Afterburner. Because the reader has to download the multimedia file before he can view it, the size of the file is a concern. Afterburner compresses Macromedia's multimedia files so that they can be more easily downloaded when embedded in a Web page.

Figure 13.13.

You can find the latest information on Shockwave at Macromedia's Shockwave Central Web page located at `http://www.macromedia.com/shockwave/`.

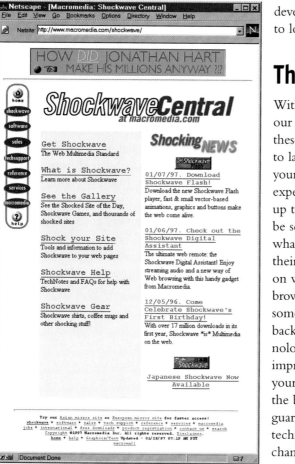

For the average Web designer who wants to develop Shockwave applications, the price for Macromedia's authoring tools might be a bit hefty. But for a designer who wants to learn multimedia development that can be used on computers as well as on the Web, Macromedia development tools might be worthy applications to look into. (See Figure 13.13.)

The Bleeding Edge

With so much new technology being shoved in our faces every day, one has to wonder which of these new, fancy thingamadoobobs is really going to last. Using the latest, greatest technology on your Web page might be an awesome learning experience, but if your readers have not caught up to you in the technology department, they'll be scratching their heads trying to figure out what in the world you are trying to do and why their browsers are crashing every time they click on what seems to be a harmless link. A crashing browser is probably not the best incentive for someone to stay on your page, much less come back. It might be wise to wait for the new technology to develop and show signs of continued improvement before diving in and redesigning your sites around it. Using a technology that is the biggest and best new technology today is no guarantee that it will be around tomorrow. If a technology does not develop and adapt to the changes, it might eventually go the way of the woolly mammoth. So research the technology before you decide to invest your time in learning how to use it.

With all the newbie surfers on the Net these days, a designer has to consider the usability of his site. Imagine surfing the Web for the first time and hitting a site that has buttons labeled `Java Enabled`, `Shockwave Enabled`, `RealAudio Enabled`, `ActiveX Enabled`, `Java with ActiveX Enabled`, `Shockwave and ActiveX But Not Java Enabled`, `Java and RealAudio But Not ActiveX Enabled`, and `Glow in the Dark Enabled`. It would be absolutely frightful for the surfers who would have to download and install enough plug-ins to fill their 1GB hard drive. Technology is great and should be pursued, but the basic HTML Web page will continue to be the foundation on which to build Web pages.

Summary

Now that we have gone through interactivity on a Web site, let's review the major points in this chapter:

- ✦ Video files can become very large, so try to make them small by using a smaller frame size and reducing the number of frames.

- ✦ Clearly label a downloadable video file with the content, size, and format of the video.

- ✦ Because there are many types of systems on the Net, try to convert audio files into more than one format.

- ✦ To reduce the size of the audio file, reduce the sample rate, bit depth, and number of channels (mono/stereo).

- ✦ Each audio file should be clearly labeled with the file extension, description of the content, total time of the clip, clip size, and recording information (sample rate, bit depth, and number of channels—mono/stereo). This allows the reader to select the files that are compatible with his hardware and software.

- ✦ Try to use new technology on a Web site sparingly. Designing with the basics in mind ensures the widest range of usability.

Q&A

Q What if I have a five-minute video that I want to play over the Internet?

A You can do a few things. One is to pray that your reader has the mega-patience to wait as the download indicator bar ever so slowly inches its way across the screen. Another thing you can do is reduce the screen size to the minimum size possible, being sure that the video still will be recognizable when it plays. You also can compress the file for downloading and hope that the reader doesn't mind the extra step of uncompressing your video file before it can be played. Looking toward the future, watch for the development of streamed video across the Web. Just as streamed audio has allowed longer length audio files to be played over the Net and people to hear live audio transmitted files, the continuing development of streamed video should open up the same possibilities.

Q With all this new technology coming out for Web page designing, how do I know which one to choose, and how do I keep up?

A Always remember that HTML is the foundation of Web page design. It might seem to be a classic, but it is still the most reliable way to get your information across the Web. As for new technology, try keeping up with newsgroups, visit the developer's site, surf around and look at what is being used and what is not, and read magazines that focus on Web design. Get a number of opinions (make sure that it's not just propaganda) and consider the options. Remember that an informed decision is usually a good decision.

Challenge
Yourself

In this section, you will explore the possible plug-ins and development tools used to design interactive Web pages.

Case Study

Follicle Follies, your new client, is paying you to research the newest Web technologies on the market. They want you to recommend to them which of the new technologies is worth implementing on their Web site.

Your Mission

Pick a few new Web technologies and research the pros and cons on the Net. You can ask yourself the following questions to help start you off in your exploration:

- How new is this technology?
- Is it in the beta stage, or has it been released?
- Is there good support for it from the developer?
- How many people actually use it?
- Is there a good third-party support for it, or do I have to constantly go back to the developer?
- Are functions or code available to be viewed or even downloaded?
- Do a number of professionals consider it a leading technology that will stick around?

The Future of Web Design

What does the future hold for the development of Web page design? Nobody knows for sure what's going to happen in the world of Web design, but we can all contribute in some form by discussing the issues that need to be addressed. In this chapter, we give you a wish list of what we want to see happen to the Web, HTML, and anything else that deals with the Internet. We also look into the crystal ball and discuss the changes that may be on the horizon and the changes that are happening on the Web today.

A Designer's Wish List

It will be a dream come true when all browsers recognize the importance of typographic and layout elements on a Web page. Giving designers more control over the appearance of a page will make our jobs a lot easier. We have put together a little wish list that we hope will become a reality one day soon.

Small Caps

It would be nice if we could have an HTML tag that allowed us to apply SMALL CAPS to some of our text. Right now, the only way to achieve this is to use the SIZE attribute in the <FONT> tag. We know that having the capability to have a small caps tag would only have an aesthetic purpose on a Web page. But wouldn't it be great to be able to apply small caps to headings or pullquotes, for example? Perhaps this is a silly wish, but it's a wish all the same.

> **Note**
>
> With *small caps*, all the letters in a word are in capitals, and the first letter is larger than the rest of the text. The word FANTASTIC is displayed in small caps, for example.

Give Us a Footnote Tag

We would like to see a footnote tag become a standard in the HTML 3.2 specifications. Currently, we only have two options to format a footnote. The first is to place the footnote at the bottom of the Web page and manually format the text by italicizing it or using the `<ADDRESS>` tag. The other option is to use hypertext to point to the footnote information located on a separate Web page. More likely than not, a reader won't bother to click on the link just to read the footnote.

Printing Capabilities

Although the Web is not meant for the paper medium, it would be nice to be able to control what we print out. Have you ever tried printing out a Web page that contained a background image? If you have, you might have noticed that the printed copy of the site does not contain the background image. Okay, we agree that most people can probably live with that. What bugs us is printing what we think is a single Web page, only to find out too late that the page being printed is actually 20 pages and is causing our little bubble-jet printer to go into convulsions. It is impossible to guess the length of a Web page just by looking at your screen. Right now, the only way to work around this is to go to the print preview screen, look at the footer information to see which page you want printed, and then select the desired page number from the Print command itself. Why put readers through this torture just for one stupid page? We suggest that browsers add a button to allow the reader to print only the current screen of a Web page, or give him the choice to print what he wants instead of what the browser wants.

Are There Any Smart Search Engines Out There?

Have you ever used a search engine to search for something specific on the Web, only to get 1,468,290 irrelevant matches to the keywords you typed in? Wouldn't it be wonderful if we had search engines that were capable of accurately bringing up Web sites that relate to what you are actually searching for on the first try? We once did a search specifically on the topic of Web design tips, using the advanced power search techniques that the search engine offered. But instead of getting links to what we were looking for, we got a list of links to commercial Web design companies, a cartoon knowledge site, a greeting card site, an editorial cartoon site, and other unrelated sites. On that first page, there was not even *one* accurate hit to a site that contained Web design tips. (See Figure 14.1.)

As a Web designer, it is frustrating to launch a site, only to find that when you try to bring up your Web page on a search engine, your site comes up as 5,344 on the search list. Sure, you could use as many fancy `<META>` tags in your HTML code to help search engines index your Web pages, but it would be much nicer to see a search engine that does more than match the most number of keywords on a site.

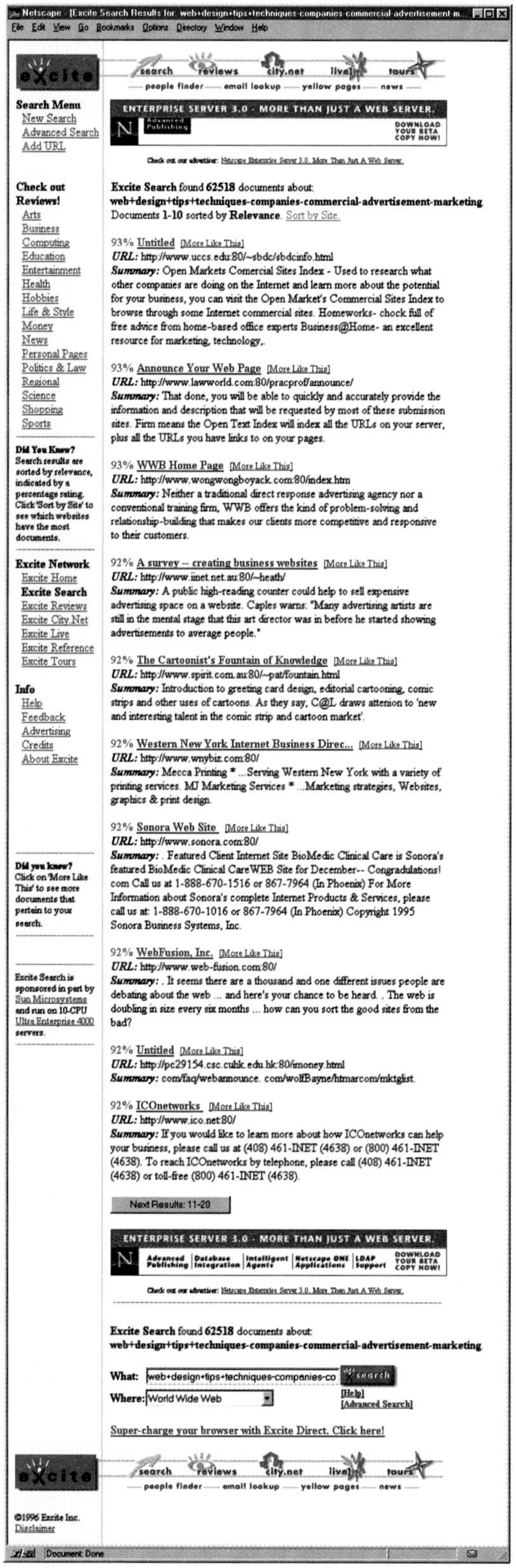

Figure 14.1.

Now can you find any links to Web design tips on this search results page?

How about a search engine that can match a user's search query to the exact topic and content of a particular site? Or a search engine that can filter out crappy, useless Web pages from honest-to-goodness informative and appealing ones? Okay, that might be asking way too much, but there's no harm in asking. Hopefully, though, someone out there will be able to design the perfect search engine that will bring up accurate and intelligent search results that inevitably will benefit both users and Web designers alike. Ya never know…

Give Us a Style Sheet Editor

Style sheets soon will be adopted by the latest and greatest browsers in the market. Some browsers today already support a number of style sheet features, such as Microsoft Internet Explorer 3.0. What we need is for someone to develop a WYSIWYG or text-based style sheet editor that makes designing style sheets for Web pages much easier. HTML is one thing to master, but having to learn style sheet properties and attributes is another thing. Yeah, yeah, we know we're just whining. Once we start designing a few style sheets, it probably won't be so bad. Still, a style sheet editor would be a nice treat, don't you think?

Transparent JPEGs? Are You Nuts?

It would be wonderful to make 24-bit color, transparent images. The capability to make multiple colors transparent would help eliminate the slight noise effect that JPEG compression usually creates in an image. If we could assign transparency to multiple colors in a JPEG image, we could choose a single color in the background of the image to be made transparent. Perhaps if we were able to make more than one color transparent by controlling the tolerance level of the transparency, we could make the whole background area of a JPEG image transparent. Being able to make both JPEG and GIF images transparent would give Web designers better control over the design of their graphics and the look of their Web pages.

JPEG Animation

How about an animated JPEG image? Is this a farfetched idea or what? We mention this wish because we often have the desire to use photographic-quality images for our animations. An animated GIF currently is restricted to 256 colors. We would like to see a JPEG animation format supported by all major browsers. The file size of an animated JPEG would be yet another issue to discuss, though. More colors in the color palette of an image could mean a bigger file size for the JPEG animation. Perhaps someone out there could address all these issues and design a format that would allow an animated JPEG to compress to a smaller file size without deteriorating the quality of the image. Or, perhaps someone could design a completely new, 24-bit color animation format that could compress the file size considerably while maintaining the clarity of the images in the animation. Until that time, or when video over the Internet becomes the norm, we will have to settle with using animated GIFs for our Web design.

HTML 3.0 Specifications for Cascading Style Sheets

Speaking of style sheets, what in the world are they? The idea of style sheet formatting isn't something that was dreamed up by some colorful Web visionary undergoing a transcendental, out-of-body experience. In fact, advanced desktop publishing software has supported the idea of style sheet formatting for years. Okay, that still doesn't explain what it is, but we're getting there…

Style sheets eliminate the redundant formatting of every single element on a page by defining the properties of the elements separately from the content of the page itself. In plain English, when you define an element, such as a heading, you only have to do it once. That's right! No more formatting the <FONT> tags for all the different textual elements on your page. No more worrying about having to reformat the style of individual elements every time your client decides he wants to change the font color and size of all the headings on his pages.

With style sheets, you only have to redefine the property of the element that needs reformatting, which in this case is a heading, and—voilà—the headings on all the Web pages that link to the style sheet information are reformatted automatically.

Link, Global, and Inline Style Sheets

You can implement style sheets on a Web site by linking them to separate HTML pages, embedding them at the top of the HTML page, or applying the style to the element itself.

A *linked* style sheet has the advantage of being able to format numerous Web pages at once. This style is great when you need to apply fancy, complicated formatting to more than one Web page.

An *embedded* or *global* style sheet definition is used to apply formatting to an individual page. The style properties are defined in the <STYLE> tags in the head of the HTML file. Here is an example of a page that uses the embedded feature:

```
<html>
<style type="text/css">
<!--font color: blue}
p   {font-size: 12pt color: green}-->
</style>
<body> </body>
</html>
```

An *inline* style sheet definition applies style formatting directly to individual elements. If you want to format a hypertext link to have the font size of 25 points with a purple Comic Sans MS type, for example, you would format it as follows:

```
<A STYLE="font-size: 25pt; color: purple; font-family:
Comic Sans MS" HREF="http://www.link.com">More links to
see</A>
```

Note

All three style sheet features (link, global, and inline) can be used simultaneously on any given Web page. These style sheets are described as *cascading* style sheets because of the browser's capability to override one style with another. If more than one style is applied to a page, the global or embedded style overrides a link style, and the inline style overrides all styles.

Beware

For Web designers who apply design principles to their work, style sheets are the answer we've all been waiting for. In the hands of wanna-be Web designers who lack any sense of design skill, however, style sheets can be a tool of destruction. Many self-proclaimed Web designers who know a few HTML tags already are polluting the Web with hideous and grotesque pages. We don't need style sheets to help them add to the ugliness.

One more thing to stress is that style sheets are in no way going to replace HTML. HTML is

Figure 14.2.

The HTML source for Microsoft's sample style sheet.

the language that provides structural importance to the elements on the page, whereas style sheets are the means by which to format the elements based on their structural definitions. Pages designed with a style sheet still should incorporate proper HTML structure tags throughout the page to ensure that the page is viewable on style sheet–disabled browsers. A reader with a style sheet–disabled browser should be able to understand the page. The reader with a style sheet–enabled browser should not only understand the page, but also see the wonderful (or not so wonderful) enhancements defined by the style sheet properties.

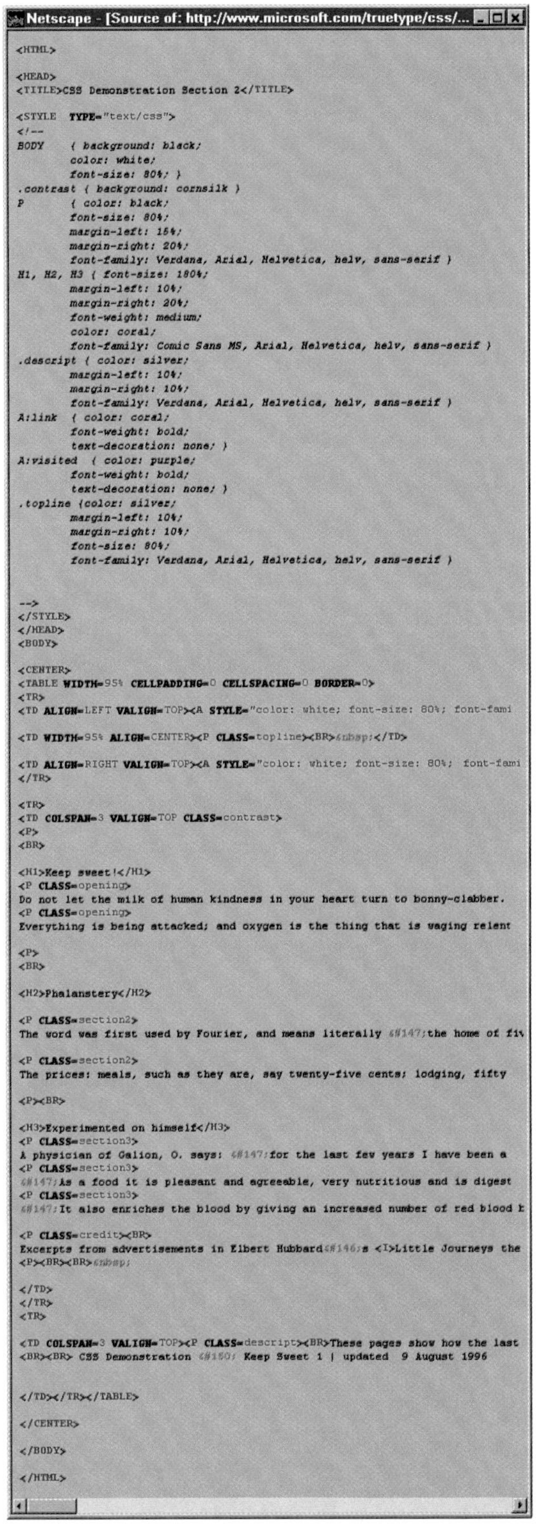

The Future of Style Sheets

Currently, the *World Wide Web Consortium* (W3C) has recommended the specifications for cascading style sheets, which hopefully will be implemented by updated versions of browsers within the year. Microsoft Internet Explorer 3.0 currently supports some cascading style sheet features and probably will support even more in a newer version. Netscape Navigator probably will support the CSS standard in Navigator 4.0. You can find more information about the proposed standards for cascading style sheets at http://www.w3.org/pub/WWW/Style/ and http://www.w3.org/pub/WWW/TR/.

```
Netscape - [Source of: http://www.microsoft.com/truetype/css/...

<HTML>

<HEAD>
<TITLE>CSS Demonstration Section 2</TITLE>
<STYLE TYPE="text/css">
<!--
BODY    { background: black;
          color: white;
          font-size: 80%; }
.contrast { background: cornsilk }
P       { color: black;
          font-size: 80%;
          margin-left: 15%;
          margin-right: 20%;
          font-family: Verdana, Arial, Helvetica, helv, sans-serif }
H1, H2, H3 { font-size: 180%;
          margin-left: 10%;
          margin-right: 20%;
          font-weight: medium;
          color: coral;
          font-family: Comic Sans MS, Arial, Helvetica, helv, sans-serif }
.descript { color: silver;
          margin-left: 10%;
          margin-right: 10%;
          font-family: Verdana, Arial, Helvetica, helv, sans-serif }
A:link  { color: coral;
          font-weight: bold;
          text-decoration: none; }
A:visited  { color: purple;
          font-weight: bold;
          text-decoration: none; }
.topline {color: silver;
          margin-left: 10%;
          margin-right: 10%;
          font-size: 80%;
          font-family: Verdana, Arial, Helvetica, helv, sans-serif }

-->
</STYLE>
</HEAD>
<BODY>

<CENTER>
<TABLE WIDTH=95% CELLPADDING=0 CELLSPACING=0 BORDER=0>
<TR>
<TD ALIGN=LEFT VALIGN=TOP><A STYLE="color: white; font-size: 80%; font-fami

<TD WIDTH=95% ALIGN=CENTER><P CLASS=topline><BR> </TD>

<TD ALIGN=RIGHT VALIGN=TOP><A STYLE="color: white; font-size: 80%; font-fami
</TR>

<TR>
<TD COLSPAN=3 VALIGN=TOP CLASS=contrast>
<P>
<BR>

<H1>Keep sweet!</H1>
<P CLASS=opening>
Do not let the milk of human kindness in your heart turn to bonny-clabber.
<P CLASS=opening>
Everything is being attacked; and oxygen is the thing that is waging relent

<P>
<BR>

<H2>Phalanstery</H2>

<P CLASS=section2>
The word was first used by Fourier, and means literally &#147;the home of fri

<P CLASS=section2>
The prices: meals, such as they are, say twenty-five cents; lodging, fifty

<P><BR>

<H3>Experimented on himself</H3>
<P CLASS=section3>
A physician of Galion, O. says: &#147;for the last few years I have been a
<P CLASS=section3>
&#147;As a food it is pleasant and agreeable, very nutritious and is digest
<P CLASS=section3>
&#147;It also enriches the blood by giving an increased number of red blood b

<P CLASS=credit><BR>
Excerpts from advertisements in Elbert Hubbard&#146;s <I>Little Journeys the
<P><BR><BR> 

</TD>
</TR>
<TR>

<TD COLSPAN=3 VALIGN=TOP><P CLASS=descript><BR>These pages show how the last
<BR><BR> CSS Demonstration &#150; Keep Sweet 1 | updated  9 August 1996

</TD></TR></TABLE>

</CENTER>

</BODY>

</HTML>
```

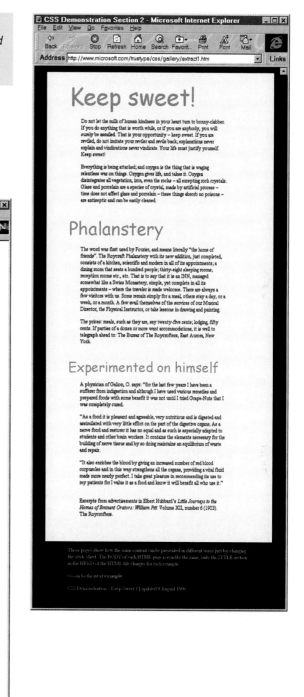

Figure 14.3.

Microsoft's style sheet example, which you can find by going to http://www.microsoft.com/ truetype/css/gallery/extract1.htm.

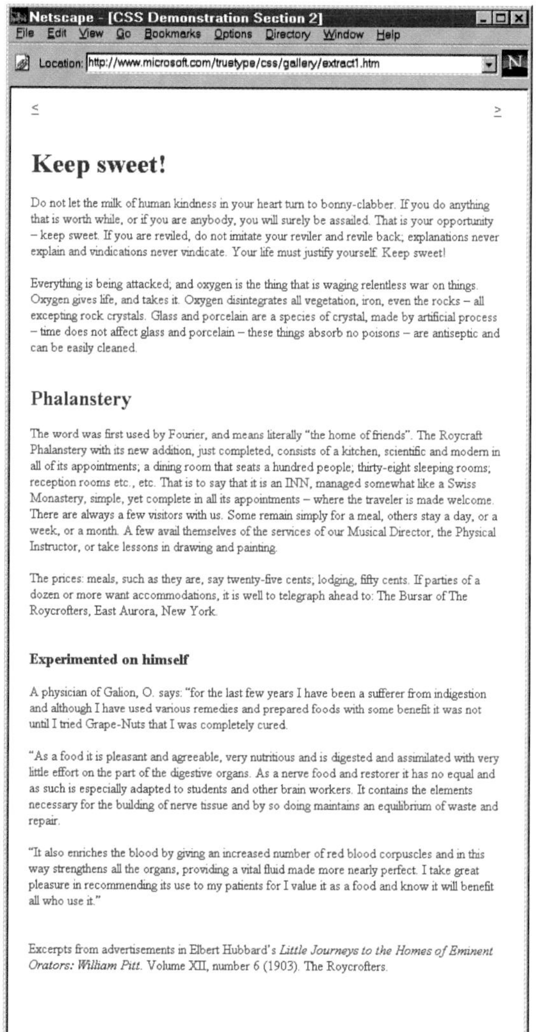

Figure 14.4.

The same page shown in Figure 14.3 when viewed on a style sheet–disabled browser.

Adobe PostScript: The Designing Possibilities

Currently, font format standards do not exist on the Web. The proposal for using Adobe's PostScript language or Microsoft's TrueType fonts as a standard for the Web is an idea that excites many Web designers. With standardized fonts, Web designers can anticipate that their designs will appear the way they were intended to be seen. The Web designer can specify the line spacing, heights, and text widths without worrying that the page layout will be altered because the reader does not have a particular font.

The problem is how to implement the standard so that it is supported by many platforms. Will a reader have to download a package of fonts before he can see them on a Web page? Will he have to purchase the fonts first? When he receives the fonts, is he expected to install them himself? Now, realistically, a reader probably will laugh in your face (or at least at your Web page) if he sees a note on your page like this:

```
To view this page with the proper fonts, please download
a Fonts Package for only $19.99. To download the fonts
package, click here now. You will find a read-only text
describing how to install them onto your hard drive.
Please read it carefully before installing. Thank you,
and have a nice day.
```

A Possible Solution

One solution to the lack of font-formatting standards would be to transport read-only, embedded fonts over the Web. This solution would provide two main benefits. First, the quality of the font would remain intact on the reader's screen. Second, the font would not be used for any other purpose than to display on the Web page. It then would be the Web designer's—not the reader's—responsibility to purchase the fonts he needs for his Web page. Using embedded fonts in an HTML document also relieves the burden of having the reader install the fonts himself.

Using TrueType Fonts

Microsoft's answer to cross-platform Web fonts is TrueType fonts for the Web. Microsoft provides a collection of free TrueType fonts, a royalty-free TrueType rasterizer program that enables any platform to view the fonts, and the technology to embed the fonts into your HTML page when desired. It seems that with these things happening, Web designers and Web audiences alike can have their cake and eat it, too.

> **Note**
>
> Microsoft's *TrueType* fonts are outline fonts that contain instructions for the rasterizer to interpret. A *rasterizer* is a software program that interprets how to display the appearance of the font as a bitmap image.

What we want to know is, *what's the catch*? At this point, only Internet Explorer 3.0 supports TrueType fonts. In addition, you have to download the fonts onto your hard drive. If you think about it, font files can be quite large and probably would take up a lot of space. Other than that, it seems that Microsoft is paving the way for Web font capability on the Web. (See Figure 14.5.)

Figure 14.5.

Microsoft's Typography page at http://www.microsoft.com/truetype/fontpack/default.htm.

OpenType Fonts

Adobe and Microsoft are working on a new font specification called *OpenType*, which will increase the font capabilities on the Web. This font format combines the PostScript and TrueType technologies as one standard font format for the Web. OpenType promises to be supported on many different platforms, to give designers more control over typography, and much more.

> **Note**
>
> *OpenType* is a font format that will give Web designers the capability to place high-quality fonts into their Web pages. These fonts are supposed to give Web designers control over the textual look of the Web pages without the worries of increasing the download time. You can find more information about OpenType fonts at Microsoft's site (http://microsoft.com.:80/truetype/faq/faq9.htm).

Type Control

Because we are on the brink of finally having a standard for Web fonts, there are still a number of things to consider.

Embedding Fonts

If embedding fonts is really going to be the wave of the future, readers still should have the overall choice of deciding whether they want to view an embedded font. People who are visually challenged, for example, might not be able to view a font-specified page. Also, some people just prefer to use their own fonts and view the Web the way they want to, instead of the way a Web designer tells them to.

Font File Size

We must also mention that the file size of the fonts should not increase the download time of your Web pages dramatically. If embedded fonts make a Web page 10 times slower to download, no one will be willing to use them.

Typographic Capabilities

Web designers would like to have kerning, tracking, and other typographic support for their designs. Yes, we know that we're asking for just a little too much, but we thought we'd ask. We are hopeful that cascading style sheets and the promise of a Web font standard will answer this wish; until then, we can only wait and hope.

Kerning and Tracking Capabilities

Currently, the only way to manipulate the spacing between textual elements is to create a graphic of each textual element and to manually increase or decrease the space between the graphics. Style sheets will give us the capability to control the word and letter spacing in our documents without having to use graphical workarounds. The capability to fix uneven spacing between certain characters and punctuation is something to look forward to after cascading style sheets become the standard for a majority of browsers. To learn more about typography, you can visit Razorfish's awesome site at `http://www.razorfish.com/`. (See Figure 14.6.)

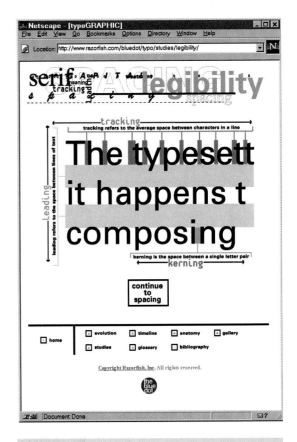

Figure 14.6.

The Razorfish Web site at `http://www.razorfish.com/bluedot/typo/studies/legibility/` *is an excellent source for typographical information.*

Leading Issues: Controlling Line Spacing

Currently, the only ways to control the spacing between lines is to use the <BR> or <P> tag, tables, or—in moments of desperation—a graphical image.

Thanks again to cascading style sheets, we now can specify the line height of all our textual elements. After all the browsers get their acts together and support style sheets, we can start controlling the readability of our Web pages. The only thing to worry about is the misuse of the line-height flexibility. If someone wanted to squeeze all his information into the top portion of the screen, he could quite easily decrease the line height to accomplish it. Let's hope we're not giving any ideas to anyone!

> **Note**
>
> A possible downside to controlling margin space is the potential abuse some people might inflict to accomplish a cheesy effect. If someone used negative margins, for example, they could give a Web page a certain effect. Using style sheets for cheap effects, though, will only degrade the value of the Web page when viewed on another browser.

Controlling Margin Widths

What? No more tables to control margin widths? Surely you jest! Yes, it's true, boys and girls: With cascading style sheets, we can determine the size of our Web page's left, right, top, and bottom margins. Style sheets will enable us to make the margins on all our documents consistent.

Controlling Text Alignment

Currently, HTML does not give Web designers the capability to determine exactly how an image or a table will align beside text. We do have the ALIGN attribute in the image and <TABLE>, however, which can increase the vertical and horizontal alignment and space around the element. Cascading style sheets will give Web designers more options for controlling the vertical alignment of inline elements with values such as text-top, text-bottom, baseline, subscript, and superscript.

Unifying Standard Plug-Ins for Audio and Video

One of the major headaches when listening to audio and viewing video on the Web is that there are a large number of formats floating around out there, and each needs its own plug-in to access the file. With all these plug-ins bogging down a browser, it's a wonder that it can function at all. The amount of space needed for these plug-ins is no small matter. It's time to worry when the total size of all the plug-ins loaded on your hard drive is 20 times bigger than the browser application itself.

A way to reduce the bulkiness of all these different plug-ins would be to create a single, uniform, standard plug-in that could simply be added to the browser in one shot. With a standard, the reader could go to any page containing audio or video without worrying about whether he has the correct plug-in to access it. The stress on the user who has to install all these plug-ins would be reduced, bulkiness of the browser would be reduced, and a good chunk of the hard drive space would be reclaimed and put to better use. (See Figure 14.7.)

Figure 14.7.
The universal, all-in-one plug-in.

Designing Great Multimedia with Increased Bandwidth

Waiting for an animation, multimedia, or anything that requires a plug-in to download can seem like an eternity. It's great when you have to go out, fill your car up with gas, pick up some groceries, and grab a café mocha on the way back. Maybe when you get back to your computer, you will be able to enjoy whatever it was you were downloading in the first place.

The problem with multimedia on the Web is that most users do not have the bandwidth required to quickly download sizable files. Currently, multimedia files have to be watered down or reduced in quality in order to create the most compact file possible.

An increase in bandwidth will bring an improvement in the type of multimedia presented on the Web. With higher bandwidths, users will be able to tolerate downloading multimedia files. This means that more Web designers can incorporate larger multimedia files on their Web pages. Without the dark shadow of file-size issues looming over them, multimedia files will become fuller and richer in content.

Summary

Here are some points about the future of Web design that we covered in this chapter:

✦ Style sheets eliminate the redundant formatting of every single element on a page by defining the properties of the elements separately from the content of the page itself.

✦ With style sheets, only the property of the element that needs to be reformatted must be redefined. This means that you only have to reformat one element instead of all the elements on your page.

✦ A linked style sheet has the advantage of being able to format numerous Web pages at once. This style is great to use when you need to apply fancy, complicated formatting to more than one Web page.

✦ An embedded or global style sheet definition is used to apply formatting to an individual page.

✦ An inline style sheet definition applies style formatting directly to individual elements.

✦ If more than one style is applied to a page, the global or embedded style overrides a link style, and the inline style overrides all styles.

✦ *HTML* is the language that provides structural importance to the elements on the page, whereas *style sheets* are the means by which to format the elements based on their structural definitions. Style sheets are in no way going to replace HTML.

✦ With standardized fonts, Web designers can anticipate that their designs will appear the way they were intended to be seen.

✦ A way to reduce the bulkiness of all the many different plug-ins on the Web would be to create a single, uniform, standard plug-in that can simply be added to the browser in one shot.

Day 7: Multimedia and What the Future Holds

- Currently, multimedia files have to be watered down or reduced in quality in order to create the most compact file possible.
- Adobe and Microsoft are working on a new font specification called *OpenType*, which will increase the font capabilities on the Web.
- Multimedia files will be fuller and richer in content when bandwidth is no longer an issue.

Q&A

 With all the new tools that will make putting up a Web page so easy, who cares about typography? Isn't the content of the page more important?

Content is the most important part of a Web page, but it doesn't mean anything if it can't be conveyed properly to a reader. So it is very important to use good typography to place the content in a format that makes it easy for a reader to find the information. If typography weren't used, all the written information available would be in clumps of unformatted text. It would make for a very unpleasant reading experience for everyone. To ensure that readers visit and absorb your Web page's content, you should place it in a format that is pleasant to digest.

 Where can I find out what the latest trends are in Web design?

Here are few sites on the Web where you can find out more about what's to come in Web design and multimedia:

Browser
http://www.zdnet.com/wsources/filters/topindx.html

Dvorak's News, Views, and Snides Aside at *PC Magazine* Online
http://www.pcmag.com/insites/dvorak/jdindex.htm

Feed Magazine
http://www.feedmag.com/

Info World—Electric
http://www.infoworld.com/

PC World
http://www.pcworld.com/

Salon Magazine
http://www.salonmagazine.com

The Future Chronicles
```
http://www.futurecast.com:80/futurechronicles/
```

The Hot Spot
```
http://www5.zdnet.com:80/cshopper/filters/
onlhsp.html
```

The Mac Week
```
http://www.macweek.com/
```

Web Developer
```
http://www.webdeveloper.com/
```

ZD Net's Registry
```
http://web1.zdnet.com:80/wsources/content/0397/
regrev10.html
```

Challenge Yourself

Now write your own wish list about what you'd like to see HTML and Web pages be able to do. Next, travel the Net and look for sites that address your wish list and the issues that it brings up. You might be surprised to find that someone out there has the same wish list that you do. Some companies might even be addressing those very issues you have brought up. It would be wise to keep up-to-date with your wish list issues. You might even want to discuss your ideas with the World Wide Web Consortium at `http://www.w3.org`. Who knows? Maybe one day soon, your wishes will become reality.

Top 30 Design Tips

These tips will help you design better sites. Read them. Learn them. Use them.

1. Don't, and we repeat, don't, use frames unless there is an absolute reason to do so. Many people consider frames a nuisance. If you are going to use them on your site, give your users a choice to view your site without frames.

2. Make sure that you have a reason to be on the Web. A Web page without content is like a pizza without topping.

3. Don't overuse free clipart and animated GIFs on your page. The Web is already cluttered with pages using the same free clipart and animated GIFs. Be original and design your own graphics.

4. Don't use every plug-in under the sun to enhance your Web pages. Keep your pages simple and to the point. Only add a plug-in that will genuinely contribute to the overall quality of your site.

5. Keep the length of your Web pages to no more than 1 1/2 screens. Extremely long-winded Web pages that force a user to scroll endlessly should be blown off the Net.

6. Keep the information on your Web pages fresh. A stale page wastes space on your server and on the Net.

7. Always be aware of the size of your files. Nobody wants to wait 10 minutes for your files to download.

8. Make the information on your site short, sweet, and straight to the point. Don't be tempted to add irrelevant information on your home page. Not everyone is going to want to see your photos taken on your most recent trip to Disneyland.

9. Try to make your Web pages flexible so that they can be viewed on many platforms.

10. Use white space to add breathing room around your elements. Web pages without white space can suffocate the life out of your site.

11. Don't announce to everyone that your site is under construction. If your site is not ready to be seen, wait until it *is* ready before putting it on the Web.

12. Check your site regularly to make sure that all the links are working. A collection of dead links on your site is like a block of moldy cheese sitting in your fridge, four weeks past its expiration date.

13. Use colors on your Web page sparingly. Don't try to blind your users with yellow, red, and orange stripes blaring from your page. Not all of us can take large doses of psychedelic color schemes without getting a migraine.

14. Pick your colors wisely by using a color wheel. It will save you the hassle of trying to figure out which colors work well together and which colors don't.

15. Create margins on your Web page to increase readability. Your users will appreciate it.

16. Design your Web pages with your 640×480-pixel-width audience in mind. Remember that not everyone has the pleasure of owning a super-huge monitor.

17. Don't add a Java script or Java applet to your page if there is no purpose for it being there. Java scripts and applets can be time-consuming to download and, in some cases, may even cause a browser to crash. If you can produce the same effect without using a Java script or applet, use that alternative instead.

18. Keep the file size of your image maps small. A large image map can take forever to download and can drive your user bananas. Also, make sure that the clickable areas on your map are obvious. Don't assume that everyone visiting your page is going to know the hot-spot regions of your image map.

19. Don't design your animated GIFs with the Benny Hill syndrome. Animated GIFs that move at hyperspeeds are extremely annoying to see. Be sure to add enough delay between frames to make the motion in your animated GIF smooth. (Benny Hill, for those of you who are not familiar, is a British actor who had a wonderfully funny show that used to feature skits where a group of people would be chasing him at super-fast speed. In some shows, he would speed up the chase scenes even more to add humor to the scene.)

20. Try anti-aliasing your graphics to give your images a soft, professional look. Don't use anti-aliasing on your transparent GIF images, though; this gives your graphics ugly outlines or halo effects.

21. When saving your graphics, keep the number of colors in the palette as small as possible without destroying the quality of your image. The smaller the number of colors, the smaller the file size of your graphic.

22. If you want to simulate text in a colored box, consider using an HTML table with the BGCOLOR attribute instead of using a graphic. If you can use HTML text to create the same effect as a graphic, then use it. This will help keep the download time of your Web page to a minimum.

23. Don't forget to use the ALT attribute in your <IMG SRC> tags for browsers that do not support graphics or for users who have turned off their browser's graphics capability.

24. Use the HEIGHT and WIDTH attributes in your <IMG SRC> tags to help decrease the download time of your graphics. These tags will enable certain browsers to lay out your Web page the first time they receive information from your server by not having to send extra requests to the server to determine the dimensions of the graphics.

25. Don't add annoying sound files that play when someone lands on your Web page. If you want to have sound files play in the background of your page, by all means add them in, but let your user decide whether he wants to listen to them.

26. Don't make your counter the center attraction on your home page. A page that reveals that only 125 people have visited the site is pretty pathetic. On the other hand, a site that brags that a person is visitor 15,284,393,100 is just as annoying. We're not saying that counters are bad. Just don't make the counter the focus of your page. If you decide to add a counter to your page, put it at the bottom of your page. That way, people who are really interested in knowing how much Web traffic your site attracts can easily find your counter, while others who couldn't care less don't have to have it shoved in their faces.

27. Learn good HTML. If you want to be able to apply proper design techniques, you can't escape from knowing your HTML. Bad HTML shows through a Web page like sweat on a silk shirt.

28. Don't misuse HTML tags to create cheap design effects. The effect on your Web page as seen on your browser will more likely lose its effectiveness when viewed on other browsers.

29. Don't use the Web to rant about your personal opinions. There are enough sites out there that have nothing better to say than *I hate this and I hate that*. The Web is not a soapbox for people to slam other people or other sites. If you have something to say, say it constructively or don't say it at all.

30. Have some fun with your designs. Web designing is a lot more fulfilling when you are having a good time doing it. By maintaining a sense of humor, Web designing can be a very entertaining process.

Color Reference Guide

RGB Hexadecimal Table Reference

Figure B.1 shows all 216 ditherproof colors in the 6×6×6 color cube.

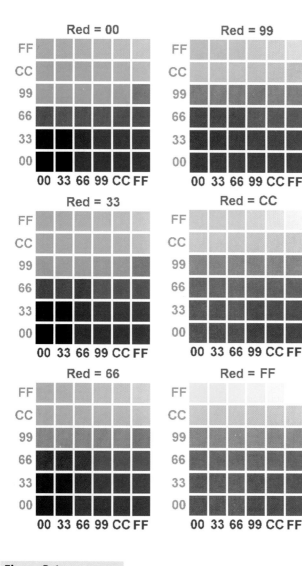

Figure B.1.

The 6×6×6 color cube.

Complementary Colors Guide

This guide shows the relationship between the colors on the ditherproof color wheel.

Figure B.2 shows the ditherproof color wheel, and Figure B.3 shows the table of hexadecimal values for each color on the wheel.

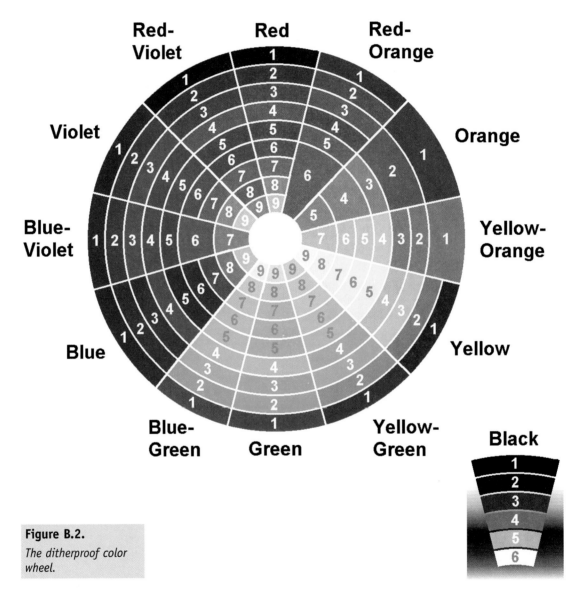

Figure B.2.
The ditherproof color wheel.

Figure B.3.

The corresponding hexadecimal values of the colors in the ditherproof color wheel.

Red

1	660000
2	993333
3	CC3333
4	CC6666
5	FF0000
6	FF3333
7	FF6666
8	FF9999
9	FFCCCC

Red-Orange

1	993300
2	CC3300
3	CC6600
4	FF3300
5	FF6600
6	FF6633

Orange

1	996633
2	CC6633
3	FF9900
4	FF9933
5	FF9966

Yellow-Orange

1	CC9966
2	CC9933
3	CC9900
4	FFCC00
5	FFCC33
6	FFCC66
7	FFCC99

Yellow

1	666600
2	999900
3	CCCC00
4	CCCC99
5	FFFF00
6	FFFF33
7	FFFF66
8	FFFF99
9	FFFFCC

Yellow-Green

1	336600
2	339933
3	66CC00
4	33FF00
5	99FF00
6	99FF66
7	CCFF00
8	CCFF66
9	CCFF99

Green

1	006600
2	009900
3	00CC00
4	99CC99
5	00FF00
6	33FF33
7	66FF66
8	99FF99
9	CCFFCC

Blue-Green

1	006600
2	339999
3	00CC99
4	66CCCC
5	00FFCC
6	33FFCC
7	66FFCC
8	99FFCC
9	CCFFFF

Blue

1	000099
2	333399
3	3333CC
4	6666CC
5	0000FF
6	3333FF
7	6666FF
8	9999FF
9	CCCCFF

Blue-Violet

1	660099
2	9933CC
3	9966CC
4	CC33FF
5	CC00FF
6	CC66FF
7	CC99FF

Violet

1	663366
2	993399
3	996699
4	CC33CC
5	FF00FF
6	FF33FF
7	FF66FF
8	FF99FF
9	FFCCFF

Red-Violet

1	660033
2	993366
3	CC3399
4	CC6699
5	FF0099
6	FF00CC
7	FF6699
8	FF66CC
9	FF99CC

Black

1	000000
2	333333
3	666666
4	999999
5	CCCCCC
6	FFFFFF

The *primary* colors are red, yellow, and blue. All other hues are derived from these colors. (See Figure B.4.)

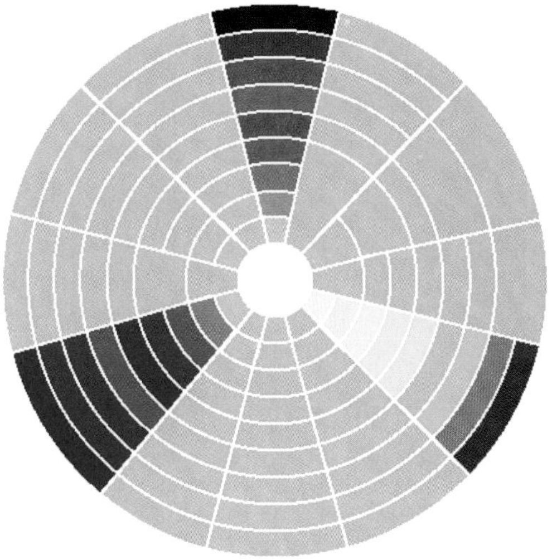

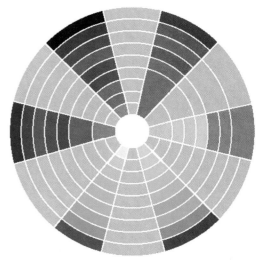

Figure B.4.
The primary colors.

The three *secondary* colors are orange, violet, and green. These colors are between the primary colors at even intervals. A secondary hue is composed by combining the two adjacent primary colors equally. (See Figure B.5.)

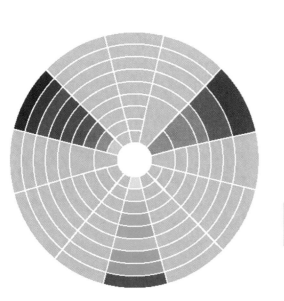

Figure B.5.
The secondary colors.

Between the primary and secondary colors are the *intermediate* colors. Like the secondary colors, they are the result of evenly mixing the hues beside them. They are sometimes referred to as *tertiary* colors. (See Figure B.6.)

Figure B.6.
The intermediate colors.

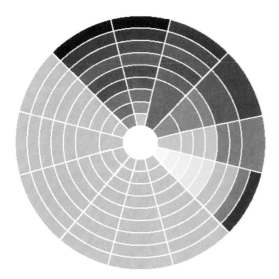

The colors ranging from red-violet to yellow are referred to as *warm* colors. Orange is considered the extreme of warm. Warm colors are vibrant and active. (See Figure B.7.)

Figure B.7.
The warm colors.

The colors ranging from violet to green-yellow are referred to as *cool* colors. Blue is considered the extreme of cool. Cool colors are relaxed and subdued. Creative color selection starts with a few basic color schemes. (See Figure B.8.)

Figure B.8.
The cool colors.

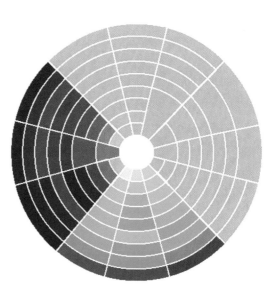

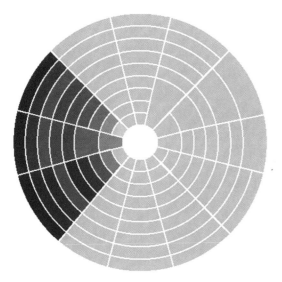

Analogous colors are any three consecutive color segments on the color wheel. Analogous colors produce a palette that blends well and conveys a feeling of harmony. (See Figure B.9.)

Figure B.9.
This wheel uses blue, blue-violet, and violet as analogous colors.

Complementary colors use two hues that are directly opposite. Their strength can sometimes also be their weakness. This color selection is very powerful and provides high contrast, but it sometimes can be quite jarring and hard to view over long periods of time. (See Figure B.10.)

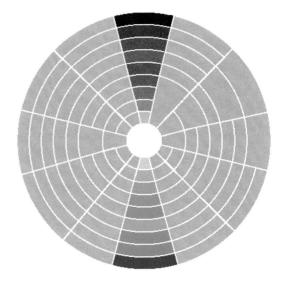

Figure B.10.

This wheel uses the red and green segments as complementary colors.

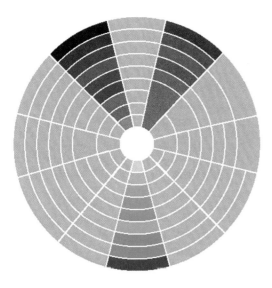

Split complementary colors consist of one hue and the two segments adjacent to its complement. This color scheme is vivid and not too overpowering. (See Figure B.11.)

Figure B.11.

This wheel uses the green, red-violet, and red-orange segments as split complementary colors.

Monochromatic colors use all the hues of one color segment. A monochromatic color scheme conveys harmony through gradual tone changes in the single-hue segment. (See Figure B.12.)

Figure B.12.

This wheel uses the blue segment as monochromatic colors.

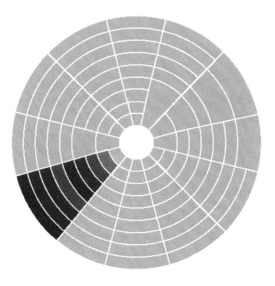

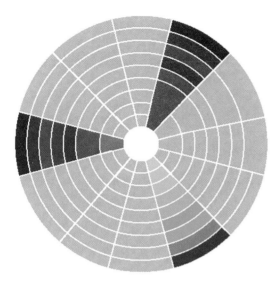

Triadic colors use three colors that are an equal distance from each other. These can include the primary, secondary, and intermediate colors. This color scheme gives a sense of balance between the colors. (See Figure B.13.)

Figure B.13.

This wheel uses the blue-violet, red-orange, and yellow-green segments as triadic colors.

Foreground/Background Color Suggestions

When deciding which foreground/background color combination to select, you should review a few basic points.

Q **A** **What is the basic color scheme of my Web page?**

Make sure that the text and background encompass part of that color scheme and do not clash with other elements.

Q **A** **Is there a background image?**

If there is a background image, you might need to modify it to allow the text to be seen on top. If there is no background image, you simply can add the color for the background to the <BGCOLOR> portion of the body tag.

 Is the text supposed to be subtle, blended, or vibrant?

Monochromatic colors give a pleasant, subtle effect as a foreground/background color scheme. The colors need to have a certain level of contrast in order to be legible. In Figure B.14, the monochromatic colors are chosen from the color wheel. The left column contains colors from the red hue segment. The middle column contains colors from the blue hue segment. The right column contains colors selected from the yellow hue segment.

Figure B.14.

Three sets of monochromatic color schemes.

Appendixes

Triadic colors give a balanced color scheme. The hues in this color scheme blend well together. In Figure B.15, the triadic colors are violet, orange, and green. They are also known as the secondary colors. The left column shows orange and green text on two different shades of violet. The middle column shows green and violet text on two shades of orange. The right column shows violet and orange text on two shades of green.

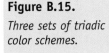

Figure B.15.
Three sets of triadic color schemes.

Complementary colors provide a high contrast and a vibrant color scheme that is easily noticed. Selecting a balanced amount of contrast gives a vivid, highly legible text foreground/background color scheme. If the colors selected have too much contrast, the effect will be quite jarring to the reader's eyes. In Figure B.16, various shades of the complementary colors of red and green were chosen. The left and middle columns show vibrant and legible foreground/background color combinations. In the right column, the colors have a high amount of contrast and therefore have a jarring effect. This color selection would make large amounts of text difficult to read.

Figure B.16.
Three sets of complementary color schemes.

Metaphoric Examples

Metaphors

Remember that a *metaphor* helps represent unfamiliar elements of your Web page by substituting those elements with the description and functionality of objects that are familiar. You therefore should make sure that the metaphor will be understood by your reader. Almost anything can be considered a metaphor. The following categories contain a few possible metaphors and color-selection techniques that should give you a jumpstart in designing your own metaphoric Web pages. You can see these colors in the colorwheel in Appendix B, "Color Reference Guide."

Business

an office tower, a briefcase, a reception area

Color Selections

In a business-style Web page, traditionally solid, low-key colors and shades of gray and black are used to enhance a professional look. Some colors to use for these metaphors are

Black 1, 2, 3, 4, 5, 6; Red 2, 3, 4, 5; Yellow 2, 3, 5, 9; Yellow-Green 1, 2, 3, 9; Green 1, 2, 3, 9; Blue 1, 2, 3, 4, 5

Kids

a toy box, a playground, a comic book

Color Selections

Kids love bright pages. Lots of bright, primary colors should be used to attract and keep their attention. Some colors to use with these metaphors are

Red 5, 6, 7; Red-Orange 4, 5, 6; Yellow 5, 6, 7; Yellow-Green 4, 5, 6; Green 5, 6, 7; Blue 5, 6, 7; Violet 5, 6, 7

Generation X

a hip magazine, an Internet café, a grunge festival, an abandoned warehouse, a messy bedroom (Have you ever seen the movie "Joe's Apartment?"), an alternative concert with a Lollapallooza theme

Color Selections

Depending on the type of site you are designing, a mixture of wild colors or a set of depressing colors could reflect the mood of the site. Here are some suggestions of colors to use for these metaphors:

Red 3, 4, 5, 8; Yellow-Orange 4, 5; Yellow 5, 6, 9; Green 1, 2, 3, 4, 5, 6, 7, 8, 9; Blue 2, 3, 4, 5, 9; Blue-Violet 3, 4, 5, 6, 7; Violet 2, 3, 4, 5

Retro

an old-style appliance shop; a drive-in restaurant; the house with the white picket fence, 2 cars, and 2.5 kids

Color Selections

The retro look is marked with an abundance of pastels and mixtures of primary and secondary colors. Some colors to use for these metaphors are

Red-Orange 1, 5, 6; Orange 1, 2, 3, 4, 5; Yellow-Orange 3, 4, 7; Yellow 2, 3, 5, 6; Yellow-Green 1, 2, 3, 4, 5, 6, 7, 8, 9; Blue-Green 1, 2, 3, 4, 5, 6, 7, 8, 9; Blue-Violet 1, 3, 5, 7; Red-Violet 3, 4, 5, 6, 7, 8, 9

Just for Fun

a joke novelty display, a comedy club, a novelty store, a carnival

Color Selections

Splash it on or paint it on. Just-for-fun colors are usually vibrant and eye-catching. Some colors to look at are

Red 2, 3, 6; Red-Orange 5, 6; Orange 4, 5; Yellow 2, 3, 5, 7, 8; Green 2, 3, 5, 8; Blue 3, 5, 8; Violet 2, 3, 4, 5

Friendly, Warm, Gives-You-That-Fuzzy-Feeling

a baby nursery, a puppies and kittens playpen, Grandma's house

Color Selections

Friendly color schemes usually are represented by the warm colors on the colorwheel. These colors are inviting and energetic but not overpowering. Some colors to try for these themes are

Red 6, 7; Red-Orange 5, 6; Orange 1, 2, 3, 4, 5; Yellow-Orange 3, 4, 5, 6, 7; Yellow 2, 3, 5, 8, 9; Yellow-Green 2, 3, 5; Green 1, 2, 3; Red-Violet 5, 6, 7, 8, 9

Trendy and Funky

a night/dance/disco club, a fashion show featuring the latest styles, a hair salon

Color Selections

What's trendy today can be out tomorrow and trendy again 10 years later. When picking trendy colors for a page, remember that trendy colors and elements will change over time. If your site is supposed to be up-to-date with the latest trends, you have to make sure that you keep up with the styles and change your site when necessary. Some trendy colors for the '90s are

Orange 2, 4; Yellow-Orange 1, 5; Yellow 7, 8, 9; Yellow-Green 1, 2, 3, 4, 5, 6; Green 1, 2, 3, 4, 5, 6, 7, 8, 9; Violet 3, 4, 5

Die-Hard Romantic

a reclusive rose garden, a fireplace setting, a moonlit night on the beach

Color Selections

Romantic colors are soft and warm. The colors for these metaphors should give a feeling of surrealism and a dreamy air. Some colors to use for these metaphors are

Red 7, 8, 9; Red-Orange 4, 5, 6; Yellow-Orange 6, 7; Yellow 7, 8, 9; Green 2, 3, 7, 8, 9; Blue-Violet 1, 2, 5, 6, 7

Scientific

a laboratory, atoms & molecules, an experiment

Color Selections

It's difficult to list a number of colors for scientific metaphors. There probably would be two types of scientific sites. The first would be a site to teach or inform the reader about the selected subject; in this case, these colors should be fun and attractive. For professional, scientific research types of sites, it might be good to stick to a more professional- and business-looking color scheme. Some color suggestions for these metaphors are

> Red 2, 3, 6; Red-Orange 5, 6; Orange 4, 5; Yellow 2, 3, 5, 7, 8; Green 2, 3, 5, 8; Blue 3, 5, 8; Violet 2, 3, 4, 5

Some professional-site colors are

> Black 1, 2, 3, 4, 5, 6; Red 2, 3, 4, 5; Yellow 2, 3, 5, 9; Yellow-Green 1, 2, 3, 9; Green 1, 2, 3, 9; Blue 1, 2, 3, 4, 5

Environmental/Nature

a forest, an ocean floor, rivers and lakes, mountains

Color Selections

Nature has a wide array of vivid colors. Knowing what part of the environment your page is focusing on helps narrow the selection of colors to use for these metaphors. Each of the earlier examples has its own unique blend of colors. When your page is about the forest, many different shades of green naturally will predominate. In the ocean, a huge variety of blue should be available to choose from. On the mountain top, snow may cause the peaks to be white, while the green trees grow up the side of the mountain right beside the crystal-clear blue waterfall. So, the best thing to do when you need to choose colors related to a particular natural habitat is to get pictures of the area and select colors that closely coordinate with the colors you see. There are some inherently natural/earth colors. Some of these colors are

> Orange 1, 2, 3; Yellow-Orange 1, 2, 3, 4, 5; Yellow-Green 1, 2, 3, 4, 5, 6, 7, 8, 9; Green 1, 2, 3, 4, 5, 6, 7, 8, 9

Informational

a magazine, a newspaper, a TV newscast

Color Selections

When delivering information, you need the content to be clear, interesting, and fun. Therefore, a mixture of splashy colors and traditional print colors could be combined to make an attractive splashy page that delivers its contents. Some colors to use could be

> Black 1, 2, 3, 4, 5, 6; Red 5, 6; Orange 1, 2, 3; Yellow 5, 6; Green 1, 2, 3, 4, 5; Blue 1, 2, 3, 4, 5; Violet 1, 2, 3, 4, 5

Commercial

a department store, a vending machine, a great big shopping mall

Color Selections

With these metaphors, you have to give a subliminal message to the reader to Buy! Buy! Buy! To convince a customer to do that, the commercial Web page needs to be catchy and attractive. Some complementary colors would work well in grabbing the reader's attention, but be careful that you don't overuse them so much that your page becomes one huge eye-throb. Also look at the products that are to be featured. You can take your color scheme from the colors used on the product or the packaging of the product. At least make sure that the product colors do not totally clash with your color scheme. Some colors to catch the reader's attention are

Red 5, 6, 7; Red-Orange 4, 5, 6; Yellow 5, 6, 7; Yellow-Green 4, 5, 6; Green 5, 6, 7; Blue 5, 6, 7; Blue-Violet 2, 3, 4, 5; Violet 5, 6, 7

Sports Junkie

a sports equipment store, sports cards, various playing fields (ice surface, soccer field, basketball court)

Color Selections

Colors for a sports-related Web page can come from a variety of sources. If the page focuses on a single team, the team colors can be used as the page colors. The color of the playing surface also can be selected. You also can select the colors of a number of team logos and paint them onto the page. The following color selections should be reviewed if they are to be added to a page with existing team/league colors. You need to make sure that the colors do not clash and cause an unsightly site. Some suggested colors are

Black 1, 2, 3, 4, 5, 6; Red 5, 6; Orange 2, 3; Yellow 5, 6; Green 2, 3, 4, 5; Blue 2, 3, 4, 5; Violet 2, 3, 4, 5

The Graphic Genre

Although graphics come in a wide variety of types (illustrated, photographic, and three-dimensional), styles (cartoonish, surrealistic, and realistic), and categories (object, person, and animal), they usually can be classified into specific genres. With graphical genres, graphics easily can be classified and grouped together. When they are grouped together, looking for a specific graphic brings up various other related graphics that you might never have thought of using before. Groups of these related graphics then can be selected and placed into various Web page metaphors. To give you a start, a few examples of some genres and a few of the types of graphics that relate to them follow:

The Old Wild West

dusty, dirt-road towns; horses; saloons; wagons; inns; guns; gunslingers; arrows; cowboys; farm animals; Indians; wheat fields

Roman Time Period

Roman soldiers, coliseums, Roman army, gladiators, roads, Roman statesmen, mules, statues of ancient gods, columns

A Medieval Time Period

knights, kings, serfs, queens, damsels, princes, horses, princesses, knight's armor, barons, jousting, armies, medieval weaponry, cavalry

The Roaring '20s

Ford Model-T cars, nightclubs, men in suits with hats, people dancing, telegraphs

Modern Warfare

handguns, fighter planes, machine guns, bombs, officers, explosions, soldiers, missiles, civilians, battleships, tanks, aircraft carriers, bomber planes

Modern Day

cars, airplanes, TVs, trains, computers, telephones, microwaves, cellular phones, cities, faxes, houses, washing machines, CDs

Futuristic Outer Space

spaceships, satellites, colonies on other planets, planets, astronauts, solar systems, space suits, stars

Gloomy Futuristic Earth (Cyberpunk)

computers, hackers, microchips, corporate businesspeople, cyborgs, corporate office buildings, mainframes, run-down apartments, leather-clad hoodlums, the Internet

Fantasy

dragons, orcs, elves, monsters, dwarves, magical items, gnomes, gold, goblins, jewels, centaurs, treasure

Superheroes

superheroes, effects of superpowers, supervillains, superpowers in action, sidekicks, people in distress, secret identities, superjails

Horror

blood, green slime, bodies and body parts, unsuspecting victims, monsters, deranged killers, knives, chainsaws, gloomy houses

Espionage

spies, top-secret documents, overcoats, microfilm, spy gadgets, video tape, spy cars, surveillance equipment

What's on the CD-ROM

On the *Teach Yourself Great Web Design in a Week* CD-ROM, you will find all the sample files presented in this book, the "Challenge Yourself" resources, and a wealth of other applications and utilities.

> **Note**
>
> Please refer to the readme.wri file on the CD-ROM (Windows) or the Guide to the CD-ROM (Macintosh) for the latest listing of software.

Windows Software

HTML Tools
✦ HomeSite 2.0 demo

✦ HomeSite Free 1.2

✦ Hot Dog 32-bit HTML Editor

✦ HoTMeTaL HTML Editor

✦ HTMLed HTML Editor

Graphics, Video, and Sound Applications
✦ GIF Construction Set for Windows (16-bit and 32-bit)

The GIF Construction Set for Windows software included with this publication is provided as shareware for your evaluation. If you try this software and find it useful, you are requested to register it as discussed in its documentation and in the About screen of the application. The publisher of this book has not paid the registration fee for this shareware.

✦ Goldwave sound editor, player, and recorder

✦ Paint Shop Pro 4

✦ LView Pro

✦ SnagIt screen capture utility

✦ MapThis imagemap utility

✦ ThumbsPlus image viewer and browser

Explorer

- ✦ Microsoft Internet Explorer 3 for Windows 95 and NT 4

Utilities

- ✦ Adobe Acrobat viewer
- ✦ WinZip for Windows NT/95
- ✦ WinZip Self-Extractor

Macintosh Software

HTML Tools

- ✦ BBEdit 3.5.1
- ✦ BBEdit 4 demo
- ✦ WebMap v1.01f imagemap creator

Graphics, Video, and Sound Applications

- ✦ Graphic Converter
- ✦ GIFConverter
- ✦ Fast Player
- ✦ Sparkle
- ✦ SoundApp

Utilities

- ✦ ZipIt for Macintosh
- ✦ ScrapIt Pro
- ✦ Adobe Acrobat

Electronic Books

About Shareware

Shareware is not free. Please read all documentation associated with a third-party product (usually contained in files named `readme.txt` or `license.txt`) and follow all guidelines.

Web Site Design

We have put together a collection of the best design resources on the Web. Here you will find great stuff to help you design your Web sites.

Typography Resources

Adobe Internet Conference 1996
`http://www.adobe.com/events/aic/main.html`

This site contains the session handout for the Adobe Internet Conference for 1996. It is an excellent resource for tips, techniques, and explanations to help create dynamic Web pages.

The following are some interesting and informative articles at this site:

"Building Sites Right!," by Wendy Govier

"Creating Visually Rich Pages for the Web," by Judy Kirkpatrick

"Advanced Web Design," by Lisa Lopuck and Sheryl Hampton

"Optimizing Images for the Web," by Neil Robertson

"How the Web Works," by Nathan Shedroff

"Keep it Snappy: Encouraging Return Visits," by Ben Benjamin

Art and Zen of Web Sites
`http://www.tlc-systems.com/webtips.htm`

This site contains an essay about Web design—including deciding the goals for your Web pages, creating clear navigation, designing a friendly user interface, designing image maps, designing images, and creating frame-based sites.

Dmitry Kirsanov's Top 10 Web Design Tips
`http://www.design.ru/ttt/`

This site contains a wonderful collection of brief tutorials, advice on different HTML topics, Web page design and layout, and Web graphics.

Professor Pete's Webmastering 301
http://www.professorpete.com/

This site provides a good, detailed tutorial on designing a business Web site. Its online, interactive tutorial is a lot of fun to use and will teach you the things you need to know about designing a commercial Web site.

Project Cool Developer Zone
http://www.projectcool.com/developer/

This site offers tips and techniques for building effective and interesting Web sites. The site contains many Web tips that cover the conception phase to the HTML programming phase of a Web page.

Publish RGB: The Electronic Publishing Authority
http://www.publish.com:80/

This magazine site provides excellent articles on a wide variety of topics, such as layout design, typography, illustrations, image map editing, and more. It also includes reviews of the latest software and hardware Web developers might be interested in. At this site, you will find many articles with tips on improving Web sites using case studies to illustrate various techniques. Another interesting thing at this site is the extensive archive of previously released articles, which are accessible via a search engine.

Razorfish
http://www.razorfish.com/

This site contains a section called "TypoGRAPHIC," which focuses on type and typography on the Web and in digital media. The information is presented clearly and contains lots of visual content.

Tables Seminar by John Newsom
http://www.ckcs.org:80/seminar/intro.htm

This site has a fun, step-by-step, online tutorial that teaches creatively using HTML tables to help you construct informative and attractive Web pages.

Typography on the Web by Microsoft
http://www.microsoft.com/truetype/hottopic.htm

This site discusses how font support is being brought to the Web. The site also leads into discussions about the use and advantages of cascading style sheets on the Web. It offers solutions for lowering the file size of a Web page by using creative typography and reducing the use of graphics.

Typsetting the Web by Kevin Ready
http://www.publish.com:80/1096/online/

This article provides a typography technology overview. It focuses on using HTML to improve the legibility and look of a Web page.

W3C: World Wide Web Consortium
http://www.w3.org/pub/WWW/

This is the organization that was created to standardize the evolution of the World Wide Web. Led by Tim Berners-Lee, the creator of the World Wide Web, this is the site that gives the latest standards for HTML and information on the Web's future development.

Web Page Design for Designers
http://ds.dial.pipex.com/pixelp/wpdesign/wpdintro.htm

This is an excellent site that focuses on a variety of design concepts, from typography to graphical design. Designed for those who already know HTML or are using a WYSIWYG Web page editor, this site discusses what goes into creating great Web pages.

Web Pages That Suck
http://www.webpagesthatsuck.com/

This site teaches good design technique by showing bad Web design. It covers the elements of design by commenting on a variety of unappealing sites on the Web. If you want to learn about Web design and get a few laughs while doing it, you should definitely check out this site.

Web Review
http://webreview.com/

This online magazine discusses many issues on Web design, from HTML and graphics to multimedia. It is packed full of informative articles, design tips, and reviews.

Web Wonk by David Siegel
http://www.dsiegel.com/tips/

This site provides a number of writings that deal with typography, Web design tips and tricks, HTML, and frequently asked questions. David Siegel's site is a great place to gain a solid foundation in basic Web page design.

Webweek
http://www.webweek.com/

Webweek is an online magazine that deals with the Web and Web designing news. Topics for articles include intranets, Web industry news, and the latest software. The site also provides a good resource list of Web tools.

Why the Web Sucks II
http://www.spies.com:80/~ceej/Words/rant.web.html

This page, written by C.J. Silverio, is an article that discusses how many Web pages suck because of a lack of good content and design techniques. This is an interesting article that brings up many good points on the reasons why some Web pages are boring and uninformative.

Developer's Resources

Creating Killer Web Sites
http://www.killersites.com/

This is a great site that contains design tips on color, graphics, and compression. The site includes an excellent resource for developer tools.

The Digital Artisan
http://www.interspin.com/digitalartisan/

This is a great Web design resource directory with articles, resource pages, and a searchable freelance directory.

Dmitry's Design Lab
http://www.webreference.com/dlab/

This site provides a tutorial and useful tips on creating great Web page logos. You will learn everything from the design to the finishing touches of creating an effective logo.

The Pixel Foundry
http://the-tech.mit.edu/KPT/

The Pixel Foundry site contains tons of Web graphics tips, and the infamous Kai's power tips and tricks for Adobe Photoshop. In addition, you will find an archive of background images, a graphics forum, and a KPT discussion area.

Web Design Group
`http://www.htmlhelp.com/`

The Web Design Group is an organization founded to promote the creation of Web pages that are supported by all platforms. It emphasizes that Web design can be seen by all users in the same way without being boring and nongraphical. The site contains an outstanding HTML reference, great Web authoring tips, and feature articles related to Web design.

Web Developer Magazine
`http://www.webdeveloper.com/`

This online magazine contains great articles specifically related to Web page design. You can learn about everything a Web developer needs to know by going through the extensive archive of back issues.

Interactive Script Resources

Cut-N-Paste JavaScript
`http://www.infohiway.com/javascript/indexf.htm`

Cut-N-Paste Java Script is an excellent site filled with interesting and useful Java scripts that can be cut and pasted into any HTML document. If you want to add some exciting Java script to your Web pages, this is the place to go!

Cut-N-Paste Tool Kit
`http://www.imastudios.com/`

This site contains a collection of useful cut-n-paste Java scripts. It is one of the best sites

to get the latest and greatest scripts and code for your Web pages.

Graphics Resources

The Animated GIF File Archive
`http://www.euronet.nl/users/fairy/ani.html`

This site contains a collection of animated GIFs that you can download for your Web designs.

BoZine Web Graphics
`http://www.bozine.com/`

This site includes very useful help pages dealing with the development and design of efficient, effective Web graphics.

Club Unlimited Animated GIFs
`http://www.wu-wien.ac.at/usr/h95a/h9552688/local.html`

This site boasts an impressive collection of more than 1,500 animated GIFs. The GIFs are divided into a number of categories for easy reference.

Creating Graphics for the Web
`http://www.widearea.co.uk/designer/`

This site contains relevant Web graphics creation topics. It includes tips and techniques pertaining to Photoshop and anti-aliasing.

Free Art @ Solarflare
`http://www.solarflare.com/freeart/index.html`

This site contains tons of free graphics, including theme sets of rules, bullets, and background images.

The Free Graphics Store
http://ausmall.com.au/freegraf

This site contains many free graphics, including backgrounds, icons, rules, and animated GIFs.

GrafX Design
http://www.grafx-design.com

This site contains great graphics tutorials that show step-by-step instructions on creating buttons and rules, using tricks with masks, creating transparentized GIFs, and generating 3D text designs.

Home of the Horizontal Rule
http://www.wanderers.com/skull/
hor_rule.html

This site contains a nice collection of free horizontal rule graphics that you can use for your own Web designs.

Lynn's Web Mastery
http://fly.hiwaay.net/~nlf/
graphics.htm

This site is a collection of great links to the best design resources on the Web. It is an outstanding resource for graphics on the Web, including animation, backgrounds, bullets, and clipart. It also has links to sites that feature sound and sites that contain useful Web tools.

SSA's Gallery
http://www.ssanimation.com/
gallery.html

SSA's Gallery an excellent site that contains a number of free animated GIFs that can be downloaded and added to enhance your Web page.

Web Creation
http://www.axicom.net/~shawn/web.html

This site has archives for backgrounds, balls, and bar graphics. It also has a list of HTML editors and graphics programs that you can download to help you with your Web designs.

The WDVL: Graphics for the World Wide Web
http://WWW.Stars.com/Authoring/
Graphics/

The WDVL site is a wonderful resource for graphics techniques, HTML seminars, 3D graphics, images, and icons. You will also find a list of useful graphics tools that you can use for your own designs.

Shareware Resources

Awesome Webmaster Tools
http://www.isecure.com/webmaster/
hotsites.htm

This site is an excellent resource of links to a variety of software relating to 3D and VRML animation, counters, scripts, backgrounds, color indexes, browsers, HTML, clipart, photos, icons (arrows, bars, bullets, and buttons), image maps, GIF tools, Java, Real Audio, Internet Phone, Internet Video, Winsock, video/audio players and encoders, music, sound effects, and video clips.

Shareware.com
http://www.shareware.com/

This site offers a powerful and detailed search engine, the *Virtual Software Library* (VSL), that contains more than 160,000 software files—including freeware, shareware, demos, fixes, patches, and upgrades that can be downloaded.

TuCows

`http://www.tucows.com/`

TuCows is one of the best sites for Internet software for Windows and Macintosh platforms. You can probably find all the tools you will need for Web developing here. This site rates almost all the tools in its database with a cow rating. (A five-cow rating means that the software is highly recommended.)

Windows95.com

`http://www.windows95.com/apps/`

Windows95.com contains a list of the latest shareware, freeware, and commercial demos for the Windows operating system. You will also find walkthrough tutorials for some of the software at this site.

Index

Index

M

Q - R

T

Index

W - Z

Laura Lemay's Web Workshop:
Netscape Navigator Gold 3, Deluxe Edition

—Laura Lemay and Ned Snell

Netscape Gold and JavaScript are two powerful tools to create and design effective Web pages. This book details not only design elements, but also how to use the Netscape Gold WYSIWYG editor. The included CD-ROM contains editors and code from the book, making the readers' learning experience a quick and effective one.

CD-ROM includes fully licensed version of Netscape Navigator Gold 3!

> *Price: $49.99 USA/$56.95 CDN*
> *ISBN: 1-57521-292-7*   *400 pp.*

Laura Lemay's Web Workshop: 3D Graphics and VRML 2

—Laura Lemay, Kelly Murdock, and Justin Couch

This is the easiest way for readers to learn how to add three-dimensional virtual worlds to Web pages. It describes the new VRML 2 specification, explores the wide array of existing VRML sites on the Web, and steps the readers through the process of creating their own 3D Web environments.

CD-ROM contains the book in HTML format, a hand-picked selection of the best VRML and 3D graphics tools, plus a collection of ready-to-use virtual worlds.

> *Price: $39.99 USA/$56.95 CDN*
> *ISBN: 1-57521-143-2*   *400 pp.*

Laura Lemay's Web Workshop:
Graphics and Web Page Design

—Laura Lemay, John Duff, and James Mohler

With the number of Web pages increasing daily, only the well-designed will stand out and grab the attention of those browsing the Web. This book illustrates, in classic Laura Lemay style, how to design attractive Web pages that will be visited over and over again.

CD-ROM contains HTML editors, graphics software, and royalty-free graphics and sound files.

> *Price: $55.00 USA/$77.95 CDN*
> *ISBN: 1-57521-125-4*   *408 pp.*

Laura Lemay's Web Workshop: JavaScript

—Laura Lemay and Michael Moncur

Readers will explore various aspects of Web JavaScript and interactivity, graphics design, and Netscape Navigator Gold—in greater depth than the *Teach Yourself* books.

CD-ROM includes the complete book in HTML format, publishing tools, templates, graphics, backgrounds, and more.

> *Price: $39.99 USA/$56.95 CDN*
> *ISBN: 1-57521-141-6*   *400 pp.*

Laura Lemay's Web Workshop: Microsoft FrontPage

—Laura Lemay and Denise Tyler

This is a hands-on guide to maintaining Web pages with Microsoft's FrontPage. Written in the clear, conversational style of Laura Lemay, it is packed with many interesting, colorful examples that demonstrate specific tasks of interest to the reader.

CD-ROM includes all the templates, backgrounds, and materials needed!

Price: $39.99 USA/$56.95 CDN
ISBN: 1-57521-149-1   *672 pp.*

Laura Lemay's Web Workshop: Creating Commercial Web Pages

—Laura Lemay and Brian K. Murphy

Filled with sample Web pages, this book shows how to create commercial-grade Web pages using HTML, CGI, and Java. In the classic, clear style of Laura Lemay, this book details not only how to create the page, but how to apply proven principles of design that will make the Web page a marketing tool. Illustrates the various corporate uses of Web technology—catalogs, customer service, and product ordering.

CD-ROM includes all the templates in the book, plus HTML editors, graphics software, CGI forms, and more.

Price: $39.99 USA/$56.95 CDN
ISBN: 1-57521-126-2   *528 pp.*

Laura Lemay's Web Workshop: ActiveX & VBScript

—Laura Lemay, Paul Lomax, Rogers Cadenhead

ActiveX is an umbrella term for a series of Microsoft products and technologies that add activity to Web pages. VBScript is an essential element of the ActiveX family. With it, animation, multimedia, sound, graphics, and interactivity can be added to a Web site. This book is a compilation of individual workshops that show the reader how to use VBScript and other ActiveX technologies within his or her Web site.

CD-ROM contains the entire book in HTML format, a hand-picked selection of the best ActiveX development tools, scripts, templates, backgrounds, borders, and graphics.

Price: $39.99 USA/$56.95 CDN
ISBN: 1-57521-207-2   *560 pp.*

Teach Yourself Web Publishing with HTML 3.2 in 14 Days, Professional Reference Edition

—Laura Lemay

This is the updated edition of Lemay's previous best-seller, *Teach Yourself Web Publishing with HTML in 14 Days, Premier Edition*. In it, readers will find all the advanced topics and updates—including adding audio, video, and animation—to Web page creation. Explores the use of CGI scripts, tables, HTML 3.2, Netscape and Internet Explorer extensions, Java applets and JavaScript, and VRML.

CD-ROM included.

Price: $59.99 USA/$81.95 CDN
ISBN: 1-57521-096-7   *1,104 pp.*

Add to Your Sams.net Library Today
with the Best Books for Internet Technologies

ISBN	Quantity	Description of Item	Unit Cost	Total Cost
1-57521-292-7		Laura Lemay's Web Workshop: Netscape Navigator Gold 3, Deluxe Edition (Book/CD-ROM)	$49.99	
1-57521-143-2		Laura Lemay's Web Workshop: 3D Graphics and VRML 2 (Book/CD-ROM)	$39.99	
1-57521-125-4		Laura Lemay's Web Workshop: Graphics and Web Page Design (Book/CD-ROM)	$55.00	
1-57521-141-6		Laura Lemay's Web Workshop: JavaScript (Book/CD-ROM)	$39.99	
1-57521-149-1		Laura Lemay's Web Workshop: Microsoft FrontPage (Book/CD-ROM)	$39.99	
1-57521-126-2		Laura Lemay's Web Workshop: Creating Commercial Web Pages (Book/CD-ROM)	$39.99	
1-57521-207-2		Laura Lemay's Web Workshop: ActiveX and VBScript (Book/CD-ROM)	$39.99	
1-57521-096-7		Teach Yourself Web Publishing with HTML 3.2 in 14 Days, Professional Reference Edition (Book/CD-ROM)	$59.99	
		Shipping and Handling: See information below.		
		TOTAL		

Shipping and Handling: $4.00 for the first book, and $1.75 for each additional book. If you need to have it NOW, we can ship product to you for an additional charge of approximately $18.00, and you will receive your item overnight or in two days. Overseas shipping and handling adds $2.00. Prices subject to change. Call between 9:00 a.m. and 5:00 p.m. EST for availability and pricing information on latest editions.

201 W. 103rd Street, Indianapolis, Indiana 46290

1-800-428-5331 — Orders   1-800-835-3202 — Fax   1-800-858-7674 — Customer Service

Book ISBN 1-57521-253-6

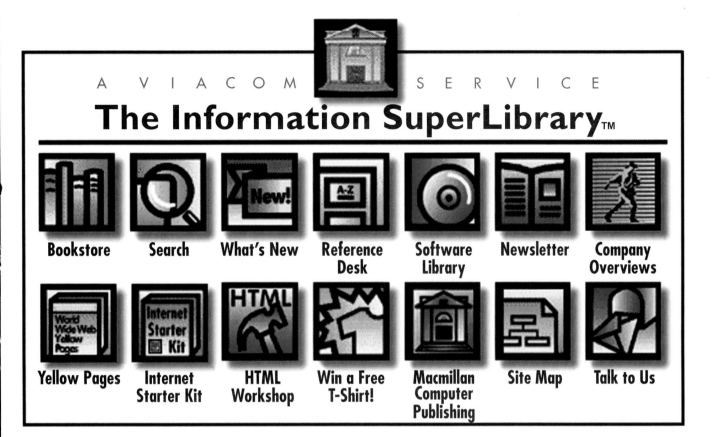

MACMILLAN COMPUTER PUBLISHING USA

A VIACOM COMPANY

If you need assistance with the information in this book or with a CD/Disk accompanying the book, please access the Knowledge Base on our Web site at **http://www.superlibrary.com/general/support**. Our most Frequently Asked Questions are answered there. If you do not find the answer to your questions on our Web site, you may contact Macmillan Technical Support **(317) 581-3833** or e-mail us at **support@mcp.com**.

Installing the CD-ROM

The companion CD-ROM contains all the source code and project files developed by the authors, plus an assortment of evaluation versions of third-party products.

Windows 95/NT 4 Installation

1. Insert the CD-ROM into your CD-ROM drive.
2. From the Windows 95 or NT 4 desktop, double-click the My Computer icon.
3. Double-click the icon representing your CD-ROM drive.
4. Double-click the setup.exe icon to run the CD-ROM installation program.

Windows NT 3.51 Installation

1. Insert the CD-ROM into your CD-ROM drive.
2. From File Manager or Program Manager, choose Run from the File menu.
3. Type **<drive>\setup**, where **<drive>** corresponds to the drive letter of your CD-ROM, and press Enter. If your CD-ROM is drive D, for example, type **D:\SETUP** and press Enter.
4. Follow the on-screen instructions.

Macintosh Installation

1. Insert the CD-ROM into your CD-ROM drive.
2. After an icon for the CD-ROM appears on your desktop, open the disc by double-clicking the icon.
3. Double-click the Guide to the CD-ROM icon, and follow the directions that appear.